GOD'S BROKER

By Antoni Gronowicz

Biographies
God's Broker
Béla Schick and the World of Children
Sergei Rachmaninoff
Modjeska: Her Life and Loves
Gallant General; Tadeusz Kosciuszko
Paderewski: Pianist and Patriot
Chopin
Tchaikovsky

Novels
An Orange Full of Dreams
Bolek
Four From the Old Town
Hitler's Woman
The Hookmen

Poetry
The Quiet Vengeance of Words
Polish Poems

Plays
The United Animals
Shores of Pleasure   Shores of Pain
Chiseler's Paradise
Forward Together
A Painted School
The Lost Money
Recepta
Greta
Rocos
Colors of Conscience

Essays
The Piasts
Polish Profiles
Pattern for Peace

GOD'S BROKER

The life of John Paul II

Antoni Gronowicz

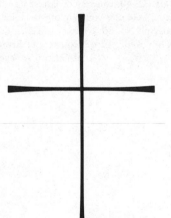

RICHARDSON & SNYDER
1984

ISBN: 0–943940 10–9
LC Catalog Number: 84–60108

Typography and case design by Mr. Joseph Ascherl
Jacket design by Mr. David Gatti
Composition by *Paragraphics*, New York City
Printed by Book-Crafters, Inc.

PHOTOGRAPH CREDITS:
Photograph Nos. 1–21, 24–26, 30, 35: courtesy of Pope John Paul II.
Photograph No. 22: courtesy of Wojciech Staszkiewicz, Cracow
Photograph Nos. 23, 28, 29: courtesy of Adam Bujak, Cracow
Photograph No. 27: courtesy of Antoni Litwin, Cracow
Photograph Nos. 31, 39, 42: courtesy of Tadeusz Zagozdziński, Warsaw
Photograph Nos. 32, 40: courtesy of Janusz Czerniak, Warsaw
Photograph No. 33, 34, 38: courtesy of Marek Langda, Warsaw
Photograph No. 36: courtesy of Felici, Rome
Photograph Nos. 37, 41, 43: courtesy of Arturo Mari,
L'Osservatore Romano, Vatican City

To My Family

CONTENTS

Book Six: Christ's Deputy

PHOTOGRAPHS *(in sequence):*

PROLOGUE

GOD'S BROKER is based on research that spans nearly nine years. Much of the material comes from private conversations in Europe and America with Pope John Paul II, Cardinals and other high officials of the Roman Catholic Church, as well as with the cultural and political personages of Poland.

I am grateful to the late Stefan Cardinal Wyszyński, Primate of Poland, who introduced me to the Pope, acquainted me with Vatican circles, and convinced the Holy Father that he should bypass the Vatican Department of State and grant me private interviews.

I am also thankful to Primate Wyszyński for giving me many days of his own precious time in Warsaw and Rome for his interpretation of church and state matters, as well as for his contribution of numerous stories about the Vatican, the papacy and most especially John Paul II. I am indeed fortunate that this outstanding humanist gently paved the way for my smooth relations with his successor, Józef Cardinal Glemp, the present Primate, that enabled me to complete this book.

It has been my lifelong practice as a writer to record in my own shorthand the details of conversations as soon as they have taken place. The dialogue in this book is therefore often not verbatim, but is never far from an accurate paraphrasing that reflects what was expressed.

In my specific conversations with the Pope, who is also a born actor and dramatist, I certainly could not use any mechanical recorders; but in my own shorthand I succeeded in capturing his various dialogues with people from his past as well as the narrations of stories and legends in which the Pope imitated the voices and gestures of real and fictitious figures. As a result of those verbal exchanges, which the Pope called "dialogues in dialogue, and dialogues again," an extra dimension was added to the biography of this remarkable man.

Book One: Green Years

1

Crucial Test

"To write a book about the living Pope you have to have the imagination of a poet, the intellect of a philosopher, the patience of a saint, the cleverness of a Jesuit, the knowledge of an encyclopedist, and, above all, the confidence of cardinals—especially those who sit in the Vatican and take care of daily church affairs in the Curia. Naturally, it helps if you know the Pope," said the Reverend Stefan Cardinal Wyszyński, Primate of Poland, to me in June 1979.

The Primate had called me to meet with him at his palace on Miodowa Street in Warsaw. Our friendship had grown over the past twenty years during my frequent visits to Poland. I was working on a different book at the time, and his help in my research was generous. He had arranged for me to meet Pope John Paul II the next day.

"I don't know if I will succeed," I replied.

I first met John Paul II on June 2, 1979, in Warsaw, when not yet Pope for a year, he visited his native Poland. He is built like a soccer player, yet gentle in his relationships with people who come to see him. His smile is that of an innocent child; his blue eyes widened as he said, "It's a pleasure to meet you..." He shook my perspiring palm while his left hand rested on my shoulder. There was a moment of silence, and then we started our conversation. Before it ended, he had invited me to visit him at the Vatican.

Within the next few days, Cardinal Wyszyński began to arrange a series of meetings between me and the Holy Father. To make those arrangements, he would have to convince the Pope to bypass the Vatican State Department, which usually approves all formal audiences. But a formal, fifteen-minute meeting with the Pope would hardly be enough time for me to gather all the material I would need for a book. Yet to circumvent the State Department, an arm of the Curia—the organiza-

tion of Cardinals and their staffs that run the daily business of the
Church—could create animosity between me and the Curia and make
my task in Rome difficult to accomplish. I needed the confidence and
support of the Primate of Poland in order to navigate successfully
through this difficult course.

I met with Cardinal Wyszyński at his palace again later that summer.

The Cardinal told me, "If there ever was a holy Pope in history, John
Paul II is the one." A faint blush on his cheeks accentuated a wart on
one side of his face. His eyes were pale blue like those of the Pope. "I
met the future Holy Father many, many years ago, and quickly discovered in him a great spiritual being, an unusual intellect, a deep love
for humanity and a tremendous capacity for prayer. About a quarter of
a century ago, I told Karol Wojtyla that he would be the Pope some-
day." His fingers combed his thinning gray hair. His thin lips formed
words that didn't materialize. A warm but slightly ironic smile appeared.

I waited no longer. I asked, "If I understand correctly, you were a
candidate for the Papacy. Am I wrong?"

The Cardinal replied, "I am a man of deep faith. I believe that God
leads us all." With assurance, he continued. "Karol Wojtyla was chosen
by God. Why? Because he is young. The youngest Pope since 1846,
when Giovanni Maria Mastai-Ferretti was elected and took the name of
Pius IX. He remained the Pope until 1878."

He continued his observations on John Paul II. "Karol Wojtyla
studied theology under the Nazi Terror. He was active in the Polish
community and church affairs during the Stalinist era. The Holy Father
is an economist and champion of human rights and justice for the
Third World. He supports the workers because he himself was a worker. The Pope is trying to find a *modus vivendi* with the Soviet Union,
other Socialist countries, and Western democracy. He is a pacifist by
conviction who is already trying to prevent another war and save humanity. Do you think the Holy Ghost inspired the Cardinals wrongly
to elect this man?"

"But you, my Primate, helped the Holy Ghost a little bit, did you
not?"

My candor surprised him and he replied, "All of us listen to the voice
of the Holy Ghost. All of us believe deeply in God and His doings."
Iron discipline and efficient organization are the basic elements of the
Church's power in Poland. Out of 36 million Poles, there are 20,234

Catholic priests and 39 different orders, the largest among them, Franciscans, Salesians and Jesuits. The Primate of Poland is in charge of this spiritual army. That seat was held until his death in May 1981 by the Reverend Stefan Cardinal Wyszyński, to whom Pope John Paul II once said, "Beginning this new Pontificate, I am full of love for God and confidence in Him. But if you, Primate, did not have the enormous belief and heroic hopes that are characteristic of you and of your great work for the Church, there would be no Polish Pope."

Behind the Primate stands Bishop Bronislaw Dąbrowski. Officially, the Bishop is the secretary of the Polish Episcopate, the Council of Bishops. In fact, he is the Primate's right hand; his outstanding diplomatic skills help bring both moderate and militant bishops together in support of the Primate, who desires peace and cooperation with government. His talent was recognized by the then Cardinal Wojtyla, head of the Cracow Archdiocese. Bishop Dąbrowski helped Cardinal Wojtyla in his relations with "17 Miodowa Street," the Primate's residence, where the Church's power is concentrated.

Bishop Dąbrowski also has a passion for secular politics. When Solidarity was being formed, he, in the name of the Primate, advised its members and relayed messages from the Primate or even from the Vatican. It was no surprise that the Bishop was received by the Pope for a long audience on February 13, 1981, the day after he arrived in Rome during the height of Solidarity's membership and power.

Toward the end of our meeting, Primate Wyszyński said, "If the Holy Father should invite you to a Mass performed by him in the private chapel of his Vatican apartment, the news of this will travel throughout the Curia. All doors will open for you, and only then can you write an authentic biography of the Pope."

"How could I arrange that?" I asked.

The Cardinal had no time to answer my question. Two men appeared and stood at either side of him. They were the Primate's personal secretary, Reverend Bronislaw Piasecki, and Bishop Bronislaw Dąbrowski.

Warsaw, July 1980. I was invited to supper at the apartments of Bishop Bronislaw Dąbrowski, at number 1 Dziekania Street, to discuss my forthcoming trip to Rome, although a definite date for an audience had not yet been set. According to Cardinal Wyszyński, the Bishop was supposed to instruct me in the intricate etiquette involved in meeting the Holy Father. But I was reluctant to discuss only etiquette. Instead I wanted to talk about the Vatican Curia, and the role the Primate played in the election of John Paul II. I had carefully prepared dozens of questions, because I knew the Bishop was a determined man and would hesitate to divulge information. But I also knew that because I had the support of Primate Wyszyński, the door to the Vatican was already open.

Dinner with the Bishop was on Thursday, July 24, at 7:00 P.M., but I decided to leave my hotel early in order to walk to his home and observe the people on the streets. I asked the porter in the Forum Hotel where I was staying where Dziekania Street was. He took me outside, pointed to the red brick of the Royal Castle and replied that Dziekania was behind that palace. The Castle's roof gleamed gold in the sun. I thanked him, and started off in that direction.

The evening air was balmy and the gray buildings contrasted sharply with the deep greens of the trees and parks I passed. When I reached Ujazdowski Park, I decided to rest on one of the benches near the sculpture of a gladiator. Children walked quietly along the paths, holding hands, and I thought of the contrast between the conduct of these children and those in American parks. I recalled a poem entitled "Children," written by the future Pope in 1958:

They grow unexpectedly through love and suddenly
        they're grownups,
holding hands, wandering in great crowds
their hearts are caught like birds, profiles fading into the dusk.
I know they ponder the pulse of all humanity in their hearts.

Holding hands, they sit on the bank of a river,
trunk of a tree and earth, imprinted on the moon,
a triangle still smoldering…whispering…
the dew has not yet risen, but the hearts of the children
        grow above the river.

Do you think it will always be like that, I ask, when they arise
        and begin their going?
Or another way: chalice of light bent among green stalks;
discover in each one the unknown bottom
all of those things which began in us.

Will they be able not to spoil them,
will they always know how to separate good from evil.

A man sat beside me on the bench. His gray hair was thickest behind his ears; his eyes were deep-set and penetrating. He wore dark pants, a denim jacket and a priest's collar. "Probably a Catholic priest of Polish descent from the United States, looking for his roots, or about to confront the Polish Episcopate with some problem or other..."

Before I'd finished my thought, he grabbed my hand, shook it, and said in Polish, "Reverend Doctor Peszkowski, from St. Mary's College in Orchard Lake, Michigan."

At that moment a ball rolled toward me, which I stopped with my foot. I picked it up and saw a girl, about six, blonde braid hanging down her back, dressed in green, her eyes almost the same color, slowly approach me. She looked at me, the ball and the priest, one after the other.

"Why don't you talk to me?" I asked.

She looked at the ball and replied, "Mother told me not to talk to strangers. Besides, you know what I want."

The priest laughed loudly and the girl stepped back. I rose from the bench and handed her the ball. She said, "Thank you" and ran away. I said good-bye to the priest and went on my way.

I hastened my step and on Victory Square hurried past the *Tomb of the Unknown Soldier*. I didn't look at it.

Uncertain as to exacatly where Dziekania Street was, I asked a young militiaman.

"Not far from here. I am going in the same direction and will show you the way."

"I am looking for number one."

"Ah, you are going to the Polish Episcopate?"

"Yes," I replied. "I was invited to Bishop Dąbrowski's for supper." After a moment I wondered whether I should have divulged my destination to this person.

"He is a smart man," said my guide as we passed the Royal Castle.

"And how do you know that he is so smart?"

"Because I've talked with him a few times. Our police station is not far from the Bishop's offices."

"So you are neighbors."

"Here is Dziekania Street."

At this moment a priest rushed toward me from the other side of the short street. By his wide smile and aquiline nose I recognized Bishop Dąbrowski.

"I guess we're going to the same place," I said.

"Sorry, I'm late," he answered.

I looked at my watch. It was three minutes to seven. "You are not."

"You seem to be under military escort."

I turned to the young man and said, "Please introduce yourself."

The militiaman saluted and the Bishop said, "We know each other."

"Your Eminence," answered the militiaman. "I think it's better to walk with me than with a priest."

"Mr. Militiaman," I said quickly, "I think you're mistaken."

"No," he replied with a grin. "When you go with a militiaman you're on your way to jail. But when you go with a priest, you're on your way to heaven." The Bishop and I laughed, and the militiaman departed.

"As you can see, we have connections not only with the government but with the police," concluded the Bishop.

"Render unto Caesar what is Caesar's, and render unto God what is God's," I replied as we entered his house.

A nun greeted us in the corridor with the words, "Let Jesus Christ be praised."

Dąbrowski and I, in turn, replied, "For ages and ages."

"Supper is waiting," said the plump nun softly.

"Thank you," replied my host. "We are going."

Bishop Dąbrowski and I walked along a narrow corridor, down some steps into a large room. Four tables stood along the walls; in the middle of the room was a large table. As we were about to sit someone entered the dining room. I turned and saw Reverend Peszkowski.

"This is Reverend Peszkowski from the United States."

"We've met," I answered.

The Reverend knelt, took the Bishop's hand and kissed his ring, then nodded to me.

We sat at the table and two sisters brought plates of ham, salads, bread and a bottle of red wine. The younger nun who had the long fingers of a pianist, poured the wine while the shorter one served the food. Dąbrowski got up, we rose with him, and he blessed the food.

When we sat down again, he said, "To your health and success," and to the priest, "Safe return to Orchard Lake."

After a few bites the Bishop looked at me with an ironic smile and said, "I hear that you knew Francis Hodur well."

"Yes, I did," I replied. "Hodur, you know, was born in the village of Zarki in Poland, and became a priest in Scranton, Pennsylvania, in 1893. He left the Roman Catholic Church and organized the Polish National Catholic Church in the United States. In 1907 he was consecrated by Archbishop Van Gul of the Christian Reform Church in Utrecht, Netherlands, and from then on he was known as Bishop Hodur. Francis Hodur was a man of great belief and love of God. He was a hard-working man, a simple man."

The Bishop and the priest were listening intently, and even the two nuns, who had brought us the next dish, veal cutlets, vegetables and plums, were eavesdropping.

I continued my friendly lecture. "In the late nineteenth century, the then Father Hodur introduced the idea of using national languages for Mass and other Church ceremonies to Polish, Lithuanian, Czech and Ukranian Catholics. At that time the Roman Catholic Church uniformly used Latin. But in my opinion, the reason the First Bishop was hated was that the German clergy in America was very influential, and hated everything Slavic. First Bishop Hodur, a long time ago, on a very small scale, was doing the same things that John XXIII and Paul VI did years later."

I fell silent, then Reverend Peszkowski, with a pleasant smile, poured wine into my glass and the Bishop's. Both of them raised their glasses in toast and said, "To your long life."

After we drank, the Bishop asked me, "And what is happening today in Hodur's church?"

"You know better than I. After the election of a Polish Pope, Hodur's church steadily shrank. Maybe in a few years it will return to the jurisdiction of the Vatican."

"That would be good," concluded Bishop Dąbrowski.

"As I get older, I think more and more that it's very difficult to judge in advance what is good and what is bad. *Post factum*, everybody is wise. But right now, I know one thing: with the election of Karol Wojtyla to the Holy See, the prestige of the Roman Catholic Church has grown."

"Pope John Paul II understands very well the constant social changes in the world, and I think he is trying to direct the Church to cooperate with the people who are pressing for radical social and political changes, even for revolution."

"What makes you think that?" asked the Bishop, raising his voice.

"The Holy Father wrote a play, " I replied, "called *Brother of Our God*. In this play the Holy Father says, 'Every one of us walks his own road. Every one of us makes his own nest. In the meantime, for so many people the roads are very crowded. There is no place to put their feet. There is no piece of land they can call their own. There is no slice of bread for which they can work. There is no child that they could bring into the world feeling that the child would not be a burden. In all of us something is lacking. We don't know yet what. We're trying to guess, but I know that this lack of justice will destroy us.' The author of this drama is today the highest authority of Christ on earth."

The meal had ended. The Bishop rose and turning to me, said, "Would you be good enough to come upstairs?"

Reverend Peszkowski got up as well. "I will wait for you here. Perhaps you'll let me take you to your hotel?"

"Thank you," I replied, "I would be most grateful."

"Maybe, Father, you could wait in the waiting room on the first floor?" said the Bishop with authority.

"I will do that," said the priest.

Upstairs, the small sitting room is filled with portraits and etchings of the Pope, the Primate, the Holy Mother of Częstochowa and memorabilia from Rome. The Bishop asked me to sit in a slightly worn but comfortable chair next to a table that held a crystal bowl laden with raspberries, gooseberries and deep red—almost black—cherries. He poured two glasses of cognac, raised his, and said, "To you." The Bishop handed me a bunch of cherries, and just as I put a few in my mouth, said, "Primate Wyszyński must go to Rome in October. You will fly with him to see the Holy Father."

I jumped up in joy, dropping my cherries. My mouth was empty, but I still could not speak. Regaining my composure, I said, "I am overwhelmed by your help and am grateful for your confidence." I stretched my hand toward his; instead, he approached and embraced me, we clapped each other on the back and even placed a few kisses on

Warsaw Cathedral, 1979. Stefan Cardinal Wyszyński with renowned composer Krzysztor Penderecki, during his concert.

Stefan Cardinal Wyszyński and the author en route from Warsaw to Rome, October 1980.

Warsaw, October 1980, in the Primate's palace (left to right): Bishop Dąbrowski,
Cardinal Wyszyński, and the author.

Cardinal Wyszyński and the author, Warsaw, 1980.

Stefan Cardinal Wyszyński, Primate of Poland, 1966.

each other's cheeks. When we returned to our chairs, he said, "But it would be a great honor to you and a tremendous help if the Holy Father should invite you to his private chapel for a Holy Mass."

The Bishop took a handful of gooseberries, and quietly said, "You must understand this thousand-year-old tradition. The Popes used to invite kings, heads of state, princes to the Holy Mass performed by them. But never a writer. If you get an invitation, it will be a tremendous exception. And I am sure, an important event in your own life. The initiative must come from the Holy Father. But to create the atmosphere from where the invitation will come—that's a different story. God's grace appears in various forms. Here on earth often the Holy Father, on the whispered advice of heaven, shows this grace to ordinary people."

"You mean, God has to give the order?"

"Not necessarily." A smile appeared on his face. There was a pause. "Maybe we can go downstairs. Some people from Solidarity are waiting for me." He turned toward the door, pulling a white handkerchief from his sleeve first to wipe his hands, "Allow me to lead the way."

We walked through the narrow corridors and down the stairs. For the first time I noticed that the walls were covered with pictures, among them, portraits of Cardinal Wyszyński and several Popes. The wooden floor, banisters and steps shone with fresh polish. On the first floor we met the Bishop's second guest, Reverend Peszkowski, who, upon seeing us, rose. I smiled at him, but the Bishop, with a wave of his hand, motioned him to sit down. He said to me, "You and I will go downstairs. I will introduce you to some Solidarity leaders." At this moment I realized that we were on the street level and that the dining room was on the floor below.

I said to the Bishop, "Our conversation has left a deep impression on me. I am an emotional man and would like to go to my hotel and think about your goodness and my opportunities. So permit me to skip meeting with the Solidarity people. And Father Peszkowski is waiting to take me back to the Forum Hotel."

"That's a nice hotel," the Bishop added, stretching his hand toward me, "Maybe you are right. Solidarity can wait—for you, that is—but not for me."

When the Bishop embraced me as we said good-bye, Reverend Peszkowski seemed surprised. He approached us, took the Bishop by the hand and kissed his ring. By this time I was at the door. A young cleric opened it with the words, "Let Christ be praised."

I was already outside, but turned and said, "Let Christ be praised." Reverend Peszkowski followed me out.

The wind was cold against my face as we left narrow Dziekania Street and turned toward Castle Place.

· The streets were becoming empty. The wind was gathering power and singing in the trees. From time to time the sounds of taxis and trams in the streets drowned out the sound of the wind. We walked without exchanging a word. Only when we reached my hotel did we shake hands and my new friend left.

At Cardinal Wyszyński's request, I appeared at 17 Miodowa Street the next morning at 10:00 A.M. We sat at a large, elaborately carved oak table with a huge bouquet of red roses, his favorite flower.

In a decisive manner, he told me, "You are going to see the Pope. Therefore, you must have a list of prepared questions." He pushed a notebook toward me. "Think out loud and write your questions here."

I was surprised, but said nothing and reached for my pen. He explained further. "The questions don't have to be in any order, but we should know what you're going to ask the Holy Father."

I had wondered how my questions to the Pontiff would be handled and suspected that they would be reviewed by Wyszyński at least, and passed on to the Pope. Church officials, in their lives on earth, contemplate the unknown every day and want to make sure that everything in this life is arranged as much as possible, to keep the unknown to a minimum.

I had pondered the questions I wanted to put before the Holy Father for over a year.

I began without hesitation, "What are your recollections, and how early do they start, of your parents and home environment? Also, I would like to have some anecdotes and stories to illustrate them."

"Good. A proper question," said the Prince of the Church. His head was bent over folded hands. The fragrance of roses floated in the large room and through the French doors into the lush garden beyond.

"Does His Holiness' deep love for his own mother have any spiritual connections with his deep love for the Holy Mother of Częstochowa?"

The Primate raised his head, and I saw that he was surprised. "I have to admit, this is a deep psychological question. I would be offended, because of Freudian undertones. There is some doubt that the Holy Father will want to reply to this question."

"Maybe you can answer this question: how and when did the Holy Father know that he wanted to become a priest? Was this great love for God really disappointment over a woman? Personal tragedy? Family situation? The early death of his sister? In other words, was there one specific thing or was it a combination of facts and experiences that influenced him? I would like to ask for analysis."

"I would not press the idea of a disappointment in love."

"Do you think priest Wojtyla thought he could become the Pope simply through hard work, intelligence and prayer? How much is Cardinal Wyszyński's behind-the-scenes work responsible? Also, in the 'making of the Pope,' what was the position of such cardinals as Prince Sapieha, Franz Cardinal König of Vienna, the Third World cardinals, some of the 'guilty' German cardinals, and, last but not least, your friend, Pericle Cardinal Felici?"

Cardinal Wyszyński looked at me, then looked again toward the garden, as if he wanted to ensure that what he said would be objectively received. "Before you ask a question like this, you have to have a basis in fact."

"I thought I would ask the Pope general questions at first, then, if he was receptive, approach him with specific ones about the election." I didn't want to abandon this important and very interesting problem, so I asked point blank: "How did the election look from the viewpoint of His Holiness? And especially the mechanism of this very intricate function?"

"This is a perfectly natural question, to which no Pope in the history of the Roman Catholic Church would answer, and I think it would be better for you and me if you didn't ask this question." He stopped, and I saw on his face a slight regret that he had involved himself with me and my project. But I also read in his proud and stubborn face that he would not disappoint me.

I poured out my questions for two hours. The Cardinal took notes and commented on each question I proposed—which the Holy Father would try to avoid, which might be reworded.

"That's an enormous group of important points, and I personally would not like to respond to them right away," said my host, glancing at his watch, "I think it would be better if you could confront the Holy Father and me with more specific questions."

"I will do that, but in the meantime I would like to ask Your Eminence for indulgence and finish with my questions to the Holy Father, to receive your acceptance later."

"Not now," said the Cardinal, looking again at his watch, "I have a meeting. I will allow you to finish another time, in a more leisurely fashion. I will be honest with you; we think a book like yours will be important for the Church. But I'm not certain whether you will succeed in being objective."

"I will try my best, providing I get accurate verbal and written material."

"I will do everything possible to fulfill my obligation to you," responded the Prince of the Church.

I closed my notebook. "I thank you very much. If I finish this book with your help, I think we should be coauthors."

"That's a clever approach, but at the same time it is an exaggeration," replied the Primate with a smile. "Please retype your questions and submit them to me, and I'll see what I can do." He rose, then I rose still not giving up.

"I would like to address one more query to the Holy Father."

"What? I think you have asked enough."

"It would be very useful to me if the Holy Father could describe one day in his life as the Pope. I'm interested not only in his prayers and meditations, but also in his thoughts and desires."

"*Bene*," said the Primate, resting one hand on my shoulder. "The replies to your questions will create harmony and present the character of a unique man."

"I am grateful that you think so."

We walked toward the door. There was time for one more favor. Pulling a white envelope from my pocket, I said, "I would like to ask you to deliver this letter to the Holy Father."

There was annoyance and disapproval on the Primate's face.

"Please. The envelope is open."

He began reading hurriedly, glancing at me from time to time.

I am writing to you in connection with my scheduled visit to Rome and my audience with you accompanied by the Reverend Stefan Cardinal Wyszyński.

At that time, I understand that you will grant me an audience in order to enable me to write a book about you, which will be both biographical and a commentary of your view on the problems and the issues which face mankind.

Among matters to be discussed are your opinions on the Middle East and how to solve the problems which that area of the world faces, relations between the sexes, and a discussion of your personal life prior to ascending to the office which you now hold.

The letter requested the Pontiff's permission to use all interview material in this book.

"This looks like a typical American business letter. I do not believe that the Holy Father will sign this or any letter pertaining to the book," said the Cardinal, folding the letter back into the envelope. "Here we are dealing on a higher level. We cannot destroy our *rapprochement* with petty things like this. Knowing the Holy Father, he will say what I am going to say to you right now, 'Write the way you feel. Nobody will censor you, neither during the writing of the book nor after it is finished. We will simply read the book after it is published.'"

"And what will happen then?"

"Later God will judge you." He opened the door. "The best document would be a photograph, and our best photographer here in Warsaw is Marek Langda."

At this moment there was a flash from a camera.

"This will be the most important evidence of our friendship," concluded the Primate of Poland. We embraced.

Before I left the Primate's Palace I thought it would be informative to see how many and what kinds of people were in his waiting room. When I peered in, I saw two priests and five well-dressed civilians. A portrait of the Pope hung on the wall under a lithograph of the Holy Mother with open arms, as though she were embracing all the people in the room. Above one of the doorways was a painting by Jacek Malczewski, *The Kiss of Death*, a self-portrait of the artist lying in the arms of the Angel of Death. Above another doorway hung a picture by another prominent Polish painter, Jan Kotowski, titled *The Harrowing*. One more landscape hung in the room; a picture titled *Heathland*, by Józef Rapacki.

"Each symbolizes for me a certain season in human life," said the Primate.

I looked at the paintings on the white walls, but my true attention was focused on the people. Although I had seen their faces before, either in a newspaper or at a public gathering, I could not recall their names.

One of the priests resembled the French Cardinal that the Primate had said was coming to speak to him. But, I thought, a French Cardinal coming to discuss religion in the Soviet Union would not be spending time in the waiting room with others. However, I didn't have time to pursue my Sherlock Holmesian speculations because someone tapped me on the shoulder. I turned to face an old, thin priest by the name of Stanislaw Kotowski who, in the court of the Primate, played the role of the 'gray eminence,' and who had been of assistance to me during the Pope's visit to Poland.

"May I help you?" he asked as we shook hands.

To disguise my reason for gazing into the room, I said, "Reverend Stanislaw, do you know that *Heathland* by Rapacki is really a copy of the original?"

"Impossible!"

"I am almost sure."

"Probably some time during the night a Communist sneaked in and switched the pictures," said the good priest, holding his thin face between long palms. Maybe he was just acting. But I noticed that all eyes in the waiting room were turned on me. I touched the forehead of the distressed Stanislaw and said, "Please, don't worry so much about trivial things like that."

In a few seconds I was outside. The warm sun and deep green of the trees refreshed me. Leaving the Palace premises through open gates, I was now on a very busy street. I felt optimistic that the gates to Wojtyla would also be open for me. Who would be my *cicerone* on this voyage? None other than the Primate of Poland, the Pope's old and dear friend—Stefan Cardinal Wyszyński.

2

Flight to Rome

THURSDAY, October 23, 1980. I rose at 5:00 A.M. and looked out of my window in the Forum Hotel in Warsaw. The sun was already up, and the people on the street were wearing coats and hats. While dressing, the telephone rang. A young man was on the other end, Zdzislaw Bień, who was my official guide. He said he was waiting for me in the lobby with my private photographer, Janusz Czerniak. They picked up my valises and left for Okęcie Airport. After a hurried cup of tea and a roll with honey, I took a taxi to the Primate's Palace on Miodowa Street. We were to travel to the airport together.

In the car, the Primate whispered that the day before, he had seen Stanislaw Kania, Edward Gierek's successor, the first secretary of the United Workers Party, in whose hands lay the highest political power in Poland.

"Did he want to convert you, Your Eminence, or did you want to convert him?"

He replied, cryptically, "It is easy to convert others, but it is difficult to convert yourself."

"I presume the initiative for the meeting came from him."

"Yes. He is a fairly intelligent and pragmatic man. His position is simple. He must satisfy the desire of the nation for a better life, and at the same time, have a good relationship with his powerful neighbors, if you know what I mean."

"But tell me—what did he ask you to do?" I pressed.

"Oh that. He asked me, as the head of the Church in Poland, to suggest to the clergy that they cooperate with his government and appeal to the people from the pulpits to quiet down and start working harder."

"But Your Eminence has already done so in your sermon at the Shrine of Jasna Góra."

"Yes, I mentioned that, but he said the Church as well as the government is responsible for the situation in this country. At this stage, everybody should have as much good will and wisdom as possible. But to fulfill our obligations, I said to him, 'For us in the Church, national, cultural and economic independence, and morality in government are necessary.'"

"And what did he say to you?"

"He said that he was quite aware of my positive activities, and that he was grateful for my constant preaching on the subject of citizens' responsibility and respect for the law."

"That's beautiful, but please tell me what Mr. Kania asked you to relay to the Pope."

The Primate was uncomfortable when I pressed him, but he gave me an honest reply. "He asked me to appeal to the Pope and intercede with western governments and banks about Poland's debt to the West."

"Does that mean that the Pope, because he is Polish, should be the *intermediario* in Polish financial affairs?"

"That was more or less the essence of our conversation," replied the Primate, looking worried. "Twenty-six billion dollars is a tremendous amount of money for a poor country. Look around. Do you see much effect from this invested money?"

I didn't have time to reply because we had arrived at the airport.

In the VIP Lounge a group of people was waiting to greet the Primate, including Jerzy Kuberski, the government's Minister of Religious Affairs. A polite, balding man, about 5 feet 10 inches tall, he greeted us, holding his hat in one hand. Only his three-quarter-length leather coat indicated that he was a functionary of the Socialist government. This type of coat was popular in Europe thirty years ago; I guessed the Minister was a frugal man. If you spoke to him, you would realize from the first sentence that he was intelligent and sincere. He had positive standing with the country's clergy. I observed him for some time while he sat with Bishop Bronislaw Dąbrowski, leafing through some notes.

Within minutes, a line began to form, headed by the Primate and Minister Kuberski. Bishop Dąbrowski drew me into the line directly behind them. Before we entered the minibus that would take us to the plane, the Primate nodded, and all thirty people in his entourage – including his doctor and a nurse, both women—gathered for a photograph. The Primate turned to me and said, "This is for your book."

In the airplane, the Primate occupied the front seat by the window. His personal secretary, Reverend Piasecki, sat me beside him, then helped the Primate to fasten his seatbelt. His Eminence smiled with embarrassment, then opened his briefcase and began to write. I borrowed his paper, the daily *Zycie Warszawy* (*Warsaw Life*), and began reading. Moments later, Bishop Dąbrowski asked if he could sit in my seat and have a few words with his superior and Minister Kuberski. They huddled for several minutes, discussing something in whispers; the Minster left the airplane and the Bishop and I returned to our seats. The plane taxied down the runway.

The first words the Primate said were, "If there is a saint living among today's cardinals, he is John Paul II." At this moment, the airplane jerked upward. "If there is a great philosopher among Christian philosophers, it is the man who sits in the Vatican today. You should remember this when you converse with His Holiness."

"Thank you for reminding me and for your constant help."

He didn't reply; but reached for his breviary and immersed himself.

A stewardess brought breakfast. The Primate didn't look at the meal spread before him; his lips were silently forming words from the breviary. Every once in a while a passenger got up to see if he had started eating; out of politeness they wanted to wait until he began. I didn't touch my meal either, as I was sitting beside him. Noticing this, he put his breviary aside.

"You see my eyes concentrating on the breviary, but God sees my stumbling heart." He reached for a roll. I turned around and saw the other passengers begin their breakfasts with noticeable relief. The Primate didn't turn around; yet he smiled about the same thing. The way he picked at the ham on his plate with his fork told me he wasn't really interested in eating. Almost everyone knew that for a long time he had been having problems with his stomach. One of the members of his entourage whispered to me that he suffered from cancer.

I looked at the Primate's gray face, and thought that he might be dwelling on his sickness. My first reaction was to try to cheer him up. But he was quicker than I; he interrupted our moment of silence.

"Anyone who has a full stomach is digging his own grave with his teeth," he said, trying to smile. "Even if the teeth are false."

I decided to divert him from the subject. "Allow me, Your Eminence, to tell you a joke about an American priest."

"Go ahead."

"On a street in Detroit, Michigan, a man stood kicking his motorcycle and cursing because it wouldn't start. A passing priest heard the blasphemy and said to the young man, 'My son, raise your thoughts to God and ask for forgiveness. Maybe then your motorcycle will start.' The motorcyclist looked at the priest and quieted down. Raising his head toward the sky, there was a short pause; then he kicked the starter repeatedly, jumped on the bike as it started to run, and zoomed away. 'Goddamn it,' the priest muttered to himself. 'I just performed a miracle.'"

The stewardess approached us and asked, "Coffee or tea?"

"I would like tea," replied the Primate. Turning to me, he said, "I beg you, when you see the Pope, behave with dignity, because he is an unusual man and deserves all your respect. Anything he touches he makes better. I don't want him to think I introduced you for some ulterior motive."

"Your Eminence, before I told you this joke, I asked your permission. No one can say that I haven't behaved improperly toward the clergy, although I haven't kissed anyone's ring."

"I think you were discussing Hell in the airport today with one of the priests."

I was surprised that news about me had travelled so fast and so far.

"Yes, I said that according to Christian and Mohammedan theologies, Hell is fire and that according to Hindu religious teachings, Hell is flame. So judging by religious belief, God is a baker."

"Yes, I think that's what you said and I'm glad you're not deceiving me now."

"Your Eminence, I just quoted Victor Hugo."

"But why do you have to repeat all these negative things?"

"Perhaps I shouldn't discuss sin, punishment or salvation with anyone; after all, they are heavy subjects. But I think a little joke can lighten a heavy subject, and make it easier to bear the unknown. Besides, deep in my heart, I feel God will forgive me. And if God forgives me, I think Your Eminence should too."

The Primate replied, as if to himself, "I think you are an honest man, but unintentionally, you will create some problems for me at this stage of my life which I don't need."

"What kind?"

"I think, unintentionally, you will ask the Holy Father some embarrassing questions."

"I submitted questions to you and will stick to them. I even signed a paper saying that I would."

"You don't have to do that. Nobody would judge you severely if you didn't. Maybe God will, but then I don't know his attitude toward you. The Holy Father agreed to see and talk to you, and from now on, this is his problem." He paused. "This I leave to your own conscience. But again I must emphasize that John Paul II is a unique man who is introducing to the world God's plans for humanity. I hope he will live long and have time to raise humble people closer to God, and engage mighty people in helping the suffering masses to a better standard of living. But I have observed tremendous opposition to his plans already. In the East, socialist regimes are saying that the Pope is upsetting their order. In the West some major industrialists and landowners are saying the Pope is trying to destroy the free enterprise system. I know that there are those in powerful circles who would like to get rid of him."

"But the Pope is a wise man, as you have said. He has started reforms already with the cooks and servants in his papal apartment. Now they only have to work eight hours a day, and they even get days off."

"Yes, as a matter of fact he's begun everywhere simultaneously and he's perceptive and decisive. For this work, he needs a long life and trusted advisers." The Primate looked out the window. "We are approaching Rome. About these things we will speak many times later, but remember, don't disappoint me."

I felt the plane descend. Primate Wyszyński leaned toward me, "For us, with the will of God, it is important to have as holy a Pope as John Paul II.

At the Rome airport, we landed into a sunny day. While disembarking, the Primate offered me accommodations with him. Valuing my independence, I declined, but said that I would like to see him often during my stay in Italy.

"I'm here to help you," he said in a friendly voice.

In all my travels, I have never arranged accommodations in advance. And traveling with the Primate of Poland, I did not worry about my hotel because I knew that the Church people would make sure I was taken care of. In this case they knew that I was a special guest of Primate Wyszyński and they could not afford to ignore me.

The Primate was the first to descend from the plane. I started to follow him, but Bishop Dąbrowski nudged me aside, saying, "I have to be close to the Primate." I let him pass, along with the Primate's secretary and two priests. When Cardinal Wyszyński reached the ground, a tall man in a gray suit approached him, knelt on the ground, took his hand and kissed his ring. Moments later this man led the Primate to a waiting Fiat; they were followed by Bishop Dąbrowski and the Primate's secretary. As the car started the Primate waved to me through a window. Waving back, I proceeded with the rest of the entourage to a minibus and we rode to the airport building.

The Customs officials let me through quickly. Janusz Czerniak, my photographer, joined me in the waiting room. Suddenly someone tapped me on the shoulder. I turned and saw my American friend Hulbert Aldrich, banker and Hamilton buff.

"Huck, what are you doing here?" I asked. "Spying on me?"

He laughed and remarked, "I noticed that you are on good terms with the Primate."

"If you like to think so."

"I have just arrived from a conference in Vienna and am waiting for my wife Amy to join me."

As I began to leave with Mr. Czerniak, a tall, fortyish man with an ascetic face approached me from the side and asked my name. When I told him, he introduced himself.

"I am Father Casimiro Przydatek, a Jesuit priest and the secretary general of Corda Cordi, the pastoral center where you will be staying."

This disclosure surprised me. I didn't expect the Jesuits to offer Czerniak and me a place to stay. My mind wandered back through the years to my early days at school, when I had stayed with the Jesuits. The great-nephew of Wlodzimierz Ledóchowski, the General of the Jesuits between 1914 and 1942, was a classmate of mine at *gimnazjum* (high school) in Wlodzimierz. In exchange for tutoring him in his classes, I lived with his family. The offer to stay in Corda Cordi was most welcome, and we left with Father Casimiro. A porter followed with the suitcases.

A second priest waited for us in the parking lot. He was of medium height, had short, grayish hair, and wore a black suit with his priest's collar.

"I am Reverend Mieczyslaw Maliński from Cracow," he said. We took our places in a black Fiat. I sat in front with Father Casimiro, my photographer took the back seat with Maliński. The sun was hot; we all rolled down the windows simultaneously. Casimoro maneuvered the car through the heavy traffic toward the Eternal City. None of us had exchanged a word, until Reverend Maliński said,

"Sir, please call me Mietek. This way we will save lots of time." I asked him to call me by my first name.

The Jesuit interjected, "You will please call me Father Casimiro."

"At what hotel are you staying?" asked Mietek.

"Our guest will stay with us in Corda Cordi. That's the understanding I have with the Primate."

"You have also been invited to stay with Bishop Dąbrowski," Mietek said to me.

The Jesuit renewed his offer, "If our modest place would be comfortable for you, you may stay. Otherwise, you may go with Mietek to the Bishop's."

"Anything is okay with me, provided I can pay for your hospitality."

"We don't take money from distinguished guests like yourself," replied Father Casimiro, drawing each word out distinctly. His voice resonated with authority.

"If you won't take money for room and board, please take me to the Primate's headquarters or the Bishop's apartment," I said, trying to emphasize my independence.

The Jesuit noticed this and replied, "It is all right with me; I will give instructions to the sisters in Corda Cordi to accept your donation."

We went through Rome quickly and reached Via della Conciliazione, directly in front of St. Peter's Basilica, turning left into a short dead-end street called Via Pfeiffer. The car stopped in front of a door above which a sign read Corda Cordi. A short, stocky Italian man emerged and bowed politely. Father Casimiro said, as if to emphasize that he seldom drove the car, "This is Sergio Minante, my chauffeur and handyman."

I grabbed the chauffeur's hand and introduced myself and the photographer.

He replied, "I am Sergio."

Three sisters in black robes with white collars appeared, and Casimiro introduced us. Medarda, the Sister Superior, was short and plump with soft eyes and unusually warm hands. "I will help you with your suitcases," she said, then nodded to the others. One looked like a girl fresh from the village, her cheeks still pink, her pleasant smile revealing white teeth. These attributes, combined with her blonde hair, conjured up for me the picture of a village saint. The second sister was tall and handsome, with black hair, deep brown eyes and pale skin. Her look and movements resembled those of an aristocrat.

"It is a pleasure to meet you," I said.

Sergio carried the suitcases upstairs; the sisters and I followed. My room was at the end of a corridor on the third floor. It was clean and there was a lot of light.

"It is good there are two beds, so Janusz can sleep on the other," I said, thinking aloud.

The sisters looked at one another. "Why do you think so much about your personal photographer?" Sister Superior Medarda asked.

Sergio put my suitcases down and she said, "Thank you. You may go."

I took five dollars from my pocket and offered them to Sergio. He blushingly refused. I asked, "Did I do something wrong? I'm sorry."

He spoke quickly in Italian to Sister Medarda. I recognized only two words: coffee and rum. When he left, Sister Medarda said, "He felt offended; but to make it up, he wants you to be his guest for coffee and rum."

"What do you mean?"

"He works without pay. He loves Father Casimiro, and considers himself to be Casimiro's equal. Sergio is a little peculiar; but we are thankful to God for giving us this man."

I simply nodded in agreement with the Sister Superior. Still standing in the middle of the room, I said, "I have a feeling that someone has doubts about my photographer. Are you aware that he is being financed by me?" I opened my suitcase, intending to show her the letter of agreement between us.

Czerniak, an active member of the Communist Party in Poland, had come highly recommended by Wlodzimierz Wilanowski, the director of the Polish airline, Lot, and an old friend. In exchange for $100 per day and hotel accommodations, Czerniak had agreed to give me exclusive rights to any photos he took of the Primate and of the Pope.

"I don't need proof. But some would say that you should discharge him."

"Why?"

"I don't know, exactly, and please don't quote me. But they don't want him to be close to the Holy Father."

At that moment a thought crossed my mind that some people in the Curia, which is composed of a few thousand employees and is an executive body of the Vatican, had already checked on my innocent photographer. Then I asked her, "Who are 'they'?"

"I cannot say. But I advise you secretly and honestly," emphasized Sister Medarda. "It would be more complicated if some Vatican official asked you to get rid of him."

"How could they? We have a contract. I am taking responsibility for his behavior."

"You are writing a book about the Pope, are you not?"

"Yes."

"You want to have access to the Holy Father?"

"Certainly, I do."

"As one friend to another – please get rid of him. You will argue, and you will get upset and nervous in a complicated situation; and finally, Mr. Czerniak will have to be sent back to Warsaw. You will not win against the Curia."

"But Mr. Czerniak already took many photographs of the Primate and me at the airport, and in the airplane. He was accepted by everyone."

"In Warsaw, Cardinal Wyszyński is the supreme authority. Here, the Holy Father's people are."

"Understood," I concluded, ending the discussion.

"Let's have lunch," Sister Medarda said, leading me down the stairs.

I didn't know who had a grudge or something tangible against my photographer, but I knew that my paramount objective was to create a friendly atmosphere with all kinds of people in the Curia, and to spend as much time as possible with the Pope. I felt that Sister Medarda spoke in the name of someone higher.

At the first opportunity, I talked with Janusz and explained, without mentioning any names, my predicament. I was surprised that he created no opposition; nor did he question me. Instead, he asked if he could remain in Rome for a few days before he returned to Warsaw and use the facilities of my room. I consented and gave him $400 with the agreement that during this stay he would take photographs of the Vatican and Rome for possible use in the book. Czerniak kept his promise.

The next day, Arturo Mari from the Servizio Fotografico de *L'Osservatore Romano* offered his services to me. I accepted.

3

Holy Mass for a Sinner

SISTER MEDARDA left me at the door of the dining room. When I entered, eleven men dressed in clerical garments were seated at a long table, among them my host, Father Casimiro. Plates with cold meat, cheese, bread and fruit were on this table; carafes of red and white wine circled a vase of flowers. As I approached the table, everyone rose. Father Casimiro introduced me to his guests, priests of various rank, some of whom worked in the Vatican while others were in Rome for a meeting of the Synod of Bishops. He offered me his seat. Instead, I found a vacant chair.

"I am hungry," I said to my host, who looked at me intently. I reached for a piece of bread; my hand was trembling, and I dropped it.

The priests began talking among themselves about death and immortality. One young man—probably the youngest—who was called Jan Musial, began to talk about Hell. I didn't know much about Hell from a theological or metaphysical viewpoint, so I did not take part in the discussion.

A private audience with the Pope is usually arranged through the Vatican State Department—a process that takes approximately three months. During that time the State Department conducts an investigation to assure themselves—and the Pope—that no embarrassment or physical harm will come to the Holy Father if the request for an audience is granted.

But in order to collect enough material for a biography, I needed to talk with the Pontiff not once but several times. Cardinal Wyszyński made the arrangements, privately and directly—what is known in the Vatican as "going through the kitchen." And the State Department set about their examination of my character, secretly and subtly, during the days I was in Rome to see the Pope.

"Father Casimiro asked me point blank, "Do you believe in God?"

"Yes, I do," I replied, thinking, 'You judge me and my attitude toward God by my actions.'

"What kind of God do you believe in?"

"I believe in the eternal energy which exists in all people and in everything, organic or nonorganic. This energy condemns us to birth, to life, and to death; it allows us to love, even to kill, to sacrifice, to create things, to admire the universe – this energy, which was, is, and will be, both the governor of us and the universe, is a tremendous mystery and is my God. I think this God is just and to this God I pray for a peaceful life and for the creative time which is assigned to me."

The room was so quiet that I could hear a fly buzzing around the salami. No one said a word. I broke the silence, "A few days after the death of André Gide, his good friend, the Catholic writer François Mauriac, received a telegram, which read, 'There is no Hell Stop You can sin Stop This information was given by St. Peter Stop André Gide.'" Everyone smiled politely.

"Are you not mistaken?" Father Casimiro asked.

"A man who believes and is not mistaken, and wood which does not burn – these things do not exist."

"Casimiro, this is above your head, even though you are a Jesuit," said a Benedictine monk named Karol Meissner, "Leave our guest alone."

The Bishop tapped his wine glass against his plate. "You are an experienced and wise man," he said.

I thought for a moment. "I think Plutarch said to Xenophon that there was no more pleasant sound than the sound of a praising word." After which I added, "You will judge my wisdom through my writing. About my experience, Oscar Wilde observed that everybody tries to cover up their mistakes with the word experience."

They bypassed my quoted thoughts and Father Meissner spoke about women and family. I didn't prevent myself from asking, "How do you know so much about women and the family if you've never married and you have no family?"

The Bishop offered me an explanation, "Reverend Doctor Meissner, along with other ecclesiastical scientists from all over the world, has just finished preparing a tract which was read a few days ago at the Bishops' Synod, which the Holy Father attended."

"Would my learned friend give me some of his time to discuss the position of the Church on the problems of present-day families in general, and particularly on the subjects of women, sex, abortion and extramarital affairs, which, I presume, were discussed during the Bishop's Synod?"

"I am sure that Brother Meissner will work with you," said the Bishop, displaying his authority. "But now, why don't you tell us something about your marital life?"

"Yes, please do," said Father Casimiro, "although, regrettably, your wife is not here."

"Although we were married at City Hall, I have been married to the same woman for forty years." The distinguished guests looked at one another, and I added, "But you already know this." There were visible signs of embarrassment, so I introduced a lighter tone, "I agree with Molière who said, 'When you discover that a woman is bored when you are far away, you should have definite hope that your success is beginning; but when you discover that a woman is bored in your presence, retreat, because your relation with her is surely finished.'" The Bishop and other guests laughed.

After lunch, I received a telephone call asking me to appear that evening at 38 Pietro Cavalini, for a meeting with Cardinal Wyszyński.

The Primate greeted me at the door, "I had a terrible dream last night and can't shake it off."

"What happened?" I asked the Prince of the Church.

In his eyes I read terror. He took my arm and replied quietly, "I dreamed that lions were chewing the walls of my stomach. A terrible sensation. I don't think I will live long—maybe a year. I know you have started research on this book, and I would like to present my views of the battle with Communists in Poland; reflections about my dear Holy Father; about Solidarity; and my life. I would like to know that what you write comes from my lips..." He stumbled on his thoughts and words. I felt sad that so wise a man was beaten down.

I didn't know how to deal with the situation; I thought maybe I should create a lighter mood with a story.

"My friend, a missionary, told me a story about a lion who was running toward him in a desert. My friend found only one solution. He knelt and began praying. At this moment the lion stopped and did the same thing—knelt on his hind legs and raised his front paws to the heavens. My friend was dumbfounded and could barely articulate a few quiet words: 'Are you a Christian lion?' 'Yes, Father,' replied the lion, 'I always pray before a meal.'"

"I have a cancer," said the Primate, dryly. "If I find a free moment here in Rome, or in Warsaw, I would like to tell you about my life, including the secrets which I hold about the Curia, the Holy Father, about how he was elected, my work for peace, my achievements, my mistakes, my sorrow. Let posterity know the truth," he said with what seemed his last strength. I took his arm and led him to a chair.

"I am available whenever you feel the need to talk."

Everything moves at a turtle's pace within the Church. At the end of two days, I still had no word as to when I would see the Pope. I was disappointed and decided to seek some diversion. I began going to restaurants and cafes, spending days sitting by myself, drinking coffee or wine and eating very little.

One day at the restaurant *Zarazá, la tavernetta da Gino*, 21 Via Regina Margherita, a man dressed in a dark suit and wearing a priest's collar asked to join me at my table. We began to talk about Rome, drinking white wine and waiting for a meal. "I have a feeling that you have connections in the Vatican," he said, "and access to the archives. You may be interested in the history of Pope John VIII – how much is fact and how much is fiction.

"Joan Anglicus, a slim, red-haired girl from Cologne sought knowledge and power and climaxed her adventures in a sensational way by becoming the only female Pope in history – Pope John VIII. She was a mysterious and intriguing woman, her reign set against the dangers, lustiness and pageantry of the ninth century, when the city of Rome was under the inauspicious control of the prostitute, Theodora, and her two daughters."

My interlocutor continued, "You should research the eyewitness account of the Italian monk, Anastasius Bibliothecarius, who saw Pope John VIII many times and spoke with her. He wrote his observations and quoted those of many prominent people of the time."

The stranger in priest's garb paused for a moment, but I made no comment, and he went on. "The Irish-born priest Marianus Scotus chronicled her life. He was positive that it was Joan who was elected

Pope in 853. Your compatriot, Martin Polonus, who was also a monk, collected material on the subject in Rome. He wanted to publish his work, but he was interrupted by the Holy See. For the price of the bishopric in Poland, he abandoned the project and handed some material to the Pope. In 1278, while travelling to Poland from Rome, Polonus mysteriously vanished. But he was a clever man; he had left the rest of his writing *Chronicon Pontificum et Imperatorum* with friends in Rome. In this piece, he stated without qualification that the nun Joan, as Pope John VIII, occupied the Holy See for two years, five months, and four days (853–855), the years between Popes Leo IV and Benedict III."

Why was he telling me this? I knew there were dozens of books on the subject but I'd thought they were fairy tales written to compromise the Church.

Finally he asked me outright, "Don't you have an opinion about this?"

"No, I don't. I never heard such things."

I couldn't think straight when I left the restaurant. I suspected that this was a kind of provocation, but from whom? Or maybe, because of my progressive upbringing, the deep-rooted suspicion of religious organizations overpowered me. Nevertheless, I had an undefined feeling that conservative groups of the Curia didn't want me to write this book.

Still, I started looking through the Vatican library for books on the subject. They were in the Vatican Archives. My request for access to those papers was presented to Antonio Cardinal Samore, director of the Archives, but I received neither permission nor a denial of my request. It was merely ignored.

The Polish representative to the Vatican, Kazimierz Szablewski, called and picked me up on Via Pfeiffer. A journalist named Zdislaw Morawski, a correspondent of the Polish Press Agency called to arrange a meeting. I had interesting conversations with both of them about the 'Italian Curia' and the 'Polish Mafia,' that exist in the same Vatican Curia; each competes for the Pope's ear.

Everyone was pleasant, including the old friend of the Pope, Reverend Andrea Maria Deskur, whom the Holy Father had made Archbishop. His sister Helena Ostromęcki told me Deskur had hoped to be a cardinal but had suffered a crippling stroke; thereafter, he was confined to his luxurious Vatican apartment.

My research in the Vatican Library and my travel up and down the Vatican corridors were soon brought to the attention of Reverend Agostino Cardinal Casaroli. I presume news also reached Reverend Wladyslaw Cardinal Rubin, Monsignor Julian Petz, and perhaps Monsignor Stanislaw Dziwisz.

Cardinal Rubin was a confidante of and the two monsignors were secretaries to the Holy Father. I had been in Rome five days and there was still no indication of when I would see the Pope. After all, I did have Cardinal Wyszyński standing behind me, and, I presume, Cardinal Rubin, with whom I had attended Lwów University where he had studied theology and I, philosophy. During an earlier trip to Rome, I visited my friend Rubin many times at 34 Via Conciliazione, at his offices, and at 15 Via delle Botteghe Oscure. We discussed various difficult topics like the Middle East, or religion in the Soviet Union. He trusted me, and I had confidence in him.

I clung to Wyszyński's promise that I would meet with the Pope. But my nights were not passing quickly, and as I tossed and turned in bed, my mind tossed and turned from bad to worse. Would I succeed in getting material for the book?

But then came the evening of Thursday, October 30, 1980. I ate supper at Corda Cordi that night feeling extremely isolated, although, as usual, I took part in the conversation at the table with Father Casimiro and his guests. As soon as I had finished my meal, I went into the corridor and asked the sister sitting at the concierge's desk for my key. When I reached the elevator, a young, modestly dressed woman asked for my autograph. This uplifted me, because in clerical circles in Rome, nothing is spontaneous; everything is deliberate. She gave me her name: Dorota Lan, and mentioned that she read my novel *The Hookmen* in Polish translation. I thanked her, went to my room and lay on the bed. Unable to sleep, I reached exhaustedly for a book *Poetry and Dramas*, by Karol Wojtyla. I tried to read from *In Front of the Jewelry Store*, and could not concentrate. I closed my eyes hoping that I eventually could sleep.

There was a knock at my door and a woman's voice. Without getting off the bed, I called, "Please enter."

I turned toward the entrance and saw a nun whom I had not yet met. Before I could ask her reason for this nighttime intrusion, she said in a clear, loud voice, "Tomorrow morning, punctually at 7 o'clock, you, *Professore*, will appear at the private chapel of the Holy Father to attend Holy Mass."

I jumped from my bed, looking quickly at my watch. It was 10:15 P.M. I asked, walking slowly toward her, "And where is this chapel?"

"In the Papal apartment, Vatican City."

My ignorance amazed her, but I pursued my questions.

"How do I get there?"

"*Professore* ..." the nun emphasized the title ironically. "You go to St. Peter's Square, and turn right toward St. Anna's Church." She hesitated. "St. Anna's Gate ..." The woman stepped outside the door, with a final gesture. "And, *Professore*, please don't take your overcoat." She turned the corner.

I closed and locked my door, and returned to bed, overwhelmed. I felt groggy, so I got up and opened the window. The cold, wet wind slapped my face. I was shivering, but my mind was clearer.

Although the Vatican today occupies only forty-four hectares of the city of Rome, in comparison with the eleventh-century Roman Catholic Church State, which occupied 33 percent of what is today Italy, the moral influence of today's Church is, in my opinion, greater.

Pope Gregory VII excommunicated Henry IV, who was Emperor of the Holy Roman Empire of the German Nations, yet in the year 1077, Henry, dressed in the clothes of a penitent, went to the Papal Castle in the village of Canossa in the Reggionell' Emilia province of northern Italy. He was forced, personally and politically, to come under the control of Gregory VII. (In 1871, Chancellor Otto von Bismarck, in order to signify the power of the Church over the State used the expression, "Going to Canossa".) In modern times, state leaders, from their own goodwill, look to the Holy See for assistance in solving various international problems.

During the Pontificate of John Paul II, the influence of the Pope has grown rapidly among Catholics in both capitalist and socialist countries. Despite his indisputable ecclesiastic conservatism, he has enjoyed great popularity for his drive for social and economic reform. The door was opened for him by Pope John XXIII, who "was born poor and died poor," his successor, Paul VI, who died in August 1978, and probably also John Paul I, who had little time but good intentions (he died in September 1978, after 33 days of rule). In October of the same year, John Paul II, a foreigner, became Bishop of Rome. This unique man has tasted deprivation, poverty and suffering, understands the meaning of the words brotherhood and justice, and has an uncompromising stance in the struggle between the haves and the have nots. Both in the Philippines and in Central and South America, the Pope was notably in opposition to the ruling elite.

John Paul II is determined to be the Pope of the oppressed peoples, against the philosophy of the rulers on the left and the right, both of whom are for *status quo ante*, or, as it was expressed by John D. Rockefeller III during one of my discussions with him on world politics, "Let's not rock the boat."

A majority of the cardinals in the Curia wanted to preserve the status quo, but, charmed by Karol Wojtyla, outmaneuvered by cardinals from the Third World, who were led especially by the active Cardinal Wyszyński, and with the help of the Holy Ghost, they set the climate in which he was elected Pope.

During his coronation, John Paul II, so as not to create a fuss among the conservative cardinals, reluctantly wore the tiara for the first and last time. Through the ages the symbol of papal power has been a triple crown called a tiara. The custom of the papal tiara dates from the traditions of the hairdressing of ancient Persian kings. In the course of a papal coronation, the senior cardinal, who is the leader of the holy congregation, places the tiara on the head of the Pope and says, "You are receiving this tiara decorated with three crowns to remind you that you are the Father of princes and kings, the leader of the world, and Our Master Jesus Christ's representative on this earth."

Pius XII was the last Pope to wear the tiara during all religious functions. John XXIII and Paul VI each wore the tiara only once – during their coronations. Paul VI gave his tiara, which had been beautifully made by an Italian artist, to Francis Cardinal Spellman, to take to New York. John Paul II wore the tiara throughout his inaugural Holy Mass, saying, "You should judge me by nothing else than my deeds for humanity."

The high ecclesiastical and political circles were stongly displeased by his pledge to the people, especially Cardinal Siri, but when the Pope learned of their negative feelings, he paraphrased Aristotle: "Anybody can be angry—that's the easiest thing. But to be angry with the right person, for the right cause, at the right time, to the right degree, is not easy. Not many can do this and still have a clear conscience." His magnanimity was without limits, but he was loyal to his beliefs, insisting on going his own way.

These reflections kept me from sleeping on this memorable night. At 5:00 A.M. I rose and began to dress. I remembered that the nun told me not to bring my coat. It was very cold out, so I put a white, long-sleeved sweater between my undershirt and shirt. I wanted to reach St. Peter's Square as soon as possible in order to observe the Swiss Guard in their Venetian helmets and orange and violet uniforms. These pompous, stiff young men protected a simple man, Karol Wojtyla.

I left Corda Cordi and walked down the empty Via Pfeiffer. The air was thick with dew. I neared Via Conciliazione and turned left, coming face to face with the powerful Bernini columns that guard St. Peter's Basilica.

Above my head were dim electric lights; underneath the lights, emptiness. There were no guards, priests or nuns, no civilians—just sticky, wet emptiness. I was almost frightened by the enormousness of the columns and the facade of the Basilica.

I glanced from the top of the columns toward the horizon, and saw a black figure. Doubling my steps, I hoped to approach this person and ask directions to the private chapel of the Holy Father, but the form disappeared. Again, there was emptiness.

The quiet was interrupted by a conversation among the pigeons hidden in the columns. Walking to my right, I felt again an emptiness inside of me; I hadn't thought this would be my road to the Pope. I wanted to talk to someone, so I said out loud to my wife, who was in New York, "You see? I will be with the Pope!" My loud voice scared the birds. They flew nervously over my head from one side of the square to the other.

At that moment I saw the massive marble steps of St. Peter's; a priest appeared and asked, "Are you the *Professore* Gronowicz?" (If you are not a priest and your hair is gray, everyone in the Vatican calls you professor.)

I felt strength and confidence return.

"Yes," I replied, softly, as if I didn't want to wake up more pigeons. "This way, please." I walked beside him, an obedient goat. At the top of the stairs two Swiss Guards saluted, and let us pass between them. We reached an enormous corridor; the priest pointed to another staircase and said, "That way, please."

I climbed, looking to the left and right, behind and before me, but saw no one except the smiling priest below.

The walls were crowded with mosaics which represented religious scenes. The faces of the figures in the mosaics had melancholy expressions and I feared they might fall on me. They watched, observing me and every difficult step I took. And I, the sinner, whose last confession was when I was eleven years old, climbed higher and higher. I don't know if the Pope knew that my last confession was so long ago. I felt sure that the Curia knew, as well as the holy figures on the walls.

The holy faces in the frescoes seemed to look at me with surprise. How did I know all of those things? They also seemed puzzled as to why the Holy Father didn't have me take the elevator to his private apartments. I imagined one of the holy men explaining to his *confrères*: "He is a sinner; it's enough that the Pope sees him. On top of that, you want him to go to the Pope easily, in an elevator?"

Another holy man replied, "He hasn't been to confession for a long time. The Holy Father is either seeing him out of pity or because they come from the same country. Anyway, the Holy Father had a terrible struggle to convince the Curia that they should let him in."

When I heard this dialogue inside my soul, I said to the holy figures, "Have mercy. As an eleven-year-old boy, I went to confession and told the priest I had eaten meat on Friday. And for that, he gave me a tremendous penance. If I had fulfilled the penance, I would have had no time for studying or even for eating."

Another holy man said to his friends on the wall, "You see? If you were alive today, it wouldn't matter. You could eat meat on Friday and not be punished."

I interrupted: "I was skinny. I was hungry—raised on potatoes and cabbage. Anyhow, I paid for my meat. I was tutor to a boy whose father was a butcher. For helping him, his father gave me meat."

"But you were eating like a pig," said a saint with a long beard. "It is a sin to eat like a pig."

"I was young and didn't use a fork. I didn't have table manners."

Another, more severe saint, with the face of a beautiful angel (he was probably very young when he died), said, "But you didn't fulfill your obligation to the priest."

"I admit, I did have a choice: to fulfill my penance and obligation or to study. I chose the latter."

An old, roundish saint at the top of the second floor said to the young, angelic saint, "You know, to work hard and eat only potatoes is a penance already."

A third saint offered his observation. "He should be forgiven because he was young."

The fat old saint with a bluish face said, "His Holiness Giovanni Paolo II is a smart man; who knows, maybe the smartest Pope in history, He will know what to do."

Yet a different saint replied, "You say that because you want the Holy Father to give the order to restore you. A few weeks ago I heard that the Holy Father said that your face had a peculiar color and was starting to peel, and that you had to be given new life." The conversation was becoming heated.

Then, I heard the sound of a female chorus.

I hurried toward the music, arriving at huge double doors which swung open before I had time to wipe the perspiration from my face. Two tall Swiss Guards dressed in shining uniforms saluted me by banging their halberds on the ground; two civilians standing behind them pointed to me. I assumed I should walk along the narrow red carpet lining the corridor. After taking fifteen steps, a girl, no more than twelve, crossed my path. The white blouse and colorful skirt she wore and her straight, dark brown hair suggested that she might be Polish, so I asked, in my mother tongue, "Can I speak to you for a moment?"

"Later, I am in a hurry," she replied, in that language as she grabbed the brass banister and ran down the stairs. The singing engulfed me and I gave no more thought to the girl.

There are no words to describe my mood as I listened to the abstract and beautiful melodies coming from the papal sanctorum. I am not a religious man, yet the beauty of the chapel and the choir of voices stirred complex feelings.

I walked a few dozen steps and noticed an open door. Beyond it, to the left, a small, narrow chapel ornamented with pastel paintings. On either side were rows of nuns, perhaps eighty in all, the source of the beautiful singing. The altar was suffused in gold and light. In the middle of the chapel, the Holy Father knelt, head bent, immersed in prayer. I looked at the altar and saw a sculpture of Christ carved in gold. To my right, at the level of Christ's feet, hung a small dark painting, in a gold frame, encrusted with gold and jewels; a picture of the Virgin Mary of Częstochowa.

The chapel as well as my heart were full of love, but at the same time, a feeling of the smallness of man. Nobody could be so blind as not to have noticed the beautiful colors of the chapel, nor could one have been so deaf as not to have heard the overwhelmingly beautiful melodies. I was neither cynical nor so deprived of human feelings as not to recognize the truth that life is finite and yet has immortal dimensions. Personally, I had not completely decided to say yes or no to these propositions; to speak either of those two words is easy; to take responsibility for believing one of them was the greatest burden on my conscience.

A nun disappeared, returning moments later with a chair. She nodded for me to sit. I have always adhered to the maxim that it is better to sit uncomfortably than to stand comfortably in someone else's door. Yet I decided to stand, and witness this *misterium* from a slightly higher level. Everyone was standing, except the Pope, who was kneeling and praying.

My head was clearing, probably because of the lovely Middle Ages frescoes, the abundance of gold and the intricate and clever arrangement of lights in the chapel.

The Pope became more and more engrossed in prayer and the singing more mellow. I was impressed by the sincerity and the piety of the Pope kneeling between the black and white rows of the singing nuns. I was certain at that moment that John Paul II was the only leader in today's world who had a deep feeling for peace, together with the power and determination to do good. These combined qualities could make him a positive and powerful factor in solving the problems of today's world. I knew he was aware of these powers, and that despite the millennia-old ecclesiastical trimmings which contradicted his personal simplicity, that he was a humble man who prayed to God to help him in his work for man.

The singing continued. The Holy Father rose from his *prie-dieu*, gray with gold trimmings, and slowly, his hands clasped together, walked toward the altar. A hand pushed me forward. I was excited, more so than I had ever been in my life: not in the sense that my pulse was racing at 120 beats per minute – there was a curious kind of peace in it. Blood rushed to my cheeks. I hesitated where the Pope had been kneeling. He was now at the foot of the altar, where again he knelt, made the sign of the cross, rose and continued forth. Two priests emerged from behind the altar. From the right appeared Stanislaw Dziwisz, from the left, Julian Petz. Two nuns in white garb followed with the papal garments. The priests began dressing the Pope for the celebration of the Holy Mass.

It was an emotional experience for me to observe all the steps leading to the performance of the highest mystery of the Roman Catholic Church, celebrated by the Supreme Pontiff, the representative of Jesus Christ on earth.

In substance and in form the Holy Mass is not only a mystery but represents the philosophy, theology and viewpoint of 800,000,000 Roman Catholics the world over.

The chorus abruptly stopped. The first part of the Holy Mass began as the strong voice of the Holy Father rose in a melodious chant: "In the name of the Father, and the Son, and the Holy Spirit. Amen."

The gathering repeated after him; I think I heard only the word, Amen, because I was so absorbed in thought. Why was I here and why had this Mass been arranged for me? Am I worthy? The people in the chapel took a more active part in this expression of love for God.

> ... Judge me, O God, and distinguish my cause against an ungodly notion; deliver me from the unjust and deceitful man.
> O send out Thy light and Thy truth; Thou hast led me and brought me unto Thy holy hill, even unto Thy tabernacles...

Once again the Holy Father lifted his voice in prayer, and was joined by his two assistants and the faithful gathering:

> I confess to almighty God, to Blessed Mary, ever virgin, to Blessed Michael, the Archangel, to blessed John the Baptist, to the Holy Apostles Peter and Paul, to all the saints, and to you Father, that I have sinned exceedingly in thought, word and deed, through my fault, through my most grievous fault...

The second part of the Holy Mass, called the Sacrifice, begins with the Offering:

> ...Receive, O Holy Father, Almighty and Eternal, this spotless Host, which I, Your unworthy servant, offer to You...for my own countless sins, transgressions and failings...

A dialogue between the celebrant and the congregation that introduces the most important part of the Mass:

> The Lord be with you.
> And with your Spirit.
> Lift up your hearts.
> We have lifted them up to the Lord.
> Let us give thanks to the Lord our God...Be pleased, O God, to bless this offering...that it may become for us the Body and Blood of Your dearly beloved Son, our Lord Jesus Christ, Who, the day before He suffered, took bread into His holy and venerable hands, and with His eyes lifted up to Heaven...He blessed, broke, and gave it to His disciples, saying: 'Take and eat you all of this, for this is My Body...'

I was moved by this Mass, performed for me. My thoughts were confused. The Holy Father approached me, the chalice in one hand, the white wafer now transformed into the Body of Christ in the other. He looked into my eyes as he spoke:

> Behold the Lamb of God, Behold Him Who takes away the sins of the world...May the Body of our Lord Jesus Christ preserve your soul to life everlasting. Amen.

Throughout my life I have been a suspicious, cynical man. Nothing could dissuade me from a rational, materialistic way of thinking. This outlook has resulted in a hard existence. I rarely received anything for free, and early in life, when I did, paid for it three times over with bitterness in my heart. I was closed within myself, and even when someone approached me with kind words or deeds, I thought there was a scheme behind it. My perceptions were developed on Polish soil. With age, a person may become mellow, due to physical, emotional or intellectual weaknesses or strengths.

Those were my thoughts as I looked into the Pope's eyes, at his hands, which offered me Holy Communion, and at the shining golden chalice, in whose reflection I saw my own pained face. I thought that this ceremony influenced me because of its two-thousand-year-old tradition, and that it overwhelmed not only a simple man like myself but also the Pope.

The ceremony, at this particular second, changed me. I began to think that religion had a positive place in one's life. For how long?

The most distinguished Celebrant looked at me again with understanding or pity, his delicate smile pregnant with compassion. I swallowed the Communion, he looked at me once more, smiled and slowly turned around. As he walked toward the altar, I stood motionless. The songs seemed more joyful now.

> …Grant, O Lord, that what we have taken with our mouth, we may receive with a pure mind, and that from a temporal gift it may become for us an eternal remedy…The Lord be with you.
> And with your spirit.
> Go, you are dismissed.
> Thanks be to God.

The Mass had ended, but fragments remained with me:

> In the beginning was the Word, and the Word was with God, and the Word was God. The same was in the beginning with God. All things were made by Him, and without Him was made nothing that was made. In Him we live, and the life was the light of man; and the light shone in darkness, and the darkness did not comprehend it…That was the true light, which enlightened every man that cameth into His world. He was in the world, and the world was made by Him, and the world knew Him not. He came unto His own, and His own received Him not. But as many as recieved Him, to them gave He power to become the sons of God; to them who believed in His name, who were born not of blood, not of the will of the flesh not of the will of man, but of God…

The echoes of the singing slowly died and the nuns filed out of the chapel one by one, leaving in their place a stillness. Reverend Dziwisz and Reverend Petz removed the Pope's vestments and handed them to two white-robed nuns. Then they followed the nuns carrying the garments from the presbytery.

I don't know when I discovered that I was alone with the Pope. He wore a well-pressed cassock. I was motionless. The Pope approached me, put an arm around my shoulder, and smiling broadly, said, "Let's have breakfast."

I was awakened from my dream, brought back to reality with the thought that the age of eleven was the last time I went to confession and took Holy Communion. I did not have the strength to say this out loud, but he said, as if in reply: "Don't worry. I know. The Pope is privileged to give you complete absolution." We looked at one another, but had no words to exchange.

And so our friendship began, and so this book began.

On the way to breakfast, I related, "I have a strange feeling in my heart, or, if you prefer, my soul; maybe it's my usual premonition, but something tells me to warn you that you should watch out for your life."

His face paled and he looked at me; I noticed a dark shadow in his blue eyes, as though in that brief moment he was trying to remember all the people, pictures and scenes from his life.

Then he spoke, "I pray for everybody, and I work for the salvation of souls and the well-being of physical bodies. Is there a man on this earth who would like to harm me?"

On the way to the dining room Primate Wyszyński joined us and the Pope remarked, "If you don't object, the three of us will try to recollect our bygone years at breakfast."

"Bygone just for me," said the Primate.

"And for me too," I added.

"Why should you be unhappy?" the Pope asked, "You who should be the happiest of us all, simply because your time is your own, free to think."

"Your Holiness is right," the Primate exclaimed, "I never have time to eat breakfast slowly and in peace. Only when I visit the Holy Father do I really enjoy my meal."

We three looked at each other and smiled simultaneously.

When we reached the pastel colored room, the large table which could seat at least twelve, was set for only four; evidently someone else was expected. There was a large silver bowl, placed off center, with fruit, red apples dominating the bowl. The china bore the crest of Pope Paul VI; I presumed that Pope John Paul II's had not yet arrived, or perhaps this was a sign of his thriftiness. Religious paintings hung on the wall and crystal vases filled with flowers sat on two credenzas; white venetian curtains covered the tall windows. In a moment we all become aware of the enticing smell of coffee.

"I would not exaggerate if I said that my nose never experienced such a fantastic aroma." I expressed such enthusiasm for this beverage that Cardinal Wyszyński added, "I cannot concur with you." The Pope gestured for us to be seated. The Primate commented as he took his place, "At this juncture in my life, even coffee is poison for me."

We made ourselves comfortable and the Pope remarked, "I had an old friend in Cracow who drank many cups of coffee during the day. One time when visiting me in my office he become ill. I summoned a doctor who after examining him asked, 'Do you drink a lot of coffee.'"

"'Yes,' he whispered.

"The doctor was either trying to teach him a lesson or frighten him by his next remark, 'Sir, coffee is slow poison for many parts of the body, especially the heart and stomach. Please stop drinking coffee immediately.'

"My good friend replied to the doctor's warning, 'I agree. Coffee is slow poison. I have been drinking it all my life and am now eighty-five.'"

The three of us burst into laughter, which is a good prescription for everything, especially in the morning.

Three nuns entered the room, bearing silver trays filled with tall glasses of orange juice and a basket filled with freshly baked rolls – rosetta and panino – their aroma hung over the table.

The nuns left and two returned almost immediately with boiled eggs in antique silver holders and a platter of fried bacon and sausages. The third nun walked in majestically carrying a graceful silver pitcher with steaming fragrant coffee and a second pitcher of hot milk.

The host graciously inquired, "Who prefers hot milk, coffee, or perhaps both? As you can see, this is a much different breakfast from the one in Cracow, where there is less variety."

We began eating and discussed the sunny weather in Italy, then turned our conversation to our lives in Poland.

As we ate and talked, the Pope drank orange juice, two cups of coffee, and ate only one boiled egg, and a rosetta.

The Primate tried everything, but I stuffed myself not only with food, but with stories.

Book Two: Origin of Configuration

4
Land of Legends

"WHEN I look back," said the Pope, "I see how the road of my life has wandered through the milieu of Wadowice, through my parish and through my family, taking me to one place: the baptismal font in the Holy Mother Church of Wadowice. Through the grace of God's Son, my Redeemer, I was accepted at this baptismal font into the congregation of His church on June 20, 1920. During the celebration of a thousand years of Christianity in Poland when I was Archbishop of Cracow, I kissed the baptismal font. I kissed it again on the fiftieth anniversary of my baptism, when I was a cardinal; and I did it a third time in June 1979, when I came from Rome as a successor of St. Peter."

The Pope was reminiscing about the history of the church dedicated to the Holy Mother, the church where this particular baptismal font was placed. The church's presbytery had been built in the fifteenth century, its nave and aisles in the 1700s and the church completed in the nineteenth century. The entrance sat on one side of a market, and was always full of fresh flowers. Surrounding the market were two-story, dull gray houses which contrasted with the vivacious flowers.

The town of Wadowice borders a small river, the Skawa, in the Galicia area of southern Poland; it was built as a village in 1327 by a family of nobles called Wadowit. It grew rapidly, and at the end of the fourteenth century was reclassified as an *oppidum* (town).

In the surrounding countryside, which was heavily forested, lived outlaws and thieves. Major east-west trade roads ran through the town which bustled with commerce and social activity.

"Those parts of the country, you might say, produced more legends than any other." The Pope related, "They sprang up like the mushrooms which grow in the area in abundance and variety. The people of the Beskidy region believed all of those stories; after all, they created them; and, through this process, developed imagination and creativity." Here my host paused.

The subjugated Poles, more than any other people, developed a keen feeling for their history. In the course of any discussion they usually reach out into the past to support their arguments or viewpoint. The Polish Pope is no exception. One of the by-products of this stimulus was the creation of legends, especially on Polish-German themes. The Germans, more than the other two invaders, tried very hard to deprive the Polish nation of national and Roman Catholic awareness. So it should be no surprise to anyone that the Pope during a conversation even with me followed this national trend.

From 1772 until 1918 Poland was divided between Russia, Prussia and the Austro-Hungarian Empire. Wadowice was controlled by the Austrians and during this 146-year occupation, legends sprang up around outlaws and political activists, creating an atmosphere of immortality, mystery and romance, set against a background of destroyed castles, crumbling churches and old cemeteries. The pictures of saints hanging in these churches were to protect people who were just and the heroes of these legends.

"One of a thousand legends was about the priest Otto who sold himself to the German Lucifer. Although there is little difference between German, Polish and other Lucifers, perhaps a German would be more persistent and organized than a Pole, but from the viewpoint of the Church, Lucifer is Lucifer.

"The peasants in this region noticed that their sheep were disappearing. They suspected Otto of stealing and selling them to Austrian or German traders. Although the peasants, thanks to Otto's efforts were getting good prices for their sheep, they thought, 'What profit will we receive if, during the year, we sell ten sheep at a good price but lose five other sheep near the ruins of the castle?' Otto tried to explain that they didn't understand arithmetic and that they really weren't losing the sheep.

"The peasants also objected to the Germans who spread Luther's propaganda among Catholic believers. They went to the Reverend Otto and complained that he, a Catholic priest, should protect the villagers from the Lutheran church. To their surprise, Reverend Otto explained that Martin Luther was an honest and ethical man, and that they should be tolerant of different branches of the Christian religion. But here a problem with Otto's pronouncement interfered. When he said Luther, they thought he said Lucifer. The people of the neighboring villages became divided between one group which believed Reverend Otto and his tolerant approach to Martin Luther's teaching and his German followers; and another which believed in a Polish curate who detested Lutherans. They saw Otto as a goodwill emissary for the Germans, who, under the pretext of paying good prices for their sheep, was trying to create an atmosphere of confusion and dissent. But no one could solve the problem of the missing sheep."

The Pope continued his story, "In every village there is at least one smart peasant. In this village his name was Janus. This lean, self-educated man convinced the peasants that the ruins of the castle had something to do with the problem. It seemed certain that neither the Lutherans nor Lucifer were responsible for the sheeps' disappearances. Janus went to the young curate and said, 'Once and for all, we must resolve this issue. Reverend Otto is the reason for the turmoil in our village. If we get rid of him, we will probably also solve the mystery of the lost sheep.'

"Weeks later, Reverend Otto died suddenly and was buried in the local cemetery. But to everyone's surprise, the sheep kept disappearing. The peasant Janus decided to act on his own. He stood watch over the castle ruins for half of each night, while his son stood guard for the other half. Their surveillance produced no results, but they decided to continue until German merchants arrived for their annual buying of the sheep.

"One night, a human figure, dressed in animal skins emerged from the ruins and headed for the meadows. The figure dropped onto all fours, made the mating call of a ram, and crawled back to the castle. A commotion started in the herd. The human dressed as a ram repeated the process several times. To the surprises of Janus and his son, a dozen of the fattest, most beautiful sheep followed the ram toward the castle, past the crumbling walls of the ruins, inside. Father and son ran after the last sheep toward the castle, but when they arrived, could find nothing. They walked around the castle, but found no exit.

"'There must be an underground passage leading to the other side of the mountain and into the forest,' ventured the older Janus.

"'Yes,' replied his son. 'We'll watch tomorrow and the day after—until the German merchants depart.'

"A few days later, the ram appeared again and repeated his performance. The men jumped on him, pinned him to the ground and undressed him. The ten frightened sheep returned to the fold.

"Suddenly, the elder Janus yelled, 'O my God! It's Reverend Otto!'

"The son said, 'It's a real resurrection!'

"'Certainly, it's a resurrection,' agreed the father.

"'Yes, you stupid peasants, I am resurrected, and you'd better pay me your respects!' shouted the ram.

"Father and son remained on top of the Reverend, both shivering with excitement.

"'Fools! Get off me, and I will explain.'

"'Oh, no,' said the son.

"The father added, 'Let's tie him up.'

"'Agreed,' the son replied. 'Then we will call the villagers here.'

"They removed the rope from his shoulders and tied Reverend Otto's arms and legs. His eyes were closed.

"After making sure the Reverend was well tied, they left.

"When they reached the village, they announced the capture to the peasants. Most of the village returned with them to see whether it was really Reverend Otto.

"The children reached the captive first. 'The body's not moving! He's dead!' one yelled.

"The elders untied the Reverend who lay immobile. Someone looked at the priest's pale face. 'He died of fright.'

"The crowd rushed back to the village to consult the curate. A small group, along with the curate, went to the late Reverend Otto's apartment. It was full of German books and boxes of gold ducats. They touched nothing, and the elder Janus said, 'Who is in the cemetery, in Father Otto's casket?'

"'Probably the village fool, Piotruś,' answered an old woman who worked at the parish house and knew that he had been sick.

"The villagers returned to the castle, put Reverend Otto's body in a casket and brought it to the church. Along with the curate, they prayed for the soul of the misguided father."

The Pope paused and looked out the window as though he were trying to find a deeper moral in this story about the nationalistic stubborn Polish people and their aggressive western neighbors. Then he concluded,

"It was late afternoon when they went to the cemetery, dug up Reverend Otto's grave and found Piotruś' body in his casket. They knelt and prayed for the fool's soul and for Reverend Otto's soul; then they dug a fresh grave and buried the two side by side. 'Piotruś never expected to be buried alongside this priest,' the elder Janus remarked ruefully. After the sermon, they prayed some more.

"For the next hundred years, anyone who walked along the serene roads and paths of Beskidian valleys during the night heard the alluring voice of a ram and the excited voices of sheep. The wind mixed the sounds of the voices with the sounds of the trees and carried them far away."

It was toward the end of our breakfast, and for a moment silence reigned. Primate Wyszyński took advantage of this moment and said to the Pope, "With the permission of Your Holiness, I would like to excuse myself and leave the table because there are many administrative matters that have to be attended to."

The Pope smiled and replied, "In other words you would like to leave us alone."

"You are right. I want you to tell our author the early story of your family life, which I think should be recorded and preserved."

He rose slowly and approached the Pope, embraced him and left the room.

The Pope without any further ado took me to a large adjacent room. Upon entering he motioned to two brocaded chairs; we both sat down and he immediately began his narration. I, in turn, continued with my notes which I later *paraphrased* in the following form:

Forty kilometers southwest of Cracow, at the foot of the mountains Zar and Lanckorona, there is a place called Kalwaria. In this area, located not far from Wadowice, there are forty-four chapels, which resemble the holy places in Jerusalem. The history of Kalwaria dates back to the seventeenth century, when the *voivode* (governor) of Cracow province, Mikolaj Zebrzydowski, gave the village to the Benedictines and agreed to build them a church and monastery. Seven years later, the buildings were completed. Over the ages they were destroyed and rebuilt, but parts of the original archways and chapels remain.

In 1641, the nobleman Stanislaw Paszkowski, from Brzezia, donated a painting of the Holy Mother to the Benedictines. Soon after, legends grew of miraculous cures of the afflicted who prayed before the Holy Mother's painting. In 1658, the Church decreed that anyone who prayed in front of this painting would receive special grace.

The Kalwaria area is renowned for its architecture especially the Church of Jesus Christ's Tomb. Inside the church is a wooden altar on top of which is a reclining figure of Christ. The ceiling of the cupola is covered with beautifully sculptured angels.

The southwest wall is supported by Tuscan columns and semicircular arcades, and once inspired Father Marek, the poet of Kalwaria to write,

"Here every rock calls, every rock cries, and reminisces about the past...and here both kings and common people have worshipped through the ages." To this day, every year, the faithful come from all over the country to pray in front of the Holy Mother's picture, and to follow Christ's Golgotha.

One faithful person was a girl named Emilia Kaczorowski, who was poor and had no cart or horse. It was her custom to walk barefoot, to save her shoes. One July day as she walked along the dry road, her feet began to hurt, but Emilia was determined to reach the place of worship and ask the miraculous Holy Mother of Kalwaria to help her find a husband.

Miss Kaczorowski was handsome: her face was round, her hair light and her eyes blue. Her only fault was that she was shy. Because of this, she had no friends, either among the girls or boys of her age group. Emilia was already twenty-one and had lost hope of getting married.

The sun was hot, flowers burst with fragrance; nearby, a group of pilgrims was singing. But in these quaint surroundings, Emilia was alone and on the verge of tears.

The buildings of the monastery were in sight. She sat on the grass under a tree to put on her shoes. She looked at her feet; they were bleeding. How could she put her shoes on? They would hurt; and how could Emilia then talk to the Holy Mother or to anyone else? The crowd continued to pass her by. No one looked at her, although lots of people were in a similar predicament—walking barefoot as was common among the peasants, in order to save their shoes. She looked around and noticed that everyone had gone on ahead. She felt helpless and started to cry.

As the church bells pealed, calling people to prayer, Miss Kaczorowski sat looking at her feet. The Holy Mother gave Emilia no sign
to guide her.

A cart with several people rushed by; she bowed her head so as
not to be noticed. A young man jumped from the fast-rolling,
squeaking wagon. Short, slim and wearing the uniform of an Austrian Army Corporal, he walked slowly to where Emilia sat.

"Can I help you, young lady?" he asked, with concern, bending
toward her. "What happened? Why are you crying?" Then he saw
her badly blistered feet. Then he sat on the grass and removed his
jacket, pulled a handkerchief from his trousers pocket, and said,
"May I bandage your feet?"

Emilia said nothing, nor did she look into his dark eyes.

He tore the handkerchief in half and bandaged her most injured
toes. They burned with pain, but she didn't react. He began to
dress the other foot, but not having enough material, tore a piece
of gray muslin lining from his coat.

Emilia was so surprised she spoke, "I'm sorry you did that, but I
can sew your lining. I have a needle and thread with me."

He smiled. "Maybe some other time." He pulled a second handkerchief from his jacket and suggested that she wipe the tears from
her face.

"My name is Karol Wojtyla."

"You are Polish?"

"Yes."

"Then why do you serve in the Austrian army?"

"Because there is no Polish army, " he replied in the manner of a
teacher speaking to a young pupil.

"You know that young men must go into the army because of
conscription. So before the call, I went as a volunteer and was able
to choose my occupation—working in the commissary. I don't have
to carry a gun there. Besides I like army life with good regular pay.
Now you not only know my name but my occupation and the reason for it. I don't even know your name."

"Emilia Kaczorowski."

"Emilia, Emilcia, Emilka," he repeated. "A melodious name."

She did not reply, but instead, searched in her bag for a needle and thread.

"What are you looking for?"

"Something to sew with."

"Don't you know that today is Sunday, and you're not supposed to sew?" The young man removed his own shoes.

"Why are you doing that?" she asked, starting to get up.

"Don't worry. Sit down," he commanded. She obeyed. Karol removed his socks, then put his shoes back on. He shook the socks out, stretched them with his hand, and said, "They are very thick."

"So what?"

"Put them on so you can walk."

"What an idea. I should walk in a stranger's socks so I can make holes in them, so I then have to buy him a new pair? I don't think I could even get such military socks in the market around here."

"I'm not a stranger. I'm a Pole, like you."

He liked her. "So, we aren't strangers anymore. Call me Lolek. Everybody does."

"All right, everybody calls me Emilcia. I guess you can too." She bowed her head to hide the blush spreading across her fair cheeks. He noticed this, but said nothing. Instead, he rose and stretched his arm toward her.

"Please, get up. Let's go."

She jumped up, ignoring his outstretched arm. "Where do you think we can go?" Emilcia brushed green clover from her red and black striped skirt.

"To church," he replied with a grin. "Are you a religious girl, Emilcia?"

"Average. Not too much, not too little," Miss Kaczorowski responded not knowing what his attitude toward religion was, "But everything that I have, I give thanks to God."

"Hold on to me," said Lolek. "It will be easier for you to walk. Later when we're closer to the church, I'll let you go by yourself so you're not embarrassed. Go ahead. Hold on to me. Don't be bashful."

"I'm not bashful because of other people. Besides, I've done nothing wrong, except for destroying your socks." So they started walking energetically.

The church bells stopped pealing. In the silence, the sound of nearly a thousand people singing was heard. These people had gathered not only from neighboring villages, but from other towns as well. The sun was hot; the heat shimmered in the air as colorful butterflies danced through it. They passed clover patches buzzing with bees busy gathering nectar. It was a perfect day.

When Emilcia and Lolek approached the crowd of worshippers surrounding the church, she dropped his arm and drew away. He said, "You have to hold my arm, otherwise you'll get lost in the crowd. I don't even know where you live—in what town or what house."

She did as he asked without speaking, and together they made their way to the church entrance. The sound of many people praying and singing together, combined with the strong but pleasant smell of incense overwhelmed them. The powerful church organ pulsed out the melodies of Bach, although neither of them knew the difference between Bach and any other composer. They knew only two things: the music suited them, and they were together. They didn't look at each other even once; the feeling of their hands in each other's reassured them. They couldn't get near the altar, but they could at least see it. Kneeling, they immersed themselves in their prayers.

After the Holy Mass, the church slowly emptied; but Lolek and Emilcia were so deep in prayer, they didn't notice.

The sexton found the young couple an hour later. In a hurry to close the sanctuary, he approached them, and as politely as possible, whispered, "It's getting late, and I have obligations that I cannot attend to until I close these gates. If you would move away from the sanctuary you could kneel outside and pray there to the Holy Mother." They woke from their thoughts and prayers, and left the church grounds.

Not far away, green grassy slopes bordered the river Skawa. "Let's have something to eat," said Corporal Wojtyla. He pulled bread, a piece of cheese and a hard-boiled egg from his jacket pocket. Opening the towel in which the food was wrapped, he spread it out on the grass. The appetizing aroma of cheese tantalized Emilcia. Both were hungry for food and for more information about each other. They ate; and while they ate, they told each other stories about themselves.

"My family came from the village of Czeniec, not far from Andrychów town," began Lolek. "My father, Maciej, who was a tailor, owned a small piece of land. Because the village was poor, and my father didn't get enough business from the neighboring villages, he left Czaniec and settled in Biala Krakowska town. Every summer we return to the village to visit the family.

"My mother was also from peasant stock," he said, stopping to brush pieces of egg from his trousers.

"But I don't know anything about you. It's your turn to talk."

"About me there's not much to say. I was born on March 26, 1884. I love to sew and cook. My mother's family comes from Silesia; her name was Maria Szolc. My father's name is Feliks." She turned to her companion, "You didn't tell me how old *you* are."

Lolek looked at her. "I was born on July 18, 1879."

On February 10, 1906, Karol Wojtyla and Emilia Kaczorowski were married. They rented an apartment on the first floor of number 2 Kościelna Street in Wadowice, a building with winding stairs and a wrought-iron banister.

The entrance to this drab, grayish building was through an iron gate which led to a small courtyard that surrounded the well and protected the area children from traffic in the street outside. The only drawback to the courtyard was the smell emanating from the garbage containers in its two corners. The children didn't mind, however, preoccupied as they were with a ball or playing hide and seek.

Around the corner was the Church of the Holy Mother of Eternal Help, the center of religious and social activity in the neighborhood. Sundays were especially lively and noisy. The bells pealed their musical call to Mass, and people hurried so they wouldn't be late.

To reach their apartment, the Wojtylas had to climb the steps and walk along a narrow balcony. Their home had a small foyer which led into a large room with five windows. One window looked out onto the courtyard, another the street, and the other three faced the beige walls of the church across the street. There was one other small room and a kitchen. It was a railroad flat—one room leading directly into the next. The toilet was in the corridor shared with two other families on the floor. To take a bath, the Wojtylas had to fill the wooden tub in the kitchen.

The walls of the rooms were covered with family photographs; among them, prominently placed, was their wedding picture. On the center wall of the large room hung a chromolithographic picture of the Virgin Mary, and above it, a wooden cross with Christ on it, carved by a local artisan. The apartment was furnished modestly with rustic oaken furniture. A big brick stove dominated the kitchen. Emilia cooked delicious borscht, cabbage and sourdough soups during the week and served a hearty meal with meat, usually chicken or porkchops on Sunday.

The life of the young Wojtylas centered around the kitchen and large room with the windows; the smaller room was the domain of Mrs. Wojtyla, a dressmaker for well-to-do ladies who resided in the town.

After his marriage, Corporal Wojtyla was promoted to Warrant Officer, with a corresponding raise in salary. However, his wife worked constantly in order to save money because she was expecting her first baby.

In this part of the country, rich in scenery and legends, people were poor. They called their destitution "Galician misery." The Austrian rulers put high taxes on the villages and towns because the Austro-Hungarian Empire, which was composed of many Slavic nationalities, needed a strong army to prepare itself for any military eventuality. Emilia and her husband were not only hardworking and thrifty; they also tried to improve their intellectual standards. They had a deep sense of justice and sincerity and believed in working for what they wanted.

On August 27, 1906, their first child arrived. They named him Edmund, "protector of wealth," and nicknamed him Mundek.

The next child, a daughter, died so young that they didn't have time to christen her. The death had a tremendous impact on Mrs. Wojtyla; in fact, Karol thought she had collapsed mentally. He talked to her more often on religious subjects. They went for long walks, sometimes on excursions to the mountains. He prayed with her in church and at home; and on rainy days, read books to her.

During our long and very private breakfast meeting, the Pope several times mentioned how much influenced his parents were by the historical novels of Poland's Nobel Prize winner Henryk Sienkiewicz and the writings of the Russian mystic Dmitri Merezhkovsky. I detected that my host went further and tried to draw a sketch of Merezhkovsky as his mother and father would do it. I felt compelled to add this to the book to show certain influences on the Pope's early spiritual portrait. Both parents were engrossed in Sienkiewicz's novels but eventually turned to the mystic writing of Merezhkovsky, especially his work *Christ and Anti-Christ*.

A central figure in this three-part novel, Julian the Apostate, fascinated and enchanted Emilcia. Although she was interested in the book's descriptions of life in Europe at the time of Leonardo da Vinci, she was engrossed with the spiritual values of this Russian mystic. She tried to paraphrase various sayings of Merezhkovsky and repeat them to her husband. It is difficult to say how many passages she memorized or paraphrased, but her favorite saying was,

With each evil word or deed, we prove and confess that Christ never existed; but with each good word and deed we assert that Christ is a real factor in human life... To live again, and live better, we should read again the *evangelium*, then we will be reborn... Our world—despite the shallowness of life—is so deep and full of meaning, and the reason for it is that some time ago, on this earth, Christ existed...

5
The Spirit of Old and New

WHEN OUR breakfast meeting ended, I asked my host for another appointment to continue his story. He graciously agreed, and set the date for the first week of November 1980.

During this meeting, which took place in the Pope's private library, he highlighted the history of the country and interwove it with the point of view and experiences of his parents, especially of his father in the Austrian army. As usual, I took notes, and on return to my quarters in the Corda Cordi hostel, I rewrote and added dates to show the continuity of his account.

In the Wojtyla family, the reading of Polish history was as important as the reading of daily prayers. Practically every free hour during the day and on Sundays and holy days, Warrant Officer in the Austro-Hungarian army Karol Wojtyla read about the past happenings of their country to his wife, and later, to his sons.

He took special pride in the history of the kings of the Jagellonian dynasty (1386–1572), when Poland was probably the most powerful country in Europe. Next came the period of electoral kings, and with it, shady political and economic dealings between Polish noblemen and their Russian, Prussian and Austrian neighbors. Gradually, the state of Poland slid toward political disaster until the country was so weak that the army was unable to repel invasion and conquest by Prussian, Austrian and Russian soldiers at the end of the eighteenth century.

Officer Wojtyla had difficulty explaining to his family the bribery, treachery and political murder which took place in his Catholic country.

Mrs. Wojtyla could not understand how these things happened, how her country was, in 1772, 1793 and 1795, partitioned completely by aggressors from the east, west and south. Her husband told her that the Polish nation, many times afterward, revolted against its occupiers, only to be crushed and to have its young people arrested and sent into Russia and Prussia as slaves. She asked her husband, "Did the Pope try to help Catholic Poland?" Her husband told her that Pope Gregory XVI, a former Camaldulian monk, Mauro Cappellari, was not only opposed to a change in Poland's political status, but was also against any liberal movements in his own Italy. Immediately after the Polish insurrection of January 1831, Gregory XVI sent a message to the Polish bishops, saying, "Any insurrection, or revolutionary movements against the authorities are foreign to the Church's spiritual teachings."

In 1832, Pope Gregory XVI issued an encyclical in support of the Hapsburgs, who ruled the Austro-Hungarian empire. In *Cum Primum*, he openly condemned any Polish attempt to regain independence.

Pius IX (1846–1878), successor to Gregory XVI, who was trying to latinize the rites of the Uniate churches in Russia, also reached a compromising agreement with the tsar. He not only advised the Polish clergy to stop supporting the revolutionary movement, but he condemned outright any efforts on the part of the Catholic nation to regain its independence. But Rome was far from Poland; the Polish people ignored the advice of these Popes and began to organize an underground army.

As the political turmoil in Europe grew, so did the Polish underground. Not only the intelligentsia but also workers and peasants, Catholics and Jews, all patriots who dreamed of creating a just and better country merged into a movement inspired by the feats and thoughts of Napoleon, who was for an independent Poland.

This part of history was close to Mrs. Wojtyla's heart because she and her husband helped to shape it. In the territory of Galica and Lodomeria, which was in part controlled by Austria, two underground paramilitary organizations existed; one was *Strzelec* (Rifleman), and the other, *Druzyny Strzelecka* (Rifle Brigade), which later became a part of the regular Polish military force.

Many Polish officers of all ranks who were serving in the Austrian army joined these two secret organizations to train workers and peasants for the future uprising. They risked arrest and imprisonment for their antigovernment activities. One of the first to join *Strzelec* was Warrant Officer Karol Wojtyla. Karol worked in a supply depot of the army. He stole guns, uniforms, anything he could lay his hands on which would help the clandestine units drilling in the neighboring forests for the future war. His wife cooked, sewed and fed destitute people engaged in the liberation movement.

Then came the day of June 28, 1914, and the assassination of Austrian Archduke Francis Ferdinand at Sarajevo, by a Serb national named Gavrilo Prinzip. In August, the First World War began. On August 30, Officer Karol Wojtyla and several friends were arrested by the Austrian gendarmerie for stealing guns and ammunition. They beat him in front of his wife and took him away. He only had time to yell to her, "God should be just for me, and for you I will beg Him to have the mercy and strength to live on with our son!" She fell to the ground; Karol tried to loosen himself to run back and help her, but the arresting gendarmes prevented him and led him out. Their son, awakened by the sound of his crying mother, ran to the neighbor's house for help. When he returned with family friends, his mother lay motionless, giving little sign of life. The neighbors called a doctor; after an examination, he said that Mrs. Wojtyla had suffered a heart attack.

In the jail where Chief Warrant Officer Wojtyla had been sent, there was a man named Jan Szczepaniak, also an officer in the Austrian Army. "During the interrogation, I will play a mentally deranged man," said Jan. "Otherwise, I will get the noose."

"What about me?" asked Karol.

"Because everyone knows that you are a religious man, you should play the role of God."

"Are you crazy?"

"Otherwise, it will be the noose for you too."

Karol was confused and deeply worried about his wife and son. He nodded his head and began to cry. His friend tried to console him, "Listen. I'm telling you, I will play Napoleon, and you will play God. After all, there's nobody higher than Napoleon, except God. We can even start a conversation with each other. Don't you think it will be fascinating for the doctor to listen to a conversation between Napoleon and God?"

At this moment two men entered, wearing the military uniforms of sergeants. They shackled Karol and Jan at the wrists and took them out. "Are you taking us to Paris?" asked Jan.

"Shut your mouth," one of the noncommissioned officers said coldly.

The reached a door which opened from the inside, and the prisoners entered a small room with a window covered with iron bars. The guards locked the door and left them alone in the room.

"This must be serious business," said Karol.

"It's serious; on top of that, it's a military affair." The prisoners examined the window and the door; they had no words to continue their conversation.

Wojtyla began shaking and praying aloud. Jan looked at him with compassion then whispered, "If they have evidence that we stole military equipment, we are finished; in that case, although God is friendly with the Austrian Emperor, he won't intercede in our plight, because nobody is on the side of Poland—not even the Pope."

But Karol wasn't listening, he was too deeply immersed in prayer.

The door opened and a lieutenant accompanied by two sergeants entered.

Jan jumped up from the floor and started yelling, "I am Napoleon! Are you my army?"

One of the sergeants hit him in the face, and because Jan didn't stop yelling, he hit him again and again. Jan fell down, but as soon as he felt the floor beneath him, leaped up and shouted, louder: "You will pay for hitting Napoleon! Nobody can touch Napoleon! Napoleon is invincible, and God is on his side!"

Karol stood at attention, as military discipline required. Blood gushed from the mouth and nose of his friend. The younger sergeant stood the prisoners in front of the table, where the master sergeant sat before an opened notebook.

"What is your name?" the lieutenant asked.

"I am Emperor Napoleon!" Jan yelled.

The lieutenant's pink face revealed a faint smile. The sergeant looked at the lieutenant and smiled.

Jan continued quietly. "Don't you see that I am Napoleon?"

"I see. So you don't have to repeat it anymore. But give me a chance to say something."

Jan repeated the name of Napoleon quietly but insistently over and over.

"Sir, should I quiet him down?" asked the young sergeant who stood between the two arrested men.

"Let him yell, let him play games. He's crazy and crazy people, like normal people, have their ups and downs. He will quiet down and then we will proceed."

With these words, Jan stopped talking. He stretched his head up toward the ceiling, as though he were trying to show the lieutenant his bloody face.

The lieutenant said quietly to Jan, "I know you are Napoleon. Otherwise you wouldn't be in the army. And even Napoleon was a corporal at one time, although he wasn't a corporal in the Austro-Hungarian Army. To be a corporal in the Austro-Hungarian Army is a greater privilege than to be a general in the French Army. Look what happened to all of Napoleon's generals."

Both prisoners listened intently. The lieutenant looked at the staff sergeant beside him and at the sergeant who stood between the prisoners. Smiling, he asked, "Please tell me, who told you that you are Napoleon?"

Jan lowered his head, turned to Karol and, pointing at him, said, "God told me! He is my God."

Karol had terror in his eyes and confusion in his head. But Jan didn't notice—or perhaps he didn't want to notice—and continued his speech: "God! He is my God."

Karol turned to the lieutenant and said, "What did I say to him? Did I really say this to him?" In his head, he directed a plea to God: 'Please, God, be just to everyone. But for myself, I am a great sinner; please just have mercy on me.'

The lieutenant and the sergeants laughed.

The lieutenant got up, adjusted his uniform and, with military posture and bearing, approached the prisoners. First, he directed his words to Karol Wojtyla. "I know that you are God, because your friend tells me so with such conviction." He turned to Jan. "You are a good Napoleon. You didn't give in even when Sergeant Krantz beat you. We need such Napoleons in our army to win the twentieth-century war with France."

The lieutenant gave an order to the sergeants. In a loud, official voice, he commanded, "Unshackle them! Let them go home. It would be bad if our Austro-Hungarian Christian empire were to be threatened by two such crazy men." Both sergeants were dumbfounded. The lieutenant, noticing their disbelief, continued, "I am a medical doctor.

I know crazy men when I see them. Unshackle them, and let them go!" The sergeants stood at attention as the lieutenant left the room. They unshackled the prisoners, kicked their shins a few times and let them out.

Karol Wojtyla returned to his job in the regimental supply depot the next day.

Warrant Officer Jan Szczepaniak also showed up at his post.

"We are being watched," said Jan as soon as he saw Karol. "We have to suspend our underground work for the time being."

To his surprise, Karol, having had this terrible experience, was changed. He had become harder and more decisive. He said to his friend, "We are at war now. They are preoccupied with the idea of winning. On all fronts Austrian soldiers are dying. The Austro-Hungarian Empire is crumbling, and we should work to liberate our nation."

"The sergeant didn't bloody your face, so now you are ready to play the hero."

"That's your fault. If you had played God and not Napoleon, you wouldn't have been beaten."

Jan's swollen, bruised face showed a smile. "Now you are being clever, but you should know that this lieutenant saved our lives."

"How come?"

"Because he is a Pole, like many other Poles serving in the Austrian army."

"Who told you that?"

"I know for sure from the underground, but forget it. You never heard about it. Forget it!"

This incident had a great effect on the health of Karol's wife, although he never described to her how close he had actually come to losing his life, and even minimized his experience. But after her heart attack, she lost her appetite for life and her strength to do her daily chores. He noticed this, and in his sensitive way tried to help her as much as he could.

The First World War dragged on. Week after week, the town of Wadowice had less and less food to offer, and week after week, even the regimental commissary lost its supplies. The peasants weren't bringing their food to the town market because the army requisitioned their horses. Sometimes one could see, on a distant road, a cart loaded with potatoes, carrots and beets, being pulled by a group of farmers. Special

Karol Wojtyla (John Paul II's father) in his World War I uniform, about 1918.

Karol in his school uniform at Wadowice, aged, 8.

School excursion of the Wadowice *Gymnazjum* (high school) to the salt mines in Wieliczka, October 1936. Karol is at the far left.

Karol when he graduated from the *Gymnazjum*, 1938.

army outfits went from village to village, confiscating cattle, horses, wheat and potatoes for the Imperial Army. The whole countryside was on the verge of starvation.

Sometimes Karol would buy or dig potatoes from his friends' fields, but meat, even a half pound of horse meat, was difficult to acquire. Misery was reaching the Wojtylas' household. His modest salary did not cover household expenses and he began to sell valuables—a coat, watch and gold rings, which he had obtained before the war. Day and night, he tried to procure food for his wife and young son. With these hardships intensifying, he was more attentive to his two beloved people. Mrs. Wojtyla often said, "Don't blame yourself for the tragedy of war. We will survive somehow. The time of liberation will come and we will have better conditions."

"But now we have to learn to survive in order to see the liberation," he would reply.

Emilia received more orders to make dresses and she worked late at night. From time to time she was given money for this work, but more often the more fortunate women of Wadowice offered her produce such as milk, sugar, potatoes, beets and cucumbers. As time passed, orders for clothes became scarcer because the local people could afford less for new garments and instead saved the old ones. The daily problem of securing food just to exist was increasing. The three Wojtylas were becoming closer and closer because their prayers united them and the love in their hearts was growing.

Gradually, the powers of Russia, Germany and Austria went on the defensive; Polish prospects were looking brighter. On January 22, 1917, President Woodrow Wilson sent a message to the U.S. Senate which said that Poland would be united, independent and autonomous. On March 16, 1917 the Tsarist regime in Russia was abolished and an independent Polish army organized on Polish territory. In April of the same year the United States formally went to war on the side of the Entente. In June the president of France, Raymond Poincaré, decreed the formation of the Polish Army on French soil. Events were moving swiftly, the revolutionary movements were growing, and the three occupiers of Polish soil were falling apart. The defeat of Tsarist Russia and Imperial Germany was finally completed by the Allied Forces. At this time the Austro-Hungarian Empire was divided into a number of small national states.

On October 28, 1918 in Cracow, with the collapse of the Austro-Hungarian Empire, the Polish "Liquidation Commission" was organized and headed by the peasant leader, Wincenty Witos. Also active in this Commision was the prominent socialist member, Ignacy Daszyński. The various groups of riflemen, of which Karol Wojtyla was a member, united and chose the name of "Legions." The Legionnaires, led by Boleslaw Roja, took over western Galicia including the town of Wadowice and the complex of buildings previously occupied by the Austrian army to which the Twelfth Polish Regiment had moved. Chief Warrant Officer Karol Wojtyla was promoted to second lieutenant. On November 16, 1918 General Józef Pilsudski, as de facto chief of state, sent a telegram to the president of the United States and to the governments of France, Germany, Italy, Japan and others declaring that an independent Polish state existed on territories previously governed by Russia, Austria and Germany. The message stated that

A Polish State was created from the will of the Nation and is based on democratic principles. The Polish Government will substitute the oppression which dominated the Polish Nation for one hundred and forty years with a system based on order and justice. The Polish Army under my command will not permit any foreign army to cross the Polish borders without our consent. I'm convinced that powerful Western democracies throughout will help and will give fraternal support to the Polish Independent Republic.

Then began a very difficult time for the new state and for the nation ruined by wars and revolutions. Many Polish families whose sons were forcibly conscripted to fight on Russian, German and Austrian sides were experiencing emotional trauma and material hardships. But there is a Catholic saying, "If you have a piece of black bread and you pray hard it is enough for you to survive." Emilia and Karol Wojtyla were good Catholics and believed this, also because their daily problems were multiplying. Their son Mundek, who was insisting on becoming a doctor, was thinking of going to school outside of Wadowice and his parents didn't have any money to help him.

"In freedom we will somehow survive and even help Mundek go to medical school," Karol said, and Emilia raised her head from the sewing machine. "I think we will, with God's help, if only I could have more strength." And the sewing machine was pedaled faster, "In human life we just count small troubles; but we have to remember: it is easier to close a door before an elephant than before a small trouble."

6

The End of a Family

DURING the spring and summer of 1979, I spent many days in Wadowice and Cracow talking to various people who personally knew the Wojtyla family. The majority of them were uneducated folk who described in their own words the scenes they had witnessed, recalling even dialogues that were still vivid in their minds. I recorded it all and together with information obtained from the Pope was able to reconstruct this story and background of his life.

In the vestry of the Wadowice Church lay a book of births *Liber Natorum*. In volume IV "C" for the years 1917–1927 on page 549 was a notation in ink, turned gray, "Natus – 18, V, 1920 – Carolus Józef Wojtyla, Catholic, legitimate child. Parents: Wojtyla, Carolus – father, military functionary; mother, Kaczorowska, Emilia, daughter of Feliks and Maria Szolc." He was their third and last child.

In the same book a month later the same hand added: "Baptisatus – 20, VI, 1920. The godparents: Józef Kuśnierczyk – merchant, and Maria Wiadrowska."

Mrs. Wiadrowska was a sister of the christened child's mother and her husband was the owner of a picture framing and restoration shop in Cracow. There was a third sister who married Józef Kuśnierczyk, and although in the birth certificate he stated his occupation as merchant, he was, in fact, a restaurant owner in Cracow on the corner of Wiślna and Święta Anna Streets. Emilia obtained customers for her sewing business from the patrons of the framing shop and restaurant. Religious and family holidays were observed within the close family circle.

From the first day, Emilia called her second son not Karol, but, affectionately, Lolek or Loluś; now she had Loluś number one and Loluś number two. Neighbors still remember what she said about Lolek number two.

"You will see what a great man he will be... He will astonish the world!" She repeated this to everyone whether they wanted to listen or not. And when the neighbors came to see the child they made unanimous observations: "But he resembles you so much."

"Is that good?"

The women friends would nod their heads in agreement. "Yes, he will be a great man and we will pray for him."

"But how about me?"

"You are giving him a good start." And they would sit down for a cup of tea and discuss the future of their children.

The appearance of Lolek created a new situation for the oldest son Mundek, who was almost fourteen years old. He would have preferred to play soccer after school with friends or collect leaves to press in his books, but his mother asked for help during this time. In addition, he had lots of school work and hard studying because he wanted to attend medical school. And he could not neglect his chores in the church because he was an altar boy. So he decided to get up two hours earlier to help his mother in the kitchen or go shopping. With his father's help, he organized his day so that he had enough time for everything.

The elder Wojtyla was strict with his son. From early childhood he was introduced to an almost military discipline. Every morning before going to work he would say, "Mother doesn't feel well, so don't forget to help her. When I return I will relieve you." Mundek loved his parents despite his father's demands. Sometimes she would release him from his chores and would say, "Go and play ball, but be sure to return home before father." Mundek did not often accept his mother's suggestions to play. This was not because he didn't want to, but he felt that his mother needed him. If he had time during the day he would join his mother for soup. But mostly, he would munch on a slice of bread and help his friends with their lessons during the longer lunch break. Sometimes the parents of the less intelligent students would bring Mundek's mother produce as payment for her son's help. After school, he met mother and little Lolek downstairs and while she tied the carriage, carried his brother upstairs. While watching his mother's routine, Mundek would comment, "Who would take that old rickety carriage, especially from God-fearing people such as you and father – who are continually praying to God, and asking for his help in safeguarding our possessions?"

"My dear son," replied his mother, breathing heavily while walking up the stairs. "Always remember, before you ask God to keep your horse in good health and safe from thieves, that you don't forget to tie the horse well."

His brother Lolek was growing and healthy, but Mrs. Wojtyla was having frequent dizzy spells. Doctors said she suffered from high blood pressure and a kind of heart disease, but there was no remedy in Wado-wice for either condition. A doctor prescribed quinine and a drug called kogutek that was like aspirin.

Mundek had an opinion about this military doctor and thought, "Military doctors are good for nothing as are most of the officers." He told his father, "Maybe we should take mother to a professor of medi-cine in Cracow."

Mr. Wojtyla did not reply because he thought such ideas should come from himself and not from his son, but after a few days he took his wife to Cracow. Mundek, left with his younger brother, decided to invite one of the school girls under the pretext of helping him take care of his younger brother. Kazia was as tall as he, with black eyes and long light hair. She suspected what Mundek wanted and when they met at the door, exclaimed, "Where is your baby brother? I'm sure he's wet. We must change his diapers." She looked around the house. "Then we will put the apartment in order because it is a mess."

Mundek became red in the face. "My parents just left for Cracow and I didn't have much time..."

The girl cleaned the baby, then raising her head over the crib, said, "Do you know what they call you in school?"

"I'm sure they call me different names," he replied, attracted by the girl's professional nurse approach. "Everyone in school has some sort of nickname."

"But what nickname do you have?"

"I don't know. I really don't know," replied Mundek with slight an-noyance.

"Nursemaid," said Kazia, picking up the child.

"Why? Because I help my mother?"

"Probably."

"Is there something wrong with that?"

"No, but the girls say that you don't love them because you love your mother and are terrorized by your father. They also call you 'victim' or 'milksop.' But Mundek, I consider you a wonderful fellow, and hope that you will not be discouraged. Try to go into medicine and I will study nursing and together we will accomplish something." She kissed him on the cheek while holding his brother in her arms.

"And what should I do? Leave my parents? God put me here, and He will help me."

They sat at the table, Kazia on one side who gave a bottle to Lolek and Mundek on the other, dunking his bread in his tea.

"What should I do? You are clever and resolute. Tell me, is there a way out?"

After a moment of silence Kazia said, "Finish *gimnazjum* with the best grades. Then we will go to Cracow and you will study medicine and I will try to help you working as a nurse."

He was excited and happy, saying "I am very lucky..."

The girl interrupted him. "Tell me, what are you thinking at this moment?" She knew he might tell her that he loved her.

Instead, Mundek said, "My mother wants me to study medicine and I am sure that she is placing this thought in my father's head every day."

"That's good. In my home neither my father nor my mother want me to be a nurse."

"What do they want you to do?"

"They say that I am beautiful so I should finish *gimnazjum* then go to Cracow University just to catch a wealthy boyfriend."

"Very practical," Mundek said in a disappointed tone.

"Maybe practical, but I will not marry a man whom I do not love."

"When you find a wealthy boyfriend, people will approve because they prefer money to love."

Kazia did not have time to reply because little Lolek began to choke on the milk and burst into a loud cry.

Mundek's home routine continued, but there were bright spots from time to time, whenever he met this girl. Mundek had one other pleasant experience: his brother Lolek grew healthy, curious, talkative, and asked him lots of questions.

Many years later, Pope John Paul II recalled a story his brother Mundek had told him: In front of the church was a green lawn with a circular design of beautiful flowers. On the edge of the flower bed was a sign. Three-year-old Lolek did not know how to read and he asked his brother, "What is written on this sign?"

"Do not step on the flowers."

Sometime later Mundek took his brother to the meadows full of dark green grass and multicolored flowers where black cows with white spots grazed.

"See, there cows are grazing."

"Cows always like to eat the grass."

"But don't you think if cows knew how to read they would not destroy the flowers?"

Their father never bought flowers home. Opinions were divided. Mundek said that father was miserly. Mother explained that he was thrifty and spent money only on essential household items. But eight-year-old Lolek was not satisfied with this explanation. One Sunday during dinner when Mundek was home from medical school in Cracow, Lolek asked his father, "Why don't you ever bring flowers for our mother?"

Father looked at him through thick glasses as red spots formed on his bald head. Mrs. Wojtyla and her sons expected a burst of anger, but instead, father stretched his hand forward, placed it on the arm of his youngest son and said quietly, "The wise man never cuts the flowers, because he wants their fragrance to spread for the longest time to him and to other people."

Then father, mother and the boys looked through the opened doors at a beautiful bouquet of flowers on the table in the center of the living room—given by Mundek to his mother. All were embarrassed, especially Mundek, as a result of his father's saying. Both boys didn't know that their father, because of his poor health, had retired from the army with a salary cut, and he kept this secret even from his wife.

On April 13, 1929 Emilia Wojtyla died suddenly. A great sadness overcame the three Wojtyla men. Father became nervous and developed stomach ulcers but never told his sons of his illness. He went from one army doctor to another without relief and grew worse, physically and mentally. Only time spent with his younger son gave him peace. Mundek studied medicine in Cracow and didn't visit Wadowice often. As a result, the two Loleks, young and old, went to church

together, walked through the meadows for hours, talking, always occupied with each other. Together they read the poetry of Jan Kasprowicz, who was in love with the Carpathian Mountains and the region
of Wadowice. His masterful poetry expressed peasant sensibility and
deep religious feelings; his books of prose were impregnated with original folklore and simple mountaineers' wisdom. To this day, the youngest son of retired Second Lieutenant Karol Wojtyla can pluck from
memory many lines of Kasprowicz's poetry:

From depth of painful heart
write forever words of such meaning:
as iron ore finds its cleansing power in fire
so does a man find his in pain.

In May 1930, Mundek Wojtyla received his degree in medicine from
the Cracow Academy of Medicine. On April 1, 1931, after a short practice in the local children's clinic, he went to work in a hospital in the
town of Bielsko-Biala where his girl friend Kazia worked as a nurse.

On December 8, 1932 a notice appeared in Cracow's newspaper:
"Doctor Edmund Wojtyla died of scarlet fever on December 4 of this
year after four days of sickness. Ten days before he spent the night beside the bed of a nurse stricken with scarlet fever. On December 6 he
was buried at the local cemetery." At the open grave one of his colleagues said, "All your life you tried to help other people, to find a cure
for disease, and console the dying; when I saw your pained face for the
last time, your fevered burned lips asked me, asked everyone around
you. '*Why now, why exactly me?*'"

The grieved father and his only son returned to Wadowice to live, to
work, to pray. They repeated to themselves, "Such was the will of
God."

Years later, the casket with the remains of Dr. Wojtyla was moved
from the cemetery in Bielsko-Biala to Rakowicki Cemetery in Cracow
where Mundek now rests beside his mother and father. On his grave is
inscribed, "Victim of his profession, he gave his young life to suffering
humanity."

Those were the words of Lolek, the future Pope, who would never
forget the words of his dying brother, "Why now, why exactly me?"

7
The Bucolic Life and a Revolver

AFTER the death of his wife and eldest son, retired Karol Wojtyla become a recluse. He stayed at home, cooking and cleaning, and when there was a matter to be taken care of on the outside, he would do it quickly with few words. He went for walks accompanied only by his surviving son. Even his own family, which lived in the village of Czaniec called him *odludek* – a recluse; he neither wrote nor visited them.

On Sunday mornings, father and son went to church where Lolek later served as an altar boy. After mass they prayed at the grave of Mrs. Wojtyla, then went for a walk on the meadows. When they returned home in the afternoon, father did household chores and Lolek worked on his lessons. They would eat supper and spend the rest of the evening reading *Quo Vadis, With Fire and Sword,* or *Deluge* – three novels by Nobel Prize author Henryk Sienkiewicz, which they borrowed from the local library or Catholic Recreation Home. From time to time he and his father engaged in social or political discussions, but most frequently the topics were religious. The Catholic Church and Polish patriotism were the dominant points of view. Lolek, from his early years, was a religious boy because of his parents' influences, but he was also interested in secular culture.

In June 1930, Lolek finished grammar school and in September of the same year his father enrolled him in the local Marcin Wadowita Gimnazjum. This eight-year school was roughly equivalent to an American high school plus two years of college. There were two other *gimnazjums* in the town of Wadowice, one conducted by the Carmelite Order and the other by the Palatine Fathers. Everyone in the neighborhood was surprised that the son of such a pious man went to a secular school, although this school taught Latin and Greek in addition to Polish and German. As an army officer, Wojtyla was given a fifty percent discount and later a one hundred percent cut in tuition fees. He was not offered such a discount in the private Catholic schools.

Lolek was a good student from the start. His knowledge of the Polish language and literature was such that he began to write poetry. He'd become acquainted with German in childhood from his mother's family, who were of Silesian descent. Latin he had learned in church by memorizing the Holy Mass. Greek he loved because of the ancient culture, and because of the music and intricate grammar of the language. He earned the highest grades in nearly every subject. On his certificate beside his grade for religion are the words: "with deep interest."

Here again I would like to go back to my private meeting with the Holy Father in the Papal library in the first week of November 1980, and quote him directly on the birth of his political beliefs:

> In *gimnazjum* I read intensively not only the classics of Polish literature, but also newspapers and magazines. I then began to understand the working people and the views of social reformers and progressive leaders. Novels of Stefan Zeromski influenced me very much toward this point of view. The peasant leader, Wicenty Witos, was my idol at that time. I always thought that, properly managed, agriculture should be an important base of the Polish national economy. As far as I remember, my social and political philosophy was based on a theme of fair distribution of material wealth. All this wealth is produced by human hands and God wants everyone to participate in its benefits.

Lolek was a hardworking, well-organized young man. He was an altar boy on Sundays, participated in the Marian Society (Sodalis Marianus), a social group organized through the church that was dedicated to the Virgin Mary, played soccer with school boys in the meadows, and acted in school plays, in which he was most often the lead. Writing poetry and drama, his latest hobby, absorbed much of his time and helped free him from his father's control.

When Lolek was going to primary school his head was shaved close and he looked slightly awkward, with his large blue eyes shining against the white skin of his head. When he began attending *gimnazjum* he received permission from his father to grow his hair longer; and as he matured his figure became thinner and more manly. But his manners still showed a touch of bashfulness. These youthful characteristics together with his extreme intelligence, created an attractive young man, whom many girls secretly loved.

During his young life in Wadowice, Lolek often thought that his faith was placing him in trying situations. At these moments he would repeat his brother's last words, "Why now, why exactly me?" Then, he would go to church to pray and beg God to take him in His hands. After praying, he would regain his strength and the will to work harder in order to develop deeper inner feelings for people and religion. Secretly, he compared himself to the mountain birds who, although they experienced harsh weather and starvation, somehow survived and would appear each spring with shining plumage.

"My friend, Boguś was a clever boy, a year or two younger than I," the Pope recollected many years later.

> Our friendship began when I appeared for the first time in his parents' restaurant to buy a jar of milk and piece of cheese; as you know, his father and mother owned the restaurant and dairy shop called U Banasia. Mr. and Mrs. Banaś were good people and cared more about friendship than profits. I taught skinny Boguś to play soccer and sometimes helped him with his lessons. We lived across the street and my effort to help him was not a chore, but a pleasure.
>
> "In their restaurant, I saw a policeman several times in the late afternoon, who would take his revolver from his holster and give it to Mr. Banaś. Mr. Banaś would put the revolver under the counter or in the cash box which he would lock, and then serve the policeman vodka, saying the usual words, 'tomorrow morning on the way to work don't forget to stop in and I will give your revolver back.' The guest would not reply, just nod his head and plunge into a deep plate of potatoes and meat, gulping vodka almost after every spoonful of food. He would stay for a few hours until he finished a bottle of vodka, put a handful of zlotys on the table, and staggering, would leave the restaurant.
>
> "One day the policeman didn't show up, and he didn't show up the second and third day. When a week passed, Mr. and Mrs.

Banaś sat at the kitchen table, located on the side of the dining room, and tried to resolve the problem of what to do with the revolver. Mrs. Banaś insisted that her husband should go to the police station and deposit the gun there, but her husband said, 'If I do that he will be in trouble and might even lose his job. What if he has a large family?' Boguś was a witness to this conversation, which developed into an ugly quarrel because his mother accused his father of being a coward who didn't want to get involved, and his father accused his wife of being heartless and unaware that she could destroy the man.

"The next day I came in to pick up some milk and pay the bill and did not notice anybody except Boguś and his brother, so I said I would wait for his parents. We began talking about the ball game which was to be next Sunday afternoon, but which would collide with choral practice. Suddenly, Boguś went behind the counter, opened the cash box, pulled out the revolver, and aiming at me, yelled, 'Hands up! Give me your money!!' Then he started laughing hysterically. Judging from the distance of today I guess he felt his youthful power over my helplessness. He yelled a few more times and I felt as though my legs were giving way. At this moment the revolver discharged with a tremendous bang. I was petrified. It was difficult for me to raise my hand and touch my forehead to see if I were alive. I felt cold perspiration on my forehead, but could not take a step. Then I turned toward the window and saw part of it shattered. Turning my head back I looked at Boguś, still standing in the same place holding the revolver, but not moving, his face as pale as the milk in the jar. His younger brother burst into a loud sob and ran out. Suddenly, Mr. Bonaś appeared, grabbed the revolver from Boguś' hand, put it on the counter and began to beat him with his fists. I dropped the money on the bench and ran out. When I reached the church I fell on my knees and started to pray aloud and to cry.

"I don't know how long I did this, but when I raised my head I saw the face of the crucified Christ over the alter and was astonished. I am sure, I remember to this day, that Christ's eyes were full of tears."

Although I was sitting in a comfortable chair in the Papal library

I could not take notes carefully because I was shaken by this sad story. I looked at my host and noticed that he was deeply reliving the happenings of his youth.

Silence prevailed; and eventually I asked, "Epilogue?"

The Pope was listless. I thought he had returned from a different world. After a moment the Pope repeated, "Epilogue? Later, I don't know how much time after, my father found me in the church still on my knees. To this day I feel my knees and my burning eyes. To this day I see Christ crying for me, for humanity."

8
Karol and Halina

POLISH society in Wadowice, as well as in the rest of the southwest part of the country which until the First World War was under Austro-Hungarian domination, inherited class division. Although it gradually disappeared it still existed in those territories in the 1920s and 1930s. Four distinctive groups existed. On the top were the local clergy and high officials, together with doctors, judges and lawyers. The second group was composed of prosperous merchants. Following them were headmasters and teachers in various schools, whose members were constantly trying to climb the social ladder. At the bottom were engineers and technicians from local industrial establishments. This division was neither observed nor preserved among the young people; they looked at each other as equals and searched for friendship and love despite economic or social differences.

The population of Wadowice is a mixture of tall, handsome people of the Carpathian Mountains and blue-eyed people of the Polish plains. The youth of Wadowice are proportionately attractive. After school hours neither the church nor any secular group allowed the youth to frequent restaurants or cafes. Their place was in fields and forests, or theatrical and sports clubs connected with church or school.

In this part of Poland it could be said that time stopped during the nineteenth century, or maybe we should say that time was lost on Lysa or Jaroszowicka mountains, or in the forests where people went to pick wild strawberries, blueberries, raspberries; or in the meadows surrounding the town where young people played games or recited poetry, and recounted local legends about heroic deeds and great loves of the mountaineers. In the fall young people picked mushrooms in the forests or bagged potatoes in open fields. Who could not remember the fragrance of potatoes mixed with burning wood and hot sand?

During the winter and especially during the Christmas holidays young people went skiing, ice skating, or sledding.

The forests and fields bloomed with flowers in the warm spring sun. Young people would go to the high mountains where snow still persisted despite the sun. There they looked for crocuses, a rare white flower with deep green leaves, which by some mysterious power pushed through the layers of snow. With the crocuses grew many legends in the region about pure love, which were passed from generation to generation of young people.

Loluś was a normal boy in every respect and he had a girl friend whom he met in the spring of 1934. Halina Królikiewicz was a little younger, with a beautiful voice, big eyes, well-kept dark hair and a slim proportionate figure. Although she liked sports because this enabled her to be close to the boys and especially to Loluś, her greatest interest was the theater.

Karol Wojtyla was a top student at the *gimnazjum* on Mickiewicz Street. He also had enough time for skiing in winter and kayaking and bicycling in the summer as well as acting in the theater and serving each Sunday as an altar boy. Despite an early rebellion against his father who was constantly organizing his time, Karol, in later years looking back, was very grateful.

On May 6, 1938, the Archbishop Adam Stefan Sapieha (1867–1951) visited the Wadowice *gimnazjum* where Karol Wojtyla was studying. Archbishop Sapieha was the head of the Cracow archdiocese and a member of one of the oldest aristocratic families in Europe. He was of slim build, ascetic looking with a big sharp nose and proud of his royal title. The school selected Karol from forty-two graduates to deliver a welcoming speech, which he did from memory in a masculine and dramatic voice. The prince listened to this young boy with unusual attention and when finished, said to the local priest, Kazimierz Figlewicz, who now worked in the Cracow archdiocese, "We need such alert boys in the seminary. Do you think he would like to be a priest?"

"I do not think so," replied Figlewicz who had known Karol from boyhood. "He is a religious young man, but his masters are Polish national poets – Mickiewicz, Slowacki and Norwid. Loluś will begin his studies at the Jagellonian University this fall to become, first, a writer and then, an actor and theatrical director – not the director of human souls."

The prince, according to Stefan Wyszyński's account, squinted his big blue eyes and said, "From early morning to late at night the situation of humans is constantly changing, and everything and everyone are going before the watchful eyes of God. This boy will be a great priest."

A week after the Archbishop's visit, Karol passed his last exams and on May 27 made a farewell speech to his professors and temporarily to Wadowice.

In 1936 the Polish parliament adopted a six-year plan to reorganize the economy that included the development of an industrial region in the south. Through *Junak*, the national work brigade, young people did their part to assist in the economic recovery. As Junak volunteers, they built or repaired roads, bridges and schools, and cleaned and beautified the countryside. Karol joined Junak after graduation. For three weeks during the summer before he began classes at the university, from sunrise to sunset, Karol worked on a road that led from the village of Jablonka to the village of Czarny Dunajec, near the town of Zakopane, the ski resort in the Carpathian mountains where international winter sports competitions were held. He lived in a hut of poor, simple mountaineers in the village of Zubrzyca Górna and often shared his provisions with them. The family liked Karol's modesty and how he shared his provisions with them; but, above all, they were amazed that this young, handsome and well-educated man would get up early in the morning and kneel and pray for one half-hour at his bedside before going to work, and afterward would go in his dirty overalls to the village church and pray again. All this was the result of his early religious upbringing and family tragedies. Other young people from the work brigade, who were patriotic and sacrificing young men, would spend their time in the local pubs drinking and playing with peasant girls. The mountaineers, who made extra cash in summer by renting rooms to people from various parts of Poland, could not comprehend that such a young man as Karol could exist.

Jagellonian University in Cracow is one of the oldest European institutions of higher learning. The young Wojtyla was not only accepted to study Polish philology, but also received a scholarship.

At the end of the summer of 1938, Lolek helped his father pack their belongings and moved to Debniki, a part of greater Cracow. The

apartment the Wojtylas shared was located in the basement of 10 Tyniecka Street. The three rooms were dark and damp, the entire building, a rather ugly, gray structure, stood separately in a vegetable garden.
It resembled an old factory, especially in late fall when the vegetation
around it was dead and the dominant color was a dirty brown.

The elder Wojtyla spent most of his time inside the apartment cooking, cleaning, washing and waiting for his son to return home. Karol
would get up early and return late at night, remaining at the university
campus the entire day studying, working on a theatrical project or giving private lessons to students who were having difficulties with their
courses.

Among the faculty were philologists of international reputation –
Tadeusz Lehr-Splawinski, Stanislaw Pigoń, Kazimierz Nitsch and Stefan Kolaczkowski. Their students included a group who later became
well-known and important Polish writers –Tadeusz Holuj, Juliusz Kydryński, Marian Pankowski, Tadeusz Kwiatkowski among them. These
students and others established a literary magazine, *Our Expressions*.
They organized poetry readings, literary competitions and dramatic
performances. Karol and Halina Królikiewicz, who was also enrolled at
the university, immediately joined this circle of creativity. During his
first year of study, Wojtyla read his poems in the Cracow Catholic
Home. On October 15, 1938 poems of four writers, collectively called
Road Over the Poplar Bridge were presented at a reading. Most were read
by their authors, but two young actresses, Danuta Michalowski and
Halina Królikiewicz, read a poem recently composed by Karol Wojtyla:

> Over your white grave
> blossom white live flowers –
> How many years ago did this happen
> without you – so many years?
>
> Over your white grave
> so many years already closed –
> But always above looming
> Something like death which is not comprehensible
>
> Over your white grave
> O mother, my lost love
> For love you gave your son
> I could offer a prayer...
> I pray for your eternal rest

Later that evening the poet Wojtyla expressed his opinion on art: "Art should not be only realistic truth or a mere plaything, but a glance into the future, a companion of religion, the guide onto the road to God; it should have the scope of a romantic rainbow stretching from earth and the human heart to eternity."

In late 1980, I also spent some days in Cracow talking to various people about the Pope, among them Halina Królikiewicz, a warm and physically appealing woman who was an old high school and theatrical friend of his. At the time I was staying at Reverend Mietek Maliński's apartment at 39A Lobzowska Street. I phoned and asked her to visit me there. She refused, so we met at the Francuski Hotel for lunch. It was there that she told me numerous stories about the Pope.

From the outside Lolek looked like an ordinary university student, yet on the inside he was very complicated. He had a tremendous desire to capture in daily deeds his own belief in God, his trust in men, and to penetrate the question of death and life after death. He was reading works of St. Teresa of Ávila, St. John of the Cross and Immanuel Kant. At times he thought of becoming a member of the Barefoot Carmelite Order, where he would be isolated the rest of his life, reading, deliberating and writing philosophical and literary works.

Halina was more practical than Lolek; she wanted him to marry her and organize a theater in which she would act and he would write and direct his own dramas. Lolek and Halina had performed together in Polish plays at the Wadowice Catholic Home and in the theater at Sokól Hall under the direction of Mieczyslaw Kotlarczyk. Kotlarczyk was also in Cracow, in the late 1930s and early 1940s. The three worked together in the Rhapsodic Theater, a movement founded by Kotlarczyk, that used an economy of props and all kinds of musical effects, but which emphasized the inherent drama of the spoken word.

Lolek explained to Halina:

Some people who read novels remember only the story, the description of activity and the background, whereas other readers look for ideas, problems, their reflections and scope. This latter group is fascinated by intellectual vision and by abstract elements.

We were reaching for nonscenic, literary material, much of it original, from which we tried to create our authentic vision: the great ethical power of the theater. We placed the human problem directly in its abstract form without embroidering it with action.

The philosophy of the Rhapsodic Theater grew directly from the book of Genesis in the Bible – 'In the beginning was the Word'. The actors' gestures and mimicry flowed from the dynamism of language, basic decoration or a musical frame was introduced sometime later. We were not portraying superficially created life on stage, but rather presenting conflict itself.

Halina listened to Lolek; to his conception of the Rhapsodic Theater, to his talks on religion, to the questions of truth and the individual in society. He would talk for hours about abstract ideas and problems, but she never heard him talk about the love of a man for a woman. Does he know anything about it? Can Lolek picture himself in a relationship of male to female? She began to have secret doubts. At the same time his attitude toward other females was almost the same: polite, helpful and ready to give advice.

No doubt Karol was popular because he was good-looking, extremely intelligent, perceptive and possessed unique elements of character which would eventually mature into a charismatic individuality. When Karol talked, he looked directly at the stranger's face and one could see that his heart was full of love not only for a woman but pure love for Christ's mother. To analyze this kind of love one must remember that Karol had an unusually strong and deep love for his early departed mother and this feeling had grown despite her absence on earth. His love for Halina, his mother and the mother of Christ produced a psychological crisscross, the three loves mixing with each other and never establishing their own borders and limitations. At times Karol could not distinctly separate human love from heavenly love nor his obligation to a person who loved him or to God who was supposed to love him. His feelings for people were mixed with feelings for eternal being, and Karol could not in his mind and heart clearly specify his obligation toward physical existence and spiritual demands.

When Karol noticed someone trying to take complete possession of him, he would slip out of their hands and disappear for days or even a week. He would go to the Carpathian Mountains to ski or for a long bicycle excursion. He would lock himself in the house to read, to contemplate.

Some thought he went to a monastery for prayer and communion with God. Miss Królikiewicz was convinced that she was in love with an unusual young man who, if he did not go crazy from all his philosophical deliberations, would become a great man. Once, one of her close friends, an aspiring writer named Tadeusz Kwiatkowski, said to her openly, "Don't bother yourself with Lolek. He will never get married."

"Why not?" she asked.

"Because he is already married."

"To whom is he married?"

"To the Black Madonna of Częstochowa."

"You are really crazy, Tadek. You are blasphemous!" she responded with tears in her eyes.

"If you are not crazy now, Halina, you will become crazy eventually and this man will haunt you for the rest of your life. I have never heard a human being talk about arts, ethics and the destiny of humanity as he does. Lolek is already crazy; he sees every aspect of human development from the perspective of God and religion; and for him, the whole world is a beautiful woman whom he wants to capture forever and transform into a vision of morality and holiness."

"You are jealous."

"I and some other friends read fragments of his literary compositions such as *Job*, *David's Psalms* and *Jeremiah*. They are literary works inspired by the Bible and there is only one dominant character, Karol Wojtyla, who wants to rewrite the Bible, remake men and completely reshape the world. Remember this is not the timid boy Loluś, Lolek, Karol who served as an altar boy in the Wadowice church and worshipped only God and the Holy Mother, and who admired his priests, Edward Zacher and Kazimierz Figlewicz. This is not the boy whom you knew down there playing ball, who acted in the theater and kissed you. Here in Cracow, one of the greatest European centers of learning with its important Jagellonian University, well-stocked libraries from where not Lolek, but the grown man Karol Wojtyla has gained knowledge, prepared himself to be an outstanding activist and a reformer of the Holy Church or to be locked up in a mental institution. In each case, there is no place beside him for Halina Królikiewicz."

Halina shook with anger, "But where, in your opinion, is the place for Halina?"

"Beside me," replied Tadeusz Kwiatkowski in a soothing voice.

9

Death Was Here

WHAT was in Karol's soul he occasionally expressed to close friends, but most of his deeper thoughts were set forth in writing during the 1940s and 1950s. The mystery of Christ in human suffering is contained in his poetry cycle, "On Attempting to Understand Man." The real name of the hero of this literary work, "Brother Albert–God's Servant," was Adam Chmielewski (1845–1916), a painter.

He was a religious man who cared for the plight of the destitute, and also founded the Albertian Order. Chmielewski painted portraits of Cracow's upper class and used the money to care for the sick, lame, and the homeless. When people asked him to explain his behavior, Brother Albert would simply reply, "I have discovered in the face of the suffering Christ my own calling." And so, he led the life of a beggar, spending his own money and collecting more to buy medicine, food and clothing, and to fix the shelters of the less fortunate. To Karol, Brother Albert was an ideal servant of humanity and was a model and inspiration. He saw in Brother Albert's painting, *Ecce Homo*:

You do not resemble Him,
      whom you are supposed to resemble.
Working hard through each and every man
You will become tired.
They have tormented You
And this Being called compassion, charity.

Despite that, You are beautiful,
Most beautiful of all human sons.
Such beauty never repeats itself later–
O, how difficult is this beauty, how difficult.
Such beauty called compassion.

In the poem, "Song About Hidden God" Wojtyla's feelings about love are expressed:

Light is not what it seems.
When the sea covers you up quickly
And melts you in its speechless depths
light perpendicularly tears up the glow from the waves
and gradually the sea is ended and brightness flows in.

And then, can be seen from all sides, in mirrors
    far away and near
you can see your shadow.
How could you hide in this Light?
You are not transparent enough, so brightness comes
    from all sides.

Then — look into yourself. This is a Friend.
who is one spark, but all the Light.
Taking with your being this spark,
you don't see anything else
and you don't feel by what Love
    you are embraced . . .

Love explained everything to me,
Love will solve everything
for this I admire the Love,
    wherever she will exist.

Such were the poetic dreams of Karol Wojtyla, but the reality of his daily life was quite different. There was a law that every young man who was enrolled in the university, would fulfill his military obligations during summer vacations. According to surviving documents, in July 1939, the army gave Karol "a four-cornered hat, woolen coat, jacket, pair of trousers, shoes, belt and two pairs of socks." And so, this infantryman, together with the other university students, arrived in the town of Ozomla in the Lwów Province to build a school, one of the activities the army pursued in peacetime. His father stayed behind in Dębniki. When he returned in the fall, he went to the Wawel Cathedral every first Friday of the month to meditate and pray with his old mentor and confessor, the Reverend Kazimierz Figlewicz.

On September 1, 1939, while they were praying at the Altar of the Crucified Christ, Cracow city sirens blared and explosions shook the cathedral. The German blitzkrieg had begun. The Cathedral emptied and only he and his friend remained at the feet of the cross of Jesus Christ. As he knelt before the crucifix, the call to the priesthood came more strongly to Karol than ever in the past.

The Reverend Figlewicz arranged a meeting for him with Prince Archbishop Adam Sapieha. The aristocrat dressed in priestly raiments remembered Karol from Wadowice and his own prophetic words about him. It was a warm meeting between the aloof prince and the young man of humble background. The meeting was held in secrecy because one of the first acts of the invading Germans was to prohibit the Polish Catholic Church from accepting new candidates into the priesthood. At the suggestion of the Archbishop, Karol talked with the Reverend Jan Piwowarczyk, rector of the Cracow Archdiocese Seminary. After evaluation, the Reverend Piwowarczyk secretly sent Karol to Professor Reverend Kazimierz Klósak, head of the philosophy department at the seminary. All meetings and evaluations proved positive for the church hierarchy and Karol, and this marked the beginning of the new road for a young man whose thirst for the love of God and people demanded a more disciplined course.

On September 6, 1939, the Fourteenth German Army under General List occupied Cracow. All educational institutions, including Jagellonian University, were closed by order of the invaders, but schools went underground and tried to continue the regular education of the Polish population. Soon after, the German command invited the professors to Jagellonian University to discuss the new political reality. When the professors arrived, 186 of them were arrested and sent to the Oranienburg-Sachsenhausen concentration camp. All priests and church staff from Wawel Castle and the old buildings of the Wawel Cathedral were evacuated, arrested and sent to detention camps. Resisters were killed on the spot. The Polish name Cracow was changed to the German Krakau and the entire province came under the jurisdiction of the Nazi, Hans Frank. Work in factories, railroads and on the highways was transformed into slave labor for all males over twelve years of age. All persons were compelled to carry an identity card. Karol secretly secured forged credentials for himself and his father.

So began the occupation of Poland by the German army and the ensuing biological, cultural and economic extermination of the Polish nation. This particularly affected the Jews, toward whom no mercy was shown. On stores appeared signs, 'Germans only'; the rest of the population received ration cards for bread, marmalade and ersatz coffee. Only Nazi soldiers were allowed to buy dairy products, meat, vegetables and fresh bread. Among Poles and Jews a private trade flourished. Secretly they traveled to villages to buy potatoes, eggs, butter and meat in exchange for jewelry, clothing or shoes. Tramways, buses and trains warned: Jews and dogs are forbidden. Railroad cars and other means of transportation were divided into German and Polish sections, the latter smaller and more crowded. On the streets of Cracow appeared the army, police and Gestapo patrols who sometimes without reason shot at Poles but more often at Jews. Arrests were frequent and ordinary Poles who were arrested were sent to work inside Germany. Intellectuals and the majority of Jews were sent to concentration camps.

In occupied Slovakia, Romania, Hungary and France collaborationist governments were formed, but in Poland everything was directed by a German administration sent from Berlin. The political, cultural and social life in Cracow and the rest of the country went underground. Conspiracy engulfed the whole population.

From the beginning of the occupation, Karol Wojtyla and other young people of various religious persuasions involved themselves in political and cultural work for which punishment was a concentration camp or death. Meetings were held in a house called *Pod Lipkami* (Under the Maples), number 52A on Prince Józef Poniatowski Street, where there was a beautiful view of the Wisla – queen of the Polish rivers – and of the smaller Losiówka River.

Karol met Irena Szkocki and her daughter Zofia Poźniak through his university friend, Juliusz Kydryński, in whose apartment during the war many young people met for various discussions and theatrical activities. Karol and Juliusz were members of the University's theatrical fraternity together with the painter Tadeusz Ostaszewski, actresses Halina Królikiewicz, Danuta Michalowski, and Krystyna Dębowski.

In the beautifully furnished apartment of Mrs. Szkocki, full of antiques and exquisite porcelain, the young people formulated conspiratorial political activity while Mrs. Szkocki's husband, a musicologist and pianist, performed Chopin. Often the well-known Polish actor, Juliusz Osterwa would give instructions on acting while Mr. Kotlarczyk did the same on his "rhapsodic directing." To elude the Gestapo, similar gatherings were organized at the apartments of Krystyna Dębowski, Danuta Michalowski, and Tadeusz Kudlinski.

Many of these people took an active part in fighting the Nazis. Cracovians, living in a city with a thousand-year-old tradition of cooperation between the Polish and Jewish population, hid Jews in many places, including the Palace of Prince Adam Cardinal Sapieha. People said that even the Germans knew that the seventy-four-year-old Prince has hiding Jews, but they could not enter his palace without the permission of Goering, who had respect for the Polish aristocrat and was aware of his relationships with the most powerful families of Europe, including German aristocrats. Sapieha was also well respected by Pope Pius XII who, as Eugenio Pacelli, had been the Vatican nuncio in Germany for twelve years. His connections with the German aristocracy (through his Pontificate, March 2, 1939–October 9, 1958), did not prevent the murder of 3,000 Polish Catholic clergy during the German occupation. Toward the end of the war, when the German army was losing, the Pontiff became very active on behalf of the persecuted people, but it was too late for many millions. Every believer in God was sure that the Master in Heaven would judge Pope Pius XII accordingly.

One of Karol's underground functions was to provide working papers for hunted people, so they could identify themselves as workers in various industrial establishments and escape immediate arrest. He also secured papers for himself and in 1940 went to the Solvay Chemical works on the outskirts of Cracow in the town of Borek Falęcki, There he spent long days toiling in a quarry.

A mutual friend of the Pope and the author, novelist Wojciech Zukrowski, in April 1982, later reminisced to me about those times at his house on Karowa Street in Warsaw.

"We met during the first terrible winter of the war when we felt that God was trying to cover with snow the ruins of our cities and battlefields plowed by tanks. We started to work, I think, at the same time in this Solvay quarry. I had escaped from a prisoner-of-war hospital, and was looking for a place to hide, and Karol, because of his underground work was eager to secure a good cover for his other activities. My job was to drill rock from early morning until late at night and Karol's was to carry big boxes with sticks of dynamite to place in

holes in order to blow up the rocks. His work was extremely dangerous, but Karol considered himself lucky that he could also provide dynamite to various underground military groups. I helped by stealing
ammunition and guns from the German warehouse. The Solvay quarries were the hiding place for many intellectuals, such as the famous pianist, Tadeusz Żmudziński, and the writer and translator Juliusz Kydryński."

"What did the future pope look like at that time?" I asked my friend,
Wojciech, a short, stocky, nervous, pipe-smoking writer who, to this
day, is active in various humanistic causes, such as the Committee to
Save Children from Hunger.

"Karol did not look different from anyone else. He wore an old dirty
cap and jacket with holes and bulging pockets. His trousers were splat-
tered with cement and oil and had many holes, and he carried a tin can
in his hand. Often I saw him sitting with old workers and laborers,
counting sticks of dynamite while they recited the rosary. Although he
was one of us, he didn't like our dirty jokes, or our making fun of the
hunchbacked workers or when, after eating potato soup, we would
make loud poomps."

"Did you have many conversations with him? When I interviewed
the Pope in November 1980 he described you and your work in
positive terms."

"Yes, we spoke many times, when the weather was good and we
could sneak out and sit on the bank of the Wisla River. The water was
gray and coal barges floated toward the Baltic Sea. We talked about our
futures, about our writing and he placed his hand on my shoulder and
said, 'I see civilian life behind me; I will be just a priest.'

"This surprised me and I tried to bring to the surface his ideas about
the priesthood. 'I think you will be a writer,' I said, 'and I also have the
feeling that you have a girl with whom, if you are not now seriously involved, you will be.' Without hesitation he replied, 'No, I think you
have the wrong man. Seeing the misery, deprivation and crime around
us, I think I would like to be a priest, to help my fellow man and to
serve humanity.' Hearing this from him in such a strong voice I looked
at the slowly moving coal barges and melancholy overcame me."

Kydryński described life in the Solvay quarry:
"Karol, Wojciech and I worked in the open in all kinds of weather.
It was cold and often rained or snowed. When we were exhausted we

would sneak into the small barracks where there was an iron stove and drink a cup of ersatz coffee, eat a slice of black bread with marmalade and talk with one of the lower-ranked supervisors, Mr. Krauze, whom we suspected of being of Polish descent. He was lenient and realized that it was physically impossible for young people who were not accustomed to hard labor to fulfill their work assignment. Mr. Krauze, if he is dead, God bless his soul, and if he is alive, God help him to reach one hundred years of age. He falsified our work records and saved us from death by exhaustion and from the concentration camps. If the higher-ups had discovered his tampering with our records, the four of us would have been finished.

"Old Franciszek Labuś who was the immediate superior in working with dynamite characterized Karol: "One day the office sent me a very young man, just bones and yellow skin. I took pity on him, and did not give him heavy work, but he was always trying to do his utmost and helped without thinking about his own safety."

Another worker, Wladyslaw Cieluch, remembers such a scene: "During the night shift, at about 12:00, Karol would go into the barracks, and on his knees, pray. Some workers would join him, but most of them made fun and threw garbage at him, trying to disrupt the supplication."

A worker, Jan Wilk, recalled: "Karol was poorly dressed in a cotton uniform and wooden shoes. In winter he wore a three-quarter-length coat full of patches and cement splotches. He worked the night shift and when I first saw him praying, I said, "You will be late for work." he replied, "Would you please give me a few more minutes to finish my thanksgiving? I am in the middle of a thought in which I am asking God to help somebody solve an important problem.""

"How about some lighter moments in his life?" I asked Żukrowski.

"There were such moments, if you can call them that. We would deliberately talk about girls and sex in front of him, and at such moments he usually reached for a book and turned his back to us. One day I said that I would like to introduce him to a nice young girl because working and praying, I figured, were not enough for a normal young man. He replied, 'All my life I have admired the Holy Mother of Częstochowa and would like to put my life in her hands.'"

"You want to be a priest?"

"He replied, 'Yes, but don't talk to anyone about it because this is between God and myself.'"

During one of my meetings with the Pope in November 1980, I asked the Pope to comment on what his superior Labús was like. Wojtyla replied, "He had a strawberry-squashed nose and a saint's heart. He would ask me to go through the records of how much dynamite we used during the week, because the Germans demanded accurate statistics. He hovered over my shoulder with his eyeglasses constantly tumbling off his nose, a shaved gray face chewing a piece of bread. 'Remember, fellow, everything must be acurate, nothing missing because Auschwitz is not far away. If we do not square with the Germans on the dynamite they will say that we gave it to the underground and then *kaput*, for you and me.' Sometimes Mr. Labús called me a bookish fellow when I complained about my swollen chapped hands, he tried to get some horsemeat as a supplement to our rationing because the Germans considered us important and our work in Solvay as dangerous.

"I will always remember with gratitude the simple people who supervised me, knowing that I was a twenty-one-year-old student. They would say, 'You did your share, go take your book and study because times are changing and we need people like you'...

"When the night shift went on they would say, 'You did your work, go and nap, we will watch and let you know when the Germans come for inspection.'

"When I received orders to work the second and third shifts without rest, the old workers came to me with a piece of bread and said, 'Eat, brainy fellow, you should not go hungry, you should survive. For your bright future is coming.'"

"Yes, they were simple workers who behaved as children of God. Often they would give me warm clothes and leather shoes. You might not know, but I was wearing the same cotton clothes and wooden shoes in both summer and winter. They supplied me with leather shoes, old and worn out, but still better than sabots. I was also confronted with many personal problems which I could not solve properly even with constant praying. I was on the verge of emotional collapse."

"You mean your father was the reason for this?"

"Yes, the hopeless situation of my father who was sinking rapidly, my emotional entanglement with Halina, and of course the war and the enslavement of my country. Sometimes I was in such a state that I thought the affairs of the world were my responsibility, yet I could do nothing. All was engulfing me, only my constant prayer and poetry writing saved me from madness."

Here I recalled his poem "Quarries" written at that period and published in *Tygodnik Powszechny* (*Popular Weekly*) in 1950 under the pseudonym Andrzej Jawień:

Listen to the sound of hammers,
that I transfer to the people, examine their strength.
Listen to the electric current cutting the rocky river.
Inside of me day after day the thought grows, that the overall
    greatness of this work exists inside of one man.
The calloused cracked palm strainingly holds the hammer
and human thought in such conditions solves problems differently.
    When you separate human energy from the
    energy of the rock and cut in the proper place,
    you are cutting an artery full of blood.

The Pope continued, "More and more often I thought that my work at Solvay would never end. The physical effort and emotional strain of constantly working with dynamite was wearing me out. I would not speak to anyone and felt that I was losing my mind. Knowledge that people would not understand caused me to pray more. I placed myself in God's hands and asked Him to take me from this world, and when my thoughts went to Halina and to exciting gatherings in Mrs. Szkocki's apartment, I would momentarily regain hope, But, as I sank into drudgery and thought about wheelbarrows, rocks, dust and dynamite, a hopeless fear would overwhelm me again. Once, when I was returning home from Solvay after many hours of work, I was walking on Konopnicka Street on my way to my basement apartment. I felt hazy and thought I would collapse from exhaustion. In a split second I saw a heavy German army truck speed toward me. I did not have the strength to move far and fast away. The truck hit me. I am not certain the driver saw me or not, but the next day I woke up in a hospital, my face, my head, my arms in bandages, feeling tremendous pain.

"I saw faces over my head, faces of good people. Maybe Halina, maybe Mr. Kotlarczyk or Mrs. Szkocki, or the two actresses Krystyna Dębowski and Danuta Michalowski, or even Jan Tyranowski with whom I had prayed many times and discussed religious questions. Many people were there, but I could not remember their names or distinguish among their faces; I only remember the tears in their eyes. All of the people together with doctors in white coats were whispering something and by some miracle one of the doctors said that I would survive and this voice, I don't know, maybe it was God's voice or the doctor's, gave me strength.

"After a few weeks in the hospital Mrs. Szkocki and several other women took me to her apartment in *Pod Lipkami* for further recovery. I then learned that the truck had hit me and left me on the road to die. An unknown woman passing by pulled me from the road, bandaged my wounds and brought me to the hospital. Some said that it was a village girl who was bringing fresh milk to a Cracow store. According to one doctor the unknown woman said that she had escaped from the Cracow ghetto and was in mortal danger so that she could not get in touch with the hospital, but she would appreciate the doctor letting someone know at the store on Krowoderska Street. She insisted that I must live."

"I would say that it was a miracle."

The Pope did not reply and continued his story. "I spent three weeks in bed and decided not to return to Solvay; to hide, not in my own apartment where the Gestapo could easily find me and send me to a concentration camp. But my first desire was to find the woman who saved my life. I went to the shop on Krowoderska Street, but no one knew her. In all the stores on Krowoderska Street and near by I inquired about the mysterious woman, but no one could tell me anything. Many hours, many days I silently prayed in churches and beside my bed, asking the Holy Mother to permit me to find this woman. I did not receive any sign of hope. Later, some people on Krowoderska Street said, 'Yesterday the Gestapo arrested a woman with Jewish looks in front of our store.' Then someone said that she left for Zakopane to hide in the mountains. Others, that they knew a Jewish woman who went west to England, or that she was already in Israel. Due to my per sistence, stories began to circulate around Cracow that a young man was looking for a Jewish woman. I am still looking for her, and praying and asking God to let me see her and thank her."

10

The Rays of Fatherhood

THE Pope and I were alone at the large dining table in his apartment in November 1980, eating a typical middle-class Polish dinner: vegetable soup, boiled chicken with potatoes, and a mixed lettuce and cucumber salad with sour cream dressing—prepared by Polish nuns who had come from Cracow shortly after John Paul II's ascension to the Holy See. White Italian wine was served with the meal, which I drank straight and he mixed with water.

"Three men in my youth influenced me and I think that you can guess their names."

"Your father," I replied without hesitation.

"And who else?"

"Mieczyslaw Kotlarczyk?"

"Yes."

"The third will be difficult for me to guess," I answered after searching my memory.

"An apostle of God's greatness. God's beauty."

"Prince Cardinal Sapieha?"

"We might call the man I'm thinking of a prince of spirit, but I would prefer to call him Prince Tailor." My host put an end to further speculation.

"An ordinary tailor by the name of Jan Tyranowski," he said. "In February 1940, in the Salesian Church of St. Stanislaw Kostka in Dębniki..." He hesitated and asked, "Do you know who the Salesians are?"

"An ecclesiastical order," I replied. "Organized in the nineteenth century by St. John Bosco. The full name is Society of St. Francis de Sales. They are active, especially in education." The Pope smiled as he spooned fruit compote into a dish. "The Salesian's Reverend Jan Świerc organized the 'Life Rosary Circle' and a discussion circle. Secret meetings were conducted in the chapel as the Germans forbade any kind of gathering. In this chapel were many young intellectuals of Cracow. Most of the time discussion was directed by the famous Biblical scholar Jan Mazerski, a priest and professor at the Jagellonian University who later died in Warsaw while working with and hiding Jews. A year later the Gestapo arrested the Reverend Świerc and fourteen Salesian brothers from Dębniki; they perished in Auschwitz," he reflected. "Forgive me for discussing tragic moments of our lives and memories while we are eating."

I picked up my pipe and waited for him to continue.

"One day a man with innocent blue eyes, closely cut hair, and a pensive face, maybe twenty years older than I, appeared in the chapel at the Life Rosary Circle. He was neatly dressed, like an office clerk, his modest face was closely shaven. There was nothing extraordinary about him except that his nervous long fingers didn't have a moment's rest. He introduced himself simply as Jan. I still don't know how and when he took charge of the fifteen members of our group, the Life Rosary Circle. I don't know how this group grew into one hundred people; all of us were trying to be close to Jan, who held meetings not only in the church but in the forest and other places where we could not be detected by our enemy. Jan's explanation for the venture outside of the church was simple, 'We need to be close to nature.'"

"He lived with his old parents and younger brother named Edward, on 11 Rózana Street in a modest and poorly furnished apartment," The Pope began in a dry matter-of-fact manner. "His father, a tailor, worked out of this apartment with help from Edward. Their mother occupied herself with housework and fed the guests and strangers who visited their apartment. Jan, who finished *gimnazjum* before the war, was a bank clerk by day; the rest of the time, including Sundays and holidays, he did voluntary work for the organization Catholic Action in Cracow. During the war he left the bank and became an apprentice to his father for only food and lodging, so that he would have more time to read philosophy, practice religion, and contemplate." I was surprised that the Pope so accurately remembered facts about Jan's life and was so eager to talk about him.

"When you looked at Jan you saw in him an ascetic man with extraordinary spiritual powers. I often saw him with the book *Mysticism* written by Piotr Semeneński. He talked about spiritual problems and the history of humanity, science, the emotional development of a man and his relationship to God. He felt that the souls of people need to be nourished or reborn through a religious experience, freely, not connected with an established church, but through one's own volition. Man's religion should be based on complete trust in God and trust in the goodness of man. In his evangelical tone he said to me, 'There are powerful and good forces in your soul, which you can bring to the surface through contemplation and constant prayer. When you achieve this trust through prayer and meditation, although you can see that humanity is not perfect, you will gradually attain a power of bringing God's love and greatness to your fellow man and other living creatures, and you will radiate holiness to your environment."

Dusk crept gradually across the Vatican gardens and into the Appartamento Pontificio.

"I still don't know why he paid special attention to me. He made books available, not only religious tracts of St. John of the Cross and Henri de Montfort, but books on philosophy, psychology, pedagogy, saying that self-education should include all branches of human knowledge because knowledge gives you a tool to know God, and enables you to exist beside God, and eventually to live within God."

The Pope concluded, "We would also discuss belle-lettres and even methods of fighting for the liberation of our country, but all this was viewed from the perspective of Christian morality. Many members of Life Rosary Circle put their strength into religious work, many went into active fighting in forests and cities against the Germans. People were dying in jails, concentration camps and railroad cattle cars.

"Men left for work in the morning hungry. They did not know whether they would return: the police seized people on the street and sent them to the Gestapo for torture, to concentration camps or into Germany proper for slave labor on farms. No one could be certain that the Gestapo would not knock on the door in the night and drag people out of their apartments, never to be heard from again.

"Those of us who followed the mystic Apostle Jan Tyranowski thought that he selected, graded and sent us into the world with a particular misson. My mission, he said, 'should be clean, complete service to God.'"

"Tyranowski helped the young man from Wadowice grasp the thoughts of St. Thomas Aquinas, especially Thomistic personalism which Karol Wojtyla later defined:

> Thomistic personalism is based on a premise that the good of the individual should be subordinated to the common good to which society is striving. There are laws which every society must uphold for itself because without these laws it is impossible for the individual to develop himself properly. One of the basic laws is freedom of conscience which cannot be subordinated to the mere demands of society.

Jan was slowly dying of tuberculosis. Despite his sickness, he worked during the day as a tailor and late into the night with his students. One day he pricked himself with a needle. An infection developed in the wound, which eventually prevented him from moving his hand. He lost part of his hearing and was in terrible pain, but he continued to pray and to teach.

In March 1947, he died. Karol Wojtyla was studying theology in Rome when the letter from Mrs. Szkocki carrying the news reached him. Karol cried when he read the letter and prayed to God, asking resentfully, "Why have you destroyed a man who voluntarily gave himself to you in admiration and service? God, why?" But God has an infinite time to reply to a mortal man's question and that is probably the greatest tragedy for those who believe in God's justice.

"While Jan Tyranowski enlarged my religious horizon and deepened my belief in God, Mieczyslaw Kotlarczyk helped me develop my knowledge of theater through staging Polish classics by Slowacki, Mickiewicz, Wyspiański, Krasiński and others. They helped create an extra bridge between man and God. On one hand, creativity in the theater came from the necessities and desires of people and, on the other hand, this theater work was in opposition to the wish to entertain."

I interrupted my interlocutor, pulling a piece of paper from my pocket and read his own words: "The communion between word and gesture reaches deeper and beyond the limits of theater, to a philosophical conception of man and the world."

The Pope was surprised that I had retrieved this quotation from his writings and continued: "The superiority of the spoken word over the mode of action transforms the living human word and turns it into a source of action. Man is an actor, an observer, a listener attempting to free himself from the nagging superiority of activity which tries to stifle the spiritual being. These reflections might bring forth reservations from realists in the arts, especially dramatic art, which is based on movement and action; they are not meant to contradict the validity of realistic theater, but to help us better understand the motivation of human activity."

But Wojtyla supplemented and illustrated Kotlarczyk's concepts with his own literary work and ecclesiastic philosophy of the 'theater of the word.' He was an important innovator of his time, creating theatrical religious *misterium* such as his dramas, *Brother of Our God, In Front of the Jewelry Store,* or *The Rays of Fatherhood*. All three of these plays were later produced successfully in Paris, Rome, and London as well as in Poland, mostly in experimental theaters after the war. When Karol Wojtyla was elected Pope in 1978, his dramas provided a season of theatrical events in Poland, France, Germany and Italy.

The third man who had a great influence on Karol was his father. Although rigid and demanding, he was also loving and placed much hope in his youngest child, especially after losing his wife and other two children. While tailor Jan provided the philosophical and religious basis for Karol to be a priest, and Kotlarczyk taught him to understand and organize the theater for the people and the church, his father taught him discipline and responsibility to God, and the necessity of being a valuable citizen of his country. When Karol rebelled against his father's demands saying, "I could not achieve that," his father would reply, "If I do not ask from you things whch you cannot do, then you would not do the things which you are capable of doing."

With time, Karol understood the teachings of his father and behaved accordingly, although his father's rigidity often supported by his mother, brought Karol a three-way conflict. As the years that followed his mother's death passed, the son's attitude toward his father mellowed. A deep friendship developed between the two men and eventually blossomed into love.

"My views were influenced by my father, who had definite opinions on every subject, which he tried to transfer to me. He believed deeply in the goodness of man as a creature of God, and this characteristc was more important in my opinion than stubbornness or naiveté. His belief in man identified with his belief in God and this gave my father a lot of spiritual strength. Although, all his life he was a military man by necessity, not by choice, father was a good Christian who didn't want to harm anybody. He was straightforward and simple with a deep sacrificing strength to which his short life is a testament."

Father and son spent Christmas 1940 in an apartment of Karol's friend, the writer Juliusz Kydryński. Two days before, the Germans organized a hunting expedition on the streets of Cracow for Jewish and "Polish bandits." No one knew when and where the Gestapo would enter and make arrests. They intensified their search for intellectuals, priests, former officers of the Polish army, prominent merchants, and everyone who did not sign the *Volkslist*, indicating that they were of German descent. The enemy was systematically trying to deprive the Polish nation of educated people and preserve the young and ignorant for physical work.

It was a cold Christmas Eve. Karol and his father were slowly approaching Juliusz's apartment where his sister and mother were preparing supper. After a few stops on the streets for father to catch his breath, they reached the building where the Kydryńskis lived. The father asked his son, "When did you sign up for the underground seminary?"

"How did you know?"

"I know." He pulled out his handerchief and wiped perspiration from his forehead.

"Father, this is not the time to talk. I myself am tormented and don't know if I should go to the forests to join the partisans and fight for the country or... become a priest. I don't know which way to go."

"I know you have a girl and are thinking about civilian life. This partisan business is only an excuse." The elder Wojtyla was pale and breathed heavily. "I will not live long and would like to be certain before I die that you will commit youself to God's service. Our nation is exhausted. It needs people like you."

"Father, let us stop this discussion; leave me alone with my thoughts."

"Give me your arm and let's go up, but promise that instead of thinking so much about literature, theater, partisans and beautiful Halina that you will think more about serving Our Master and take your road to Him."

"I have been thinkng about it for a long time, but there are many ways to serve God, not only in a cassock."

The Pope touched his nose, looked at me and continued: "We climbed the stairs quietly. From under the doors arose a fragrance of mushrooms, the aroma of the forest; from the other apartments came the smell of boiled and fried fish. The cement steps became softer as though one were walking on the grass beside a lake among trees. For a short moment father and I felt that we were not in a drab building, but in the country full of color and the fragrance of flowers."

When they reached Kydryński's apartment, the two hostesses who had been making mushroom dumplings greeted them with flour-covered hands.

Juliusz said to Karol, "I have a book for you."

"And I have a fish for you. Our contribution to the supper."

They sat at the dining room table, mother and daughter brought out traditional Polish Christmas Eve dishes: sauerkraut with mushrooms, pike in jelly, *crucian* – fried doughy twists, herring in oil and onion, and in the middle of the table on a flower-painted plate, pieces of wafer. To one side was a bottle of vodka and across from this, a pile of rye bread arranged in the form of a Christmas tree; all the food was placed on a white linen table cloth under which lay dried grass.

"How did you obtain such wonderful food in so difficult a time?" asked the senior Wojtyla.

"I have spent a year buying these things for Christmas Eve," replied Mrs. Kydryński. "And you see those four empty chairs; those people who are coming also sent food. In these times we don't expect to live to the next Christmas Eve."

"Mother, why are you so pessimistic?" asked her son.

She ignored him and explained, "We will have a special guest, a guest from the forest."

"Mother!" shouted her daughter. "Don't you know that we must keep this secret because death will come to them if. . ."

"You are insulting; we are among ourselves and no one will say anything to the Gestapo," her brother scolded her, then unrolled the newspaper that Karol had handed him. Inside were four carp. "Here is a present from two gentlemen, come here mother and see." She peeked out from the kitchen and although she was happy to see the extra fish, said, "Gentlemen, how did you do that?"

"In these terrible times, everything can be done," replied Karol.

His father reprimanded him, "Not everything. You cannot steal, you must have morality."

"Father, who told you I brought stolen fish?"

There was a knock at the door and a commotion engulfed the inhabitants of the room. Juliusz went to the door, "Who is there?"

"Forest," a voice replied. He opened the door and four men dressed in German uniforms entered. Juliusz embraced them one by one and introduced them to the family, giving first names only. Everyone sat at the table, offering each other a wafer and wishing good life. A tureen of red beet soup was placed on the table; the steaming liquid served into bowls for each guest with a floating spoonful of sour cream. They warmed themselves with the hot soup and afterward reached for the fish. Mrs. Kydryński said joyfully, "But fish love to swim," and she began to pour vodka.

The senior Wojtyla just touched his soup and ate nothing else. Karol noticed this and was about to suggest something to his father, but the older Wojtyla asked the hostess, "May I lie down for a moment?"

"I will make a bed right away."

Mr. Wojtyla whispered, "Please don't do that; I will just lie down on top. I will be alright in a few minutes, I'm sorry for the inconvenience." He left, followed by his son. When Karol returned all eyes looked at him, and everyone simultaneously asked, "Is he better?"

Suddenly there was a knock on the door. The festive atmosphere changed; the four men from the underground pulled out long-barrelled Lugers and pointed them toward the entrance. Juliusz asked, loudly, "Who is there?!"

"Halina," replied a voice from outside.

"Halina!" Juliusz repeated and opened the door.

"My apartment was just visited by the Gestapo! Can I rest?" she asked with a trembling voice.

"Please sit down and have some food with us."

Karol greeted her warmly. "I must go and see my father who's lying in the other room. I'll be back in a minute and we can talk." He disappeared behind the door and saw his father lying, pale with wide-opened eyes. The son held a small bottle of medicine in his trembling hand and said, "Please take it."

"I already took my glycerine."

"This is something else, a new German drug, it's supposed to be good for the heart." He took out two pills, placed them in his father's hand, then went to the kitchen for a glass of water. Returning, he said, "Please swallow them with the water."

"Can't you see that I already swallowed them without liquid?"

Holding the glass in his right hand and lifting his father's head with his left, he said, "Have some water."

Karol sat beside his father on the bed. He reached for his palm and holding it gently, felt the radiation of love flowing from his fragile father to him.

In November 1980, the Pope described to me his inner feelings at that time, "I looked at Christ on the cross hanging over the bed and went into a deep prayer," he recalled.

"I conversed with God and many days later I put this conversation down on paper which took the form of three different voices; eventually these became the base for my drama *Promieniowanie Ojcostwa...*"

"Which can be translated into English as *The Rays of Fatherhood*," I interrupted the Pope, as though trying to impress him with my knowledge of his writing career, "produced on the stage in the 1970s and 1980s in Poland, France, Italy, Spain and other European countries."

First Voice:
...here are the people, they are coming from the gates of the smelting factory...they wear workers' overalls and leather jackets. All of them pass by us, I stand on a street corner; they do not look in my direction. Here are those who reach their homes, close their doors, but do not close the gates to their gardens. Some look back with emotion at what they left, others do not turn their eyes. All pass by, each carrying in himself an incomprehensible part of what is called humanity. All these things unite the painful experience of generations.

Second Voice:
...I am the metamorphosis of so many people. I am always confronting the same thing. I decide to exclude one man and present him as a common denominator for all of humanity. Let him be present in all man, but at the same time, let him not be one of them. Later I recognize that I am this man.

Third Voice:

I looked in the direction of those who left, who died in battle. It is true that all of us fight, but are we all soldiers? I look in the direction of those who approach. Is it true that because of my guilt, 'approaching' means the same thing as 'going to the dead'?

First Voice:

It is difficult for me to think about it.

Second Voice:

Although I am like a man who can be excluded any time and be made into a common denominator for the whole of humanity, I am still a lonely man. It is easier for me to be lonely than to think that loneliness could be a sin. Easier for me to feel loneliness than to commit a sin, but certainly I knew who Adam was and who he is now. Some time ago he was standing on the border between fatherhood and loneliness. Who cut him off from the people, who made him lonely among all of them? Or did he become lonely only to inject loneliness into others? Can we say today that it is easier to feel loneliness than guilt?

Third Voice:

Ah, he was saying that about himself. I could not elevate myself to fatherhood, I could not bring myself to it. I felt completely helpless. And to think what was a gift became a tremendous weight! I discarded fatherhood as something burdensome. Was I destined to be a father? Or only an association in the thoughts and actions of the people with the idea of Father?

Second Voice:

He is lonesome. I thought, what can make me resemble Him, more.

Third Voice:

I am sure that you could leave me in a sphere of fertility and I could manage somehow with nature, but why did you leave me in the depth of fatherhood with which I could not cope! Why did you implant this thought in my soul?

First Voice:

Let people multiply from me and cover the earth.

Second Voice:

If you could make me from clay and say to it, 'Clay, continue the making.' Then I could make everything. Do you have to touch my thought with your knowledge? Did you have to touch my will with love?

In winter 1980 in Cracow, Halina Królikiewicz recalled the following happenings which I am presenting in this form:

When Karol left his sick father's bedside and returned to the festively decorated dining room, his cheeks were flushed and Halina asked, "What happened in there?"

"How is your father?" Miss Kydryński approached him with a worried look.

Karol replied, "Nothing happened to me and father is asleep." Looking around, he asked, "Where are our underground guests?"

"They finished supper, thanked us and left," replied Juliusz.

His mother added, "They cannot stay in one place for long."

Miss Kydryński interjected warmly, "You should finish your supper, Karolek."

"I am not hungry."

Halina did not take her eyes off Karol. "I too must go. Thank you for your hospitality, but I must attend to something urgent." She arose, nodded her head to everyone with gratitude and went to the door. Karol went after her. Halina while putting on her coat whispered something into his ear, opened the door and left.

He returned, pale, and sat down in his chair.

Miss Kydryński noticed his expression, "What happened to you?"

"Nothing. I'm sorry to be so moody today."

"You will have a drink with me," said the girl's brother, and not waiting for a reply poured vodka into wine glasses, "For your happiness."

"For everybody's happiness," replied Karol. They touched glasses and drank.

Gun butts pounded on the door. There was no time for words. They looked at each other and knew what was coming. With a tremendous crash the door fell. Six soldiers and two civilians, all with drawn guns, surrounded the participants of the Christmas Eve supper. With rifles and guns trained on the people one of the invaders in civilian clothes yelled, "Where are they?!"

"Where are you hiding them?!" yelled the second civilian.

No one had the strength to reply. Two soldiers guarded them while the other soldiers and two civilians searched the rooms. Minutes later they returned with looks of surprise on their faces. Mrs. Kydryński regained her compusure, sat on the chair without asking permission and said, "There is nobody here except a sick man lying down in bed. If you had entered the house as civilized people you would have found the same result."

His sister, looking toward Karol commented, "It is a good thing that I took the dishes from the table after our forest guests left."

"You saved our lives," he said, without conviction, in a tired voice.

It was the last Christmas Eve supper for retired career soldier Karol Wojtyla. On July 18, 1941, on his way home from work, Lolek stopped at a friend's apothecary to pick up pills for his father. Then he went to the Kydryński's home to get a jar of hot soup and clean laundry for his father, and accompanied by Miss Kydryński, walked slowly home, both commenting on the day's events and feeling a warm friendship for each other.

When they reached the basement apartment on Tyniecka Street, Miss Kydryński went to the kitchen. Karol went to his father's room. In a moment he burst into the kitchen, sobbing, "Father is dead. Father is dead."

They went to the elder Wojtyla's room, Karol turned his face to the girl and asked in a barely audible voice, "Can you leave us alone?" He fell on his knees and prayed aloud. He prayed all night.

Karol was alone in the world.

Book Three: Catalyst

11

An Alchemy of the Priesthood

THE year again was 1980. The Pope and I were alone in his library. The day was gloomy as most November days in Rome are. My host reached for a glass of water, took a sip and began his conversation with me.

"The deaths in my family—my sister in infancy, my brother in the prime of his life, and my mother and father in middle age—made a tremendous impression on me. From my early years I was convinced of the fragility of man. In 1940, prior to the death of my father I had decided on the Christian ministry to help people who were involved in the Second World War."

"Were there other reasons as well?" I asked.

"Yes, there were reasons not connected with the tragedy of my family, youthful psychological reasons: the loss of belief in human goodness and spiritual purity, the promises of friendship and love. I prayed a lot, thinking that in some way I could integrate my literary life with my life as a priest. Yet I wanted to separate my clerical role from my writing, so I selected pseudonyms."

"Andrzej Jawień, Stanislaw Gruda, Piotr Jasień?" I asked.

"I don't think I used those pseudonyms early in my career; I don't remember exactly what year I began. At the start I used my own name because I thought I would be a writer and a man of the theater. I believed I could flourish in both professions because of my physical and intellectual strength. But God inspired priests on my earthly path; men such as 'Tailor of Souls'—Jan Tyranowski, and Prince Sapieha, who opened my eyes and established me deeply in the House of God. Certainly I could not forget the religious atmosphere created by my mother and father, who developed in me the thirst for eternal truth.

"My personal tragedies and the war also pushed me toward prayer and conversation with God. During one conversation God said, 'You cannot serve so many professions. It will be better if you choose one as soon as possible.' I prayed again, asking him to lead me toward the direction I should take."

"The Germans at that time were winning on all fronts; and on the walls of the Polish city appeared huge placards, *'Viktoria!* Germany is winning on all fronts!' On July 22, 1942 SS Commander Herman Hoefle began the liquidation of the Warsaw Ghetto. Jewish organizations resisted with arms. Thousands died but the struggle continued until May 16, 1943 when General Stroop telephoned General Krüger in Cracow with the report, 'Former Jewish section of Warsaw no longer exists.' Ghettos in other Polish cities were also being liquidated and on August 1, 1944 the Warsaw insurrection began. After a bloody battle and the near total destruction of Warsaw, the freedom fighters surrendered and were deported to concentration camps.

"In Cracow, August 6, 1944 became known as 'Black Sunday.' Germans arrested the entire male population on the streets and in their homes."

Young Wojtyla prayed while trapped in his basement apartment waiting for arrest.

"To be in Cracow and smell the burning bodies and look at the eyes of death every moment was another experience. God was with me; one day while I was hiding in my apartment, the Germans searched Tyniecka Street, but they missed Number 10. If they had not overlooked my building, I would not be here. I had mentioned to various people that I wanted to be a priest, but my final and irreversible decision came in that damp, dark basement on Tyniecka Street.

"Mr. and Mrs. Kotlarczyk and their older daughter were living with me at the time. We were to rehearse for the underground theater Wyspiański's drama *Zygmunt August* (the sixteenth-century Polish king). Halina and I were to play the leading roles.

"Halina had not yet arrived nor had the rest of the cast. I knew that God could not wait any longer with my indecision. Zofia Kotlarczyk was talking with her daughter. I took Mieczyslaw Kotlarczyk, who was to direct the play into the kitchen, and said to him in a straightforward manner, 'I will never act again because I am going to be a priest.'

"Mieczyslaw was upset upon hearing this, but said nothing. He sat on the kitchen stool with his elbows on his knees and his head between his palms. I waited for his reply. Zofia appeared and looked at the two of us. She opened her mouth to say something, but her husband lifted his head and said, 'You are making a mistake. In liberated Poland, as an actor, you would have a great future. Why are you doing this?'

"Mrs. Kotlarczyk grasped the situation immediately, and added, 'Besides, you are a good writer and director. We need people in the arts who can rebuild, we need creative people who will bring love and vision to the citizens of this tragic country, especially to our youth...we need...we need...'

"He repeated these words and gave more arguments and I, with my bowed head, said nothing. What could I say?

"Then and there I got the idea for my poem "Song About the Hidden God,"

> Please come out Master out of me
> and my faulty thought
> don't condemn me for such feebleness,
> my weakness...

"I hesitated to tell Halina about my irreversible decision. She learned of it from the Kotlarczyks. Poor Halina. But what could I do? I had decided to sacrifice myself completely for God and the Church.

"Maybe the Almighty sent Tadeusz Kwiatkowski, whom I had not seen in weeks, to me. By accident we met on the street and he said that he was going with Halina and wanted to marry her. I was relieved of my guilt. But I did not forget her.

"I began working on a poem about Veronica, the one who gave Jesus Christ her kerchief to wipe his brow as he carried the cross to Golgotha. When Christ returned the kerchief to her his face was imprinted on it. The poem later embraced a different shape and a long title, "Redemption Looking For A Way To Enter Into The Restlessness Of All People.

First Veronica spoke:

> We are growing together
> Up into the sphere of greenery
> Supported by the heart.
> We go against the wind and
> Suddenly drop into the leaves, to grow inside
> And to discover
> How deep we put in our roots...

When I call you sister
Then I think that every meeting
Not only carries in itself communion of the moment
But also the grain of immortality

. . .

Your shape, Veronica, continues to be drawn
In the perspective of extinguished day.
And this day is searching solitude
Which we call Redemption.

After a short silence, the Pope resumed his narration in a subdued voice:

"When I met Prince Adam Sapieha for the second time in his palace in Cracow, in the autumn of 1941 – as you know, the first time I saw him was as an altar boy in Wadowice – I timidly said that I would like to enter the Carmelite Order. He frowned; his forehead, his entire face crinkled up as though the sun was burning it, '*Ad maiores res tu es*,' he said, 'You are for greater things… We need priests who will work directly with the people.'

"Archbishop Sapieha asked me to move to the palace where thirteen other seminarians lived.

"At the beginning of 1942 I began my new life studying hard in the underground theological department of the Jagellonian University, temporarily located in the archbishop's palace and called Seminarium Clericorum Archidioces Cracoviensis. We immediately received cassocks to protect us from the German patrols; they would think that we were already priests in the service of Prince Sapieha…

"Every day I arose at 5:30 A.M. and took a cold shower. Under the supervision of Reverend Stanislaw Smoleński, our spiritual father, fourteen of us spent time in meditating and participating in the Holy Mass. Breakfast consisted of a piece of black bread with marmalade and coffee made from grain. There were lectures until lunchtime when we ate vegetable soup and a dish of mashed potatoes enhanced with fried onions. After lunch, during my free time I would study the French or German language, read Kant, and sometimes Marx, whose theories interested me. After evening prayers in Prince Sapieha's chapel we went to bed. Even during the so-called sleep period, I would steal an hour or so to read. This habit never left me.

"It was at this time I became acquainted with the philosophy of St. Thomas Aquinas. During this most horrible of wars, I found Thomistic philosophy, with its emphasis on creation of a society composed of individual people whose goal is the common good, inspiring.

"It helped me when I would sneak out in my cassock and after an hour or so return in the shadow of the evening with people whom the Gestapo were looking for. They would remain in underground passages of the palace for a day or two until I could secure proper papers for them that would enable them to leave the city and go into the forest and join the underground army."

Suddenly he stopped for a second and interjected a very personal remark, "I can never forget the woman who pulled me out from under the German truck...I would like to see her once in my life and kiss her hands..."

The liberation of Poland began in July 1944 and continued into the spring of 1945. On January 15 Kielce city was freed from the German army, the day after, Radom city, then Warsaw. Two days later, Polish and Soviet armies entered Cracow. At the end of January the First Polish army under the leadership of General Stanislaw Poplawski reached the banks of the Oder River. From February 4 to 11, 1945, Churchill, Roosevelt and Stalin conducted the Yalta Conference, which resulted in the declaration that decreed Poland should be a "strong, free, independent and democratic state."

"Winter was severe; Cracow covered with snow," the Pope began. "Famine and death were everywhere. The city was encircled, the Germans were scattering out of the center to the outskirts where they were captured by the Russians. From the distance of the Prince's palace we heard bombs bursting between the rounds of machine-gun fire. A colossal wave of thunder and the walls of the palace shook, loosening plaster and bricks. We were disoriented; Prince Sapieha appeared and asked us to sing religious songs, but when more plaster and bricks fell, he ordered us to descend into the deepest parts of the old palace. He and his confessor stayed on the ground floor. After an hour or so, his confessor came down the stairs without our Archbishop and before we could ask him a question, he announced that the Prince had sent him downstairs and told him to stay with us.

"'If anyone goes upstairs,' said the Prince's confessor, 'he will be punished.'

"Around Cracow and in the city the Germans put up a strong resistance to the Russian attack. Throughout the night both sides used airplanes, artillery, machine guns and handguns. We experienced emotional anguish, yet could do nothing, but wait. The fight continued and in the morning, when we left the cellar, painful silence engulfed us. Snow was sifting through three ground floor windows; no one was in the streets. After several moments of silence we heard the roar of hundreds of motors. We looked onto these streets as hundreds of Russian tanks rolled in. Cracow was free of the German army. The first thing we did was replace the windows, clean the debris and try to secure food, but there was no food for us, nor for the Cracow population.

"I tried to establish contact with my friends. The day following the liberation of Cracow, I left the Archbishop's palace and walked across the frozen Wisla River.

"The bridge to Dębniki had been destroyed. To my left and to my right were slaughtered horses; dead soldiers lay frozen and partly covered with snow; rifles, broken machine guns and ammunition were scattered among the dead. As I neared Dębniki my heart filled with trepidation; I did not know whether Halina Królikiewicz was still alive nor what had happened to Mr. and Mrs. Kotlarczyk, or to the Szkocki or Kydryński families. If they were alive, did they need food, clothing or medical help? I thought, How can I help them?

"I reached my basement apartment at Tyniecka Street where, to my surprise, I found the Kotlarczyks and Halina. It was tearful embracing without words. When Mieczyslaw and his wife left for the kitchen to prepare tea, I asked Halina, 'What do you need?'

"'Love, which for me will be food, clothing and security…'"

"How could I give it to you?"

"'You could. You are not yet a priest, you are not yet ordained…'"

"But you are going with Tadeusz?"

"The Kotlarczyks returned from the kitchen. Mieczyslaw carried on a plate a few slices of bread and tiny pieces of cheese with onion, and Zofia held a bottle of vodka covered with dust. They offered us this modest treat which, at that time, was a feast. Mieczyslaw turned to me and said, 'Recite something which you have written recently.'"

"His wife added, 'To cheer us up.'

"'Please do,' Halina quietly asked. I looked at her face, which was sallow and sad.

"I searched my memory for a fragment from my drama *Jeremiah*, picking up the Hetman's (leader) dialogue:

> At the feet of Truth we need to put Love,
> At the corners, on the ground.
> This Love will take hold even on the crossroads,
> Will build, will bring up, will change
> In your call for the Truth...

"I looked at the faces of my friends and could see that they were absorbed, and I recited from the same play the dialogue between Brother Andrew, who symbolized human sacrifice, and Father Peter, who stood for the permanence of the church:

Brother Andrew:
They will cut my body into pieces
Curse, spit and stamp on it
But Master, if you will sacrifice me for the nations,
My body will be regained and the angel will defend me.

They will dress my body in priestly raiment
Cover it in white communion clothes.
When you come in to take my casket
You will see it has not been touched.

Father Peter:
Into that body Power will descend God's Power!
Such Power you cannot conquer.

And young people will come in to put the casket
    on their shoulders
They will see in the casket the Power of the Resurrection
The legend and admiration will go to the people
That this body is invincible and holy.

Listen all of you who are going to the City!
I give my body to the struggles of those days
But I survive as Strength and Herald
And I am Unshaken and Invincible.

"I am sure that Halina understood and the Kotlarczyks too, that although there were temptations in my life and tragic experiences, I would follow God's voice."

On November 9, 1944 Karol Wojtyla received tonsure (shaven crown), and in the same year ostiary (the church doorkeeper) and lector (one who reads the church services) degrees; on December 21, 1945, he began to assist the minister in ecclesiastical duties including exorcism.

The year of 1946 was eventful, for on October 13 he was conferred as subdeacon and seven days later as deacon. On November 21, Prince Sapieha, in the Archbishop's palace, ordained Karol Wojtyla a priest. It was a great distinction for Karol and an indication by the Prince that he was placing faith in the future of this young man.

The first three Holy Masses performed by Reverend Wojtyla were on November 2, All Souls Day, in Cracow's Wawel Cathedral at St. Leonard's altar in the Romanesque crypt. Here lie the remains of King Jan III Sobieski who, in 1683 at the battle of Vienna stopped the Turkish invasion of western Europe. Also resting there are the remains of other great Polish figures such as King Michal Korybut Wiśniowiecki, Prince Józef Poniatowski, and the friend of George Washington, the rebel and reformer, General Tadeusz Kościuszko.

I went through my research papers and found an eyewitness account of this ceremony related to me in the summer of 1980 by my fellow writer Wojciech Żukrowski:

> The dark walls of St. Leonard's altar mysteriously reflected the lights of two dozen candles and in those lights Karol's old confessor and friend, Reverend Figlewicz looked like an apostle come down from the walls of the cathedral. This fragile old priest had introduced the young priest to the mystery of the mass. He acted as manuductor or leader, the adult who takes a younger person by the hand and directs him properly. In his first mass Reverend Wojtyla celebrated the memory of his parents, sister and brother. The second was in memory of all departed souls and the third for humanity and peace.
>
> In this chapel with Roman and Gothic styles, round arches and walls full of history, Karol's face shone in the yellow candlelight.

When he turned from the altar for the first time during the mass, he saw a multitude of dear faces from Cracow, and even Wado-wice. Halina and Tadeusz Kwiatkowski were there kneeling beside Mrs. Szkocki, who had organized a reception in her apartment for the young priest and all his friends from far and near. It was a Dutch treat reception because everyone brought something to eat–not only bread, but fish, meat, homemade pastry, vodka and even Hungarian wine.

"It was the most memorable reception in my life," the Pope later reminisced in his Vatican apartment (Fall 1980). "Lots of food, but most of all, many tearful faces. To this day I see sad and happy eyes which to the end of my life in my memory will never die." Here I noticed that my host was crying. After so many years, his emotions were still fresh.

"Also in November I celebrated a mass in my native town where my manuductor was my high school confessor, Reverend Edward Zacher. There, too, in Wadowice, in the home of my friend, Zbyszek Siklow-ski, we recalled our early youth, ski excursions in the Carpathian Mountains, long walks and games among the boys and girls of the *gim-nazjum*; here too we were moved to tears over our departed young years."

"Was Halina there?"

"Yes," he replied quickly, as though indicating that he didn't want to talk about this.

12

On the Road to the Source

IN AUGUST 1946, Karol Wojtyla finished the theology department at the Jagellonian University, and according to his professor, Reverend Ignacy Rózycki performed "valde bene" (very good) on twenty-nine examinations. In November of the same year Prince Sapieha sent Karol for two years of further study in Rome at the prestigious Pontificum Institutum Angelicum de Urbe. It was at this time also that his "Song of the Hidden God" was printed anonymously in the Carmelite paper *Glos Karmelu* (Carmel Voice), and was discussed widely in Polish church circles. In addition, he left for Rome with an almost finished treatise written in Latin, on the question of faith in the writings of St. John of the Cross, *Quaestio de fide apud S. Joannem a Cruce*. He later submitted this thesis to the famous professor in Angelicum, Father Reginald Garrigou-Lagrange for evaluation.

"I brought with me to Rome a picture of this Immortal City based on history, literature and Christian tradition. For many days I walked about looking for my preconceived images, but it was difficult to reconcile the historical concepts with the reality of a modern city composed of one million inhabitants, Italians and other people from all over the world. I thought I would find God and love on every street and in every human being in this center of Western Christianity. I was disappointed," he said to me in November 1980.

"Do you still have the same opinion?"

"Not when I went to the catacombs and discovered the city of the first Christians, of apostles and martyrs, of the beginnings of the Church and of the great culture which we inherited. Only then did I begin to look at Rome and its modern life with different eyes.

"On my first day at Rome's railroad station I tripped and fell. The priest who greeted me remarked, 'Don't worry, this is not a bad sign. The exact thing happened to Julius Caesar, but in a different place.'"

"I don't understand."

"'When Julius Caesar reached the shores of Africa and disembarked from his ship he fell on his face. His noble entourage throught that it was a bad omen, but still lying on the ground, he opened his arms and said, 'O mother earth, O beautiful Africa! I take you in my arms.'""

The Pope described his acquaintance with Rome to me: "At the beginning, in my imagination, the Vatican hills covered with olive groves were the hiding place of fortune tellers, a place of magic containing secrets of the Etruscan gods and Ural or Altai mountain shamans who believed in an invisible world of demons and ancestral spirits. The legend persisted that they had the power of communicating with the world beyond, healing the sick people, making them happy or unhappy, changing or controlling events and the future..."

"Then, Christianity..." I interjected.

"You are right. Christianity entered and St. Peter entered Rome, the capitol of the Imperium. Prosecuted by pagans, he found final rest in these Vatican hills. Tradition says that on St. Peter's grave was built a modest church transformed through the ages into today's magnificent Basilica. According to Tacitus, persecution of Christians began in the year 64 by Emperor Nero, who used the burning of Rome as a pretext to arrest many Christians, including St. Peter, who was crucified head downward. The excavation which began in 1939 under the reign of Pope Pius XII proved that where the Basilica and other Vatican buildings stand today was an enormous private circus where Christians died on crosses or were torn apart by wild animals. On June 26, 1968 Pope Paul VI announced that the remains of St. Peter were authentic."

I interjected perhaps not so politely, "They were remains of a Christian probably, but not necessarily those of St. Peter."

He looked at me with irritation and did not reply. "Further discovery showed that under the Papal Palace were walls seventeen meters long, five meters high and over two meters in width. Those walls were closed from the east by compartments where circus horses, chariots and harnesses were kept. Other places of similar dimensions were built for lions and other wild animals, and for condemned Christians."

The Pope raised his head from his notes and books, looked into my eyes and I knew immediately that stubborn Wojtyla did not forget my doubts expressed a minute before. At this moment I felt that the Holy Father was trying to enchant me – the agnostic – with the glorious history of the Church. Although from time to time he referred to the papers lying on his desk, I felt that his photographic memory retained all the information that he ever acquired through reading various historians of Christianity.

He resumed, "Workers also discovered one large grave in which they found the remains of only one man and around it smaller graves of other Christians. On the large grave they found the Emperor Vespasian's seal. In the year 160 the Romans built another wall, which, for some reason or maybe out of respect for the remains of St. Peter, bypassed his grave."

"My belief could be explained by my ignorance," I said.

The host smiled and in his eyes I noticed a gleam of forgiveness. "The first and second successors to St. Peter's throne, Linus and Amicetus were mentioned by Gaius in his Roman chronicles. They built a monument over the grave of St. Peter and other Christian martyrs. For many years pilgrims came to pay their respects to St. Peter. They left graffiti on the walls in which they expressed their love and admiration for the first successor of Jesus Christ. Then, the Roman Emperor, Constantine the Great, took Christianity as his religion and that of his people and built a church over St. Peter's grave. Constantine's church was eventually plundered and destroyed by Visigoths and Vandals, and later required the efforts of five different popes and architectural geniuses, such as Bramante who prepared the plan; Giacomo della Porta and Maderno who corrected the plan and directed the construction; Michelangelo who created the dome; and Bernini who finished the construction. The foundation of the Basilica began in 1513 and the building was consecrated by Pope Urban VIII in 1626."

Although I enjoyed his interesting story of the beginning of the Roman Catholic Church, I did have the urge to say, "It is rather fascinating that you know so much about Rome and early Christianity, while others don't seem to."

"I would not agree. For example, right now I am reading you a story based on someone else's research and writing."

"I am thinking about Italian youth."

"They are being taught in schools."

"That is what I mean. Here are a few examples of this teaching."

"What kind?"

"I admire Italians for their joyous way of living; they know when to work and when to enjoy life. When I'm in Rome I wander on streets for hours in wealthy and in poor sections of the city, and I especially enjoy conversations with young people. One day I stopped a teen-age boy and asked him, 'Who was the founder of Israel?' And he replied without hesitation, 'David who killed the giant Colgate.'"

"The influence of American advertising," the Pope replied smiling.

"The other day while walking on Via Cavallini, I stopped a girl eating an ice cream cone and asked, politely, 'Please tell me, have the Popes always lived in Rome?' She looked at me, her dark brown eyes bursting with ironic laughter, as though she were saying to herself, stupid tourist, and she replied, 'Yes, the Popes always live in Rome, from father to son in lives of celibacy.' Encouraged, I asked, 'What was the name of the first Pope?' Swallowing the last part of her cone, she pulled a silk handkerchief from her purse and wiped her mouth, 'The first pope? The first pope? I am certain his name was Romulus.'"

My host covered his face with both palms and laughed loudly.

I continued, 'In Città del Vaticano just a few steps from Sant' Anna I met some American nuns, one who was in her thirties. I smiled and she smiled back and I said, 'I am a worshiper of Mohammad and I would like to know who betrayed Jesus Christ and for how much?' She looked at me with suspicion and replied in a New York accent, 'Judas, naturally, and he received thirty dollars for it.' But enough of my humor, I prefer to hear your stories about the Vatican."

"The history of the Vatican has fascinated me from early childhood. I read about it and memorized so much that I don't know what is based on my own research and knowledge or someone else's such as Bishop Paul Poupard whom I recite now; then, thanks to Prince Sapieha, I had the opportunity to see and touch it with my own hands. Many examples of religious art located under the dome of St. Peter's Basilica greatly fascinated me, especially a bronze canopy made by Lorenzo Bernini, decorated with golden fringe which later became one of the most important elements in Papal liturgy. The Papal throne, an oak chair encrusted with ivory, is the center of my admiration. This royal throne, presented by Emperor Charles the Bald to Pope John VIII is placed on a bronze pedestal and supported by four doctors of the Church symbolizing the universality of the Christian faith.

"The greatest artistic achievement is the Bernini Colonnades, one hundred eighty-seven meters long and one hundred fifty meters wide. The crowning point of this colonnade is one hundred and forty figures of saints. The structure was built over three hundred years and when illuminated by the sun or even electric light gives me a feeling of spiritual power and immortality."

"It is difficult to explain but the obelisk in the center of St. Peter's Square has an almost equal impression on me," I said.

"Understandable because this obelisk is related to paganism and Christianity and you seem to feel warmly toward pagans. Please remember that this obelisk was standing in Nero's circus and could tell a lot about the sufferings of Christian martyrs."

Not everyone would have the opportunity to listen to such a distinguished guide as I did.

"Five bronze gates lead to St. Peter's Basilica decorated with bas-relief. One of them, the 'Holy Gate,' is opened once every twenty-five years to commemorate the Holy Year. In 1300, Boniface VIII announced the first such celebration and to this day it continues. The second gate also is covered with sculptural relief. The third was executed by Giacomo Manzù, a friend of John XXIII, and represents the secrets of death in the form of Jesus Christ being taken down from the cross, the Holy Mother in 'final sleep,' the deaths of St. Joseph and Abel; the artist showed death by hanging, death in an airplane crash and the death of a mother. There is also on this door a bas-relief of Pope John XXIII kneeling on the bare ground. The fourth gate is the 'Gate of Sacraments.' The fifth gate, the 'Gate of St. Martha,' is dedicated to prayer. On its lower left-hand side can be seen the eye of God in which is reflected the Virgin Mary's portrait."

In due reverence to my host I took a different approach, "In the humble opinion of a great ignorant I would give everything for the Pietà."

He continued, "In 1964 Paul VI gave permission so that people who didn't have the means to travel to St. Peter's to see the Pietà would be able to admire it. Priests and art lovers the world over trembled while the Pietà was in the United States because they were afraid that something might happen to it. The sculpture returned safely to its place in the Basilica, and on May 21, 1972 a great tragedy occurred. A mentally deranged artist by the name of Lazlo Totha almost destroyed this masterpiece with an iron hammer, which through the ages has been attributed to various artists. But this tragedy had a happy ending and an interesting discovery."

"What happened?" I asked with anticipation.

"During the restoration, which was successful, the Vatican people discovered that in the lines of the left palm of the sculpture was camouflaged the letter 'M'."

"You mean, Michelangelo was the artist?"

"Certainly."

"Is it true that Michelangelo was only twenty-four years old when he executed the Pietà?"

"Yes. He was also a good businessman."

"How could he be? We know of stories where he worked on his sculptures for long hours with little pay, and that he was exploited by the aristocracy and the Church."

"I do not know why I am in such a mood, but I feel like telling you more stories, maybe to prove that I know so much." He smiled mischievously.

"Cardinal Jean de Bilhères de Lagraulas was ambassador representing two successive French kings, Charles VIII and Louis XII. His mother, Petronelle, was thinking about ordering a sculpture of St. Petronelia, who according to legend, was the daughter of St. Peter. The sculpture was to be one of the Virgin Mary, mother of Christ, and placed in St. Petronelia Chapel. The Cardinal Ambassador, upon the request of his mother, approached Florentine businessman and banker Jacobo Galli to 'help me find a suitable sculptor.' The banker, a collector of jewelry, visited a 'jewelry and art shop' owned by the brothers Ghirlandaio, and there he met a boy named Michelangelo Buonarroti whom both held in high opinion. They recommended Michelangelo, and the banker not only paid his expenses while sending the young sculptor to Rome to see the Cardinal Ambassador, but helped him sign the contract. The young sculptor promised he would create the most beautiful sculpture in all Rome for four hundred fifty golden ducats."

I interrupted, "This history is fascinating, but knowing that you cannot spend as many hours with me as I would like, may I ask about the present – namely the structure of the Vatican state, and specifically the Curia, which is composed of people from all over the world who are there to carry out daily chores and on the Holy Father's order to create policies and execute them for the good of the Roman Catholic Church."

"I understand, but I don't think I am able."

"Why? It would be interesting and historically important to hear those things from the lips of the Pope. But, let's try to compromise. Please give me a short description of the religious and political influences of Rome on the world."

Once again he glanced at his notes and books.

"We must go back to Constantine the Great's march on Rome in 312 when he saw in the sky a flaming cross; this vision helped him defeat Emperor Maxentius and led to his proclaiming himself master of the Roman Empire. It was Constantine the Great, who issued the Milan Decree in which Christianity was adopted as the official religion of the Holy Imperium. Believers in Jesus Christ were no longer persecuted. Then Pope Gregory II became the first Pope to bestow blessings upon the kings of Europe. Seventy-five years later Leo III became the first to physically place a crown on a secular ruler. He was Charlemagne and Leo proclaimed him Emperor of the Romans. In return Charlemagne gave the Pope a present of vast estates. Thus also began the donations of European secular rulers to the Church, which soon grew to tremendous proportions, so that by the Middle Ages the Roman Catholic hierarchy controlled vast wealth. For example, in the seventeenth century the Archbishop of Cracow possessed more land and souls working on it than did the Polish king.

"Then came deep social changes, revolutions and other upheavals; secular powers grew and began repossessing the Church. As a result, in 1870, Pope Pius IX announced the excommunication of all who participated in the takeover of Church property. He rejected the Italian government's offer that the Vatican state should consist only of the Lateran and Vatican palaces, the Pope's vacation retreat at Castel Gandolfo on Lake.Albano, and the Pope's pension from the government. Three succeeding popes took the same stand and considered themselves prisoners in the Vatican. Only Achille Cardinal Ratti, elected as Pope Pius XI, decided to break with the tradition of not venturing out from behind the walls of the Vatican and began discussing the settlement between the Vatican and the Italian government under the leadership of Benito Mussolini. In 1929 the Lateran Treaty was signed, which established an independent Vatican state, 'with complete sovereignty, and independent administration and courts.'"

"Was there also a financial arrangement?"

"According to the treaty, the Holy See would receive over 700 million lire and stocks and bonds worth one billion lire with 5 percent interest, for relinquishing various properties on Italian soil."

"No doubt this arrangement between the Holy See and the Italian government enhanced the prestige of the Church?"

"Not only that, this arrangement sped up the reorganization of the Curia, which had begun in 1908 with the so-called *Sapiente Consilio* This constitution or guide, put in legal form the way the Curia should modernize their external relations and functions inside the Vatican, as well as enhance the position of the Papacy by bringing it closer to the people of the world." He paused and with a playful smile added, "You should remember that to this day reforms in the Curia are still being introduced because in the Vatican nothing goes fast. I presume that the Vatican citizens have learned patience from the Almighty."

"And what about the Vatican citizens?"

"The number of permanent dwellers in the Vatican is small, a little over one thousand and half have Vatican citizenship. The rest are residents: cardinals, bishops, prelates and fathers of various orders who live there while performing their duties on the territory of the Papal State. When their obligations are completed and they return to their home countries, they lose their status of Vatican residency. Brothers of civilian officials and their male children have a right to Vatican citizenship until the age of twenty-five. The sisters and daughters of such officials have the right to citizenship until their marriage. Besides this thousand, there are approximately 3,000 other officials of which half are citizens of foreign countries. Although they work in the Curia they live beyond the borders of the Vatican, many in Rome."

"But the Pope is a dictator," I observed good-humoredly.

He smiled. "The real dictator, if you can use this word, is the Holy Spirit who directs the successor of St. Peter to perform papal duties in various ways; although the Pope, according to Vatican law, is the supreme figure in all three branches of government."

"And what is the role of your confessor Monsignor Stanislaw Dziwisz? Everyone in ecclesiastical circles calls him Numero Duo."

"There is no secret about him; he is my friend and adviser. In any profession the chief executive usually has a trusted personal secretary. Also, as you look through the history of the Papacy, many popes brought their closest relatives to the Vatican for advice, consultation and help on relations with the outside world. I have no such people, and this place, after so many years of working in Cracow, is taken by Monsignor Dziwisz. No one else except God knows me so well, inside and out, and many times he has proven his loyalty and made sacrifices for which he receives from me only brotherly love."

The judiciary power of the Pope is supreme. This power is divided into the Tribunal of First Instance whose decisions may be appealed to a higher papal court, the Rota. The highest court is called the Tribunal of Apostolic Signature from whose decision there is no appeal.

Because the Pope was not eager to talk to me about the security forces of the Vatican and its history, he referred me to Bishop Paul Poupard who, some time later, explained this subject. "On September 1970, one hundred years after the disappearance of the Vatican state, Paul VI in a letter to his secretary of state ordered him to dissolve the military corps. But an exception was made for the Swiss Guard, the Papal Gendarmerie and the so-called Martial Guard, which were reorganized into one Civilian Corps of Security. The Palace Guard, created in 1850 and composed of lower- and working-class Italians, also disappeared.

"When was the Swiss Guard organized?" I asked. "And what was their real duty?"

"In 1506 Pope Julius created this military unit whose duty was to defend the Pope and his palace. There are seventy-five members of the Swiss Guard including three officers, all of them under 25 years of age. They are recruited from Swiss Catholics and they sign up for a minimum of two years to work in the Vatican. According to tradition their gala Renaissance uniforms which they wear to this day, were designed by Michelangelo. The new civil guards of security, composed of 87 men, are dressed in dark blue uniforms with the insignia of the papal tiara with two keys on the lapels of their uniforms. They are posted at the entrance to the Vatican State and in Castel Gandolfo and their duty is to check the documents of the visitors as well as bring these visitors to their appointments. Also, they patrol the Vatican gardens and palaces for twenty-four hours. Gone forever are the times when the Pope was the head of the secular state. Paul VI described the new situation in these words, 'Everything which is around the successor of St.

Peter has religious character; the inspiration comes from the simple words of Evangelia, according to the spirit of the Vatican Council and aims of the people.'"

"You did not want to talk to me about the 'military side' of the Vatican," is how I started my next conversation in November 1980 with the Pope in his library, "But I do not think you should object to telling me about the social security of an employee of the Holy See?"

"I am interested in the welfare of the people working in the Vatican, and the institution which takes care of this is called Fondo Assistenza Sanitaria to which everyone belongs. The membership entitles them to medical care and the Vatican apothecary supplies them with necessary drugs. When a family needs loans they apply to the Fondo Assistenza; retirement pensions are also distributed through this organization. As you know, the Vatican treasury is supported by donations from churches throughout the world."

"St. Peter's pence."

"Yes, but on the Vatican premises you can buy practically anything with a discount because we are satisfied with a marginal profit. As a young priest I used to collect beautiful Vatican stamps that are unique in the world. In the Banco Vaticano, tourists with the help of the priest accompanying them could exchange foreign currency and get the best price, but now we are thinking of not competing with other Italian banks."

"How about Vatican money?"

"The Vatican mint releases one lira and five lira gold pieces which are accepted not only in the Vatican but in all of Italy. In addition to this should be added all kinds of valuable medals, but I collect just the stamps."

"I should praise the Vatican post office, which in my opinion is the most efficient organization," I said. "Sometimes I would send a letter on the same day through Rome's post office and another through the Vatican's, and for some reason the letter sent from the Vatican arrived in New York a week earlier than the one mailed from Rome. I guess angels are helping the mail delivery."

"You should not forget the Vatican telephone which is efficient, and when I was a theological student I often took advantage of it."

"Today you are lucky because your telephone is free."

"It is worthwhile to be a Pope," and we both smiled.

The rest of the information on Vatican communications I knew well, such as the Vatican radio which broadcasts twenty-four hours a day in thirty-two languages, and the paper *Osservatore Romano* which publishes its weekly edition in seven languages. I am not forgetting that the Vatican press releases many works ranging from science to propaganda.

"I would like you to explain the institution of the papacy, the 'competition' between the Pope and the Curia, and above all the mechanism by which the Pope is elected."

On his face appeared a smile with a puzzling undertone, and he answered, "It is impossible, it is a great undertaking, I don't know..."

I interrupted in the middle of his sentence. "For you everything is possible. You were there. You are the Pope, only God is above you and in my heart God is saying ask him this question."

He got up, stretched out his hand and with a friendly squeeze said, "For this you have to wait."

13

The Worker-Priest

THE Pope recalled to me in November 1980 that when Prince
Cardinal Sapieha sent him to study in Angelicum in the fall of
1946, the Prince had said, 'You will smell cypresses and eat
oranges, but you must study every minute of the day.'"

The Pope continued, "I sat on the edge of a chair, looked across the
antique oak table into the eyes of the Prince and listened intently to his
instructions: 'During your vacation you will not return to Poland but
will go to France and Belgium to study new methods of religious ministry. Two priests, Godin and Danièl, authors of the book *La France, Pays
de mission (France, Country of Missionary Work)*, are philosophers of this
new movement. In Belgium, the organization Jeunesse Ouvrière
Chrétienne, is trying to help the working class by protecting them from
exploitation and teaching them Christian ethics. In France, such work
is conducted by the Mission de France. In factories, priests of both organizations work beside laymen, sharing experiences, material gain and
a Christian attitude towards the world. I would like to know..."

Karol who knew these things listened impatiently yet politely.
"...how much of what is going on in Western Europe can be introduced in our country? We have cynics who say that if we introduce
those radical reforms, priests will be confronted at the confession by
workers demanding a guarantee of their constitutional rights; in other
words, conservatives say that the radicalization of the Church would
destroy the structure and discipline of the priesthood.'" Reverend Wojtyla knew that Prince Sapieha was giving him a lot of responsibility;
that he wanted him to be the leader of new ideas in Poland and bring
the workers close to the Church – and if this was not possible, to bring
the Church to the workers.

"'Observe what is going on and bring it here; but when applying those methods I don't want you to be Machiavelli, but at the same time don't be an intellectual hobbledehoy. I say this in advance because I don't know if I will live long enough to see you perform.'" With those words he rose. Karol Wojtyla left his chair, kissed his ring but said nothing. The Prince took him in his arms. They embraced and Reverend Wojtyla left the palace full of emotions and thoughts.

The last sentences of his superior puzzled him, especially the reference to Machiavelli. He recalled what this Italian statesman and writer had said, "There are three classes of intellectuals: the first sees reality and understands without help; the second evaluates things with the help of others; and the third doesn't understand the analysis of others." The young priest did not know in which class Prince Sapieha placed him. Maybe life itself will give the answer, he told himself.

During his stay in Rome, Karol spent time with his friend, also a priest, Stanislaw Starowiejski. Together they explored Rome and her churches as well as the life of ordinary Italians, trying to find harmony between Italy's glorious past and the sameness and frequent brutality of her present political and daily life. They could not comprehend how the Italians had built the Appian Way, the queen of roads with monuments lining it such as the Church Domine Quo Vadis, the catacombs of St. Sebastian and St. Calixtus and the Circus Maximus, but could not solve their traffic problems. When Karol asked the Italians to explain the discrepancy between early Christianity and today's, they just shrugged their shoulders.

One day, on the steps of Piazza di Spagna, the Polish priests met an Italian priest and asked him the same question. The Italian, when he discovered their Polish accents, asked them questions about Poland and after each reply would say, "*povera Polonia* (poor Poland)." It was a disappointing conversation between the young Polish priests and the old Italian who did not know how to explain his country to a foreigner and did not comprehend the politics beyond the borders of Italy. Italian priests seemed not to be following reformist trends which were being introduced in other countries and Karol throught, "Such mentality is being cultivated in the Curia and could be a tragedy for the Church. How wise was prince Sapieha and how far-sighted his observations..."

When Karol returned to his room in the Belgian College, he lay on the bed staring at the ceiling and thinking about existentialism. He fought within himself, trying to figure out how the Church could inspire in thousands of ordinary priests a curiosity for life and a search for knowledge through various human endeavors and not only through prayer. He remembered that Jean-Paul Sartre said, "A free man is a man without God, without the degrading knowledge of the Absolute...man by himself can create his own being and his own laws...only the weak fold their hands to pray..."

This wisdom was contradicted when he thought, "Man comes and announces who he is...that to be a man is to achieve unity with God, but then becomes God's desire."

Karol was nevertheless taken by the reality of the time. "Are those thousands of priests, monks and nuns in black, grey, white and brown on the streets of Rome also searching for God? Why are Roman churches half-empty while nightclubs and restaurants full? Are there too many churches and not enough nightclubs? Are tourists who throw coins into the water of the Fontana di Trevi paying for their salvation or playing a game? I need simple piety and deep belief in God and man." He slid down from the bed to kneel and pray.

> Existence is not being absorbed, she is growing, and gradually
>> changing into a whisper...
> You must work and trust.
> And go into yourself to know of your conceit.
>> This is already humility.
> Check your will.
> Sometimes a dramatic explosion of feeling
>> happens but does not grasp God.

Wojtyla changed his mood and began reciting a poem about a worker in an automobile factory:

> From under my fingers luxurious models of cars are traveling
>> the streets.
> But I am not swimming in them on unknown highways.
> I am not directing the traffic —
>> this is being done by the policeman.
> Cars are talking, my voice was taken away.

I have an open soul and would like to understand
with whom I am fighting, for whom am I living?
     Here the thoughts are stronger than words.
There is no answer. Do not ask such questions aloud.
Like everyday return at six in the morning to the factory.
How do you know that on the scale of the world that
     man is given most weight?

A thought came to mind. 'I must go to Marseilles, to Paris, and meet
the workers,' and 'You should not forget the town of miracles –
Lourdes.'

In Paris, Karol met the Reverend Henri Godin, who expressed his
philosophy of the priesthhood among the working-class people: "The
clergy working solely among laborers should understand that their paganism would overwhelm them. To resist this temptation one must remain in close contact with priests working in different factories, offer
mutual support, and above all, pray. Priests active in workers' districts
should specialize according to their inclinations. There should be priest
specialists for work among children, teenagers, students and retired
people. Priests doing missionary work among factory workers should
not only spend time in the factory but live with the workers, share their
burdens, expenses, eat with them, play with them and pray with them.
Above all, working priests should not be different in dress or appearance from ordinary people. Besides praying, the liturgical element of
this mission should include a united fight for social justice and political
recognition of workers."

In this speech by Reverend Godin, Karol did not discover anything
new. A long time ago, before becoming a priest, Karol had visualized
himself in such a position. This vision is expressed in his writing which
in many instances shows his admiration for a man who toils with his
hands and doesn't receive his just share. In his poem *Worker in Muni-
tions Factory*, he assumes the manner of a toiler:

I do not influence the faith of the world, I do not start wars.
I am not going with You, I am not going against You –
     And I do not know.
But I do not sin.
I am tormented because I am not influencng anyone and
     I am not sinning,

Karol as a priest, 1944.

Karol in his first parish, Niegowić, 1940.

First Communion at Niegowić, 1948. Karol is seated, center.

Karol with young people of St. Florian parish, Cracow, 1950.

Karol (center) at Cracow University with Izabela and Edward Owoc, May 1953.

only making small screws and preparing the parts of destruction
I am not grasping the totality and I am not embracing
    human misery.
I could create different things and different faiths
    but how could I without the use of small
    parts?
In which I myself as well as any other man
    could be the great achievement, honest, holy
    which no one can cross out
    and no one could express a lie.
The world which I am creating is not good—
    but I have no intention of creating a bad one!
Is this not enough?

Next Reverend Wojtyla traveled to Belgium and observed the activities of worker-priests known as Jeunesse Ouvrière Chrétienne which was under the supervision of two priests, Marcelle Eulembroeck and the other, known by his last name, Cardijn. Here, as in France, he confirmed that the key to the future of humanity was five words: 'God, economic and political justice.' On his return to Cracow, Reverend Karol Wojtyla summarized his opinion in an article *Mission de France*, published in *Tygodnik Powszechny* (*Popular Weekly*). He was careful but objective in his presentation of working priests, saying "This movement is one expression of God's spirit and uncovers new roads to the Church."

14
Curate of Souls

THE following account is based on the notes which I took during one of my conversations with Primate Wyszyński in 1980 in his apartment on Miodowa Street in Warsaw. According to the Primate his friend Prince Sapieha showed him a confidential report on Reverend Wojtyla's relations with worker-priests in France and Belgium. The Prince was ecstatic: "This young man must be sent to a village where there is no electricity, no sanitary facilities, and where drinking water must be fetched from a distant well. Let him show what he can do!" To his secretary who was puzzled as to why such a bright priest was sent to this place, the Prince replied, "If Karol can endure the hardship there after experiencing civilization in the West, he will be on the road to great things."

It was decided that the village would be Niegowić in the western Carpathian Mountains between the towns Bochnia and Wieliczka. In 1049 a wooden church had been built. Sometime later this tiny house of God burned from a candle fire; in 1788 a new wooden church was erected and dedicated to the Holy Mother. To this day a picture of Her in a golden frame hangs over the altar.

On July 18, 1948 Reverend Karol Wojtyla began his first pastoral services there as assistant to the old rector Monsignor Kazimierz Buzala. Reverend Wojtyla rolled up his sleeves and began working, but this doesn't mean that he didn't complain to himself. "I am a doctor of holy theology and I was placed in the worst parish in the country. I don't know why. What is the Prince doing to me?" But he did not complain to Buzala or to anyone else in the village.

"He was coming from the direction of Gdów village," recalled the old parishoner Stanislaw Subtelny, "He wore grey cotton trousers, a faded black vest, worn shoes, and under his arm was a briefcase which I, as a peasant, would be ashamed to carry to the village market. He asked me the way to the village Niegowić and I replied, 'Why are you going there?'"

"'I am going to work in the local parish.' He thanked me politely and walked toward the village, stopping about 500 meters away by the cross on the side of the road decorated with flower garlands where he knelt and prayed. When he got up he waved to me, and continued on his way."

A few months later when Prince Sapieha's emissary visited Niegowić, an old peasant, Jacaszek, told him the following story: "It was a sunny day; flowering lindens spread their scent throughout the village and in the air one could hear the traffic of bees; but in the church 'Reverend Doctor,' which we all called him, was preparing to christen a child. He asked the parents, 'What name have you selected for this lovely girl?'"

'Bernadetta Frederika Katharina,' replied the parents and godparents in unison. Reverend Doctor smiled and turned to the altar boy, 'More water please.' To the parents he said, 'Instead of one dozen eggs for the christening you will have to pay us two dozen eggs because we have to go far for the water.'"

"The parents were surprised because they didn't know why they had to pay extra for three names; they thought it might be a joke on the part of the young priest. But the father of the child said, 'I will pay because this is my first child, and I will pay not in eggs but with money.' The Reverend Doctor smiled broadly."

After the christening ceremony the Reverend Doctor invited the parents, godparents and their friends to the parish house for a small reception. When the priest was handed the money for the christening he said, 'Tomorrow you will show me a savings account book with the name of your daughter on it, and in this book should be noted the amount that you are now giving me. When Bernadetta Frederika Katharina gets married she will have a dowry.'"

The young curate was instrumental in getting electricity brought into Niegowić together with other twentieth-century facilities. As to the beautiful wooden church, he suggested to Prince Sapieha that it be moved intact to the vicinity of Chrzanów town where more people could admire the eighteenth-century relic. In its place his parish should receive a larger brick church. The Reverend Doctor organized a parish theatre, chorus and sports club. He took part in all the activities of these organizations and even led young parishioners in various excursions to the mountains or played soccer with them. In a short time, Monsignor Buzala discovered that his helper was the most admired and sought-after priest and he envied him. Here again, Jacaszek reminisced. "The Reverend Doctor was young and wise but not pompously wise, and anyone at any time could reach him and ask for advice. He walked about neighboring villages and inquired as to whether people needed help or advice. He knew how to listen. During holidays, church and state, hundreds of people crowded around him posing questions from purely family to social and political. In a short period of time the young Reverend Doctor became a source of inspiration to people in our village, and in surrounding villages."

When Halina Królikiewicz, now Mrs. Tadeusz Kwiatkowski, heard that Karol had set up a theater in Niegowić she went to assist him. Halina reasoned that since they had known each other for so long and had worked in various theater groups in Cracow, why not in Niegowić? However, it was unusual, especially in the minds of peasants for a married woman to leave the cultural center of Cracow in order to help a priest organize a theater in the village. No doubt Halina still loved Karol, but he could not understand why she had married so quickly.

Despite his writing, Wojtyla could not define exactly his opinion about women and their relationship with men. He spent time reading the opinions of philosophers and writers on this subject, but was not satisfied. For him, woman was a more mysterious creature than man and he attached to them extra characteristics of perception, intuition, beauty and inspiration. He came across the works of Eliza Orzeszkowa (1841–1910), an important nineteenth-century Polish novelist who he felt comprehended her sex. Mrs. Orzeszkowa said, 'In general, Polish women exaggerate when expressing their emotions. As a result, they are full of exaltation and fantasy.' To fortify himself mentally during Halina's visit, Reverend Wojtyla reminded himself, 'I am persuaded by the Lord Jesus that nothing is unclean in itself; but it is unclean for anyone who thinks it is unclean.'

During Halina's visit, he intensified his excursions, prayers and visits to the other side of the Raba River where the poorest people in the village of Kleczany lived. He asked the standard questions about how the government officials treated them and what the church could do to lessen their burdens. He concluded that the function of a priest should not only be as intermediary or broker between God and people, but between people and government. In addition to preaching the gospel, he wrote petitions, and called police stations and other state institutions to intercede on behalf of the peasants.

Once, he met an old woman on the road whom everyone called Tadeuszka and considered to be the village eccentric.

"Why are you crying?" he asked her as she walked slowly with her head bent down. She stopped sobbing, looked at the priest, and tried to grab his hand to kiss it. Reverend Wojtyla pulled away and repeated "You did not say why you were crying."

"I was robbed," and again she started to cry.

"Of what?"

"Bedding, pots, pans, bread, cereal, everything," she began to think of what else she was missing, "Everything, everything..."

He did not say anything but took her arm and began to walk.

"Where are we going?"

"To my place."

"You will make me your servant?"

They continued walking and the young priest said out loud, "I have no servants. Let's go to church and pray."

It was noon and the church was empty because the peasants were working in the fields or were in their homes having a meal. A cool breeze caressed their faces as all entrances were open, creating a gentle draft. Together, they knelt and prayed in silence. Afterward he said, "Tadeuszka, let us go to my place and have a cup of milk and bread."

When they finished their nourishment he went to his room, pulled up bedding from the floor, adding to it a pillow and blanket, then returned to the kitchen, picked up pots, a bag of potatoes, loaf bread, a bag of cereal, a jar of tea and dumped them on the bedspread. When Tadeuszka saw what he was doing she began to cry again. "If you continue to be a crybaby I will not give this to you."

"I am not deserving of all those things. I am robbing you." Again she reached for his hand to kiss and again, he pulled it away. "Don't thank me, thank God." He reflected for a moment and corrected himself, "Before you begin your prayers, go to the sacristy and ask the man to bring the horse and cart to my place because you cannot carry all these things yourself." When she left he looked to see what else he could put in the bundle.

Local state authorities did not like the social activities of Reverend Wojtyla which, according to them, were demoralizing and counter-revolutionary.

"We have one Christ and don't need a second one," the head of the village militia said. When inspectors arrived from Warsaw to scrutinize Wojtyla's activity they told the village council to "prove that the local curate does not act properly." It was difficult and silly for the Police Chief and the Village Council head to complain that the Reverend Doctor gave pots, food and bedding to the village outcast because she was robbed and the militia could not catch the culprit. So they concocted the following: "You see Comrade Inspector, Reverend Wojtyla does not permit Party activists to sit in the front benches during church services. We have tried hard, politely and persuasively, to get him to change his mind.

"Nothing happened. He is as stubborn as a mule," complained the Militia Chief.

"So what did you do?" asked the Inspector.

"Collectively we decided to step up the class struggle with this stubborn priest," said the head of the Village Council.

"We decided to teach him respect for the people's authority," the Militia Chief added.

"Finally, what did you decide? What did you do?" the Inspector asked impatiently.

"We decided that no militiaman and no member of the council would carry the Holy Canopy over the priest's head during the Corpus Christi procession."

While he was the rector's assistant in Niegowić, Wojtyla travelled several times by bicycle from his parish to Cracow to report on village concerns to the Prince, who in turn received information about Karol from his superior Monsignor Buzala.

Wojtyla was agitated not only by the outside world's problems, but more importantly by torment in his heart and soul which later as Pope he described to me, "For many years I lived as a man banned from the depths of my personality while simultaneously condemned to penetrate it. Often, I thought that I had lost my self and that my personality was being washed out in the processes of history where decisions are made by quantity, through the masses and the state. I must meet each man and examine everything he brings forth, while my personality enters the process of devaluation. Many times I thought I should erase my footsteps, so I could identify with every man whose record is being written by the masses. The thought that I should find myself in every man returned to me all the time – the thought that I should not look from outside myself but from inside is very persistent."

15

Philosophy of Life and Grain of Prophecy

THE autumn day was gloomy and lifeless. During such days you feel like locking yourself in your house, pulling down the shades, pouring a glass of cognac and listening to Chopin. Cardinal Wyszyński and I were sitting in a garden of the Primate's palace on Miodowa Street in Warsaw. Ruffled clouds hung low, almost touching the trees in the garden. It looked like rain and the atmosphere felt as though it would remain for several days.

The Primate continued his story, for a broader and deeper portrait of Karol Wojtyla, "As you probably remember, on October 22, 1948 Cardinal Hlond died, making the primate's position vacant. At that stage I was the bishop of the Lublin diocese. Times were hard for the Church as the regime was doing everything possible, including arresting and imprisoning priests, to make our work difficult. On November 16 I received news that the Holy Father Pius XII had nominated me as Archbishop of Gniezno and Warsaw and also as Primate of Poland. In this capacity I made my first speech in Warsaw."

He withdrew a sheet of paper from the pile of papers and books lying beside him on the garden bench and showed it to me.

It was a fragment of his speech, "I am neither politician nor diplomat, nor even a social reformer. I am your spiritual father, your bishop, the pastor of your soul. I am an apostle of Jesus Christ. The Queen of Poland, Our Lady of Częstochowa, will remain on the shield of the Primate; she will continue to be our Queen and I shall be her humble servant. She will allow me, with your help, to be faithful with all my heart and soul – *Soli Deo*..."

When I had finished reading his speech he continued the autobiographical tale, "Soon after I heard that old Prince Sapieha was sick, I went to Cracow to visit him, and to discuss various Church matters including the selection of the Polish clergy which we would try to send to work in the Vatican Curia. For quite some time we had the idea that the Curia should reflect all nationalities and above all Poland which remained a faithful Catholic country. It was a difficult task, even for the Prince.

"He said to me with a glow in his fading blue eyes, 'I have under my wings an interesting priest, who is well educated, a good writer of poetry and drama, wise, tactful, loved by his parishioners, but above all by the youth. Most importantly, he is a man with a strong character and philosophical in his approach to the reality around him.'"

"I tried to interrupt because, as Primate, I felt this was too much praise."

"Above all, he is a very religious man and gives in to Christ and the Holy Mother...'

"I asked with authority, but pleasantly, 'My esteemed Prince, is there such a priest living today in the world? I do not believe that such a man could function in twentieth-century society.'"

"The Prince adjusted himself in bed and continued, 'I have known this young man from childhood. He is material for export to the Vatican! Not merely as some official but for the top position.'

"To be frank I confess that I thought the Prince either crazy or senile. But I am patient, especially with one who has served so well, so I kept silent and he continued, 'I tested this young priest by sending him to study and travel, and then to work in the poorest village. He passed all tests and even made a minor revolution. I recalled him from the village and placed him in the position of curate to help Reverend Tadeusz Kurowski in St. Florian parish. And you know, in this district of Cracow – Kleparz – many high school and university students come to the Church, and this young priest is doing such fantastic work among them that St. Florian is full of prayers every day of the week. I don't know how he does this, but I consider it to be a minor miracle.'

"'For God's sake,' I said, jokingly, 'as the Primate of Poland I am giving you the order to divulge the name of this young man.'

"He slowly, almost spelling each letter, said 'K–a–r–o–l W–o–j–t–y–l–a.'"

The Primate coughed and reached for a glass of water and sat quietly sipping it. Watching him, my mind at that moment recollected that

while traveling around Poland searching for fresh material about Wojtyla, I visited St. Florian Church in Cracow which had been protected
by kings throughout Polish history. The church had been consecrated
by Bishop Wincenty Kadlubek (?–1223), an outstanding historian and
teacher. Among its pastors was the first Polish cardinal, Zbigniew Oleś-
nicki, and in the years 1949–1951 the Reverend Wojtyla worked in this
famous church with unusual skill and an original approach. No one
could remember such great numbers in attendance at the church as
when Karol Wojtyla conducted services, for the crowd spilled out of
the entrance onto the sidewalk.

I spoke with the old sexton Wojciech Pasiowiec. Frankly I was
searching for negative facts in Wojtyla's life which would enable me to
develop a full-bodied man. Each time I approach someone who knew
him I always posed the standard question, "Please give me something
critical about this man; I have plenty of positive things. Give me a
colorful incident which shows Karol at least in a grey color..." They
would listen and reply not to my satisfaction. It was the same with old
sexton Wojciech, "He was young, but you saw in him a special nobili-
ty, humility and peacefulness. One Good Friday while churches were
packed we had to go to services for a dead parishioner. I had forgotten
about this matter, although I was supposed to remind priests about our
obligations. An hour before, Reverend Wojtyla found me and said, 'I
do not wish to bother you but I would like to remind you that we are
supposed to go to the house of the deceased and pray; would you like
to go with me or not?' Such a thing had never happened in my lifetime,
a priest reminding a sexton of his duty. After he had left the parish for
good, he would return on Sundays to pray and to counsel young people waiting for him in the sacristy. Sometimes when he was late the
youths wouldn't talk with any other priest because they were certain
that he would come and speak with them for awhile."

"Can you give me some incident, not a very pious one?" I asked.

"I already said that I cannot find anything bad in my memory but
here is one incident. Reverend Wojtyla and I were standing in a packed
tramway and beside us, also standing, was an old woman; in front of
her a teenager sat on a bench. Reverend Wojtyla noticed this and asked
the teenager, 'If I give you ten zlotys, will you give the seat to the lady?'
the boy nodded, put the ten zlotys in his pocket and got up. 'Lady,
please sit down,' said the priest and she replied, 'I will not take this seat
for which you paid.'

"'Please, lady, sit down, this way we will teach the boy manners.'

The woman sat down, thanked the Reverend and motioning for the boy to lean toward her, whispered, 'Grandson, did you thank him for the zlotys?'"

The same day when I talked to sexton Pasiowiec I also spoke to Andrzej Kijowski, a Cracow writer. "What was Wojtyla's attitude toward students and what kind of logic did he use in conversations with them?"

"Everything he said was known to us, but his form of expression was uncommon; his interpretation of Christ's miracles, of Lazarus' resurrection, and his story of Mary Magdalene and many other incidents from the New Testament all possessed a definite contemporary application. His literary analysis of Jesus Christ was so dramatic in form that you felt the Son of God was among us.

"He knew a lot about me from my mother who complained of my irreverence toward anything connected with the Church. I was afraid he would convert me. I was twenty-one years old and he was thirty. He wore a worn-out cassock under which one could see grey trousers. His shoes were full of holes and on his head was a worn-out beret. Most of the time he walked fast and kept his hands in the pockets of his coat as though to prevent himself from using too much energy.

"One day I had just left my apartment building and was walking with my hands in my coat pocket. I looked down the empty street and saw a lone figure approach me, with hands in his pockets. I dug my hands deeper and resolved to pass by. Karol slowed down and took his hands out of his pockets as though trying to greet me, and I continued walking maybe thirty more steps before feeling a burning in my back. 'What the devil is this?' I thought. Turning around, I saw Reverend Wojtyla standing with open arms, waiting for me to come."

"And what next? Did you improve your standing with the Church?"

"I approached him and we talked. I was deeply moved. Now I believe more in the goodness of man."

My thoughts snapped back from the past and returned to the present reality when Primate Wyszyński put his empty glass down and continued his story about the Prince and Karol Wojtyla.

"Prince Sapieha, who became a cardinal at the end of his life was gradually sinking. His face got darker and thinner, only his blue eyes shone with the fire of wisdom and compassion. One day in May 1951 he invited Reverend Wojtyla for a conversation that began dramatically. 'I am leaving all of you, those who love me and those who hate me. I am leaving for sure.' Karol had tears in his eyes and although the old Prince asked him to sit down, he would not.

"The old Prince Cardinal continued, 'You too, should leave the parish for two years to study and write. You, my son, have convinced me that you are not only an inspired preacher, but that you love people and they in return have admiration for you . . .' The Prince stopped as though to gain his strength, then asked, 'How many languages do you know?'

"'A little bit of Latin, Greek, French, German, Russian, Spanish. I have sampled all of them, but I could not say that I have made of them a meal,' replied the young priest.

"The Prince Cardinal adjusted his pillow and propped himself up. 'You claim that you know a little, but I am sure, knowing your nature, that you know them all well. I suggest you study Italian and English because these languages will be helpful. Do not neglect contemporary philosophy, especially Christian; study hard and write. I see a bright future for you . . .' Tears appeared in the eyes of the Prince. 'I only regret that I will not see this illustrious career with my earthly eyes.' Karol began to cry, approached the bed, knelt and kissed the ring and then the hand of the dying man, who whispered to him, 'I gave orders to Bishop Eugeniusz Baziak, who will take over most of my functions, that he should see about your material existence so you will have no worries. Above all, be in constant touch with Primate Wyszyński who is your great friend and admirer. You just pray and work hard; everything else God will give you."

This intimate account among the three churchmen was later verified by the author with Karol Wojtyla, John Paul II.

In July 1951 Prince Cardinal Sapieha died and was buried in the crypt of Wawel Castle. Reverend Wojtyla left the position of curate at St. Florian Church and moved to an apartment of his professor's, the Reverend Ignacy Rózycki, at the Jagellonian University, 19 Kanoniczna Street. He plunged into study and discussion about a fairly new philosophical trend, phenomenology, whose creator was the German philosopher Max Scheler who died in 1928. The cocreator and continuator of this philosophical trend was a Polish professor at the Jagellonian University, Dr. Roman Ingarden. Karol Wojtyla spent many hours of discussion with Professor Ingarden and two other professors of the same Cracow university, Wladyslaw Wicher, Adam Usowicz; and a professor from Lublin University, Stefan Świezawski; together they analyzed and argued about ethics in Thomism and phenomenology. This last theory claimed that intuition is the basis for knowing phenomena outside everyday life. According to Max Scheler's teaching, the phenomenon of religion is one of the basic elements in human consciousness. Karol Wojtyla produced a work entitled, "Evaluation of the Possibility of Building Christian Ethics Based on Max Scheler's System," that criticized the German philosopher for not noticing that the 'person' is embodied in the Absolute of God.

Professor Roman Ingarden radicalized Karol Wojtyla not only in the philosophical sense but socially and politically. The future Pope, like many students before and after, heard the famous saying of Professor Ingarden: "No religion is worth a shred of cotton if it does not have the vision of a brighter future, if it does not help man on earth to rid himself of oppression, any oppression, material or moral!"

Karol Wojtyla took those words to heart and an immediate result was a poem written in 1952, "Our Conversation From Which Some Sentences I Remember":

Our conversation is existing in growing suffering.
When you say that suffering always accompanies
    the great changing,
that a man will wake up during his most painful work —

oh, how right you are,
    how much truth there is in your saying!
But I think that a man suffers most
    when he lacks vision.

16

The Prince and the Priest:
Two Characters in Search of the Third

"I WOULD like to know," I began, delicately, my next conversation with Primate Wyszyński, "what was this great secret between you and Prince Sapieha?"

"I promise to tell you, but in order to keep the story going I would like to present the situation in the country in 1950 and how I, as primate – forgive me for this immodesty – helped the Church; although at the beginning Monsignor Domenico Tardini, the Vatican Secretary of State was against my diplomatic activities."

"Let's begin with Prince Sapieha who headed Caritas, the national charitable organization founded with the help of the American Catholic League. Caritas had branches in all dioceses and helped poor people, especially children, senior citizens and retired priests. On January 23, 1950 government authorities made inspections in all the branches of Caritas, confiscating documents, arresting some functionaries, and the following day accused the bishops of exceeding their authority in many ways including the use of Caritas' funds for propaganda purposes."

"I guess they deliberately hit the Church in the pocket?"

"You are correct. The next day I sent a telegram to President Boleslaw Bierut: 'I am deeply distressed and shocked with this type of control and with the attacks in the press. I am lodging a protest in the name of the Polish Church and asking the government to change its behavior.' President Bierut did not reply, and on January 30 the national council of bishops gathered in Prince Sapieha's Cracow palace to deliberate on the situation of the Church and its relationship to the state. The result was three letters.

"The first, directed to Bierut, accused the government of trying to destroy Caritas by accusing Polish Catholics of dishonesty and of dividing the country. Together with a virulent press and radio campaign priests and nuns were forced to attend anti-Catholic meetings.

"The second was a pastoral letter to all clergy in which the Episcopate warned priests not to take part in political activity, nor act in ways that would not reflect God's and canonical laws. This letter was signed by all members of the Episcopate. It was really a strong warning to behave or be excommunicated."

"Oh, I see, you and the Episcopate were worried that the government and other churches would entice some priests, especially in poorer regions of the country, to anti-Vatican activities?"

"In the third letter to all Polish Catholics, read from the pulpits of every church in the country, the Episcopate attempted to explain its position on the Caritas affair as well as that of the Church on various other matters relating to the Vatican and Warsaw."

"Here, I would like to tell you that you are a modest man because at the time, a difficult time for both nation and Church, you were instrumental in starting a dialogue between an atheistic government and the Catholic Church. Although you suffered much opposition among the Polish clergy and almost total opposition from the Vatican you succeeded. On April 1, 1950 the Polish Episcopate and the government signed an agreement which defined the relationship between the Church and the socialist state. This was a milestone, for it demonstrated how communists and Catholics could coexist.

"A few months before Cardinal Sapieha died, he sent me a message saying that he was ill and could not travel, but would like to see me right away to discuss an important matter. I knew that he had a few problems which he wanted to resolve before his death. I went to Cracow. It was raining when I arrived and the Prince's palace had a cold, damp atmosphere. Upon reaching his bedroom I felt sad; after opening the door I noticed the small figure of the Prince standing in the middle of the room. Slowly, he approached, grabbed me and said, 'Take me for a walk.' He squeezed my arm and I felt his fingernails. I embraced him and thought, 'This will be our last meeting.' He added, 'I need physical movement because I am taking so many pills that I feel numb.'

"'Let's go,' I said, taking his arm. He was small, skinny, and his face was grey; in contrast to my physique he looked like a child but his mind still worked well."

"'The Holy Father more than anyone else thinks globally...'" he began as I walked slowly with him through the corridors of the palace. I nodded my head and squeezed his hand as a sign that I agreed. I knew that Eugenio Pacelli was a good diplomat and before becoming Pope in March 1939 was a Vatican diplomat. I also know that he was on excellent terms with Prince Sapieha primarily because this aristocratic Polish family was well connected with European royalty.

"'During my many private meetings with the Pope I said to him politely, do not zigzag in politics; once you hit capitalism and twice you hit Marxism, and as a result people do not believe you.' The Pope was shocked by my opinion and said, 'You are different now.' I replied, 'If you knew more about the suffering of my nation you would also be different.' He asked in a conciliatory voice, 'What should I do, my beloved Prince?' I replied from the top of my head, 'You should work right now so that the next Pope will not be Italian. I think he was shocked, but did not reply right away.'"

Primate Wyszyński said to me, "I knew that Prince Sapieha never hid his opinions but his relations with the Pope were warm. I paused with the Prince at the bench and asked, 'What did the Holy Father say to you?' Then I helped him sit down and while waiting for a reply listened to the rain hitting the roof. The Prince answered in a dull voice, 'Pacelli said, 'not so simple my friend.' I was disappointed with his reply and said, 'Right now I know a cardinal who would not refuse the election to the Holy See. I am not thinking about myself...'" He embraced me and said, 'You served Christ and the people well and I appreciate your suggestions but...' I lost my temper. 'You have in your approach in later years too many buts. There is a great difference between the affairs of God and those of the people. Human problems due to the morality of the people should be solved as soon as possible and to their satisfaction. Almighty God must give direction to the Church to cooperate with the people, to help them. After all, God is immortal.'

"'I see that you are impregnated with the spirit of socialism,' the Pope replied.

"'This has nothing to do with socialism. The present-day situation of the Church demands that we cardinals should elect to the Holy See a Frenchman, an Irishman, or even a Pole.'

"Pacelli was dumbfounded, but knowing that I was old, I pushed my thought further, 'If, for example, we elect a Pole we could bring new vision to the millions of Christians in Eastern Europe, South America, and even the Soviet Union, and bring the Church to a moral and social renaissance. The people would then say that the Vatican is going with the spirit of the times and helping the world emerge from spiritual confusion...the Roman Catholic Church is going with the people.'

"He interrupted me, 'Are they not talking today like that?' Then added after a moment's reflection, 'A good idea, as a matter of fact, it is very good, a non-Italian Pope would introduce real reverence which could bring people closer to the Church...Whom do you have in mind my dear Prince, which cardinal?'

"Without hesitating I replied my candidate was not yet a cardinal. The Pope said with a smile, 'You mean Archbishop Wyszyński?'

"Yes, I replied loudly."

"When the Prince told me of his conversation with the Pope, I cried," Wyszyński said, "And my aristocratic host noticing this said, 'Stefan, please do not be so sentimental. I know your value; also, I'm a realist and am aware that no one will make you Pope, but maybe your nomination for cardinal will arrive earlier as a result of this conversation. For a Pope of foreign extraction, we must wait until the next generation. Pacelli is healthy and will be Pope for several more years, maybe even ten years. After that only God knows what will happen in the world, but let us not lose hope. In this matter I have some definite ideas and would like to pass them to God and to you, my dear Primate. Before I go to a conference with God upstairs I will relate something to you...'"

"I admit that I was lost in all my speculation but out of respect for the Prince and his position in the Vatican I did not press for a clarification; instead I waited patiently and switched the subject. 'How is your health, really?'"

"The Prince waved his hand, 'Don't interrupt me...there is a young priest whom I have known almost since his childhood: He is handsome, but I didn't find anything that would disgrace him with any women or any sex. He is pious yet intellectual. A good organizer with extra appeal to the young and old. He is involved with university youth, which thanks to him, attend the Cracow churches more often now. Some young people of both sexes call him uncle, others Reverend Doctor, and the working youth in Nowa Huta factory center call him, 'our man.'

"I already knew about whom he was talking, because as a Primate, I kept a file in Warsaw on bright priests. But I was enjoying the story and so I did not interrupt him. The Prince rested for a moment.

"'Beside his regular priestly duties this young fellow who seldom dresses in a cassock organizes excursions with youths of various walks of life: some he takes to the Carparthian Mountains and others in large groups to the Mazurian Lakes. Every day he finds time to discuss religion, science, philosophy, political affairs, but most importantly he conducts regular religious services in fields or nearby local churches.' I thought at this moment I might interrupt because these were too many praises for one man. But the Prince continued on the same subject, 'I do not know how he manages his time since he also writes, gives lectures on Thomistic philosophy and on Max Scheler.'

"'I myself was young some time ago and in my long life I did not find such an amazing fellow. Yes, my investigators tried to find something derogatory; as a matter of fact, I specifically asked for such aspects of his character, but they did not find much except maybe one girl. Telling you this story I want to ask you for help...'

"With the young girl or with the young priest?"

"'Wait a moment.' The Prince slowly rose from the bench. 'The sun has come out from behind the clouds, take me to the courtyard and let me see the sky...'

"As we walked down the steps, the Prince was quiet as though he were trying to collect his thoughts. '...This priest is a young doctor of theology and despite his running around still regularly preaches at St. Florian Church...' he hesitated in the middle of the courtyard, I helped him to his knees; he folded his hands and raised his pale face to the bright sky. The Prince said in a strong voice, 'God, Holy Mother, please help Karol Wojtyla to be a Pope!' I found myself recalling the words of Plato, 'Everybody is conducting some sort of calculation which we call hope.' I took my hand from the Prince's shoulder and knelt beside him, folding my hands in prayer, but Sapieha did not interrupt his supplication, 'God, Holy Mother, please help Karol Wojtyla to become Pope...' He paused, '...Jesus Christ, if you need the Holy Mother of Częstochowa...; I leave here on earth your humble servant Stefan Wyszyński...He will help You and through You he will help Karol...please, please, help this young man to occupy the Holy See...' he let his hands down and whispered, 'Please assist me to my bedroom, I need rest.'

"We walked slowly upstairs, both crying. I said to the Prince in a trembling emotion-filled voice, 'I will do it, I solemnly promise that I will do it.' As we embraced I touched his face with mine. I don't know how long we stayed like that in silence."

On July 23, 1951, 7:25 A.M., Prince Adam Stefan Cardinal Sapieha, Archbishop Metropolitan of Cracow died at the age of eighty-four, two months and two weeks.

"I as the Primate of Poland conducted the funeral services of the Prince. All of Cracow came out into the streets to say good-bye to him. In the burial procession walked the Reverend Karol Wojtyla who did not know that on his shoulders rested the prophecy of poets and the secret prayers of the Prince and myself. I could not divulge to Karol my secret agreement with the deceased, but told him that the Prince in the last hour of his life read his poem "Mother":

This moment of all life is being experienced
    in a word,
from that time this word became the body nourished
    with blood
in elation was carried
in my heart was growing a New Man
during the time when thought was overwhelmed
    with wonder and hands
    with daily work.
This moment is at the peak but fresh
    as at the beginning,
because it finds You – there is no drop on the eyelashes
in which the rays of the eyes were melting in cold air –
but the enormous exhaustion discovers its light
    and its sense.

At the end of our meeting, Cardinal Wyszyński expressed a thought, which has been on my mind to this day. "Everyone of us has a mother and admires her, but no one loves a mother as much as priests of the Roman Catholic Church; and as priests age and climb the hierarchial ladder this love grows to enormous proportions and eventually blends with the love for the Holy Mother. Maybe in this dual love lies the eternal power of the Church."

Cardinal Wyszyński always carried in his wallet a photograph of his mother, and a picture of the Miraculous Holy Mother of Częstochowa in a specially built jewel-box case.

17

Tastes and Intelligence of Setting

THE WRITER Wlodek Sokorski and I were seated in my room at Warsaw's Forum Hotel, drinking vodka on ice and eating sturgeon canapés. He was in a good mood as he presented his cultural saga about Karol Wojtyla, "Being minister of culture in postwar Poland I received confidential information and gossip about various people in the arts, science and church circles. Even now I like to hear an occasional droll story. My favorite is about the dean of Polish novelists, Jaroslaw Iwaszkiewicz and young priest Wojtyla. Jaroslaw was visiting Cracow in order to lecture at the Union of Writers, and like all famous people, everyone wanted to exchange words with him or get his autograph. After his presentation, Reverend Wojtyla approached the writer who was well known for his love of French cuisine and good jokes. "I hope you are not upset that I criticized your latest book," Karol said. "If you are then I am sorry, but I was trying to express my sincere opinion."

"Jaroslaw looked at his cassock, raised his head and looked into his eyes. 'I see that you are a handsome priest, but do you know how to write?"

"Wlodek continued, "However you approach the character of Karol Wojtyla you must emphasize that the cultural postwar milieu in Poland had an enormous influence on him. Writer Wojtyla was well known in Cracow and throughout the country by his uniqueness of combining religious themes with socialist ideas. He was an avid reader and keen observer of social and political changes in Poland.

"I was not keen on socialist realism because I thought this trend could not capture different artistic minds which were working in surrealistic or religious approaches to reality, and I reasoned that forcing socialist realism on all people in various branches of culture would deprive the nation of great achievements. Convincing the government to recognize my viewpoint of tolerance in culture was difficult so I decided to step down from my post and spend more time writing."

"I do not think that trends are important in creativity for particular writers," I interrupted, "because history shows that we have important literary achievements in realism, naturalism, surrealism and spiritualism. I am not convinced that a writer could change his style and present the existing situation in a different manner solely to comply with a government's order."

"You are right. As a result of our efforts, artistic freedom in Poland gradually approached one hundred percent. That is the reason that during the post-Stalinist period important books appeared in various styles such as Iwaszkiewicz's *Fame and Glory*, Dąbrowska's *Adventures of a Thinking Man*, Leo Kruczkowski's *Governor*, and Zukrowski's *Stone Tablets*. In addition, new writers of great talent appeared, such as the poet Stanislaw Grochowiak, dramatist Marek Hlasko, poet and dramatist Ernest Bryll, and the poet Bohdan Drozdowski. Many talented critics, publicists and novelists stimulated and transformed Polish cultural reality. Their characteristics were intellectual courage, a search for new forms, new morality and a more critical look at the political and social trends of the country which, after 1968 reached political confrontation. During the 1950s we liquidated illiteracy and brought our universities to a high European level, and in the 1960s we endorsed the idea of universal secondary education. Simultaneously, the country experienced a tremendous political awareness that climaxed in the strikes of July 1980."

"Wasn't the single reason for this the fact that Party boss Edward Gierek neglected agriculture and emphasized the modernization of industry for which he sought large foreign loans, repayment of which did not have a base in the national economy?"

"It was not only Gierek, though he did have a poor knowledge of economics," replied Wlodek. "We have to take into consideration the psychology of the Polish people, but maybe we should talk about this later."

"I would like to share a story with you," I said. "A real happening which I think demonstrates Gierek's economic philosophy and his obsession with heavy industry.

"As you know, he enjoyed travelling on prearranged inspections and during one of these tours a worker approached him from the group of clappers who were shoved up front by the management of the factory and said, 'Comrade First Secretary, our factories are poorly managed, produce poor goods which we cannot sell on foreign markets, and as a result we cannot repay our loans.' Gierek was astonished by the courage of this worker which reminded him of his own youth, and he asked the worker what he could do to improve the situation. The worker replied, 'Fire your economic czar.'

"When the First Secretary returned to Warsaw he called the Minister of Economic Affairs into his office and said, 'You have some difficulties in your economic department?'

"'Comrade First Secretary, we have problems in many departments.'

"'For example?'

"'We do not have enough housing facilities for the people nor enough agricultural and light industry products – just a push for heavy industry.'

"'How would you solve this problem?'

"'I cannot argue the question of industrialization, especially heavy industry, because I know that you, Comrade First Secretary, are committed to it, but there are two remaining questions upon which I would like to coment: food and housing.

"'Interesting, Comrade Minister, and how would you solve these two problems?'

"'Open up the western borders and we will liquidate the question of housing...' Gierek's big well-shaped face reddened but he did not reply, and as a good politician held his temper and quietly said, 'How would you solve the food and clothing problem?'

"'By closing the eastern borders.'"

Sokorski reached for a sturgeon sandwich which I had paid for in dollars. "This is a crazy joke and does not contain much truth," he said.

"Wlodek, do not look at my hotel for the standard of living in Poland but travel throughout the country so that you will see the poor management and discouragement among peasants and workers."

Sokorski who had been an idealist all his life replied, "This is not the fault of socialist theory, but of people who are not dedicated to hard work and sacrifice. Besides, you must take into consideration the demoralizing World War II psychology when to be crooked, lazy and conniving became the national means of defeating the Nazis and surviving. Despite intensive education this type of psychology still exists and although I, an atheist, would say that the Church is working hard with the Government to eradicate this attitude among young people, we are still confronted every day with many who demand apartments, color television and cars without putting in an honest day's work in a factory or in the fields."

"Literature did not help either?" I asked

"Yes, Polish literature, especially the novel, is rather critical not only of the reality of war and foreign occupation of Poland, but of the present-day situation. A typical example is Andrzej Braun, author of novels whose heroes are moral as in Joseph Conrad's conception, who take responsibility, not only for what they did but for those things which they did not do. In such novels as *Loafer* or *Mutiny* he presents painful human stories during the occupation and the Stalinist period, but does not point to any solutions. These are clear pictures of reality without particular hope for the future. Those novels which present the Polish past and future in a negative light are being translated into foreign languages to show negative Polish characters, the bleakness of life and the failure of socialism."

"But I am sure that other writers with a positive view of socialism are published abroad."

"I do not remember," said Wlodek. "One exception may be Stanislaw Lem, a widely translated science fiction writer. But I don't think that he is talking about socialism in outer space, although he is well educated and has strong opinions about socialism. He is well liked in the Soviet Union, even by Leonid Brezhnev who likes his novels and invited him to the Kremlin. During one visit they talked about outer-space travel and the speed of cosmic vehicles and at one point Mr. Lem said to President Brezhnev, 'The Soviet Union possesses the fastest interplanetary ships...' And President Brezhnev replied, 'Yes, we have fast interplanetary vehicles but we also have fast growth of light industry and what is more, the fastest dogs...'" Mr. Lem was surprised and asked for clarification. 'I know about Soviet air and space craft, and I know about light industry production, but I never heard of the fastest Soviet dogs.'

"'Yes, special Siberian dogs...'

"'Why Siberian?'

"'Comrade writer, in vast Siberia there are not many trees; sometimes there is a distance of several miles between trees, so the dogs have to run very fast...'

"You see, there is lots of freedom in Poland; everyone tells anti-Soviet jokes, and not many people try to see the benefits of Polish relations with our eastern neighbor who helped us win independence. During the first postwar years they sent us heavy machinery to rebuild the country's industrial power and to this day we have beneficial trade agreements. But literature produced in later years, if not benign to this Polish-Soviet relation, is indifferent and sometimes even satirically bitter. We cannot move Poland to the moon, and as a result, we must have a brotherly relationship that cannot be built on critical exaggeration or on straightforward hostility."

"I know that not everything in the Soviet Union is bad and that not everything in the West is good, but I do understand one thing: you cannot ask a writer to write a novel that is only positive toward the Soviet Union, an artist to paint a beautiful picture glorifying Soviet reality, or a composer to create music to praise socialism. But the government controls television, radio and film and through these three mediums is able to push a tremendous amount of propaganda. Also there are many exhibitions of Soviet painting, books, many concerts by Russian orchestras. Did this not favorably influence the Polish nation toward the Soviet Union?"

"To be honest with you, not much. For example, I will describe to you a recent incident at Warsaw University where there was a large exhibition of Soviet books translated into Polish. It was a beautiful display, favorably accepted by booklovers, but one day or rather overnight someone changed this exhibition in such a way that the titles of the books read as follows: *We Would Like to Live...Far Away from Moscow...In the Shadow of Skyscrapers...* As you can see even with this even Western propaganda capitalized."

"So what is the solution? What will be the outcome of this national attitude toward their Eastern neighbor? Who is to blame?"

"First we must blame the Polish Workers Party which, despite possibilities, did not capture the imagination of the people, and I say that as a devout socialist. We began to build socialism right after the war when we got rid of the brutal Nazi occupation, and this antiforeigner feeling was transferred to the Russians who had helped us regain independence. Succeeding Polish governments with the leadership of the Workers Party nourished themselves uncritically with pro-Soviet propaganda. We are not sophisticated in this branch of political activity. No one would believe that everything in the Soviet Union is one hundred percent right and everything in the West one hundred percent wrong. We did not develop a political rationale to create friendly relations with both East and West. Finally the negative attitude of the Bierut regime toward the Roman Catholics alienated positive pro-government forces in the Church. It was a cardinal mistake because if we had such cooperation with the Church in the 1940s and 1950s as we have now we might have avoided the present moral and political crisis."

"I see that as a socialist you believe in the positive influence of the Church on society?"

"I know the political and religious situation in Poland; I also know church leaders such as Wyszyński, Wojtyla and others. Most of them strongly believe that cooperation between socialism and Catholicism is possible and could bring positive results in the form of national stability, a better and just life for the people."

"How could the state get out from under the present-day economic catastrophe?" I asked Sokorski.

"There are two dominant schools of thought. One is to form a strong government and go into complete economic cooperation with the Soviet Union. The other is to denationalize, bring free enterprise, and go one hundred percent with the West."

"What is your personal opinion?"

He thought for a moment and said, "We cannot destroy the positive achievements of socialism such as social security, free schools, socialized medicine and one hundred percent employment. The West will accept our cooperation if we place factories and other sources of production and distribution into private hands. But for the workers this would mean a significant loss of security."

"How about the Soviet Union?"

"We must convince the Soviet Union that the Polish nation under a broad national goverment would not be hostile or act as a base for foreign powers to attack them."

"It is a great undertaking, isn't it?"

"Yes, but if you look at the thousand year history of the Polish state you will see that we have satisfactorily solved our problems and we will solve this one too."

Taking a LOT airplane from Okęcie Airport in Warsaw to New York, I saw the well-known poet and satirist, Jósef Prutkowski at the departure gates, a wilted bouquet of flowers in his hand.

"Are you waiting for your family?" I asked, after greeting him.

"No."

"For your lover?"

"No," he replied, emphatically.

"For whom are you waiting?"

"For Americans."

"Are you crazy?"

"Why do you think I am crazy? In 1945 I waited with flowers for the Red Army."

"And what?"

"Did they not come?"

18
Cardinal's Conscience and Raison d'État

"THE year 1953 was a difficult one for Poland, the Church and for myself personally," began Cardinal Wyszyński. "The Holy Father or more precisely the Curia, and specifically, German influences in that ecclesiastical organization were against normalization of Church administration on Poland's western territories. At some point I approached the Holy Father directly and said that if he would not permit me to establish Church authority in Western Poland according to my wishes and those of the population I would resign from all Church offices and enter a monastery. As a result of this 'personal blackmail' the Holy Father gave the Curia directions to cooperate to the extent of making me sole judge.

"Not long after this exchange of views between the Vatican and myself, Polish bishops were given permission to reside in the cities of Wrocław, Opole, Gorzów and Olsztyn. The Polish government was surprised, although I had acted according to the agreement between them and the Episcopate, and on February 9 the Government issued a decree intending to curtail the activities of the Church in western Poland. As a result of this decree, the Administration started to remove clergy from their positions under the pretext that they were of German descent or antisocialist. The ensuing confusion and persecution were widely publicized in the press of the German Federal Republic."

"What position did you take?" I asked.

"It was evident that the atheistic groups in the government, despite our agreements, tried to disrupt the functions of the Church, if not entirely to destabilize it. I could do nothing about the propaganda in German papers, but on May 8 under my leadership the Polish Episcopate issued a memorandum entitled *Non Possumus*; the final paragraphs of which I will recite to you:

If outside forces would prevent us from nominating competent spiritual leaders we will not permit outsiders to interfere with Church affairs and give religious functions to the hands of the undeserving. Anyone who accepts the Church's position without our permission will be excommunicated. We respect personal views and beliefs of all people including our adversaries whom, according to Christian beliefs, we do not hate, but at the same time we demand that the religious beliefs of Polish Catholics, particularly those of children and the youth, should be respected. In all our relations with the faithful of the Church we emphasize a positive attitude by the citizen to the nation and the state; simultaneously, we demand that the Government should not prevent Catholics from fulfilling their obligations to God and the Church. We are aware of our high responsibilities and as a result, we constantly remind Catholic priests to respect and support the nation in its endeavor toward happiness and prosperity. We also demand that our priests should not be coerced into political activity which would only lead to inevitable confrontation between Government and Church. Priests should not be forced to break their allegiance to the Church and its bishops. In short, the principles of division between Church and State, as guaranteed in the Constitution, should be respected. We demand that the Government respect and protect the rights of Catholics in the People's Republic of Poland according to Article 32, point 7 of the Constitution.

"It looks like a strong ultimatum by the spiritual leaders to the political rulers of the country. You must have been aware of the consequences."

"They put us against a wall, both State and Vatican, although there was no reason for the Curia not to give permission to establish a Polish Catholic administration on Poland's western territories; the only explanation for that was German influences in the Vatican. This gave the Polish socialist government the opportunity to accuse both the Vatican and the Polish Episcopate of pro-German feelings."

"But let us be frank; in 1953 many things happened in the Soviet Union. You were taking chances being so demanding of the Polish Government whose choices, from a foreign policy standpoint, were severly limited."

"After Stalin's death, power went to three men, Malenkov, Molotov and Beria, although the latter was executed in early June. On June 4, in Warsaw's St. Anne Church in front of two hundred thousand worshippers I presented a strong sermon, saying that the Primate and all Roman Catholic Churches in Poland will defend freedom of conscience, national culture, and human dignity. I even said that I would pay for these principles with my own blood."

The Primate rubbed his forehead and added, "From hindsight you might say I was thinking about the events in Moscow and figuring out that the Warsaw government, seeing turmoil in the East, would not go strongly against the Polish Episcopate, but rather would begin to seek cooperation based on our previous agreements."

"You misjudged?"

"As a result of my preaching at St. Anne Church, the Government two weeks later called a 'national conference of Church and secular Catholic activists', the majority of whose participants supported State policies. At this conference, Reverend Waclaw Radosz viciously attacked the Polish Episcopate and me personally. The Church's and my personal situation were approaching climactic moments. Although my differences with the Government were duly analyzed in the Curia and the Pope was aware of them, I did not hear anything public from him to support me. The Holy Father, being a seasoned politician, waited. Then, on July 16, he sent me a letter in which His Holiness accepted my viewpoint and warmly supported the action of the Episcopate and my pronouncement."

"It was a tremendous victory for you," I said.

"Yes, because my attitude from the beginning was to uphold the government in social reforms and to convince them to support me in religious activities that were the logical result of our discussions and agreements. The Holy Father and the Curia were originally against my line of thinking and action, so you might say that the Polish government, seeing that I lacked backing from the Vatican, tried to harass and weaken the Church. At that time, I was between the hammer and the anvil, but being stubborn and a believer in social justice I stuck to my guns. Certainly, the Pope who said, 'We are observing you with admiration, and future generations will read about your efforts and God will reward you . . .' verified my position. And receiving such support from the Vatican, I preached a sermon on August 26 in Częstochowa in front of one hundred thousand faithful believers in which I stressed that the foundation of life and Polish culture was and will be the Catholic Church."

"This was not the end of your troubles?"

"No, but to understand these troubles we must, again, go back to Moscow. From September 3rd to the 7th, 1953, the Central Committee of the Communist Party of the Soviet Union held a conference and Nikita Khrushchev was elected First Secretary who then nominated General Ivan Serov as the chief of the secret service police, NKVD. You must remember that General Serov was a good friend of Boleslaw Piasecki. Mr. Piasecki, a clever journalist and politician was the head of the Polish Catholic splinter group called Pax. This national organization, working with the Polish government had an almost unlimited amount of funds, controlled several newspapers and a publishing house, as well as some industrial enterprises from which profits went toward anti-Roman Catholic propaganda."

"Let me interrupt. I knew Mr. Piasecki and visited him several times in his villa fenced with barbed wire and protected around the clock by vicious dogs and private guards. I asked him point blank whether he was in the service of the NKVD. He vehemently denied this connection and as to General Serov, he said that they met during the war. 'You don't think I have so much influence in Moscow as to nominate Serov as the chief of the secret police?' He admitted that before the war he had expressed fascist ideas, but now he saw the light and was supporting cooperation between Catholics and the Government. Before my departure from his well-guarded villa he mused, 'I wish that someone, some day would write a true story about my efforts on behalf of Polish national unity.' Before we shook hands at the gate he whispered, 'Yes, I have good contacts in Moscow but I have better contacts in the Vatican. The reason is that I would like to see unity not only between the Christian churches, but between all churches and communist parties in their struggle for peace.'"

"As a believer in Christ, I am not condemning Mr. Piasecki," Wyszyński said, "God will be the judge, but the Polish reality did not look so rosy as people from his camp pictured it. On September 14, in Kielce, began the military court procedure against the Bishop Czeslaw Kaczmarek and a group of priests accused of espionage on behalf of foreign intelligence services. During this trial, the military prosecutor

Colonel Zarako-Zarakowski condemned the deceased cardinals Hlond and Sapieha together with the Polish Episcopate – my name was not mentioned – for antistate activities. In his testimony Bishop Kaczmarek stated, 'All three cardinals, Hlond, Sapieha and Wyszyński sent secret reports to Rome on political and socioeconomic happenings in the country.' Prosecutor Zarako-Zarakowski went further by accusing the entire Episcopate of espionage, diversion and cooperation with the underground movement whose goal was, 'to restore the capitalist system, deprive the Polish nation of independence, and cut off part of western Poland and place it in the hands of neo-Hitlerites.'"

It was amazing how much Primate Wyszyński remembered in such detail, so I expressed my doubts and he responded, "I was there. To not be presumptuous I have to say that on trial was the Polish Catholic hierarchy and especially myself who continued to be stubborn in my beliefs. Don't forget, at the beginning, I had not only the Warsaw government against me but also the Vatican Curia."

I could not comment on these observations so instead I asked, "What happened to Bishop Kaczmarek?"

"On September 22 the military court sentenced the Bishop to twelve years in prison. Somebody who does not believe in God would say, 'The Episcopate's prayers for help and freedom did not help,' and they would be right. But during this praying we also prepared a letter to the Government protesting the sentence. The Government, I think, was also confused and in consultation with the Political Bureau of the Party who sent a delegation to First Secretary Khrushchev and General Serov. The top three rulers of Poland, Boleslaw Bierut, Jakub Berman and Hilary Minc, did not know what to do with me and felt that if something happened they would be responsible, so the wise politicans decided to distribute the responsibility. The head of the delegation to Moscow was a secretary of the Central Committee for religious affairs, Franciszek Mazur who, already at the Moscow railroad station, cried out, 'What should we do with Wyszyński!' In the meantime, in Warsaw, the Government sent Piasecki to my office. He tried to convince me to cooperate, otherwise he said, the church would experience prosecution and only those clergy who were progovernment would be permitted to perform their duties.

"This man Piasecki made a poor impression on me. He was rather tall, thin and on his dry, olive-colored face only his eyes shone as they shifted nervously from left to right. On the left cheek from time to time a nervous tick appeared. His fingers constantly rolled a pencil or his wedding ring which he often removed. As soon as he appeared in my office he said, 'For God's sake please try to save the Church; sign a letter in which you give in, just the minimum.'

"About what minimum are you talking?'"

"'Say you condemn the political activities of Bishop Kaczmarek and the Episcopate will not participate in antigovernment activities.'

"We are not an antigovernment organization. The Church is with the nation and expresses the nation's wishes."

I had also prepared a long letter to the Government which I sent on September 24. It was written in the name of the Polish Episcopate and signed by me. In this letter I held that during the meetings of the Polish Episcopate neither Cardinal Hlond, Cardinal Sapieha, nor I discussed, prepared or sent any kind of information describing Polish internal and external affairs."

"I presume you were prepared for the worst?"

"Yes, I was. The next day was Friday September 25, the day dedicated to blessed Wladyslaw from Gielniów, patron of Warsaw. At 7:00 A.M. I celebrated Holy Mass and delivered a sermon to the members of Metropolitan Seminary. At 7:00 P.M. I took part in services at St. Anne Church which was full of thousands of kneeling and praying parishioners who spilled into the neighborhood streets. I delivered a speech in which I proclaimed, 'We hear of criminals today, but history will call them saints.'

"That evening I returned to the Primate's Palace at Miodowa Street and went to my bedroom on the first floor to rest before Saturday's heavy schedule. Near midnight one of the priests knocked on the door to my bedroom. It was Bishop Antoni Baraniak and he informed me that people were knocking on the door downstairs and shouting that they had a letter to me from Minister Bida. I replied that all letters from the Polish Government to the Primate of Poland should be delivered to the secretary of the Episcopate, Bishop Zygmunt Choromański. Then I switched on the light, got dressed and while going downstairs, turned on lights to the left and right. In a few moments, the entire palace of the Primate was lighted. When I appeared in the Papal Hall, a crowd of civilians, maybe twenty or more, were waiting for me. Bishop Baraniak said, 'Those gentlemen were trying to shoot their way in.'

"Too bad they did not shoot," I said, quietly. "Then we would know this is a real holdup."

"One of the civilians announced, 'We are here on official business.' And I replied, 'Official business I conduct in my office, not in my private apartment.' I opened the door and went to the garden to look for the caretaker. The civilians followed me and just when we were in the garden our dog, Baca, bit one of them.

"I returned to look for iodine and a bandage. In the hall I met one of the sisters who worked in the kitchen and asked her to bring the first-aid kit. The nun and I took care of the wound on the intruder's leg and another said to me, 'We are here on official business and no one opened the door.' My secretary interjected, 'Gentlemen, you arrived here after midnight and tried to break into the Primate's palace. We thought you were thieves.'

"'It is true," I concurred. "We spoke with President Bierut, with Minister Mazur and other government officials and if they have something for me they should communicate during the day. What you are doing creates a poor image for the Government. We are living in a civilized world, are we not?'"

"What was the reaction of the agents?"

"They did not comment; instead one showed me the official document in which was stated that on September 24 the Government decided to remove me from Warsaw and refused to permit me to continue my duties as Primate of Poland. When they asked me to sign it I refused, explaining that I never took part in antistate activity, never even influenced anyone to behave so, and I would not voluntarily be moved from the Primate's palace.

"You acted courageously and created a sticky situation for the agents," I commented.

"For them, it was routine; two agents took me by the arm and one said, 'Mr. Wyszyński, let's go upstairs to collect your necessary personal things.'

"You didn't go?"

"Yes, I did, but I said, 'I have nothing to take. I arrived here a poor man and I will leave the same way.' The third agent who walked in front of me, reached the room, saw a valise and grabbed it, and the fourth agent started packing the valise with clothing. I turned to the priests and nuns who followed me. 'We all pledged poverty and we know the meaning of this pledge.' Next, I picked up the breviary and the rosary and left. The agents did not allow me to stop at the palace chapel to pray. In the hall I saw Bishop Baraniak and turned to him, thinking of giving him final instructions, but one of the civilian agents – I later discovered his name and rank, Colonel Więckowski, head of Department XI of Internal Security – and his deputy Demidok, simultaneously yelled, 'You cannot talk!' They looked at each other, I guess, giving eye signals and Colonel Więckowski said, 'You can speak.'

"I began loudly, as though directing my words to Bishop Baraniak, but I wanted everyone to hear, 'Bishop, you are the witness of an unprecedented violation of law. Please do not organize any kind of defense and in case of a trial, if I live, I will defend myself.'"

19
Alchemist or Plain Rascal

"I WAS sitting in the vestry of St. Mary's Church, working on parish papers," Prelate Ferdynand Machay said to me. "Suddenly a boy or girl would appear and ask, 'Is Uncle Wojtyla here?' I usually said no. Then an old man or woman would walk in and inquire, 'Is Reverend Doctor Wojtyla available?' Although I am an old pastor, no one asked for me. Everyone asks for Karol, who only occasionally performs services or listens to confessions. Such interruption forced me to move out of the vestry and work elsewhere."

"You mean this went on all the time?"

"Yes, but later the interference subsided when Karol Wojtyla was nominated as professor of moral theology and social ethics at Metropolitan Seminary. He also obtained an additional teaching job in social ethics at the Jagellonian University."

The popularity of this priest was established in a short time in Cracow, the former capitol of Poland. Here, also began the career over which Prince Sapieha watched from above and Primate Wyszyński from the ground; no one knows who influenced him more.

In 1954, Professor Jerzy Kalinowski, dean of the philosophy department at the Catholic University in Lublin, and Professor Feliks Bednarski invited him to lecture on ethics at the university. At night he would take the train from Cracow to Lublin, situated in the center of the country, 340 kilometers northeast, and would reach his destination at 5:00 A.M. the next morning. It was a rather unusual chore. One day, when I interviewed him in the Vatican I asked, "How did you manage to sleep?"

"During my train voyage I spent most of the time working on poetry and then switched to reading. After that I took a short nap. When I became disgusted with this schedule I took a cup of coffee or a pill . . . I would return in my mind to the murderous work in the quarry and sketch some poem which later became *Quarry Cycle* dedicated to my comrade workers...

> He was not alone. His muscles were growing
> > into the crowd
> until they were holding their hammer and pulsating
> > with energy –
> this thing existed as he felt solid ground
> > under his feet,
> until the rock crushed his temple
> but did not cut the chambers of his heart
>
> And again rocks were moving.
> > The carts disappearing in flowers.
> Again, an electric current cutting deep
> > into the rock wall.
> But a man took into himself the structure
> > of the world
> in which, if anger will grow
> love will explore higher.

When I met Dr. Mieczyslaw A. Krąpiec, President of Lublin University in the 1970s, he described Professor Wojtyla's lectures. "From the beginning Karol brought his students to the center of human problems in which morality was the most important ingredient. In his judgment, philosophy was concentrated in personal existence and this personal being was the highest form of reality. He accented the necessity of experience of the human personality in direct group contact. But the most intimate contact is confession. There, man is completely open showing his human experiences, morals, intentions and actions and the reason for accepting or rejecting them. The drama of human personality presented in the dialogue of confession was permanent enlargement of moral existence."

Wojtyla's popularity among Lublin students grew as rapidly as among the Cracow youth. They called him, "Uncle Karol," or "the eternal teenager." He was friendly and even intimate with most students and the familiarity grew because he was willing to make loans to needy students, saying, "When you get a job, you will repay me." Long excursions with youths were spent examining nature or taking part in philosophical discussions about "the moral existence of human beings which could be explained through individual experience."

A teacher at Lublin University, Dr. Tadeusz Styczeń, told me, "One day a group of students approached me and said that they wanted to grade their professors. I asked them how they proposed to do this."

"'We want to divide them into four groups: wise, not wise, saint, not saint.'

"But you can't divide them into just four groups because many are in between," I said.

"'We do not intend to introduce purgatory or hell, we only wish to segregate them into those four groups,' they replied.

"I could not convince them to do otherwise. Eventually, they classified Professor Wojtyla as 'wise saint,' although Karol never discovered this. You are welcome to tell the Pope now if you would like," said Professor Styczeń.

Since we are talking about classifications I should also mention that Professor Wojtyla never travelled first class, although as anyone he liked some luxury. Yet he preferred to spend his savings on loans to needy young people or on financing kayak excursions on the Mazurian Lakes which were too expensive for the students due to the travel distance, lodging and food.

One evening he almost missed his train from Lublin to Cracow and didn't even have time to change to civilian clothes. As he ran, his cassock became caught in the door and he was almost fatally caught beneath the train. The professor pulled himself out with his last strength, and coughing entered the first compartment on the left.

He looked at the people, two similar-looking women of about sixty years of age, dressed in traditional Lublin district clothes with colorful kerchiefs on their heads. They were arguing loudly with two young men with dark blue caps on their heads. The women, their voices raised, accused the men of stealing, and the men lifted their hands as if to strike them. When Professor Wojtyla entered in his priestly garb with his customary greeting, "Christ be praised," the four occupants looked at this newcomer, quieted down and replied, "...for ages and ages!...

He took his seat and the commotion on the benches quelled. Before reaching for his breviary, the professor again sized up his four companions and tried to place the two ladies, 'Their outfits were mixed, part Lublin district and part Carpathian, but the young fellows were definitely Cracow slickers...' He began reading from the prayer book, but one of the women women interjected, "Reverend, please help us; these fellows stole our money." The second pointing her finger, "They are pickpockets from Cracow. I met them some weeks ago at the Cracow market." The first added, "When they get tired of pickpocketing at the market, they go rob people on the trains." The two men quietly looked out the window at the passing countryside. Professor Wojtyla turned to the men. "What do you say to this accusation?"

The older one spoke. "They followed us to the train, accusing us of stealing their money."

The younger pimply man picked up the dialogue. "They claimed that we followed them and picked money from their brassieres."

Reverend Wojtyla turned to the women. "What is your opinion?"

The first explained, "We sold a house in Lublin which we inherited from our aunt, and we were returning to our home..."

The second explained further. "We are sisters..."

Reverend-professor, listening to the passengers' dialogues thought, 'Should I talk to the conductor or should I ask the police for help at the next station?'

The younger man said, "Reverend, we have voluntarily submitted to a search of our pockets," and the other man nodded in concurrence, figuring that the affair was now closed. The women did not comment so Reverend Wojtyla, who liked young people, concluded that the problem was solved. But closing his breviary he began thinking, 'The women look honest, maybe even pious, so why should they accuse two strangers of stealing money? Maybe they did not have the opportunity to accuse anyone else?'

He asked, "Are you religious people?"

"We are," both replied, simultaneously.

"And you gentlemen?"

They looked at one another and together replied, "We are too."

"As a priest I would like to ask all of you to pray with me to St. Anthony who is 'patron of the thieves'...

He knelt on the floor, the women moving beside him. The professor looked at the men sitting motionless on the bench.

"Would you join us? Praying is not going to hurt you."

The men looked at each other as they probably thought, 'There is no way out.' So they knelt beside the window with their hats on.

"Gentlemen," said Reverend Wojtyla, "you know that a man does not pray with his hat on..." He filled his lungs with air and yelled, "Please remove your hats because you are not only offending St. Anthony, but God!"

The men in their twenties had probably finished compulsory military service, and recognized the strong command, but they did not remove their hats. Reverend Wojtyla was upset, but determined, so he got up, grabbed the hat of the closest one, then reached for the other's. The men paled. A bundle wrapped in a handkerchief fell out from under each hat. The priest picked up the packages and in a strong voice shouted, "Get up and sit on the bench!" Then he positioned himself at the exit to prevent the men from escaping. All four obeyed his command and the priest gave the bundles to the women, saying, "Please, count your money." One of them said, "We do not have to; we can tell by the knots that they have not yet been opened." The women held their property tightly in their hands.

The Reverend-professor deliberated with himself. 'Maybe they have guns or knives...No, pickpockets don't carry weapons.'

At this moment the older man asked, with a pleading look in his eyes, "Reverend, what are you going to do with us?"

"What do you think I should do?"

"We don't know, but please don't call the militia."

The second one trembled, "We will not steal anymore."

"This would be nice on your part, but I don't know if I should trust you. I need to think about it. In the meantime, show me your documents."

The five passengers then heard a voice say, "Tickets, please." The two young men handed their documents to the priest, and began to talk fast, one after the other.

"Reverend, we will not steal anymore...we will keep our word...we promise."

"Would you go to church and pray? Would you go to church regularly? Can you promise?" At the same time he copied the names and addresses of the men.

"Yes, we will...we solemnly promise..."

The train conductor reached the five passengers and turning to the priest said, "What's going on?"

"What do you mean?" Wojtyla asked.

"My partner passed by and saw the five of them kneeling. Reverend, are you performing the Holy Mass in the train?"

"Not exactly," replied the priest with a smile. "Just a spontaneous prayer..."

The older of the thieves added, "We were praying for a safe return home."

The conductor checked the tickets and said with a grin, "In twenty-five years of working on passenger trains I never saw and have never heard of people kneeling in a car, together with a priest, praying. What's more, I thought that young people belonging to the Party were atheists. Oh my God, times are changing; the Communists are losing their grip on Poland. I don't know whether for good or for bad, but times are changing..." With a shake of his head, he departed

"Times are changing," repeated Reverend Wojtyla and to his copassengers he said, "Tomorrow at 7:00 A.M. I would like to see all of you at Holy Mass at either St. Florian's, St. Katherine's, or St. Mary's Church. Pick yourself a church and I will be there."

"St. Florian Church," said one of the women and the men nodded their heads in agreement.

But Reverend Wojtyla turned to them, "I would like to hear it in your own voice, one after the other!"

"Seven in the morning at St. Florian's Church."

"Seven in the morning at St. Florian's Church."

"Now, ladies and gentlemen, let's kneel, close your eyes and pray to God, thank Him that He created this situation to bring us together so as to become better human beings."

They kept their promise.

20
Maneuvers

WITH stoic composure Primate Wyszyński told me about his personal drama which was also a story of the Church in a time when the country and party were under the rule of President Boleslaw Bierut.

"Mr. Bierut was a cultured man, personally charming and dashing with women, but with little knowledge of economic matters and not much in tune with political affairs. He would study examples of the Soviet Union, which historically, economically and politically was much different from prewar Poland. I got the feeling that he disregarded the religious feelings of the Polish nation and though that 'what was good for the Soviet Union should be good for Poland.' As events show, the Polish nation did have specific spiritual characteristics which had been molded for a thousand years and were irreversible. Mr. Bierut was an atheist and Stalinist, and he thought that belief in God could be cut out from a man's soul by one or two directives of the Central Committee of the Polish Worker's Party.

"In September 1953 I was standing in a hall of the palace on Miodowa Street surrounded by a group of secret agents, when a man in his forties, holding the knob on the entrance door said, 'Sir, I am Colonel Czarnota, chief of this detachment from the Internal Security Corps, and there are others waiting for us outside.'

"I nodded, letting him know that I heard him, and answered, "If you and your men want to cause trouble..."

"'No, for God's sake, we're not here for trouble.'

"Sunrise is on its way," I replied. "Maybe it would be better if we waited. Why do this tonight?"

"'Better to conclude the affair tonight,' said the Colonel.

"As you wish," I answered.

"Colonel Czarnota opened the door. Snow hit my face. A group of men in civilian and military uniforms circled me. They directed me to the car, pushed me in, slammed the door, and we started our trip through the deserted streets of Warsaw.

"At Mostowskich Palace we rode over the Śląsko-Dąbrowski Bridge toward the W-Z Highway into Zygmuntowska Street. Approaching the town of Jablonna, we passed Nowy Dwór and Dobrzyń on the river Drwęca to the city of Grudziądz. To mislead me they drove through small towns and villages, and finally we arrived at the town of Rywald. Right away I recognized a Capuchin monastery. I was taken to a room on the first floor where the Colonel said I would be staying. He ordered me not to look through the window; not that I could see anything, since it was glued with heavy paper. I was occupying a monk's cell. I asked, "Is this the way you want to hide the Primate of Poland from the world?" When I received no reply, I added, "You must remember that the world is interested in the well-being of this particular Cardinal." Colonel Czarnota ordered everyone to leave and locked the door. There was only one comfort left for me and that was the picture of the Holy Mother with the words written at the bottom, 'Mother of God, please give solace to distressed people.'"

"This is how your life of confinement began?" I asked.

The Cardinal elaborated. "Every morning I performed Holy Mass in the cell. At 7:00 A.M. a guard would bring me a cup of coffee with milk and a slice of bread. My cell was guarded around the clock by twenty uniformed men; I heard their footsteps all the time. To block this rhythmical sound I would pray or read books."

I was sad and motionless in my seat.

"For lunch I would receive a piece of meat and a spoonful of mashed potatoes. Supper was a repetition of breakfast.

"On September 26 I was supposed to deliver the sermon at the Holy Cross Church in Warsaw. Because of my arrest, I could not keep this appointment with God and the faithful. Somebody pinned a note on the locked door of the church stating that I was being detained by the militia. On the same day, in the government paper *Trybuna Ludu (People's Tribune)* an article appeared, signed by hard-headed Polish Stalinist, Edward Ochab."

"Here the Primate handed me a photocopy; one of the paragraphs read,

For Primate Wyszyński the signing of the Understanding with the Government was only a maneuver that the public and the government should take at face value, but for him it was a smoke screen to conceal political activities of the church against the nation and against the people's state. Primate Wyszyński is responsible for breaking the Understanding and for accepting the help of West German crusaders as well as the Anglo-American attack of our nation and defaming People's Poland...

Stefan Wyszyński, interrupted my reading. "As you probably know, Mr. Ochab was an entrusted man of Moscow." I continued reading,

Although warned by the Government, this disciple of the Vatican did not change his attitude. He should remember that Peoples' Poland is not noblemen's Poland where discords are tolerated by the ruling class and where Vatican agents are the real power in our country.

I finished reading and the Primate returned to his story.

"Bishop Zygmunt Choromański, Secretary to the Polish Episcopates, announced a meeting of the twenty-two members of this organization to be held September 28. The Chairman was a bishop from Łódź city, Reverend Michal Klepacz, an energetic man with a first-class brain. On the day of the meeting, as if to intimidate the conference of bishops, the Government issued a communiqué about my arrest, stating that in spite of countless warnings, I was continuing my subversive activities and constantly breaking the signed Understanding with the Government. 'Even the court procedures of Bishop Kaczmarek show that he was active in undermining the legal Government and giving aid and comfort to Western enemies of the Polish state.' As a result, they decided to deprive me of my right to perform my functions as a high official of the Church."

The Primate looked at me as though he were trying to find in my face a positive reaction to his plight. "Besides, Mrs. Julia Brystygier, Director of the Religion Department in the Ministry of Security, called in each of the twenty-two bishops and tried to intimidate them in various ways, including the threat of confinement. Consequently, the Episcopate issued a statement in which they announced that they would support the April 1950 Understanding between the Church and Government, and that they would not tolerate anybody from the clergy who was acting against the best interest of the nation or against the Government. Furthermore, the Episcopate agreed with the Government that a favorable situation should be created in which the State and Church would work together, according to the Understanding, to strengthen the unity of the nation."

"It was a rather conciliatory declaration," I said.

"You have to take into consideration the Stalinist atmosphere in Poland at that time. But the Government directed Vice Prime Minister Józef Cyrankiewicz to issue a declaration which said that the Government would adhere to the Polish Constitution, which guaranteed freedom of conscience and full recognition of Church institutions. The Government also stated that it would unequivocally resolve all Church claims and grievances in such a way that the nation and the Church would benefit."

"I see here a compromise on both sides."

"I presume President Bierut and his advisers came to the conclusion that by arresting me they did more harm to themselves than good. So the Preisdent invited to his official residence, Belvedere, the delegation of the Episcopate, which consisted of three bishops: Michal Klepacz, Zygmunt Choromański and Tadeusz Zakrzewski. In their presence, Mr. Cyrankiewicz announced that the Primate was not in jail but in a monastery, although he did not say in which monastery. President Bierut asked the bishops to make an official declaration concerning normalization of relations between Church and State. The Episcopate delegation said it needed to consult with me. I accepted the declaration, the highlights of which were that the Understanding between the Government and the Polish Episcopate be retained, and that the Episcopate would ask all the faithful to pray for both the heirarchy of the Church and the Polish Republic. This Declaration was suposed to be read from all pulpits on the first Sunday in October."

"It looks like your imprisonment forced President Bierut to compromise."

"I think that outside pressure was important, although I did not know at the time that the Holy Consistorial Congregation, under the leadership of Pius XII, issued a renouncement:

The sacrilegious fact of raising a hand against the most esteemed Cardinal of the Roman Catholic Church, Stefan Wyszyński, Archbishop of Gniezno and Warsaw, and interference with his church duties, led the Holy Congregation to announce that everyone who participated in committing these crimes is subject to canonal law 2.334, n.2 and 2.343 par. 2. and excommunication...

I interjected, "I do not recall the last time that a Pope excommunicated a government, but it certainly was a tremendous blow and important propaganda victory."

The Cardinal continued, "The President of the United States, American Congress, British Parliament, Chamber of French Deputies, as well as cardinals the world over protested against my imprisonment and demanded my immediate release. But Bierut's government did not give in. During one of the meetings, Prime Minister Cyrankiewicz said to Bishop Choromański, 'Your Primate is a prisoner, but we could not hold him for long in one place, because church processions are forming and going to his place on their knees. As a result, we have to move him from place to place in complete secrecy.'

"From Rywald I travelled to Jablonowo Pomorskie, Ostróda, then to Olsztyn city, Dobre Miasto, and then Lidzbark...

"At the beginning the international protest did not have much effect on the rulers of Poland. Within the first days of October they arrested my secretary Bishop Baraniak and in Olsztyn city the Reverend Wojciech Zinek, accusing them of organizing illegal protests against my imprisonment. During my trips from monastery to monastery, my 'protector,' who was quiet and would not engage in conversation, always sat beside me in the car. We travelled at night and many times were lost, although there were always three or four cars in my convoy. I guess the drivers were foreigners or 'blinded by the night.'

"My next stop was the town of Stoczek Warmiński. The monastery building was very old, two stories high with small windows and hidden behind tall trees. The fence around the monastery was high and covered in regular intervals with special searchlights; almost every tree near the fence was rolled in barbed wire. The inside of the building was moldy and sometimes the walls were covered with ice. My guardians gave me two rooms on the first floor, one as my living quarters, one as a chapel. On the same floor in a separate room, a priest stayed and on the other side of the corridor there was a room for a nun. The three of us lived together; although they were supposed to help me, we shared equally all of the chores. Every morning the man in charge would ask me how I felt or did I want something, but when I expressed my wishes he would never comply with them. I presume that it was a psychological trick which did not bother me, and eventually I dismissed his questions with a smile. On the grounds around the monastery were twenty or thirty men in civilian clothes who walked aimlessly; I presume they were guarding my well-being."

He stopped, and I felt his reliving the events had become too painful. I said, "Permit me this digression, but some time ago I asked why you carry the case with a picture of the Holy Mother of Częstochowa."

"Yes, you did. This Holy Mother of Bright Mountain was protectress of Juliana, my natural mother."

"I did not know that."

"I was nine years old when my mother died; she was dying for almost a month. Although I insisted on sitting with her, she sent me to school every day, but I could not concentrate on my lessons; I thought about the huge bells. When they would ring I would know that my mother had died. One day, near the end of October, I returned from school and went to my mother's bed. She looked at me and said in a faint voice, "Stefan, get dressed, prepare yourself...' So I left her room thinking that she was sending me for some errand. I put on my coat and returned. My father was standing in front of the bed too, and seeing me in an overcoat, said, 'She didn't mean that.'

"I don't understand."

"'She meant something else; she meant to prepare yourself with virtues and to dress yourself with good things for the road of life.

"Those were the last words of my mother, and to this day I don't know if I succeed in collecting virtues. It is difficult to reply to this inner human fear. Every man should ask his conscience if he fulfills God's will. We know that He gives this blessing to everybody, but the fulfillment of the grace, or let's put it in a more realistic way, the success of God's grace in the human soul, depends on the attitude and work of each individual."

"If you don't mind, and if you could bear with me, please return to the story of your imprisonment."

"I was incarcerated for three years in half a dozen places and each time I asked my guardians if I could write a letter to my still-living father. On October 17, 1953, I received permission. I will not bother you with the complete text, just a fragment, although I remember the letter to this day by heart.

> My dearest Father, I beg you not to worry about me, but only to pray for your son. I would like to thank you for teaching me the truth, and because of this teaching, my life is peaceful and full of hope. Although I cannot serve my country and my people by hard work, I can in this condition only serve with constant prayer, I beg you, my sisters and my brother and everybody from the family and our friends, not to worry about me and to have faith. Nobody should hear from you or our relatives about my imprisonment. I only need your prayer and your hope. I kiss your hands, my dear Father, for everything that you have done for me...

When the Cardinal recited those words, I saw tears in his eyes, and said, "Let's have something to drink or a little walk in the palace garden."

He did not move from behind the oak table, but his pale face became bright. "This is a long story, not only my own, but the Church's. You induced me to tell you and I agreed, so let's continue. Drinks, meals and walks we will have later."

"Fine with me. I would love to hear more in your own words."

"On March 12, 1956 Boleslaw Bierut, the leader of the Party and Polish government, died in Moscow. With him the Stalinist era also died in Poland. In June an anti-Stalinist group, under the leadership of Wladyslaw Gomulka, took control of the Party and the Government. On October 29, I was freed and I said to the crowds who greeted me, 'I rejoice that I am again able to talk to you. Let us pray, for your country looks to you for calm and for positive, honest work in every endeavor for our own benefit and above all for the benefit of the nation...'"

"And what did you think about Gomulka and his reforms?" I asked at a moment when a young nun brought tea and apple cakes on a tray. I presume she was listening to our conversation behind the door, and when she discovered the Cardinal's voice develop a dry melody, decided to bring something moist.

My host thoughtfully stirred his tea, "Gomulka began our first meeting with a joke which was unusual for this dull man. 'Primate,' he said, 'can you tell me the difference between the May first manifestation before the war and today in our socialist country?'

"I shrugged. 'I never went to the May first manifestation.'

"'Before the war participants were courageous people, because they were not afraid of the government's repressions. Now workers are afraid that if they *don't* go to the manifestation they will be punished by the government.'

"He laughed at his own joke and so did I, although neither of us had laughed much during our lives. He pulled out a cigarette, cut in half, put it in a cigarette holder and smoked. The man was well known for his thriftiness in his personal life as well as in state economical affairs. They he said something startling, 'I am thinking about changing rules and regulations so that our people will work, demonstrate and play in peace.'

"You have great aspirations, and I am sure that your motives are noble. Do you think that the Soviet Union will permit you?"

"'They are not as stupid as the West think. They built Socialism in their own country in their own vision, and we will build Socialism in the Polish way. I said to Nikita Khrushchev that each nation, according to its social and cultural background, as well as its psychological moods, should build Socialism in its own way.'

"It is good that you believe Mr. Khrushchev."

"'Comrade Khrushchev insisted that I use the Party to tighten control over religion. But, as you can see, we released the Primate. If agriculture and small industry would work better in private hands, the Government will also allow that. If the Church would work for the nation and stabilization of the country without looking to the Vatican, your church would have complete freedom.'

"It was a surprise to hear such sincere words from a lifelong Communist, and I listened intently, thinking that a new era was coming. I thought I would say something in praise, but Mr. Gomulka concluded, 'I know the meaning of the word freedom, because Stalinists imprisoned me and still sit in the Government on many levels, especially in the Ministry of Foreign Affairs, where they quietly ridicule me as a simpleton and accuse me of anti-Semitism and being against Israel. In both cases they know they are wrong, because immediately after the war I was for the creation of Israel and supported this idea on a national and international front. If I disagree with Israel's internal or external policy and express my sincere opinion, this does not mean that I am anti-Semitic.'

"I knew that Gomulka's wife was Jewish and that he was touchy about this subject. As he broke cigarettes and smoked half after half, I thought of introducing a relaxing moment. 'Do you know what joke is making the rounds among people in Warsaw?' I asked.

"'I don't know much about jokes, and you saw that I do not handle them well.'

"A man asked a friend, 'What is the difference between Zionism and anti-Semitism?'

"'I don't know,' replied the friend.

"'If you don't like Gomulka, you're a Zionist.'

"'So what's the big deal?'

"'But when you don't like Mrs. Gomulka, you're an anti-Semite.'"

Not knowing how to support my host, the Primate, in his effort to be more relaxed, I said, "I think there's a lot of truth to this."

"Mr. Gomulka did not laugh, but reached for another cigarette. Digressing, I would like to mention a true story about Gomulka, that I heard from Yugoslav clergy."

I was impressed by the Primate's effort to amuse me, so I listened intently to what would develop further.

"It's a well-known fact that Broz Tito, dictator of Yugoslavia, loved gold and diamond trinkets, and decorated himself with jewels like a Christmas tree. When Mr. Gomulka visited Marshall Tito, he received a gold cigarette case studded with diamonds as a farewell present. The reason? When Mr. Tito saw a cheap cigarette case in Gomulka's hands, he said in a comradely way that a high state official should not carry a low-priced object. Mr. Gomulka accepted the present politely. But do you know what he did with it when he returned?'

"How should I?"

"He had the cigarette case appraised, since he thought that a Marshall of a poor country like Yugoslavia should not give away real diamonds. When Mr. Gomulka discovered that the value of the cigarette case was estimated at thousands of dollars, he asked his secretary to sell it quietly in London. He received the money in cash which he counted carefully, and donated it to the Polish War Invalid Association."

I was amazed because I didn't know this side of Gomulka or even Wyszyński and I started laughing.

The Primate continued, "Soon people recognized that the head of the Party was a good-hearted man; simple, without any trace of corruption, and believed deeply in the ideals of Socialism. My only criticism was that he would not acquaint himself with world culture or even with Polish cultural achievements, although he had many opportunities to do so. He did not read novels or poetry, nor did he go to plays. He was stubborn, but he was honest. To illustrate this a bit further, I will tell you one more story."

"I guess you were grateful to him for releasing you from jail."

"You may be right, but listen. His daughter-in-law was expecting a baby. As a matter of fact, it was a girl and they named her Hanka. So his son called his father and asked him if he could send the official car which was faster and more comfortable, to deliver the laboring mother to the hospital. And do you know how Gomulka responded? He told his son, 'Official cars are for official business and you take a taxi for your private business.'

"It looks like you don't have anything bad to say about him."

"I could not blame him much for things which were going on in Poland because of the great pressure from our powerful Eastern neighbors. He was doing the best he could considering the political limitations and his strong belief that our country should have the best relations possible with the Soviet Union. But he was constantly saying, 'Why do you have all these religious processions on city streets and in the countryside. Why can't you express your love for your God in your soul, in your home, in your church? Why do you have to wear out so many pairs of shoes for nothing?'"

"And your response?"

"Knowing that he liked the great and beautiful novelist, Zofia Nalkowska as a woman – although he never read anything of hers – I asked, 'You are acquainted with Zofia?'

"'What does my sympathy for a woman have to do with your processions?'

"You must know what she said – that belief should be enhanced not only by love, but by rituals and ceremonies.

"I regret that I did not seek more meetings with Wieslaw to convince him of moderation in his political and social moves. From a distance, I see that I should have worked with him more, because I hoped that this man of solid character would work to bring to our country humanistic, Christian Socialism."

"I don't think you should feel regret, because you have to take international conditions into consideration."

"You may be right, or maybe you are wrong; I have my doubts too, but I will tell you my deep secret. I did have hope in him, as I did in a young priest named Karol Wojtyla, from the time I talked about Karol with Prince Sapieha. Both Karol and Gomulka were always on my mind and I thought we would create a just system with those two men. I knew in my heart that the Reverend Karol was a unique man, maybe the only one in our country who would play an enormous role. Eventually, Gomulka lost power and all my hope was transferred to Wojtyla."

21

In Front of the Jeweler's Shop

THE July sun was setting for the last time embracing the tops of trees surrounding the lake. The stillness of the air was interrupted only by chirping birds and jumping fish as they splashed on the surface of the Warmian lake.

When you look between the trunks of the trees you can see the village of Swieta Lipka. The picture of the Holy Mother, displayed in her baroque church, brought pilgrims to the Olsztyn province from all over the country. Every year people prayed and asked Her for blessings. Naturally, they found time to fish, pick berries and mushrooms, and to relax. This part of the country was a favorite place of young people who loved kayaking and swimming. From early spring to late fall visitors could hear youthful voices or see groups of students enjoying a meal or rest on the banks of the many lakes in this region.

On this particular day, travellers passing through could see kayaks at the edge of the lake and under a lightning-struck pine a group of sixteen young men and women. Among them stood a mature man in gray trousers and green windbreaker whose voice rang with excitment.

"People often say that the clergy has no right to take part in discussions on sexual subjects. The reason is that priests are not married and have no involvement in family affairs. Ergo, they have no personal experience..." stated the Reverend Karol Wojtyla, defending his latest literary endeavor, *Love and Responsibility* to his students.

They had arrived by bus, some from Cracow, others from Lublin, to spend their vacations and listen to and discuss the 'ethical study' of the young priest-professor. Among them were men and women from Jagellonian University as well as students from Lublin's Catholic University: a group of serious, young people interested in Christian ethics.

"At the outset, I have to mention that one of two sources of information for this book was personal experience..."

Girls walked around and looked at each other and boys controlled their smiles, but the professor continued, "...experienced based on daily pastoral work. This activity often puts clergy eye to eye with the sexual problems of parishioners of varying gender, ages and occupations and creates unequaled experience for the priest. I agree that this experience with sex is an outsider's experience, not personal; however, the priest who hears confessions sometimes has an even deeper understanding than the superficial experience of active participants..."

"We have to revise the ideas of virginity and celibacy, and make a clear separation of the love of partners from the pure religious subtlety as a separate happening which leads to the realization of supreme saintly excellence. A person is of such high value and goodness that he should not be used as the object to achieve a purely physical goal. Along with this concept exists the norm that the proper and full-value approach to a person is through love. This is in accordance with the concept of the person, what he is and what kind of value he represents. Ergo, such an attitude is fair. Fairness, is a higher norm than usefulness which only recognizes utilitarianism. Although this utilitarianism does not discard everything, it subordinates all of the elements of goodness in its attitude toward the person, who exists in the realm of love. Love of two people in the first place is the desire to meet certain emotional and ethical conditions which demand complete justice toward the loved person, and should come from ethical and religious norms. This problem, perceived in the spiritual and physical dimensions is not sufficiently discussed in philosophical literature. Love is one of the processes in the universe that creates synthesis and brings together all those elements which divide and enlarge other things which are narrow and confined. As a result, we are enriched."

A young woman asked, "Uncle Karol, what I am going to say doesn't mean that your philosophical approach to love is not interesting, and I don't know if everybody agrees with me, but you expressed the same idea in your poetry and drama better."

"Poetry is great and mysterious, and you have to give her all of your time. I was not fair to this beautiful muse because the Ministry absorbed me completely." Without interruption he went into a more complete explanation. "The Ministry is a sacrament and a calling.

Poetic creativity is the function of talent, although talent in my subjective opinion and particularly in my case, is a decisive element in a calling. We should put the question to ourselves: In what sense do the two callings, ministry and poetry, coexist and to what extent do they penetrate one another in the same man? This question relates not only to created works, but also to authors. This particular process is the personal secret of each of us. Does the process of writing not open the curtains of this mystery? Eventually the basis of grasping this mystery will be left to the creation of poetry or drama or any other artistic endeavor. To some extent don't the souls of priests reveal some mystery of creation? This question and the search to resolve the mystery of creativity helps us relate to art and to enrich ourselves. This is our goal on earth." He stopped, looked around, and was surprised that everybody was listening, not only with widely opened eyes, but also with open mouths.

"I am now working on a poem or drama, let's say a poetic drama, through which I would like to explain my view on love in literary form. Of course I am not a great poet such as Paul Valéry, or a great dramatist like Stanislaw Wyspiański..."

"But with your unapocalyptic style you dominate them both," said a girl sitting in the middle of the group. "We know from your work and our preparation how to stage your drama about three couples, a play about human love which through the ages constantly fights the hard laws of daily life and its unmerciful consequences."

"Where did you obtain my unfinished drama?"

"Are you speaking about *In Front of the Jeweler's Shop*?" asked a man in his early twenties.

"I do not know if I am going to keep the title," replied Uncle Karol.

"Please don't change it!" rose voices from the group. "We know that the Jeweler is Providence...God, and Andrzej–you!"

A feminine voice added, "...and Teresa symbolizes ideal love..."

"Please don't go too far. What would happen if you were mistaken?" Uncle protested.

"At least you will not deprive us of the knowledge of reading it..." someone said. "I am an actress and know how to read dramas."

A sober masculine voice exclaimed, "Let's not talk! We should read the script right now, on the meadow! Agreed?!"

And a chorus of voices yelled, "Agreed!"

A dark, tall boy with laughter in his voice said, "Working and studying philology in the library at Jagellonian University, I came across an interesting piece of information – a few letters from abroad asking for a literary work of Karol Wojtyla. Who knows, maybe in the near future, dramas by our Uncle will be translated into many languages..."

"I will read fragments of the role of Teresa!" said Halina.

"And I, Andrzej," added a young man by the name of Jerzy.

Other voices made various observations on the staging of the play during the first reading on the bank of the blue lake. Uncle Karol was pleased and in a resigned voice, exclaimed, "Do what you want, but I beg you, I don't want to hear the complete reading, just fragments, so we will have some basis to judge the dramatic possibility..."

Teresa:
Andrzej chose me and asked for my hand
That happened today between five and six this afternoon.
The exact hour, I don't remember, I did not have
the time to look at my watch
I didn't notice the town hall clock
in such moments nobody looks for time,
the moments are growing above human time.
If I remembered that I should look at the clock,
I would have had to look over Andrzej's head.
We were walking on the right side of the market when
Andrzej turned to me and said, "Would you like to
be my companion for life?"
"Yes," I replied, but he did not say,
"Would you like to be my wife," only,
"Would you like to be my companion for life."
Saying that he looked far away, as though afraid
to read in my eyes and at the same time trying to
indicate that in front of us was a road whose end
we could not see.
My reply, yes, had been determined for a long time.
We knew that going through the past we were reaching
a distant future.
I remember that Andrzej did not turn to me right away
but for a long time he looked toward the road
which was before us.

The Reverend Mieczyslaw Maliński and Karol, 1956.

Karol and young people camping at the Mazurian Lakes, 1958.

Young Bishop Wojtyla officiating at a marriage ceremony, 1958.

Bishop Wojtyla in a pensive mood, 1960.

Andrzej:
I was moving toward Teresa for a long time. I did
not find her right away.
I don't remember if during our first meeting we
had a premonition, and I don't know what 'love at
first sight' means because my senses were being
fed at every step by the charm of women I met.
But when I tried to go after them, I met deserted
islands. Then I discovered that reachable beauty
for the senses could be a difficult gift, even
dangerous; I met some persons who led me to
other wrongs and so gradually I learned to appreciate
beauty. I decided to look for a woman who could be
a second me... I met a few girls who captured
my imagination, even my thoughts; at that time
when I was occupied with them, I discovered that
Teresa was in my subconscious, in my memory.
And how do I base Teresa's existence in me?
Why does she appear in my soul?
What guarantees her the place in my eye?
And what created around her this unique resonance,
this 'you should'?
Love grows to some extent from negation
love could be a happening in which two people
deeply realize that they should belong to each other
despite absence of moods and excitements.
This is one of the processes in the universe
which creates synthesis and brings together all
those things which are divided, and enlarges other
things which are narrow and confined.

Teresa:
His proposal did not find me completely unprepared
because I felt that I am for him
and that I could love him.
Yes, I did have a feeling that I loved him.
Only that. I could not bear to carry in myself
a feeling which could be without answer.
To this day I have to admit to myself

that is was not easy.
I remember one month, in this month, one evening
we were walking in the mountains
the group was cohesive, maybe more than friends
we understood each other well.
At that time Andrzej was interested in Krystyna.
But he did not spoil my wandering in the mountains
I was always strong like a tree
which could only be destroyed by itself
I cried about my fate but not because of love.
Today when Andrzej asked me if I would like
to be his companion for life
I said yes and after a moment, I asked him if he
believed in signals.

Andrezej:
Teresa – Teresa – Teresa
A bright point in my growing up
not any more a prism of make believe rays
but a real human being. I could go no further
I knew I was not going to look any more.
I only tremble about the thought that I
could have lost her. Lost Teresa.
For a few years she walked beside me and I didn't know
that she was living and growing. I was hesitant to
accept a thing which is a most important gift for me.
After several years I see now clearly
that the roads which are supposed to part
reach one another.

Teresa:
We were looking together through the window
of the Jeweler's shop
where in small boxes lined with velvet
all kinds of gems were shining.
We were speechless.
Then Andrzej took me by the hand and said,
"Teresa, let's enter and select wedding bands
for ourselves."

The young audience reposed on the grass and listened with great concentration; you could hear only the birds in the trees and buzzing bees together with the noise of leaping fish on the surface of the lake. This unique orchestra provided a musical background for a perceptive play by the young priest, who leaned against the tree with folded hands, looking above the heads of the performers, immersed in thoughts. You don't have to be a psychologist to know that this drama was written from personal experience; that Andrzej in the play was Karol and Halina Królikiewicz read her own role.

The author raised his hands, "Please stop!"

Everyone looked at him with surprise and Halina asked, "Is it too painful for you?"

He did not pay attention to her question, "You have a general picture of this immature work, and the eternal problem."

The audience protested. "Not enough! Let's hear more!"

But the author was insistent. "Please, instead of this youthful outburst, let's have something to eat. I am hungry and am sure everybody else is too. Besides, our knapsacks have been lying in the sun for a long time and the sandwiches might be spoiled." He moved to the center of the circle and took the scripts from the actors, "Please, do me a great favor and obey the vision of the elder of this group."

For a moment the enthusiastic group sat quietly. Then they started whispering among themselves, as though developing tactics on how to overrule their leader. Somebody noticed a boy running toward them with an envelope. When he reached the group he said, "A telegram for Reverend Doctor!" One of the men took the telegram and gave it to 'Uncle Karol' who read the text.

"Here is a real reason for interrupting your performance. Reality has caught up with us. A message from my superiors. Please read the contents."

He handed them the telegram. The group passed around the piece of paper on which was typed, "Reverend Doctor Karol Wojtyla, please report immediately to His Eminence the Primate in Warsaw."

The gathering speculated that Uncle Karol was nominated to the position of bishop by Pope Pius XII; the reason was based on the knowledge acquired before they departed from Cracow on this excursion. Recently gossip had been circulating around university and church circles that Primate Wyszyński submitted a list of priests for various nominations to the Vatican. Among them was Uncle Karol. But they did not know what kind of position he would get in the church hierarchy, nor where he would be sent. They were sad, not only because they could not hear the rest of the drama, but also because they knew the author should soon depart.

(To keep the chronology straight it should be mentioned that this was one of the last lists of nominations approved by Pius XII who died on October 9, 1958 in his summer palace, Castel Gandolfo.)

As a final expression of reverence to Uncle Karol, the students put him on their shoulders and carried him, singing, "Sto lat! Sto lat! niech żyje nam!" ("Hundred years! Hundred years. Let him live for us!")

From the village Święta Lipka, Wojtyla was to take the bus to Warsaw; the students repeated to themselves, "He will not return. He will not."

Uncle Karol replied, "You should remember what St. Augustine said..."

"We know. He said many things!" the students shouted in a chorus. One exclaimed, "*Roma locuta – causa finita!*"

Uncle Karol nodded in resignation and added, "Don't worry, I will find an excuse and return to you. I will always return..."

The bus was waiting, packed with passengers and ready to depart, but Uncle Karol still hugged student after student, saying "I will return...you will see, I will return...I will."

Halina yelled as though purposely for everyone to hear, "Before the word 'return' you should say the word 'maybe'...'with God's help'...'who knows'..." Everybody looked at her. She quieted and explained, "You should know that this is not my saying. I took it from..."

Another girl added, "...from our woman novelist, Eliza Orzeszkowa."

Stubborn Halina, holding her tears, continued, 'But I am sure nobody knows Orzeszkowa's exact words or expression, and recited, "'Besides all of those great and melodious words such as love, admiration, gratitude, faithfulness...life directs us to use other words such as maybe...a little bit...at this moment...for the time being.'"

Halina did not finish, because she could not hold back her tears. Consternation overwhelmed the group and no one knew how to react to such reality. Was it a stage performance? Was it a cruel life? No time for reflection. Uncle Karol disappeared into the bus which rapidly moved away. The young people returned to their interrupted vacation. Uncle Karol travelled to Warsaw for an urgent appointment with the Primate. From there he would begin his world journey.

22

Procul Eeste Profani

A T THE subsequent chat in his residence Wyszyński, sipping tea said, "I kept my promise to Prince Sapieha and fulfilled my obligation to Karol Wojtyla."

"Does this promise go back, far back to Wadowice?" I asked.

"Yes, once Karol was an altar boy and then he became Bishop Co-adjutor! When he appeared in the doorway at Miodowa Street, I said, 'The Holy Father nominated you as a Suffragan for the Cracow diocese.' He was weak in the knees, so I asked him to sit beside me, and continued my didactic nagging. 'Remember, you are taking the place of Stanislaw Rospond, who was close to Prince Sapieha, and remember the Prince had a special vision for you...'

"To my astonishment Karol said, 'Please forgive me, but I don't want to be bishop; I want to be a monk with time to study, to write and above all to pray. I don't want to occupy an important position in the Church...'

"I was surprised by the attitude of such an intelligent man; putting my arm on his shoulder I tried to see his position and to explain my obligation to him, although I never let him know what I was doing behind his back. 'I understand that the Deputavit Auxiliarem is a boring position. You have to constantly visit parishes, consecrate churches, ordain priests, talk to various delegations from all regions of the diocese, participate in the sacrament of confirmation, and on top of all that work, there are lots of papers in the office to take care of. I know all those things, but remember, you are the youngest Bishop and the Holy Father picked you from outside the 'club of waiting bishops.' Remember, you have to hurry, because you've got a long road to go...'

"I read on his face that Karol did not understand this last sentence. And I wanted him unaware of my influence in the Vatican, because from a psychological point of view it would be hard for this kind of man to work toward a high ecclesiastic position, and then by some fluke have everything collapse. Even for a man as strong as he was, it could be traumatic and tragic. So I said, 'I presume you will have time to dine with me and tell me about your work with the young people of Cracow and Lublin, about literature and theater, and about the actresses; I have heard a lot about your work. Naturally, I don't want to hear about everything in one session. From now on we will meet more often and for longer conversation.'

"Karol said nothing, only nodded his head.

"I wanted to warn him about getting close, personally close, to young people, but I held my tongue, thinking that too many revelations would be too much.

"He said in a quiet voice, 'I do not deserve all these things, and if Your Eminence would allow me, I would like to go to your chapel to thank God and his servants on earth for this great undeserving love and help.'

"I took him in my arms, we hugged each other and I said, 'You know the Prince used to say that the life of the departed is preserved on earth in the memory of the living.' I knew Karol understood that upstairs Prince Sapieha was asking the Almighty to help and to bless him. And on earth, without his knowledge I was the delicate instrument."

"But you did not attend the consecration of Karol in Cracow?" I asked, because Wyszyński as sponsor and benefactor should in my opinion have consecrated him.

"No, although I would like to have heard the magnificent Cracow cathedral chorus sing *Ecce Sacerdos Magnus*, and I would love to have seen Karol's face. To be honest, I was purposely absent, because I did not want to begin a precedent. As a primate I did not want to participate in his consecration for the reason that people would suspect that I favored him; also, I would have to participate in similar ceremonies all over the country. Karol was consecrated on Sepember 28, 1958 by Archbishop Eugeniusz Baziak, who was assisted by two other bishops: Boleslaw Kominek from Wroclaw and Franciszek Jop from Opole. I do not know the minute details," Primate Wyszyński added,with regret in his voice.

"I do," I said, feeling that I was contributing to the picture.

"How do you know, you were not there either."

"My friend, Reverend Mietek Maliński recounted his first-hand observations from which I took notes. Would you like me to read them?" I reached for my briefcase and pulled out some papers.

"I know Maliński. He is a perceptive observer. Hearing it would be a pleasure. Please read."

'I pushed myself through the crowd that waited outside the cathedral for the arrival of Archbishop Baziak. When I reached the main entrance, I noticed a few bishops, among them Karol with his head down, as though he were worried about something. From the main nave I turned to the side aisle, and at this moment I heard the cathedral chorus sing *Ecce Sacerdos Magnus*, and I thought, the Archbishop is entering the church. I ran to the sacristy, passing a group of smiling nuns in well-pressed coronets. When I reached the sacristy, I removed my coat and asked the vestry man to lend me a surplice. He said that other priests had asked for the same thing and that he did not have any more. So I decided to go to the presbytery in my plain cassock. When I looked from the side of the altar down onto the crowds which were like a wave flooding the cathedral, I noticed men and women dressed in colorful mountaineer and Cracovian costumes, among them also many faithful in city attire; the most amazing thing I discovered were many students, both male and female. During my work as a priest, I had never seen in any church such a mixed crowd nor so many young people. Amazingly, most were smiling and looking in the direction of Karol. When I spotted my old friend, Monsignor Bogdan Niemczewski in the canonical stall, I went to him and sat on the step below.

'What is going on?' I asked this clergyman, knowledgeable in ceremonies.

He replied, 'Reverend Chancellor is reading the papal bull nominating Karol for Bishop...'

'What will be next?' I asked Monsignor.

'Next, the examination, during which Karol will be asked if he adheres with all of his soul to the Holy Scripture; if he will obey the Holy Father, and if he will live an exemplary life in poverty and hospitality...'

The Primate interrupted. 'Please don't read the rituals, I know them by heart. I also know that after the examination Karol and the other bishops participated in the Holy Mass.'

"You didn't know and you never heard what happened next? I wonder if this happened to you when you were consecrated as Bishop?"

"What do you mean?"

"Let me read the final part of Mietek's description:

'During Karol's celebration of the Holy Mass I noticed that in the crowd of worshippers were dozens of people trying to elbow themselves out and reach the pulpit. It was an unusual scene, and I didn't know that such a thing could happen...'

I noticed surprise on the face of the Primate. "And what happened?" he asked.

I returned to my notes and read.

'The group of young people, among them a few dressed in local peasant costumes were carrying a loaf of bread, a candle and two tiny barrels of wine on a tray. It was a rare sight, its tradition going back to early Christianity. Today it is never observed.'

"You are right, it was unusual," said Wyszyński with regret in his voice. I detected that he was thinking, 'Why didn't this happen to me?'

Aloud he commented, "It was a very unusual homage of the faithful to the priest Karol."

Encouraged by this atmosphere, I returned to my notes.

'Karol received the gifts with trembling hands and returned to continue the celebration, but the enormous crowd in the cathedral was so quiet that you could almost hear every breath. After *Ite Missa est* the Consecrator blessed the bishop's mitre and put the headdress on Wojtyla's head. The chorus began singing *Te Deum laudamus*, and everyone in the cathedral joined the singing. I felt that the walls of the cathedral would burst with pride and joy. During the singing, Bishop Karol walked slowly through the crowd and blessed everybody. I did not notice one dry face. People, young and old, smiled through their tears as the new Bishop walked slowly and looked at almost each person, telling them that he loved them. Finally, from the steps of the altar, he blessed everybody once more and thanked the Consecrator in a short beautiful speech. But people would not leave the cathedral. They knelt and prayed...'

"It was a moving experience which you described to me," said my host as he took a gulp of cold tea.

And I, as though to myself said, "This youngest Bishop took as his motto the words of St. Louis M. Grignon de Montfort, founder of the missionary order and author of a thesis on perfect celebration to the Holy Mother..."

Wyszyński, hearing me well, came out with *Totus Tuus—all yours...* *I'm all yours.*"

"Karol would later say, 'In this difficult hour, full of fear, we have to direct our thoughts to the Virgin Mary, who lives in Christ and acts as our Mother, so we must say to her at all times, *Totus Tuus...*'"

I knew this would please the Primate. Reverence for the Holy Virgin among the princes of the Church is almost universal, but in each case it is unique.

Our conversation was reaching its end, and I figured that if I made the next observation about other characteristics of Karol I would elicit some interesting comments from the Primate.

"Even as a Bishop, Karol was poor. He never had two pairs of shoes. If he did, he would give one to someone else."

"I knew this and often I would send him a pair of new shoes as a present." We both laughed.

Encouraged, I continued. "He received the Bishop's mitre from the Benedictine monks of Tyniec, the crosier and a cross from the Wadowice Parish, and here you will be surprised...'

"Alright, surprise me," interrupted the Primate.

"The Bishop's garment was funded and parts of it were sewn by members of the Rhapsodic Theatre..."

"...especially by Misses Halina Królikiewicz, Danuta Michalowski, and probably Krystyna Dąbrowski, who were not only good actresses but good seamstresses," exclaimed my charming host with a twinkle in his eye. At this point I wanted to say something, but he continued. "...and Karol's aunt, Stefania Wojtyla, who was living in Cracow at number 21 Kanoniczna Street."

"How do you know the number of the street where his aunt lived?"

"I visited her a few times, inquiring about her and Karol's well-being. When she saw her nephew in his exquisite bishop's costume she said, 'Now I can die happily, because I have seen Karol as a Bishop, and I know that he will always pray for me. He will be a great churchman...'"

"It is amazing that you retain such detail."

"Forgive me, I did not intend to do that, but you remember that I have a pact with Prince Sapieha. I know almost everything about him; for example, that on a portal of an old decanol building where Karol used to live, the following words are inscribed: '*Procul Eeste Profani* — unworthy, be away...'"

"It just shows that the Church always did and still does have a good intelligence service."

"We have to protect God and the Holy Church."

Book Four: Toward the Center of Power

23

Vocabor Johannes

"**M**Y DEAR friend," said Primate Wyszyński when we were sitting beside each other in a large meeting hall, where members of the Episcopate usually gathered for conferences. There were many chairs and a few tables covered with green cloth; on the walls were pictures of popes, paintings of saints, and two or three landscapes, I presume, done by friends of the Primate. Cardinal Wyszński's mind seemed focused elsewhere and I had time to examine the background for our meeting. "I am approaching the end of my life," he said, "and have convinced myself that instead of taking secrets to my grave, I will relate them to you."

I felt badly because I knew that this honest man was dying of cancer. I had the overwhelming urge to soothe him in my own clumsy way.

"We all reach the same end; God will not make an exception for you, so let's go to the garden and there among the flowers, the greenery of spruce trees and golden oaks, God will touch us through the beauty of nature, and we might recognize the wisdom of His power and feel a part of it."

He got up and went out the door, I after him, remembering the thoughts and questions which I had prepared at the Forum Hotel.

"You remind me of Pope John XXIII," I said as we walked in the center alley of the garden, "Not in appearance, but in background and behavior."

"Don't be blasphemous," he protested energetically. "Too bad that John XXIII did not have time to finish his reforms." Then he paused and concluded, "Anyway, due to his pontificate the Church is changed forever and is closer to the people."

I ventured a big question, "I presume you too dreamed of becoming Pope?"

He was taken aback, looked at me and said, "Practically every clerk thinks of becoming a minister, corporals dream about the field marshal's baton, and scientists about Nobel prizes. A priest is no exception and he too dreams of being a bishop, and bishops think of becoming cardinals. Every cardinal would like to become Pope and I was no exception. But when I heard that Reverend Angelo Giuseppe Cardinal Roncalli, Patriarch of Venice was a candidate for the Holy See, I started working for his election."

"Although your candidacy was also mentioned in the Vatican?"

"Many cardinals were proposed: Agagianian, who led the Congregation for Propagation of the Faith and Cardinal Spellman who was eager to be a Pope and mentioned to me that if elected he would put the Vatican on a sound financial basis; as I recall a wise Chinese Cardinal Tien Ken-sin; even Eugène Cardinal Tisserant, who was engaged in the campaign for the election of Agagianian, was hoping; but we elected Roncalli, although only fifty-one cardinals took part in the election and among them twenty-two passed age eighty."

"You mean all together there were only fifty-one cardinals?"

"Yes, Pius XII postponed the nomination of new cardinals for a long time, the reason being that he could not find among the Roman Catholic hierarchy suitable candidates."

"The group of fifty-one argued and cast ballots twice a day for seven days and still they could not agree?"

"You are right; many thought that Roncalli was controversial, yet other candidates could not muster even half the votes. Finally, the controversy was resolved because they thought Angelo would not live long and therefore not 'damage' the Church too much. So, on October 28, 1958, the two hundred and sixty-second Pope was elected as successor to sad-faced Pius XII. Politicians in the Curia thought that seventy-seven-year-old Angelo would be 'an interim Pope' and not rock the conservative foundations built by his predecessor. But wise and mischievous Angelo, even when selecting the name Johannes, caused surprise."

Wyszyński sat on a garden bench and I asked, "What do you mean?"

"Five hundred forty years ago, Baldassare Cossa, Cardinal Legate in Bologna was Pope John XXII for a short time, and he made lots of trouble—imagine, at that time—for the Curia and rulers of Europe. He was more secular than a churchman and had an enormous fighting spirit. Cardinal Roncalli knew his history and liked Baldassare Cossa for his courage and vision. When members of the community of cardinals asked why he chose the name of this controversial Pope, he replied, *'Audaciter calumniare, semper aliquid haeret'* (go ahead and defame, something will always remain) and then good Angelo added ironically, 'Everything will be different after my election.' And when they asked him why he said that, he replied, 'because my goat is different.'

"He referred to the little iron stove popularly called 'goat' where the ballots were burned after each voting for Pope. This particular stove which stood for centuries in the same place and was used for this specific purpose only, disappeared after the ascension of Pius XII to the Holy See, and for the election of the next Pope the Curia, without finding the old one, bought a new 'goat.' Some disgruntled officials in the Vatican spread rumors that after his election Pius XII was instrumental in misplacing the 'goat' because he did not hold in high regard the other cardinals, and thought that the 'goat' which was used for his election and many of his predecessors should not be used again."

I interrupted the narrative of my host. "As I recall, Pius XII was friendly with Cardinal Spellman?"

"Yes, during the nineteen years of Pius XII's power, especially during Hitler's war, Spelly, as 'secret messenger of the American Government,' was a constant guest of the Pope. Spelly sent millions of dollars to the Vatican treasury."

"Didn't he want to be Pope?"

"Yes. This short, stocky man, called by some of his best friends 'piggy bank,' would whisper to various cardinals that it was time to nominate an American to the Holy See."

I added, "After the Second World War the United States was at the peak of its world power and an American Pope could have been useful to the Roman Catholic Church."

"Pius XII was a careful, envious man who could not start receiving new candidates for the Holy See. As ruler he was suspicious, and always thought that someone was trying to injure his reputation. The result was disastrous, especially during the last year of his life when he wrote his own speeches and messages and took part in all kinds of decisions. The work in the Vatican slowed down and became inefficient, because everyone waited for directives from the Pope."

"But this should not have influenced Spelly's aspirations."

"No one in the late 1950s had the Pope's complete confidence."

"Isn't it logical that it would have helped the U.S. and the Vatican if the next elected Pope had been an American. And which American, if not Francis Cardinal Spellman?"

"Yes, but here is the surprise. Through a foolish incident Spelly destroyed the possibility of his being considered a candidate for the Holy See. He was accustomed to staying in hotels during his visits to Rome. Every evening he dressed in civilian clothes and walked the streets of the Eternal City observing life, talking to people and eating in restaurants. On one such evening Spelly was approached by a hungry boy and offered to buy him a meal at his hotel. The boy turned on Spelly and robbed him of his money and important church documents."

"These days that happens to a lot of people on streets and in hotels," I commented.

"True. But if you go to a police station and cannot prove that you are a Cardinal or high Church official, what should the police do?

"Call the Vatican."

"So they did. The story not only reached high Vatican authorities, but Pope Pius XII was informed."

"And this is the American contribution to the election of Roncalli. Providence directs human ambitions in strange and mysterious ways."

"By electing seventy-seven-year-old Roncalli the more politically conservative cardinals didn't know that grandfather Angelo would bring them lots of surprises."

"No surprise for you, because you knew him well and voted for him."

"Yes, I was one of the thirty-four cardinals who voted for grandfather Angelo. He talked about his great ideas only to a few cardinals, because he knew that as a cardinal with his idealistic philosophy of the papacy he couldn't do much until he reached the throne. Once he said to me, 'A Pope is afraid of no one except the dead,' and I politely replied that the Pope should only be afraid of God. I told him a story about Antonio, the monk, who said that only a saint is afraid of nobody."

"You never told me this fable."

"During his lifetime Antonio was considered a saint by everyone in his monastery; and when he died, someone pinned a note on the door of his empty cell, "Five A.M. Antonio flew to heaven. Six A.M. nuns will remember him in Angelus.' A devotion in memory of the Annunciation usually performed at 6:00 A.M., 12:00 noon and 6:00 P.M. The tradition goes back to the year 1307. Two hours later, somebody else wrote on this card pinned to the door, 'Heaven, eight A.M., Antonio is not here yet, we are worried.' As a result, everyone in the monastery prayed for Antonio at noon and at 6:00 P.M. but the message from Heaven did not arrive that Antonio was there. Now you can see that Providence is patient and just with people, but for us it is difficult to read the writing of Providence."

I reached for a more earthly explanation and posed the question, "How did the election of John XXIII look from the inside?"

"There is a canonical order of silence for all participants in the Conclave." Cardinal Wyszyński recited from memory, "'I promise that I will keep everything in strict confidence, anything particular which was discussed by the Cardinals and pertinent to the Conclave, in any way connected with voting.' But John XXIII managed to skillfully bypass various regulations while not offending the more rigid Church dignitaries. He conveyed messages through stories or quips. One time, in my presence he called a Monsignor into his library and asked for certain clarifications, but the Monsignor was unable to satisfy him, so John XXIII good-heartedly remarked, 'It's important not to know too much, because then enemies of the Church will not try to convert you or make you into a spy.'

"After the Monsignor had left, I asked, "Holy Father, how many officials are working in the Curia?' He replied 'I don't know, but I am sure not more than one-third.' He began to laugh displaying his big teeth behind thick lips guarded by a prominent, meaty nose. He always enjoyed putting a pin in the seat of the Vatican hierarchy."

"But this critical attitude toward the Curia had, I think, some interesting background, don't you agree?"

"It goes back to when he was a young priest and personal secretary to Rodini Tedeschi, Bishop of Bergamo. He used to select reading material for the Bishop that was mostly left-wing books and newspapers, and as a result of this indoctrination, the Curia accused Bishop Tedeschi of radicalism and cooperation with the revolutionary workers. No doubt young Angelo suffered a lot, because his name was put on a special Curia list. In 1920 Reverend Roncalli was appointed to a position in the Italian directorship of the Opera della Propagazione della Fede. This institution supported mission work in foreign countries.

But for the young priest it provided a source for various stories which he scrupulously collected for future use. One he learned through reading a manuscript of the memoirs of Domenico Cardinal Svampi who was involved in the 1903 election of Pius X. According to what John XXIII told me, Cardinal Svampi took part in an elaborate feast during the election of Pius X. First a delicious soup was served with exquisite noodles, then fried liver with rice, slices of beef with green salad, broiled chicken in an extremely tasty sauce decorated with multicolored and savory vegetables, then mountains of various cheeses, fruits and bottles of old wine. But Cardinal Svampi could not eat, because his teeth hurt and his face was swollen. This was because Clausus would not permit the use of dentists or any other medical help from outside during the election. So the Cardinal suffered in cell number thirty-seven, but he had lots of time between casting ballots to think, observe and write. I will describe to you the observations of Cardinal Svampi as were copied by John XXIII and handed to me by him.

'After Holy Mass managers of the Conclave informed us that the first balloting would be at nine-thirty in the morning. We retreated to our cells. The kitchen and canteen were embarrassed; they didn't have their morning delivery of milk and bread, which we would receive later at about nine o'clock . . .

'The first balloting started at eleven-thirty. One by one the Cardinals walked slowly to the altar where three scrutators sat. Each Cardinal recited the pledge "I swear in the name of Jesus Christ that I will select the one who is meant to be chosen;" then each one placed his nomination in a large chalice.

'When the balloting was completed the first scrutator picked up the chalice and carried it to where the cardinals had gathered about a large table. He dumped the ballots from this chalice into a golden vase; then counted the ballots in front of the cardinals and two other scrutators to see if the number of ballots corresponded to the number of voters. After this, he picked out one ballot after another showing each one to his colleagues who read the name on the card aloud.

'On August 2, immediately after the opening of the Conclave, Cardinal Puzyna rose from his armchair and read a declaration in which he stated that Emperor Francis Josef of the Austro-Hungarian empire was registering his objection to the candidacy of Cardinal Rampolli, a well-known enemy of the Emperor. As we all knew, Rampolli was from the part of Italy occupied by Austria. The Emperor, taking advantage of the ancient privilege granted to him by the Church, questioned and protested the possible election of this particular candidate. All of the Cardinals were upset, because of this unique protest as well as its timing. A Cardinal, who led the election, announced that he and the rest of the members of the Conclave should not and would not take into consideration the scandalous behavior of the Emperor, who spoke through the lips of Cardinal Puzyna.'"

Here Primate Wyszyński said, "As you know, Puzyna, a Polish aristocrat, was a good friend of the Emperor, and Poland at that time was divided and occupied by Austria, Russia and Germany. To conclude this particular incident, I have to mention that Cardinal Rampolli was not elected; on August 4, 1903 Giuseppe Melchiore Cardinal Sarto ascended to the Holy See and chose the name of Pius X."

Wyszyński paused, as though looking for a bridge between that time and today, and said, "Pope John XXIII also caused trouble at the beginning, different perhaps, but interesting. As you probably know, the hidden artisan department at the Vatican usually prepares three sizes of white cassocks as well as shoes before the Conclave, because no one can guess the physical dimensions of the Pope to be elected. John XXIII suffered a lot the first day; with his big feet and pudgy figure he endured more than his predecessors. He could not wear his shoes and when he forced them on he could barely walk. The white cassock was too short and could not be buttoned, but he, a stubborn peasant, put it on. You should have seen him walking to the balcony of St. Peter's Basilica. Those viewing him from the side or back did not smile, because they were feeling compassion for him. The balcony was on the level of the fifth floor of a normal apartment building, so the public could not see his suffering, and the Holy Father blessed and smiled in pain at the enormous crowd below which knelt and shouted, '*Habemus Papem!! Habemus Papem! Habemus Papem!!!*' When he finished the blessing he removed himself from the view of the public, unbuttoned his cassock and removed his shoes; and we discovered that he didn't have socks on. He said to his entourage, 'Now I look like a simple Apostle.'"

"He was well known for his simplicity," I observed, "otherwise I don't know much about his background."

"Angelo was born in 1881, a son of a poor peasant in Sotto il Monte village. Because he was fat and short with big ears and big nose, he was ridiculed by his playmates. He did not have the opportunity to choose any profession, and because of this suffering, developed humility and a closeness to God early, as well as the tremendous desire to learn. As a result of those basic elements, by which he was burdened by nature, he chose to go to the seminary in Bergamo. In 1902 he was sent to a higher seminary in Rome where he divided his time between studying theology and history at Apolinare Papal University. He was conscripted and sent to the army. As a pacifist he suffered a lot, but remained one for the rest of his life. In 1904, Angelo was ordained a priest. During the First World War he worked on the battlefield at the rank of medical sergeant. From the front, where he caused trouble with his pacifist ideas, he was transferred to the hospital, where he took care of the spiritual and physical needs of wounded soldiers.

"After the war most of the Church superiors persecuted him for his modern, radical ideas, even when he was a teacher of history at the Papal Latyrrhenian University.

"Due to his knowledge of history and diplomacy, and after his nomination as Bishop in 1925 the Vatican got rid of Angelo by sending him to Bulgaria as Apostolic Delegate, and here again, he got himself involved in 'great royal trouble.' Italian King Victor Emmanuel II gave away his fourth daughter, Giovanna de Savoia, in marriage to a Greek Orthodox, Boris, King of Bulgaria. According to the agreement, children issuing from this marriage would be christened in the Roman Catholic faith. The Catholic wedding ceremony was performed in Assisi, but afterward King Boris was married again in a Greek Orthodox church in Sofia. Although it was a political maneuver on the part of the King, the Curia blamed Angelo for not preventing this second marriage, and accused him of not caring about differences between the Christian churches. He felt they were not right, because deep in his soul he believed that all of Christianity had the same goal of worshipping God and Jesus Christ, as well as serving all people. He suffered due to Vatican narrow-mindedness.

"During the Second World War, Roncalli was sent as Apostolic Delegate to Istanbul and immediately established friendly contact with Herr

Franz von Papen. He received much firsthand information from this German aristocrat, including news on the Nazi persecution of Jews. His reports to the Vatican were accurate and perceptive, but the Pope did not act on them; instead he tried to preserve strict neutrality. Angelo even inspired Wladyslaw Raczkiewicz, President of the Polish Government who was in exile in London to send a letter to the Holy Father. In compassionate terms, he stated that 'most of the houses of worship and especially Jewish synagogues, had been closed or converted into warehouses and the population was being persecuted. The Polish nation of various religious persuasions does not understand the silence of the Holy Father.' I could paraphrase the letter further," Primate Wyszyński said, "but it is not necessary to continue this gruesome story which tremendously impressed Bishop Roncalli and other Vatican officials. Angelo told me later that from then on, he tried to get out of the diplomatic service, but was refused; instead, he was pushed around for a long time, and finally, almost against the will of the Pope, returned to the Vatican.

"In 1953, Bishop Roncalli, for 'exceptional services,' as he defined his work to me with a chuckle, was nominated for Cardinal and Patriarch of Venice. Again, Angelo embarrassed the Curia! In February 1957, a congress of the Italian Socialist Party was held in Venice and the Cardinal Patriarch sent warm greetings to this organization.

"As you can see, Angelo had not given up his independence, although *a priori*, he knew that the Curia would not like his behavior. At such moments, he would say, 'Too bad if they demand obedience and discipline from me; I am big and fat enough to withstand them all and will save my own opinions and to hell with them.' What a man!"

Wyszyński and I smiled at each other and he tirelessly continued, "Gradually, clever people in the Curia discovered that they would have to tolerate Roncalli's progressive views, because to some extent they reflected radicalization of the world."

"I presume that because of his age the 'Vatican Mafia'—forgive me for this expression—thought that maybe Roncalli as Pope would not be a bad idea. They figured further that if his radicalism did not succeed, nothing would be lost, because he would not live long anyhow."

"You are blunt, but I appreciate your honesty. At the same time, I would say that what John XXIII did in less than five years some other popes could not do in a hundred. For example, a few days after his coronation he called in the Cardinals' Consistorium and on November 4, 1958, nominated twenty-four new cardinals whom he thought would support his 'renewal'; remember, the Church had already been waiting for this renewal for three hundred years. On January 25 of the next year, he proclaimed to the world his intention of opening a Council of Bishops in the Vatican which would consider *Aggiornamento*, in other words, preparation of Church plans which pertained more to the contemporary world. He said that the goal of the Church should be the unification of all Christian churches. This Vatican Council was to take place on October 11, 1962, and was preceded by three encyclicals: *Mater et Magistra, Aeterna Dei* and the most important of all, *Pacem in Terris*. This last one revolutionized the position of the Catholic Church toward the political, social and religious world by proclaiming that the duty of Catholics should be cooperation with all people in their work for peace using the Gospel as the source for inspiration.

"He forbade the Church to identify itself with political systems which are based on the exploitation of man; ergo the Church should be against all political groups whose view did not accord with the visions of the people."

"I guess he hit the arbitrariness of the Curia as well?"

"Yes, instead he introduced collegiality of decision. He abhorred the idea that the people in the Church were divided into two camps: a meek group of lambs and a group of omnipotent shepherds. Above all, he condemned war unequivocally."

"I think abandoning the Latin language in services touched millions of people, because they could now speak with God in their own language."

"You should also not forget that he simplified the liturgy, as well as limited the influence of the Vatican Curia over territorial churches the world over. But the Eastern Church was extremely touched when he removed the excommunication of the Patriarch Cerularius that had been imposed by Leo IX in 1054. "Such actions made enemies among some cardinals."

"Which ones?"

"For example, a cardinal from your own city."

"You mean Spelly?"

"When the encyclical *Pacem in Terris* appeared, Cardinal Spellman, as Chief Chaplain of American Military Forces, and one hundred percent for the Vietnam war, ran into me in the Vatican and said angrily, 'I could not comprehend this encyclical: What kind of Pope is he?' I politely replied, 'I know, and every messenger in the Vatican knows, that you are sending generous contributions to the Holy See, but this does not give you the right to talk like that about the Holy Father.' His round, fat, pink face became red and I figured that I should add something, although I am not a vengeful man. 'You, my dear brother in Christ, should know that the St. Peter's pence which you send are the pennies and dollars of poor American people and not yours.' Later I regretted having said that, but he made me and many others upset by his high-handed opinions and political burrs."

"I recall that newspapers the world over were divided into two groups, a conservative one condemning *Pacem in Terris* and liberal newspapers, including the Communists, who praised it. It was one more indication that people of the world were divided into two camps, one for John XXIII and one against him. The prestigious Balsan Foundation bestowed upon him the International Peace Prize."

"Judging from your opinions, it seems you think that the Holy Father did those things for publicity. That is wrong. His motto, as he expressed imself to me, was 'in order to work successfully for noble causes, you have to go to all good people of good will.' Once, against the advice of his Department of State and the whole Curia, he granted an audience to a Soviet delegation, and said to those high officials, 'We should emphasize everything which unites people and shows them the road to truth and justice.'

"On October 8, 1962, I led a delegation of twenty-five bishops who arrived for the Vatican Council of Bishops, to a private audience with the Pope. It was an emotional meeting in which he said to us, 'I know that Colonel Francesco Nullo died on Polish soil in the January Insurrection, while fighting for the liberation of your country from foreign oppression, and I also know that in your ancient city Wroclaw a street is named after him.' He chuckled, looked around and said, 'But you don't know that I was raised on the novels of Henryk Sienkiewicz and have followed the development of Poland closely from then on, especially now when you are trying to build a bridge between Catholicism and Socialism.'"

The Primate rose from the bench and walking slowly, elaborated on the politics of the Pope and German diplomacy. "When Chancellor

Konrad Adenauer heard that the Pope mentioned in his speech the city of Wroclaw which through history went from Polish to German hands and vice versa, he was angry and personally telephoned Dr. Hilger A. von Schrepen to launch a protest against the Vatican Secretary of State. What's more the Ambassador asked to see John XXIII personally, but the Pope, upon hearing about it said, 'My diplomats talk to foreign diplomats.'"

Wyszyński was paler than usual and I thought I might ask to go inside, but he ventured first. "Let's go inside and I will show you something that is most characteristic of my dear friend, Angelo."

"What's that?"

"His letter to his brother, Severo, who toiled on the family farm in Sotto il Monte and never ventured outside.

"According to tradition the Pope is supposed to stop writing letters to family and friends on the day of his election." Wyszyński approached a little chest of drawers in his bedroom, pulled out a breviary, sat on the bed and from the breviary took out a letter.

"'My dear brother Severo, today is the holy day of the great patron whose name you carry, St. Francis Xavier. I think three years have passed since I stopped writing on the typewriter which I like, and decide today to return to this pleasant chore. I would like to tell you that I have a new typewriter for my use only. This letter which I send to your address should be the voice which will reach everybody in our family, and I wish that it will be for you and them the expression of my lively and youthful affections. Although I am busy, in important service which all eyes of the world are observing, I cannot forget my loved ones; I return each day in my thoughts to them. I would like to tell you that I cannot conduct personal correspondence often, but you should keep in contact with Monsignor L. F. Capovilli to whom you can tell anything any time. Please love one another and try to understand that I could not send separate letters to each of you. Our Joseph was right when he wrote to his brother the Pope that 'you are living in a luxurious jail and cannot do what you want to do.' I know well that all of you have problems with those people who do not want to conduct themselves according to good sense. To have a Pope in the family, to whom people look with respect, and to live modestly and in poor conditions is difficult, but everybody knows that this Pope, the son of modest but respected people, should not forget anyone and should show a good heart to everyone including his closest relatives. They should know also that the material conditions of this Pope are modest. On the day of my death, I feel I would not have any less respect and recognition than that bestowed upon Pius X, who was born a pauper and died a pauper. I bless you all and think also about the wives of the male members of the Roncalli family, who bring so much joy and happiness to us all.'"

24
Spiritual Seers

"WHEN I became Suffragan or subordinate to Eugeniusz Baziak, Archbishop of Cracow on July 4, 1958," the Pope said to me in November 1980, "and was consecrated on September 28, I did not abandon my private life, creativity nor social contacts. I studied, wrote, performed church duties and met with young people in my apartment on Kanoniczna Street, where I had access to a large library in five languages. Many long hours were spent in the library discussing social, political, family and love problems with invited guests. The results of these studies and discussions were essays of varying length, such as 'Propaedeutics of Marriage,' 'The Role of a Woman in the Church,' 'Human Nature as a Basis for Ethical Formations,' 'Love and Responsibility,' 'Bringing Up Love,' 'Thomistic Personalism,' 'Observation on the Inner Life of Young Intelligentsia,' essays on psychology, and many poems on religious and social themes. I published this work under my own name or pseudonyms."

"Didn't you become very ill shortly thereafter?"

"In the spring of 1960 I developed a high fever and sore throat, together with great weakness. I thought I was developing some mysterious disease. I called my friend, Dr. Stanislaw Kownacki who right away diagnosed my illness as leukemia."

I also knew that friends and colleagues of Bishop Wojtyla were in a panic, especially Archbishop Baziak. This scare mobilized Cracow's best medical minds, and after an examination they diagnosed him as having infectious mononucleosis, otherwise known as the 'Kissing Disease,' derived from the fact that during the spring many college students contracted the illness.

Nevertheless Wojtyla's case was severe and he almost lost his life. But he never dismissed his doctor friend, who apologetically advised him to "rest from three weeks to four months in peaceful surroundings with fresh air." Relieved from anxiety Bishop Wojtyla was able to relax and take the advice seriously. He put more time into writing, reading and above all, thinking and praying.

Not long after, inquiries came from Rome to Primate Wyszyński in connection with the Second Vatican Council, announced by Pope John XXIII. Karol Wojtyla was surprised that the Curia had asked for his opinion on the subject of "returning to the source," renewing the Church in an Evangelical spirit, and adjusting to the growing social radicalism all over the world. He knew that "Pastor of the World" Pope John XXIII had said, "The voice of the Church should reverberate the world over"; and the young Bishop, with all his energy, went to work to fulfill this appeal.

"When I saw Karol, his pale countenance worried me," Primate Wyszyński said. "Although I knew he was in good medical hands, I suggested that he pray more to the Holy Mother of Częstochowa, and in my prayers, I promised the Virgin Mary that I would be closer to him, and try to prepare him spiritually for higher duty."

At that moment there was a knock on the door. Reverend Stanislaw Kotowski appeared and announced, "Dinner is ready!"

We got up, and my host continued the conversation about Bishop Wojtyla. "His work on love and responsibility, his deliberations on marriage and youth, and also his essays on the metaphysics of philosophy, Max Scheler and San Tommaso d'Aquino, and other printed intellectual exercises were well known to the Pope and the Curia, so when Karol appeared in Rome he was already a celebrity. When the Pope announced the Second Council of Bishops for *aggiornamento et accommodata renovatio* over three thousand of the most illustrious members of the Church and lay members arrived at the Vatican together with outstanding scientists in every human endeavor.

"This enormous Vatican gathering sparked conferences and discussions first under the leadership of John XXIII, who had a vision of a new church which would fit into the future world. This vision was a church liberated from the complete influence of Western culture, moving in the direction of social, political and cultural universalism, to engulf all races and nations. The church was supposed to reach all people, regardless of religion, to help them develop a system of equality and freedom. I was one of the first clergy to introduce these ideas in my native country long before the Second Vatican Council. Naturally, I should emphasize that Bishop Wojtyla had ideas too, and with more energy than I, put them into action."

We sat at the dining table and when we started our beet soup he was not silent for long. "Please allow me to jump from subject to subject, and abandon the Vatican Council for a moment. I would like to show you John XXIII's private side."

"Please do."

He reached for a piece of black bread, "I love to eat beet soup with bread." So saying, he continued, "As soon as I arrived in Rome he invited me, as he called me, 'My Beloved Son' to participate in giving the blessing *Urbi et Orbi* which was a great distinction, and I was much moved. After that, he asked me to visit him in his private apartments, which were on the right when facing St. Peter's Basilica. From St. Damascus Court I reached the Appartamento Pontificio and there, when emerging from a slow-moving elevator, saw my beloved friend, the Holy Father waiting to greet me with open arms. I went down on my knee to kiss his ring, but he pulled me up, took me by the arm and said, 'Let's go to my Chapel and pray.

"We walked slowly, like two old men, and I felt his smile on my cheek. I could not attempt to describe the beauty of his chapel, but if you are not familiar with it, you can refresh youself by reading a book on the Vatican.

"The Holy Father slowly approached a prie-dieu in the middle of the chapel. Kneeling, he pointed to a beautifully encrusted chair, as through he wanted me to sit down. I was overwhelmed by the handwork of the chair and thought how much time the artisan had spent engraving the faces and scenes. For some inexplicable reason I thought about Karol Wojtyla, who some time ago said that simple physical work sanctifies a man and transforms his work into a beautiful prayer.

"Rather than sit on the ancient chair, I knelt behind the Holy Father, looked at his bent back and prayed. My prayer was simple. I begged God to recognize Karol Wojtyla, to bring him to the attention of the Holy Father and protect him from Vatican politicians. When the Pope got up, he said slowly to me, 'I prayed for Poland; that she would find harmonious cooperation between Christianity and Socialism, and that her people would set an example on how to develop a just system based on Christian principles.'

"Again, John XXIII held my arm and directed me to the door through which we reached the dining room, and I noticed that on a table stood two crystal carafes full of red and white wine, and around them cheese, Italian bread and fruit. He said, 'This modest meal is just an excuse. The reason I've invited you here again is because this is the only place where no one can hear us. Everyone knows that during meals I do not talk about politics or philosophy; I just eat!'

"Then the Pope said something startling, 'I know that some of our Cardinals who express progressive views are sicker than those who express conservative ones. I don't know if this is God, or the people's punishment; but I will tell you that I am mortally ill. I have cancer. Yet I fooled the people, and I will fool the cancer, because I am working on my successor who adheres to the same social philosophy. The reason I brought you here is that I don't think I will survive the Second Vatican Council, and I want a man who will continue my work on the Holy See to bring the people together.'

"Holy Father, who is this Cardinal?

"He looked straight into my face and replied, 'Montini, I want you to work hard for his election.'

"He said he had been watching my experiment of cooperation between the Polish Socialist Government and the Church, and if this experiment succeeded, the Vatican could show Moscow that there was a possibility of friendly relations between an atheistic State and the Roman Catholic Church."

"But you, at some point, went to the Vatican at the invitation of the Holy Father to lecture on this very subject?"

"In 1963 I delivered a lecture on social philosophy based on my experiences in Poland. I demonstrated that even under totalitarian pressures one could convince authorities that social and personal freedom is important to everybody concerned, and beneficial for the development of the country. When the question was raised of Soviet Union interference in the Catholic Church experiment in this country, my reply was simple: If the Soviet Union saw that Christian principles did not endanger the Soviet system, they might even introduce our Polish experience into it.

"Another time when I was enjoying *cappuccino* with John XXIII in his apartment, and we were exploring the possibility of *rapprochement* with the Soviet Union, he shifted the subject and said, 'I would like your opinion on the subject of the Third World.'

"I was puzzled, but did not want to interrupt, so waited for more of an explanation.

"'Our good friend Giovanni Montini told me that Bishop Wojtyla tells jokes about Catholic missionaries in Africa.'

"This surprised me because I was thinking about how to make Karol more positively visible to the Holy See. Now, I felt that in this split second everything had collapsed.

"The Pope saw anxiety on my face, and said with a smile, 'Don't worry. I know a lot about him, and I think he is excellent material for a Cardinal.'

"He is probably the most intelligent priest in Poland today, and has come from a similar background as yours.

"The Pope ignored my words, and continued with his own description, 'A very good writer and first class Thomist.'

"I was dumbfounded.

"'Originally I heard about him from prince Sapieha, from Archbishop Baziak, above all from you, and from various Cardinals whom you indoctrinated about Wojtyla. I know also that your protégé is pious and my great defender, and now I think I'm entitled to hear his jokes, and if they are of interest we will invite the author.'

"After he said that, I rose from my seat, went to the other side of the table, grabbed his hand and kissed his ring.

"'Don't kiss my ring so often, it looks suspicious. Better return to the jokes.'

"Wojtyla vehemently supports our work with the Third World. There he envisions great achievements for Christ's Church. Just a few days ago Wojtyla showed me a poem which he had written to a brother Bishop who arrived here from Africa for the Second Vatican Council. Without asking permission I started reading the poem in rough translation:

Here, in this place, my dear Brother,
I feel in you an enormous land
in which rivers fall suddenly, and sun burning
      human bodies as furnaces melting iron ore
I feel in you a similar thought;
although our minds do not run parallel,
but one scale divides the truth from falsehood.

There is the happiness of expressing our thought
on the same scale
although in your eyes and mine they shine differently
they have the same meaning.

"'A wonderful observation, beautifully expressed,' said my host, impatiently. 'But I didn't yet hear the joke, and a good joke is better than good wine. If you don't tell me right away, I will assume the joke is not his, that you invented the whole thing to acquaint me with more material about your protégé.'

"After many years in the interior of Africa, our missionary returned to Rome and submitted his report to the Curia. Priests gathered around and asked questions: 'Please tell us, with your hand on your heart, how missionaries have improved the conditions of the natives?'

"'What kind of medical help did you give them?'

"'How did you enlighten them to Christian belief?'

"The missionary modestly replied, 'I'll just speak about myself: I spent the last two years with a tribe who fished and hunted for almost extinct fish and animals. They were starving. I tried to find a way out, but it was a difficult undertaking if you don't have animals and fish.'

"'Well then, how did you solve the problem?'

"The missionary was embarrassed, but after a pause, replied, 'When I finally left the tribe, the aborigines were killing white hunters, saying that the meat from white hunters is sweeter.'"

"The Pope did not smile, but remarked, 'Wojtyla's joke has meaning. The Church is doing little among the people of Black Africa, or in the rest of the Third World. That is why I emphasize that the Vatican Council should take stock of our missionary work all over the world. Bring this young man to me. He has a sharp mind and a youthful approach. Does he speak foreign languages? How many does he know?

"'Probably seven or more.

"'Definitely bring him here for a conversation with me.'

"I am most grateful to Your Holiness.

"On December 8, 1962 Pope John XXIII ended the first session of the Second Vatican Council. He looked pale, and could barely move. On April 20, 1963 I had my last private audience with him, during which time we talked about the ecumenical movement, relations between the United States, the Soviet Union, and the Third World.

At this audience he told me, 'Please try to help elect Cardinal Montini to the Holy See, because he would carry on my work for the benefit of all nations helping to end the exploitation of all people, and for peace on earth.'

"As I was leaving he said, 'Good-bye my dear friend. Let Madonna Nera di Jasna Góra before whose image I pray many times, lead you to victory. And don't forget to tell your Bishop Wojtyla to come to me as soon as possible and join me in an Angelus. I would like to pray with him; but let him hurry.'"

"Naturally, you told Karol about this visit?" I asked.

"Primate Wyszyński replied sadly, "When Karol appeared in the Pontifical apartment, the wise Pope said to him, 'Go on the same road as you are going. I cannot teach you anything. You are young. Wait a little bit longer. Pray to God, and you will be here forever, because there is no other man in the world who is worth more to a Holy See than you...'

"I achieved my goal, and here I would like to quote my favorite writer, Boleslaw Prus." He paused, closed his eyes and I saw that the Primate was very tired. Opening them, he repeated the words of Prus: "'Consistent and wise work of a man who is not thinking of harvesting right away, eventually conquers mountains and builds bridges over ravines.'"

On June 3, 1963, John XXIII died, with excruciating stomach pains, after a little less than a five-year reign, leaving for people all over the world, hope and a strong belief that the Christian Church could work successfully for the betterment of humanity. After his death the modest wooden casket was placed in the library of his apartment, and from there it was his wish that a simple interment should be carried out. But there was so much opposition from the people of Rome and elsewhere, that the casket was moved to St. Peter's Basilica, where the common people could say good-bye, in their own way, to this remarkable man.

25

The Pope's Logic and
The Wisdom of a Simple Story

Primate Wyszyński continued his narrative.

"During our last encounter in the spring of 1963, Pope John XXIII said, 'You deserve to occupy the Holy See after me, but who will then take your place in Warsaw? Who will continue the renewal? Without you in Poland the experiment of reforms would collapse. With your help and others like you, Poland could show that Socialism can succeed with a Christian base. Only you could make the experiment of solidarity between Church and working class a reality.'

"When I made no comment the Holy Father got the impression that I would like to be his successor and he approached this problem from a different angle, 'Yet, only Montini could contain the anger of a displeased Curia if I were to support you for the Holy See.' In John XXIII's opinion, only a *pro forma* Conclave should be held because he had selected Cardinal Montini as his successor. He was deeply convinced that only Montini could continue the policy of reforms which he had begun."

"He even ignored Canon 231 which set a maximum of seventy members for the College of Cardinals. This regulation, derived from the Constitution *Postquan Verus Illi*, goes back to 1586 to the time of Pope Sixtus V and is based on a long tradition when God suggested to Moses that he should have seventy wise elders with the experience and wisdom to help him govern the people. But good-hearted grandfather Angelo, raised the membership of the College of Cardinals to ninety. His successor Paul VI later raised the number to one hundred eighteen. They modernized both costume and electoral ceremony, and from then on cardinals were addressed not as 'His Eminence,' but simply as 'Reverend Cardinal.'

"In the beginning Christ's apostles selected successors from the people around them. Later, secular powers influenced the election of the Pope, and as a result, the Church went through much turmoil. Not earlier than the second half of the eleventh century, Pope Nicholas II through his decree *In Nomine Domini*, ordered that the Pope be elected by cardinals through secret ballot.

"When I visited Pope Paul VI during the consistorial meeting in 1967, the Holy Father asked me what I thought of his curtailing the cardinals' power.' I replied, 'The Curia would not agree. But as Pope you have the right to do this. You must choose between implementing your progressive ideas and curtailment of the cardinals' power.' On his thin ascetic face a smile appeared, and he noted, 'I would like to try this, but it is difficult to tell if success will be the result.' Already on June 28 of the same year Paul VI announced publicly that 'we have no reason to change the rules conveyed by our predecessors. Activity of the Holy College of Cardinals is truly holy and ecclesiastical, because the duty of the Holy College is cooperation with the Pope in governing the universal Church. According to the canonical law, to this duty also belongs the election of Saint Peter's successors. It is an enormously delicate function and should be protected, as it is now, by the College of Cardinals; this obligation should be permanent and free from all foreign influence.'"

The sun was going down and peeking with its red eyes through the greenery of the garden. On the face of the Primate, I noticed the irregular shadows of leaves.

"Let's say that John XXIII developed radicalism because of childhood poverty, and Paul VI through intellectual deliberation. Am I right?"

"I guess you are," said Wyszyński. "Giovanni Battista Montini was born in 1897, in the town of Brescia, to a wealthy and influential family. His father was a prominent lawyer, Catholic activist and member of the Italian parliament from the Christian People's Party which was later renamed the Christian Democratic Party. The family was progressive considering the times, and thought the Catholic Church should play a more important role in the social and political life of the country. This atmosphere of liberalism and intellectualism influenced young Giovanni as well as an inborn carefulness in expressing one's inner thoughts, secretiveness, and especially, suspicion. All those qualities were delicately molded into *savoir vivre*. Once he confided that he didn't like old men nor did he trust them, and he especially didn't like the old Church dignitaries. When he became Pope he was rigid with his cardinals.

"Montini went to school at an early age, was an exceptional student and became a priest in 1920. He was accepted at the Latyrrhenian University and Ecclesiastical Academy where he decided to become a Curia diplomat."

"Nice to have a wealthy and influential family," I said. Wyszyński continued.

"Three years later he was sent by the Curia as an attaché to the Apostolic Nuncio in Warsaw. He was small and thin, but enormously discreet, a man of few words and great intelligence, excellent material for a diplomat. I spent many hours with him in Rome during my visit to the Holy City in 1929 and 1930; he was then *aiutante* in the Vatican Secretary of State. I even gave him my work, *The School and the Rights of the Family, the Church, and the State*. In 1937 he was raised to the position of Director of Pius XII's cabinet. He became the right hand to the Secretary of State, concentrating on internal affairs. In this position he became friendly with Bishop Angelo Giuseppe Roncalli. All the while Montini was progressing in his career, he remained a Prelate because his liberalization campaign had alienated the Curia. Pius XII had sent him to Milan to be *Ordinarius* of the diocese. He stayed there until the Pope's death. This banishment provided Montini with time to think, read and examine his progressive ideas. When Roncalli was elected Pope John XXIII, he immediately nominated Montini to the rank of Cardinal, and entrusted him with organizing the Second Vatican Council. On his deathbed, John XXIII said to Cardinal Montini: 'I make you responsible for the continuation of the great work of the Vatican Council.' So this is the way the Holy See moved from John XXIII to Paul VI; from good-hearted grandfather Angelo to intellectual Montini, who brought the *Secund Vaticanum* to a successful conclusion. The words of Jesus Christ, 'You all are brothers' received an extra boost in the modern world."

"What was Karol Wojtyla doing during the Second Vatican Council?" I asked Cardinal Stefan Wyszyński thinking that involving himself with the Popes he had forgotten about the Polish Bishop.

"He was active in many sessions of the Council, and during one of them criticized Scheme XIII for not giving enough rights to laymen in Church activities. As a result, Scheme XIII went to *Subcommisio Cen-*

tralis of which Wojtyla became a member. There he met prominent theologians such as Jean-Marie Cardinal Daniélou, Father Bernhard Häring, Father Yves Congar, and many others. He also became a friend of the Archbishop of Vienna, Franz König.

"During this Second Vatican Council most of the greatest theologians and Catholic scientists and historians appeared in Rome from eight countries; among them Bishop Karol Wojtyla who with his modesty and knowledge impressed everybody, especially because he didn't waste time getting himself placed on various commissions; instead he prayed in the various churches of Rome. As a result, prominent Church dignitaries and intellectuals saw him in many places of worship, and they started talking about him. When Karol was invited to take part in a Council commission he was always well prepared and delivered a dramatic and original speech. One day Pope Paul VI told me, 'This Bishop Karol is performing excellent service to the Church. Our friend Angelo in heaven is very proud of him and no doubt you on earth are proud as well...'

"I replied meekly, 'Give him a chance.'"

"The Pope smiled, 'He has everything, the only thing he needs is a long life.' Then he asked, 'Is he still writing poetry?'

"'And how,' I said.

"'Give me some to read.'

"'I have to translate them first, then I will.'

"'He should start writing in Italian, so he would provide competition for Roman poets.'"

"'I don't know if he can do that,'" I replied. 'As you see, he is very busy, but if he became a Cardinal he would have the time to learn Italian and write poetry.

"'I see you favor this young Bishop to be nominated for Cardinal.' He smiled. This indicated that he was thinking positively. I pursued the subject further. 'Your Holiness, two cardinals in such a faithful and large country as mine are not too much.'

"He was about to depart and I saw that I hadn't made a good impression. He put his arm on my shoulder and said, 'We cannot favor your country so openly during a time when we are talking with the Soviet Union, because it would appear that we are trying to encircle Moscow with the churches of Eastern Europe. We are in a special era when we are attempting to develop meaningful relations with Russian Christian churches. But, remember, you and your country have a unique place in my heart and throughout the world a lot of positive things are happening for the Church. If you could help me...'

"I kissed his ring and said, 'I will fulfill my duty to God and to You, Holy Father.'

"He hugged me, but a thought went through my mind, 'John XXIII said the same thing and now Paul VI; only promises...the same promises...'

"This is the way we parted and I returned to my apartment in Istituto Polacco, immediately contacting Karol who was staying during Vatican II at the Collegio Polacco. I asked him to bring me some poems as soon as possible. I did not tell him that the Pope wanted to read his poetry. He sent an envelope containing a dozen poems to the Institute the same day. The receptionist delivered the envelope to my apartment and right away I began translating them from Polish into Italian. In the evening, I called Bishop Antonio Samore, who spent a good part of his life in the Vatican archives, and asked him to recommend a good Italian poet who could help polish the language."

"You were working fast."

"I always adhere to the widsom of the peasant's proverb, 'Hammer the red iron before it gets cold.' In my opinion two poems of this collection were interesting and characteristic of Karol."

"Which ones?" I asked.

"'For Travelling Companions' and 'Inspiration.'"

I reached for the first and started reading:

If you are looking for the place where Jacob was struggling
don't travel to Arabia, don't look for the stream on the maps
you will find a trace of it close
Just allow lights of the subject to appear
        in the perspective of your thoughts.

I read the last lines of this poem:

When our days are full of ordinary tasks
in which the inner of the deed
        is constantly covered by a gesture
despite that we have a certainty that this gesture

> will drop off some day
> and in our deeds only things which are really important
> will remain.

"Inspiration" began:

> The work began inside and out, there was so much space
> that palms, overwhelmed by this work, immediately reached
>   to the borders of breath,
> look, the will hits into the rock's deep bell.
> When thought receives its certainty
> then heart and palm reach the peak

And the end of the poem:

> When you want to reach from far away and enter,
>   and live inside of the people
> you have to unite those two forces with very simple speech
> (Your speech should not disburse in tensions of this lift
> which love and anger creates)
> Then nobody can pull you out from inside of the man,
>   can never rip you off of him

"I might correct the impression that Paul VI's interest in Bishop Wojtyla was not isolated," said Primate Wyszyński, "For a long time his Holiness had been considering relying more and more on bishops beyond Rome. He even created a permanent bishops' council, a type of advisory board, which was not only the source of firsthand information from all over the world, but also the power of the Curia. Paul VI knew firsthand about the works of the Curia, especially after the postwar era when Italy was governed by Christian Democrats. He used to say, 'The Tiber river should enlarge itself into a vast sea, then the Roman Catholic Church would be a universal Church.'"

Then suddenly the Primate began talking about another Pole in the Vatican.

"When Bishop Wladyslaw Rubin was nominated as Secretary of the Council of Bishops, the Curia was upset and tried to neutralize various progressive moves stemming from suggestions of the advisory board.

Gossip circulated that through Rubin the bishops' council was dominated by foreigners, especially Poles."

I noticed a shadow of fatigue on the face of the Primate and to preserve his energy for future conversation, suggested that we postpone our meeting for the time being. I knew that if I lost this unique human gold mine of information of the Vatican and personalities of the Church I would not find anybody else so well informed. He had greater knowledge of ecclesiastical matters, past and present, than Bishop Antonio Samore, the Vatican archivist.

When I started working on this book, I discovered that Wladyslaw Rubin, the wizard of Vatican intelligence was the same Rubin I had known as a younger colleague during my studies at Lwów University, and that we both were born in the southeast part of Poland, he on September 20, 1917. The Second World War interrupted his life and study of theology which he finished in Beirut, Lebanon. It was there, on June 30, 1946 that he was consecrated as a Roman Catholic priest. He began his pastoral work among European refugees as well as Arabs, and, as a hobby, collected information pertaining to the cultural, social and political life in that part of the world. His analysis and opinions were valuable to the Vatican, but he did not abandon his education, and in 1952 received a Doctorate of Canonic Law from Gregorianum in Rome. Seven years later, Rubin was nominated Papal Chamberlain. Paul VI then raised him to the position of Bishop and he was consecrated by Primate Wyszyński in the presence of Karol Wojtyla. He was nominated for the position of Secretary General of the Council of Bishops. On June 30, 1979 Wojtyla, as Pope John Paul II, recognized Rubin's great service to the Church, and raised him to Cardinal.

During Vatican II Bishop Karol Wojtyla stayed in the living quarters of the Collegio Polacco, located in the Aventino, a beautiful section of Rome; the head of this Collegio was Wladyslaw Rubin. From September 7, 1962, when Bishop Wojtyla took part for the first time in the deliberations of the Vatican Council, to the day of the closing of Vatican II, my friend Wladyslaw, was a constant companion of Bishop Wojtyla. Before him Karol practiced his speeches and philosophical tracts such as "Source of Revelation," "About the Church," "Religious Freedom," "Secular Ministry and the Church in a Contemporary World." Wladyslaw provided the Bishop, not only with original criticism of his work, but with valuable information about the Curia, and characteristics of many cardinals whose lives Wladyslaw knew inside and out. This exchange of views on personal, philosophical and political levels enlarged Wojtyla's knowledge of the mechanism of Church administration. When I asked Wladyslaw why he did this, he paraphrased Christ's saying, 'There is nothing secret which cannot be revealed; nothing is so hidden that cannot come to the surface.' (Mark 4:22)

Bishop Rubin was a deep thinking and God-fearing churchman, realistic in his observations and blunt in his opinions. He was modest in his daily life and didn't like the fact that some Church officials talked most of the time about money. He liked Wojtyla's poetry and recited fragments to me. Wladyslaw's favorite stanza was:

> The truth should not be like olive oil which we apply
>   to the wound to soothe burning
> the truth should not ride through the streets on a donkey
> The truth must be painful
> because the truth carries the man.

He was not smothered in the philosophy of humanity; he saw things from a realistic and practical view. His judgment of people, especially the clergy, was down to earth. Wladyslaw's favorite joke, which he told Bishop Wojtyla and repeated to me, was, "In a remote Italian village a woman approached a priest and asked him to arrange her husband's burial. The priest who hadn't noticed her in Church for a long time said, 'Giovanna, I heard that your Giovanni died.'

"'Yes, Giovanni died,' she replied.

"'I am sorry that he died so soon. We must go to your house to pick him up.'

"'Please come.'

"The priest wrote on a card: 20,000 lire and said, 'but we should sing at the house for a while beside his casket.'

"'Yes, you should, he was a good man and worthy of song.'

"The priest added 10,000 lire more and kept asking about what kind of church service she wanted for her deceased husband, adding more and more until he reached 80,000 lire; then he said to the grieved widow, 'Finally we have your Giovanni in the Church.'"

Wladyslaw said, "When I told this story to Bishop Wojtyla he laughed more than I had ever seen him laugh, and he repeated many times, 'Finally, we have your Giovanni in the Church.'

Later my friend Reverend Dowsilas told me that some time ago while travelling with Cardinal Wojtyla from Cracow to Warsaw he said, 'You must drink the Jana water, on doctor's orders.' They stopped at the nearest parking space, got out and opened the trunk. Another car also stopped from which a little poodle jumped out; he ran around and hopped into the Cardinal's trunk. Busy drinking, the Cardinal didn't notice the dog, but his companion Dowsilas, pointing to the animal, said, 'Finally we have him in the Church.' Hearing this, the Cardinal started laughing uncontrollably and spilled water all over himself. Reverend Dowsilas commented to me, 'I thought he would choke himself to death.'

"And is this the end of the story?"

"Not exactly," Wladyslaw replied.

"What do you mean? Did something happen to the dog?"

"When Karol Wojtyla was elected to the Holy See he gave a little libation for his close friends during which I said aloud so that everybody could hear, 'Now we finally have him in the Church!'"

26
Barefoot Bishop in Jerusalem

"AFTER supper the Primate and I, a recently consecrated bishop, sat in his apartment in the Istituto Polacco on Via Pietro Cavallini," began John Paul II. "Wyszyński interrupted a long silence and said, 'You should buy yourself a new pair of shoes. I can't stand those worn-out ones!'

"You should be ashamed, Primate," I said, smiling.

"'Why should I be ashamed to talk about your shoes?'

"Because we were talking about Jesus Christ, Holy places, Palestine, philosophy, and you comment on my shoes!"

"'You should look decent.'

"What does decency have to do with shoes?"

"'We are not living in the time of Jesus Christ. Even He had a good pair of sandals.'

"Where did the Primate read about the good pair of sandals of Jesus Christ?"

"Surprised by such a question, he replied, 'A long time ago I read Tacitus or perhaps the Roman historian Suetonius, or was it the Jewish historian Josephus...'

"I became sad. Why did he want to impress me? Wyszyński said, 'You don't have to look pathetic if you wish to demonstrate that you are good at philosophy and theology.'

"I'm sorry, I was searching my mind for the principal source of information about Jesus Christ. I was not thinking about St. Matthew or St. Mark, St. Luke or St. John, but who else at the time of the emperors Augustus and Tiberius talked about sandals? I stopped, because I noticed a trace of envy on the face of the Primate. I felt badly on account of knowing that he was trying to say that he was an intellectual equal. I was certain that he was superior to me and to many other church dignitaries. However, I could not convince him.

"Not long ago, my friend from the *gimnazjum* died, and his wife asked me to perform Holy Mass for the redemption of his soul. I replied, it was not necessary to perform Holy Mass."

"'You really said that?' asked the Primate. 'What kind of theologian are you?'"

"I'm not as good as the Reverend Primate, but remember, even during Christ's time on earth people said that 'He went about doing good.' So, as a priest, I was doing, in my own way, my good."

"'Go ahead, continue the story.'"

"I told this to the widow, and she replied, 'You know, Uncle Karol, you may be right because last night I dreamed about my Mietek—that he went to heaven and was laughing so much—that St. Peter heard his laughter, approached him and asked the reason for his joy. Mietek, in his naiveté replied, 'You are St. Peter, the right hand of Jesus Christ, and you don't see what's going on downstairs?' St. Peter shook his head to let him know that he was unaware of what was going on downstairs. Mietek took him aside and pointed down, 'You see, they are still performing surgery on me, and I am already in heaven.'

"The Primate laughed and said, 'A clever joke, but it doesn't relate to your moral attitude.'

"You are strict, Reverend Primate."

"'Maybe? When you return from Jerusalem, I am sure you will be more serious. When you are there you should pray a lot in Christ's places. You should walk the places of Christ's Passion, and pray so you will be spiritually enriched.'

"I would prefer not going to Jerusalem for these ten days with a crowd of bishops and priests, especially before Christmas."

"'You can isolate yourself and you know how to do that.'

"Tell me, my beloved Primate, what Christ would do in my place?"

"'Every time I pin you down you refer to Christ. It is a good approach. Not only on Christ, but his apostles and the saints.'

"Don't you think I'm using the best references?"

"'But with such references, you cannot get a loan from a bank,' and then added, 'Go ahead. Go to Holy Jerusalem; yes, you have to include this experience in your papers.'

"I saw a tired look on his face. I wanted him to get more rest because I saw how much time he was spending at the Vatican, talking to Cardinals and high officials of the Curia. On top of this, fragments of my poems from the 'Church' cycle were crowding my head. But the Primate was still talking about where I should pray in the Holy Land and whom I should see, while I was full of verse.

"He saw this and asked, 'Are you praying now?'

"No. At this moment I am thinking about my poetry."

"'Do you write your poems because they are more exquisite then your theological philosophy?'

I see the simple wall or rather a fragment of it
flat pilasters run on both sides of the conch
in which figures of Saints stop in its running
to relate with one move
some kind of enormous Move, which impregnates us people
from open books.

But for this wall, arches are not heavy
The people who are living far away in small rooms,
people of tired hearts, are not weighed down.
The precipice which engulfs the earth
is not heavy either
because man is being born to suck a mother's breast.

"'Why did you stop?'

"I thought I should not bother a tired man with my intellectual perspiration. It's also difficult for me to remember the lines.

"'I don't believe you. You have an excellent memory.'

"I will recite these few lines, but no more:

Each from two cities is a unity not transmittable from
heart to heart.
They have to live on expanse of everyone's heart
and every one of us again has to live
with each city,
otherwise none of us could exist,
as they would make unity from one of these two cities
(we are talking about it for long hours
above the lights of the Third City—

which evening is more itself
when we discard daily trumpery)

"'I am enriched.' He took my arm and continued, 'Go to the Holy Land, gain strength and return quickly because a great duty awaits you.'

"I didn't know what he meant. We embraced and I left. Outside, coolness and Roman street lamps engulfed me together with sounds of cars and voices of people, creating a song that acted as my star on the road to Bethlehem.

"Jerusalem made a strange impression on me. I flew there to see the immortal city of Jesus Christ; instead I saw a modernistic city with tall buildings, blown-glass foundries, and many other commercial establishments, among them churches, synagogues, monasteries and mosques. I knew that Jerusalem was the seat of the Chief Rabbis of the Jewish nation, and Third Holy Place of Islam. It's also a place of religious importance for Roman Catholic, Greek Orthodox, Anglican, and schismatic splinters of Christianity. On the streets men and women walked slowly in religious garb of various colors, but for me the city appeared bleached of holiness.

"With my entourage of bishops and priests I walked and travelled through places mentioned in the Holy Book, but I did not find Jesus Christ. Too much noise shattered my thoughts about Jesus and His Mother in Nazareth, about St. Peter on the bank of Lake Gennesaret and about Jesus in the Garden of Mount of Olives. I am sure that that time the earth of Galilee smelled with His and the apostle's perspiration; today the odor reeks of agricultural chemicals, or the perspiration of Arabs, Israelis and tourists washed in French and American soaps.

"I recalled the words of Father Peter from my poem 'Jerusalem'

Over Jerusalem clouds gather
I see them with my eyes and my soul
a storm is coming to Jerusalem
for fire you have to reply with stronger fire,
this hatred you have to combat with love
enemies are preparing against Jerusalem,
we need to send messages, to call all hearts
in helping to repel enemies from walls and gates.

I did not accept the different enlightenment,
only I took God on my lips and in my eyes
when others covered their eyes; from the walls
I noticed through the sun, through the gold—
this gold began to crumble,
and in the temple gold fell from the statues,
invasion is coming, on the walls, on the city,
a deluge is coming...we must hit with power.

"I went up Tabor mountain and repeated the words after St. Luke, 'He is my chosen Son, listen to Him.' I looked at the sky, bright with small clouds, almost as it would have been at the time of the Transfiguration. I saw the small house in Nazareth, the house of the Holy Family, and prayed kneeling before the Crypt of Annunciation; with my eyes I drank water from Jacob's well in Sychem, but about Jerusalem, I shout with vehemence:

O Jerusalem! Beg for forgiveness!
Why, by the stoning of God's prophets
are you destroying his law
Yahweh was sending?
You could not defend your walls
because in the city a plague lives
O Jerusalem! You who defile your victims
an enemy has infiltrated you
and will crush the gates.
How can goodness grow in you
when you are lying with Baal,
when there is so much licentiousness,
and so much shame
O Jerusalem! O City. Your strongholds
are for nought
because you befoul your Order and your Church
The enemy will destroy your walls and enter
into your temples.

Peace entered the room; we sat motionless, and after a moment the Pope asked,

"Why is this church over Christ's grave? Why is Jesus not attainable for simple people, thirsty for love and God's goodness? The grave should be in the sun and greenery over which birds sing. The grave should be in an open space under the blue skies. Yet all you have is commercialism and commercialism again."

He closed his eyes, tightened his lips, and in his imagination, in his heart, returned to Jesus Christ, to this long-ago Jesus Christ.

"I walked by myself from holy place to holy place in the depth of night, where silence reigned, and I didn't smell the perspiration of moneylenders. Here, I tell you for the first time, that I walked barefoot, and wore a robe bought in an Arab market. I almost looked like one of them. My feet hurt me terribly, my heart bled, but I was with the real Christ. I stopped at the place where He prayed on the road to Golgotha…and prayed. When I appeared at the walls of the Church of the Holy Sepulcher, I tried to enter, but the doors were locked, and the note pinned to the door said that the church was undergoing renovation. I went down on my knees, and kissing the walls, begged God to give me strength, to be a different man, to be a better priest for simple people. I begged Him to give me physical strength and enough brains to become, at least a shadow of his Apostle Peter; to fulfill the Will of God and my predestination to serve Him. I begged Him again and again not to give me anything more, only deep faith in His Goodness, to believe in the goodness of humanity, and that His Faith should never leave me. My hands hurt me; my shoulders hurt, my heart was beating so fast I thought it would leave me. Most of all, I felt my bleeding feet; and I have so many roads to travel. But I was happy that I could talk to Jesus Christ man to man. My thoughts were full of love for Him…

Judean Desert: It is difficult to tell this earth,
'You are beautiful.'
On the slopes the brown rocks hang and penetrate bent clouds.
Cars rip the air and rain.
It is pointless to look for a trace of green.
People have gone far away. It is impossible to live here
The road is not leading to those places,
but running away from them.
So You came to this place, not to say,
'You are beautiful.'

The place was not important. You are searching for people
To search for them everywhere You have to appear
        in some place.
You chose this one.
The whole earth is coming to this Earth and through her
becomes the thing which is
Everything through Him Who Is.
There was no meeting of this earth
with Who Is Everything
that was Called Creation...
To have for your own, to possess,
To hold in existence
Oh, earth, oh earth, no trace of freshness or beauty left in you;
Even when you were young you were not graceful
Only some of your nooks were full of beauty.

"As I boarded the airplane for Europe, a priest looked at me from head
to toe and asked, 'Bishop, what happened to you? Where are your
shoes?'

"I replied, 'I hurt my foot.'

"'It looks like you hurt both feet. Both your socks are bloody and
dirty.'

"I did not care to discuss what happened, so I replied, 'Forgive me,
but I did not remember to count my feet or even glance at my socks.'

"The priest looked at me. I'm sure he thought to himself, 'Our
Bishop is sun struck.'

"I should have said, 'Your bishop is God struck.' But I was numb. My
feet hurt terribly. In front of me was an unknown road. How could I
make that long journey?"

27

On the Foreground of a Cryptonym

IN his *Ecclesiam Suam* Paul VI had some positive things to say about atheists. "They are people directed by anxiety, and often by noble desires; they possess utopian ideals and dream about justice and progress; their goals revolve around that which in their opinion is better and almost godly."

Paul VI and Primate Wyszyński were convinced that Bishop Wojtyla was one of the few who could unite believers and nonbelievers in the name of Christian principles. In his ethical study, 'Love and Responsibility' Wojtyla pointed the way for the Church's return to the source of love, faith and moral responsiblity, thereby uniting individuals and nations. The Pope was convinced that this "man from a far away country" could be a man of destiny for the Church and for humanity. On December 30, 1963, Wojtyla received the nomination for the position of Archbishop of the Cracow archdiocese, the position that Prince Sapieha, the remarkable churchman who had discovered young Karol, had once occupied.

On March 7, 1964, the day before his formal investiture, Karol received a telegram from Primate Wyszyński, "Before your Excellency's Ingress to the archcathedral of Saint Waclaw in Wawel, the capital of Saint Stanislaw, the martyr Bishop, and blessed Wicenty Kadlubek, we the faithful greet you in common prayer, with great feeling and deep hope. We bless you with our hearts and wish you an abundance of God's grace and love."

On Sunday, March 8 the weather was cloudy and cold, but crowds of people nevertheless gathered on Wawel hill. A stiff wind ripped banners of different colors and shapes into peculiar rhythms which together with the ringing of bells created reassuring music. The conductor of this orchestra was the largest and most melodious tower bell in Cracow and the country, 'Zygmunt.' It was the spokesman and messenger of love, passing through the ancient walls of the cathedral to enter the worshippers' hearts. The costumes were as colorful as the music. Tall black hats of coal miners stood out against the red blouses worn by women from the Wadowice region. There was also the Cracow intelligentsia, including professors from Jagellonian University dressed in their academic robes, and many children. Inside the cathedral, filled both with people and ancient pictures hanging on the walls, flowers were held by young and old, or they were placed in vases on the altars, under the pictures and even around their frames in long intricate strands.

The church was full of past and present friends of Lolek Wojtyla, among them his theatrical mentor, Mieczyslaw Kotlarczyk, with his wife, Zofia, the daughter of Irena Szkocki whom Lolek always called, 'Babcia' and in whose house he had spent many memorable days. There was the writer, Tadeusz Kwiatkowski, with his wife, Halina Królikiewicz. They all knew there would be no more theatrical performances with Lolek, nor summer excursions to the mountains, no kayak races on the Mazurian lakes, nor long ski expeditions in winter. In a corner of the cathedral was Krystyna Dębowski, the present wife of the artist, Tadeusz Ostaszewski, who wept openly. On the left, close to the altar, an actress, Danuta Michalowski, waited to see the face of Lolek, who was in the sacristy, being outfitted in silk, silver and gold, as the highest Church official of the Cracow archdiocese. A fragment of Pushkin's *Eugene Oniegin* appeared in Danuta's mind. She had played the role of Tatiana opposite Lolek in the Rhapsodic Theater production. Tatiana's barely audible words came from her trembling lips:

> Why are you clinging to me so much today?
> Why do you suddenly notice me?
> Is this because I entered the great world of society,
> because I am powerful and rich,
> and because fate lifted me so high?...

Danuta looked around and noticed Halina's face streaming with tears. She lowered her head and whispered, "Everything is gone with the mountain wind."

In various other parts of the cathedral the Kluger, Stolf and Kudliński families were gathered; also the Schroeders, Góreckis, Markiewiczs and Brauns. Some were somber; others smiling. There were Christians and Jews, rich and poor, young and old; but a predominance of youth. The oldest worshipper could not remember such a variety of people.

The ceremony of Ingress began at 9:45 A.M. the Monsignor Curator greeted the Archbishop in front of the cathedral by giving him the gold box containing relics of St. Stanislaw to kiss. Next, the Archbishop climbed the steps to the main entrance of the cathedral where the metropolitan Curia greeted him and Prelate Bogdan Niemczewski presented him with the key to the cathedral. The man of this holy day then crossed the threshold of the ancient church and a great chorus started singing, *Ecce Sacerdos Magnus qui in diebus suis placuit Deo*... The walls trembled in song and emotion. Lolek walked slowly toward the main altar, looking left and right, smiling to his acquaintances, thinking, "The doors of the past are closed forever and now the doors of service to God and humanity are opened..."

On almost all the faces of his friends he saw tears. He didn't have strength enough to whisper or nod his head, because his own tears fell from his face onto the beautiful robes that weighed him down to the ground. He strove to maintain control. "I have to be strong and think only about God and the goodness of man; everything else I must put in a box, lock, and dump into the Wisla river."

But how could one throw away the happenings and emotions of so many years? Words of Paul VI, spoken at Vatican II helped, "'...If Vatican diplomacy stopped developing or disappeared, world secular diplomacy would be deprived of the example of constructive methods on how to work for peace in this world.'" Lolek tried to find a niche for himself in this diplomacy, which gave him endurance to survive the strenuous forms of Ingress.

Afterward he told me, "During this long walk from the entrance to the main altar, I recalled a message which I recently sent to the faithful from my Archdiocese,

Remembering the past gives me a deep feeling of responsibility. If this feeling does not lead me to fear, I thank Jesus Christ and His Mother who I believe and trust deeply. I must add and never forget my sincere devotion to the people. At this particular moment, my thoughts and my heart go out to all the people in my Archdiocese, to mothers, fathers, to youth, sick, suffering, to simple, educated, to everybody with whom I am united in life and Christian belief. This natural unity is the result of the effort of all people of good will.

I have to admit that this mental shift enabled me at that particular moment to clear my head and approach my speech in the cathedral with inner vigor. I began,

'To enter this cathedral without emotion is impossible. I must say more precisely, it is impossible to enter this cathedral without inner fear, because inside these walls there exists the tremendous greatness of our history, of our complete past. In this cathedral, all the monuments, sarcophagi, altars and sculptures speak to us full of names and deeds that mark a thousand years.'

"Nobody would believe, even though I never mentioned this to anybody that during this emotional speech in the royal cathedral, I was thinking about the Carpathian mountains covered with snow and of young people on skis; I was there among them, and we were going down the Kasprowy peak. Driving snow hit at our faces, obscuring our vision, and I feared that we would never arrive safely. A frozen wind pierced my clothing and stung my body. I felt this was the end of my friends and me, the end of my love...

"You know that the human brain is a great miracle and those fearful thoughts gave me tremendous energy and vision, thereby helping me concentrate on my speech in this historical cathedral.

"When I entered, my past appeared before me in detail. I thought about the faces around me covered with tears, about friends from my youth, and all those things which I could no longer do and about which I cannot talk.

Such is the detail of St. Stanislaw's sarcophagus and how much meaning it holds. Last night I took a pilgrimage to the grave of Cracow's Bishop, blessed Wicenty Kadlubek, and today I remind myself that under this altar at which I stand, my predecessor rests; his name I am afraid to mention because everyone is aware of the significance of Adam Stefan Cardinal Sapieha. On November 1, 1946 he placed his hands upon me and consecrated me for the priesthood. I must also reflect upon Queen Jadwiga...'

Here my eyes went to the faithful as I searched for Halina. I searched for confirmation of my admiration for a woman who is a source of life and love. Then I added,

'I should include in my spiritual travelling one more person, Archbishop Eugeniusz Baziak. He consecrated me Bishop on September 29, 1958. Prince Sapieha, Primate Wyszyński and Archbishop Baziak treated me like a dear brother and when I think of them today I feel warmth in my heart and eternal love in my soul...'

"After this long church service I invited a group of old friends to the palace of Prince Sapieha at 3 Franciszkańska Street. I moved there from Kanoniczna, because the Cracow Curia almost forced me to think that I should live like the Prince. This rearrangement of my life's habits caused problems for me and my coworkers, but especially for my valet, Franciszek Wicher. He often complained that before there had been peace and quiet discussions in the palace where there was plenty of space; but this space is now filled with the continuous hubbub of students, actors, bishops, nuns and others who suddenly discovered their allegiance to the Church. Good Franciszek blamed everything on my popularity, and I replied every man has his own style. But with age and increasing visits not only from the inhabitants of Cracow, but from all over the country, Franciszek's lament grew. I realized that my residence in the palace created a lot of work for my assistants who tried to ease my daily life. I considered them not as servants, but as brothers and sisters. When I had a moment, I would polish my own shoes and straighten up the bedroom. It was easy, because I never developed the habit of collecting personal belongings, the only exception was books. They developed my intellect, my friendships and enabled me to deepen my love for God."

"I presume that the reception after your Ingress was a result of your popularity, too?" I asked.

"It was a proper occasion to explain to my friends, especially to my oldest friends from the arts that, as Archbishop, I would not have enough time for them, particularly when those dear close friends barged into my private quarters any time of the day or night."

I interrupted, "A painful task, to tell your old pals that 'now I am an important person and should curtail my meetings with you.' No more kayaks and skis, no more walking in the mountains, nor conversations with God and nature. And how about group discussion on art?"

"What should I do? Push aside my old friends and play the Prince of the Church, when I had always had the feeling in my heart and soul that I am only a servant of God and the people?"

He stopped; silence reigned and then he continued, "I got up at 5:00 A.M., washed and quickly dressed, then went to the chapel to pray by myself. At 7:00 A.M. I performed Holy Mass for my household. After that came a simple breakfast consisting of two eggs and bacon or ham, a piece of black bread and cup of coffee. Most often I had this nourishment accompanied by my closest coworkers, and we discussed Church and political matters. Then I went to my study, locked myself in and worked on various Church pronouncements, philosophical tracts or poetry. About twelve o'clock audiences and meetings began, where I learned about the world and received ideas from people of many political and social persuasions. At two o'clock was lunch, as you call it in America, but we call it dinner.

"All meals were cooked by the nuns from fresh produce, because I like to taste natural goodness. The meals didn't have much variety through the seasons; in summer and fall there was plenty of fresh produce, but in the winter and spring it was scarce."

"You mean the Archbishop's kitchen didn't use imported fruits and vegetables from Italy or France?"

"I always forbade it from a moral viewpoint. I don't think it is right that if a Polish peasant and worker can survive on a piece of meat and potatoes, a high Church official should be tempted by French truffles."

"I suppose that during the winter you didn't have many guests for meals?"

He smiled and continued his story. "After lunch sometimes I would take a short rest, but if I had guests, I would take them for a walk and conversation. Many times we wandered to the Kościuszko Mound, Wolski Grove or Ojców town; other times we strolled in Planty Gardens, sat on a bench and watched the passers-by. When I returned from these short excursions, I would work until supper which usually was around 7:00 P.M. Sometimes when I had guests this final meal was a little more elaborate and lasted longer due to circumstances and my desire to learn.

After supper I would go to my study to work on routine Church matters, but most of the time I would try to spend a few hours on literary creativity. In Cracow I imposed the standard routine that lights be out by twelve o'clock except in the chapel where I prayed for a few hours or again wrote."

"Did you have the same habit during the holidays?"

"Not exactly. During my trips abroad the schedule was altered. Also, Christmas and Easter weeks I was available twenty-four hours a day to everybody who desired to see or pray with me.

"I suppose the crowning point of the Archbishop's ceremony for me occurred in the fall of 1964 when I arrived in Rome to take part in continued discussions at Vatican II and the Holy Father, Paul VI, presented me with the pallium, which he blessed and placed upon St. Peter's tomb."

"What is a pallium?" I inquired tentatively.

My patient host smiled, "You don't have to know; as a matter of fact, there are millions of people who don't know, but it doesn't mean that they are lesser in the eyes of St. Peter or His Church. A pallium is a circular band of white wool with pendants worn by an archbishop and symbolizing his authority; but above all, it is the symbol of unity between St. Peter and the Rock on which the Church is built. The Holy Father, putting this symbolic band on my head then uttered these final words, '...You should live in good health for a long time... During this ceremony, nobody could explain this cryptonym to me, and I puzzled over it myself for a long while, until I was elected to the Holy See."

28
Metamorphosis

KONSTANCIN is a picturesque town strewn in and out with majestic pine and spruce. Lying in the Mazowsze Plains and reachable from Warsaw in half an hour by car, it is an ideal vacation place with its many lush garden paths. Retired politicians, scientists and artists are more noticeable than cars, and you can engage these promenading notables in interesting and revealing conversations. I know from personal experience, because I spent many days there resting and contemplating, as well as picking the brains of prominent inhabitants of this town.

Once, I stayed in a house with a garden and little brook. Between this house and the hospital hidden by trees and encircled by a fence was a one-family building resembling an eighteenth-century nobleman's manor. In this manor lived a retired political leader of Poland, Wladyslaw Gomulka, who, between June 1956 and December 1970, was the most important single power in this country. Short, skinny and bald, but with a friendly twinkle in his eyes protected by heavy glasses with horn-rims, this man didn't want to talk to me in the summer of 1968 when I asked him a few sharp questions about the Polish economy. But after his retirement from office I will never forget his meaningful answer in the summer of 1975: "The tragedy of Polish socialism is one paramount thing, that it came with the Soviet army and was not born through the trials and tribulations of the Polish people." At that time, political enemies, such as Roman Werfel said, "Gomulka is an apologist of Polish nationalism." Another one, Werfel's friend and an important postwar boss of Polish culture, Jerzy Borejsza, added, "What will remain of the present will be those achievements which sprang from our contempt of Western culture."

Gomulka had many powerful enemies of his economic and political liberalization and was sabotaged even by faithful friends in the implementation of his program. When confronted with workers' riots in the port cities of Gdańsk and Szczecin, he gave up his power to Gierek and disappeared into the oblivion of retirement.

Nearly every day in the town of Konstancin, he would leave his house at ten o'clock and walk slowly with an ordinary dog pulling at its leash. Beside him was his wife Zosia, a bit shorter than he, who was usually dressed in a light brown leather jacket or sometimes a black one with white spots. Some fifteen steps behind them followed a body-guard who also doubled as a driver.

On Monday mornings at about twelve o'clock Gomulka went out alone with his dog while his wife and driver went shopping.

On one of these mornings I joined him, and we talked about Stalin, Khrushchev, international politics and Poland. From those conversations I deduced that Gomulka was an honest man and even more intelligent than I had suspected. Only in international affairs was he to some extent simplistic. He believed that socialist countries would have a 'brotherly' attitude toward Poland when dealing in the economic sphere; also, that because he left Stalinism and did not collectivize agriculture but rather, allowed small private industry and commerce to flourish, the United States should give Poland enormous loans and credits with low interest. This is how he described his economic tack: "The change in our policy toward trade was not a momentary one. We thought that well-developed trade was not only no threat to a socialist economy but could act as a useful supplement to it. This is why we supported growth of trade and small private enterprise." Naturally, he was again thinking that Western capitalist countries would swamp his native land with various profitable ventures. When he said that he "re-organized the work of the public security apparatus and directed it only to fight espionage and other hostile activity against People's Poland and the interest of the state," he was thinking that Western countries would consider such action as a plus. He was disappointed when nobody in the West reacted toward his liberalization positively, but in the East his moves were regarded as a "weakening of national discipline."

In September 1960, he went to the United States to deliver a speech at the United Nations, thinking that American capitalists would use this opportunity to talk to him about economic cooperation. Again he was disappointed, and instead of staying in New York, went to visit his sister, Josephine, who had been living in the United States for many years. Then, he returned to Warsaw. The next day he talked with

Primate Wyszyński. They were close to each other, because both had sat in Stalin's jail.

During one of my promenades with Gomulka he said, "Cardinal Wyszyński urged me to abandon my shallow atheism and become a practicing Catholic because, 'this change would do good to your heart and your soul.'"

"What did you reply?"

"That I am already under pressure from all sides because I let the Church function normally, and if somebody discovered that I, an old atheist, had become a practicing Catholic, the Party would consider me crazy. Then I asked the Primate, 'Don't you think I have done plenty to improve material and spiritual conditions in the country?'

"He agreed and said, 'This improvement will not last long. As I see it, the Front is being organized against you because the opposition thinks you want to slowly dismantle socialism in Poland.'

"When I asked him who the friends of our country are, he replied that the Roman Catholic Church under his leadership was willing to try to develop Christian Socialism with cooperation from the Party. Once he even handed me a piece of paper on which ten points of his 'crusade for social love' were printed."

"There was nothing wrong with his philosophy," I answered and at this moment Gomulka's dog pulled him forward. He yelled "Heel!" and turned to me, "But imagine giving the modern Ten Commandments to a modern atheist who is the First Secretary of the Party; it was rather ridiculous."

"Wyszyński was an extremely religious man and liked your being in the Party. He was the top man in the Church, and so it was an exchange between two top people. But tell me, why didn't you invite Pope Paul VI when Poland was celebrating the 'Millennium'? He was very much for the Polish Socialist experiment and you would have profited by his visit."

"It was a mistake, I admit, but you have to know that during my Party Chairmanship, I had many enemies in the ministries of foreign and interior affairs. Their motto was simple, 'If worse within the country— it is better for us.'"

We were both tired and sat on the nearest bench under a shady pine tree; the dog started digging for something beneath it. Gomulka continued, "Those Stalinists, some of them outright agents, were sabotaging my foreign and domestic policies. They spread rumors in villages that collectivization was coming and therefore peasants should not work hard since the State would take their land anyway. At the same time, factories were not delivering enough agricultural machinery to the villages, because they had received instructions from someone in Warsaw that they should slow down due to forthcoming new agricultural policies. As a result, individual farmers did not have enough harvesters or tractors to work efficiently on the land. State and cooperative farms, which work on fifteen percent of the land, didn't have use for excess machinery. Then, I dismissed the Minister of Agriculture in an attempt to correct the situation, but in the meantime we lost the harvest.

"These enemies of the Polish nation also tried to destroy its culture. They built steel and chemical factories near lovely ancient Cracow; also, a new city called Nowa Huta for the workers, saying that the tens of thousand of people living there would radicalize the citizens of Cracow who were the citadel of Polish conservatives. The result was that chemical fumes produced by the various industrial establishments around Cracow were rapidly destroying ancient churches, the royal castle, beautiful medieval and postmedieval buildings and other historical structures, such as Sukiennice. But the 'positive socialists' fumes did not influence the reactionary citizens of the ancient Polish capital. Instead, the workers of Nowa Huta demanded that a church be built for them."

"Why was there so much fuss and negative international publicity about this church?" I inquired.

"Again, this is my fault, because instead of examining the explosive situation myself which involved thirty thousand workers and their families, I relied on a report by the Director of Religious Affairs who stated that there were already two churches."

"Really, there were just two chapels."

"Probably the real reason behind these difficulties was that Bishop Wojtyla, a terrific organizer and speaker, who already as vicar in the little town of Niegowić had forced the government to issue a permit for the building of a church, was well known according to an offical report as a 'rabble rouser.' Even at that time we were collecting everything about him, including clippings of his writings. We had him under constant surveillance."

"It looks like you are talking about a real democracy where everybody can spy on everybody."

"Wojtyla's unusual popularity among people, and especially among the young population, was dangerous from the point of view of the Ministry of the Interior. I had read a few of his speeches that expressed positive opinions even from the viewpoint of rigid socialists; they were against neither the State nor the system, but against human weakness. Nevertheless, the Interior Intelligence attempted to push some beautiful women on him; however, they did not succeed. Before he became Archbishop, the militia installed listening devices in his private quarters, but somebody always disconnected them and the militia gave up."

"I see you tried in the wrong way to get him on your side. Did you try to talk to him?"

"We did. And it seems to me that he was a positive man with many progressive ideas, which were perhaps at that time reaching too far into the future."

"Instead of incurring unnecessary expense and assuming an unethical approach, you should have been reading Wojtyla's cycle of twenty-one articles, *Primer of Ethics*, printed in the weekly *Tygodnik Powszechny*. In one of these he noted,

'The Christian ethic defends not only social virtues which are the priceless inheritance of Revelation, but also the basis of human virtues, and therefore existence itself. A person is free, but this freedom is not independent of society; a person is free within the framework of social life. Freedom is used fully only when it has this social base and when it helps to develop these social virtues as the realization of common good. A human being cannot flourish nor develop outside this common good.'

Don't you think that you as a Communist could sign your name to this?"

"Well spoken and truthful. Now I see that we did a lot of wrong to this man, but you must take into account the internal political atmosphere at the time as well as the international political situation. But you are right, listening to malicious advisers, I missed the opportunity of closer cooperation with the Church."

"Wojtyla has told me that the government forceably removed peasants from villages surrounding Cracow to build the Lenin Steel

Works; afterward the government brought in thousands of laborers to replace the peasants. When those workers tried to build themselves a church, the government sent armed militia to disburse the workers."

"This happened before I came to power," replied Gomulka. "The building of Nowa Huta started in 1949."

"Wojtyla told me that in December 1965, Pope Paul VI invited him and his friend Reverend Gorzelany to a private audience during which he gave them a piece of rock taken from St. Peter's grave and said, 'Take this rock to Poland and let it be the keystone for the Holy Mother Church which you are building in Nowa Huta.' Wojtyla said, 'During this audience, the Holy Father handed us a thousand dollar gift for the church. I think it was a symbol and indication that there were great possibilities for cooperation between the Vatican and Poland. Instead, when we returned to our country, the *leitmotif* of the government's propaganda was that 'the Pope was trying to buy Poland and that Karol Wojtyla was his most trusted agent.'"

"What do you think about that?" I asked Gomulka, who at that moment bent down to pet his little dog.

"What can I say? It was a political mistake. Our constitution and our Government proclaims religious freedom and the Church was eager to work with us openly. But we were forced to consult Moscow, and at least publicly, we could not say that we were willing..."

I felt pity for this old, shrinking, bald man who was once the most powerful leader of the country. Now, sitting on a bench, he was trying to explain his difficult position at that time of opportunity when he did not have the courage to conduct his policy. Here he startled me with the following, "You should know that I met with Primate Wyszyński on a regular basis, and when people from the Party discovered this, started spreading rumors that I was ready to become a practicing Catholic and an anti-Semite, although everybody knew that my wife was Jewish and that I never divided people according to religious belief. The reason for my meetings with the Primate was to convince him that he should go among his faithful more often and persuade them to work harder and produce more and better goods which would result in uplifting economic conditions within the country."

At this moment, his dog returned to the bench with a strange companion and I asked Gomulka, "Why is this other dog wearing such a peculiar collar?"

"Every time I go for a walk with my dog this stranger appears out of nowhere, and I don't know why he loves my dog so much." It was a rather well-known fact that secret service agents used dogs to carry listening devices, but I didn't ask him about that directly. Instead, I thought I would be more circumspect.

"Is it true that during the ceremony of transferring the body of Wojtyla's mother from Wadowice cemetery to her resting place in Cracow, the Interior Ministry placed a dozen male and female agents there to pose as guests or perhaps as grave diggers? What was the purpose?"

"How should I know? I don't think anybody should worry about any grave except his own." I could tell he was peeved at this strange question.

"With regard to the intelligence service, I will admit that ours did have knowledge of Sapieha's and Wyszyński's efforts to have a Polish pope. But, to this day, I wonder what or who inspired them to choose Karol Wojtyla as a candidate."

"I presume because they recognized in him a man with character and talents."

He did not comment, just added, "We always had three men under surveillance."

"You mean Sapieha, Wyszyński and Wojtyla?"

"Yes."

"But why?"

"Sapieha due to his extensive international political connections. We thought it would be possible through him to establish economic contacts faster and at lower cost; so we tried to make a list of those prominent people who were in touch with the Prince. As for the two others, we discovered early through out political connections in Italy that John XXIII and after him, Paul VI, perhaps even more, were considering a Polish Pope. Logic led us to surveillance of Wyszyński and Wojtyla. High officials of the Vatican Curia were maneuvering underground to prevent this from materializing and you should know the reason why."

"I presume nationalism and a fear of losing power because of a foreign Pope."

"You can explain the far-sighted policy of Paul VI with only two words: Soviet Union. He thought that electing a pope from a socialist country would help develop permanent *rapprochement* with Moscow and result in a renaissance of Christian Churches in the land of the

October Revolution. That was a reason he nominated many new members who supported his policy to the College of Cardinals. But the Curia performed the 'holy double-cross' and maneuvered in such a way that Cardinal Albino Luciani was elected."

Here I stepped in and said, "I guess somebody more powerful made this 'holy double-cross' because the sixty-six-year-old newly elected Pope John Paul I ruled only thirty-three days and died suddenly."

"If you are religious, you might say that God called in John Paul I early because he had such a beautiful smile."

"I remember from the first day of his pontificate everybody called him the 'smiling Pope.' This characteristic gave him a lot of publicity in the media."

Gomulka continued his talk, "If you believe in socialism and think that a Pope with progressive inclinations could help the world, then surely you must thank god or at least the living friends of Paul VI."

Suddenly both dogs appeared at our feet and I bent down to touch the collar of the strange dog.

"Let your friend Gierek explain. He talked to Paul VI, was in constant touch with Wyszyński and naturally with Wojtyla. I am retired. Only dogs listen to me now."

"Please tell me how you career ended so abruptly?"

He rose from the bench, put his dog on the leash and said, "I have to go home. My wife is waiting. But if you walk with me, I might try to give you some bits of information."

"Surely. As I recall, at the end of the 1960s you became popular because of a saying."

"Yes, 'A Pole should have one country and that country must be People's Poland.' At that time, June 1967, war was in progress between Israel and Egypt, and all the socialist countries were on the side of Egypt. Some idiot in the satirical weekly *Szpilki (Needles)* wrote, 'We agree with the opinion of the First Secretary that we should have one country, but why should this country be Egypt for comrade Gomulka?' A Zionist group of Polish writers started campaigning against me; one of them, Janusz Szpotański, even wrote a play about me."

"It is unbelievable that a satirical weekly or a play should topple you."

"Gradually, all Polish intellectuals came out against me, spreading various rumors about my primitive approach to cultural and economic affairs. A combination of political and social riffraff in alliance with various elements in the Party enlarged this opposition. I did not have support among the young members of the Party, because I neglected to educate them in the belief that the only road to Polish socialism wasliberalization of rigid economic and social aspects of our reality. I also neglected Primate Wyszyński and his sound advice which led to destabilization. But the crowning blow, the *coup de grace* if you will was the Polish cooperation with the Soviet Union in toppling Dubcek and his democratic reforms in Czechoslovakia. People started saying, 'What is this crazy Gomulka doing supporting liberalization in Poland and helping to kill the same thing in Czechoslovakia?' They didn't know that I was trying to be neutral, but our Eastern enighbors persuaded me otherwise." He looked around, spotted the strange dog with the peculiar collar again and made a wry comment, "Even now my enemies do not trust me, and send not people but dogs to eavesdrop."

"I feel that what you say has merit, but in my opinion, the economic problems that besieged you were the real cause of your political collapse."

"You don't have to be a genius in economics or politics to understand that if you sell the West Polish coal, sulphur or agricultural products for hard currency, and then buy with this currency sophisticated western instruments for Polish ships being built in Gdańsk shipyards, which are sold for soft rubles with which you cannot do much except buy available goods in the Soviet Union that, you do not enrich your own country. You deplete it. By buying entire factories in America or Germany for dollars on loan or credit, when those factories, often equipped with antiquated machinery, only produce goods for your domestic and eastern European market, how do you repay your loans and other obligations which were originally drawn in American or German banks?"

"What was your approach?"

"Simple," he said when we reached the gates of his serene domicile, "I strove for self-sufficiency by building a sound agricultural system, one which would deliver enough produce for domestic and some for foreign markets; together with the profit obtained from the sale of Polish coal, other minerals and high quality finished industrial goods. By selling to the West, we could collect enough capital to modernize our factories and to rebuild industry to the extent that we would attain an economic balance and self-sufficiency."

"To talk about this is simple, but you would need the understanding and cooperation of your workers and peasants, as well as a hard-working government apparatus to administer this delicate balancing act."

"You also forgot the purely political element. I was naive in thinking that our socialist neighbors would understand and support me." He dropped the rest of the sentence and concluded, "Everything else you know; strikes in Baltic seaports, unnecessary brutality on all sides, and then Gierek came in."

Gomulka opened the metal gates, extended his hand and in a soft voice said, "As a Communist, perhaps I should not say this, but Karol Wojtyla could be an important man in our difficult international situation... providing he stays healthy..."

The second dog was nowhere to be seen.

29
Nikifor

"WHO does not know about this great primitive painter from Krynica?" John Paul II began his new story.

"I don't except that I saw his exhibition, some years ago, on New York's Madison Avenue," I replied, "and was impressed by his colors."

"He did have an exhibition in New York; also in Paris, London and other capitals of Europe."

"Just a few months ago I read in the papers that he was crippled and almost blind; they say he had tuberculosis. Nobody knew how he appeared in Krynica spa, everyday early in the morning, and made his way to the foot of Parkowa hill, to sit and paint." When I finished my sentence, I realized that instead of listening I was talking, but my host did not mind and pursued his story.

"He didn't know who his father was, or when he was born. All he knew was that his mother was a cripple. When he became famous in the 1950s and 1960s he went to the local church and said, 'I need a birth certificate, but I don't know where I was born, or in which church I was christened.' The old priest engaged him in conversation, and finally they agreed on the date of birth as January 1, 1895."

I laughed; "I guess in those matters the church is liberal."

"This is true, but you must remember that this man made Krynica spa famous by putting it on the international tourist map. Imagine, a crippled, almost blind man, sitting many hours, day after day, painting small-sized pictures of dilapidated wooden churches, spooky castles, priests and people with haunted expressions; also, magnificent figures of Christ, and some saints whom he poked fun at. He created such an atmosphere in this old and to some extent forgotten southern town at the foot of the Carpathian Mountains, that every year hundreds of people from all over Europe travel to Poland to see Nikifor, and buy his saints or devils, angels or gods, shining with silver luster, encrusted with red and green, yellow or blue. The world created by him was difficult to describe, but filled hearts with hope and joy as well as sadness. He executed his illusions on pieces of ordinary paper with watercolor, or a few times on pieces of cloth with oil colors. And don't forget, he was almost blind."

I was fascinated by this story and asked "Holy Father, is it true that he didn't know how to read and write?"

"Yes, not only did he not know how to read and write, but he was, as they say, as poor as a church mouse, and if he saw a man, woman or child poorly dressed, would hand them his picture for nothing, saying, 'This is from God.'

"When those people thanked him and searched their pockets for money, sometimes offering him a few zlotys, he would say, 'Give it to God, give it to the poor. I am a wealthy man. I don't need money.' Then he returned to his work and mumbled peculiar words about the Pope and Rome, about God and angels."

"I guess he figured out that not everything is right in the world, and that he should complain to somebody," I commented.

"The local priest heard his complaints about God and the Pope, went to him and asked, 'What are your complaints?' From his seat Nikifor touched the priest's cassock to hold one of the buttons and said, 'Nobody can help me talk to God, and shortly I will see him and talk myself, I don't need anyone to come between me and God. But on earth I have something to say to the Pope in Rome.' Then he let go of the button and returned to his painting.

"The clergy said, 'You know you are in the southern part of the country—a long way from Rome. You have no money. You're almost blind and a cripple, so how can you go there?'

"Nikifor stopped painting and replied, 'Certainly I do not expect help from you. You take care of holy matters and are not interested in a cripple like me, here on earth.'"

Here, I ventured, "Such a man should at least be made a bishop, and dictate his philosophy for posterity, for some priest to learn a little about Providence and people."

The Pope looked at me strangely but his patience with interlocuters is well known, and so withheld a reply. He continued, "One day the artist disappeared from the foot of Parkowa hill, and practically everyone in the country talked about Nikifor. Where was he? What had happened to him?

"Naturally, local authorities were worried because the spa had lost its main attraction."

"After a few weeks they found him in the port of Szczecin on the Baltic Sea, trying to make an arrangement with some sailors to take him by sea to Italy."

"Did he succeed?"

"When one sailor refused, he asked, 'Was Jesus Christ God or a man?' "The sailor was not religious and replied, 'I guess when Christ was in heaven, he was God, but when He visited the earth, He was a man.'"

"Naturally, I presume Nikifor would have tried to walk on the water," I said, smiling.

"Yes, he did. He tried and almost drowned. Two sailors pulled him out, and took him to the militia station. When they discovered that this small nutty man was Nikifor, they took him to the best hospital in town, and after a few days, the militia with a VIP escort, took him back to the Krynica spa and to his usual place of artistic activity. But he was a changed man. He began painting devils in cassocks dancing with young girls, and other pictures in which he expressed his bitterness."

"He was probably mad at the world, the Pope and the Church."

"I presume so. He became weaker, but still painted vigorously, although his creations were more wild and darker in color. He developed a talkative mood and repeated many times, mind you in confidence, that the Pope should visit him, otherwise great tragedy would come to humanity, 'To save the people and the earth from complete destruction, it was not a big sacrifice and humiliation for the Pope to visit insignificant Nikifor.'"

"How do you know about all this in such minute detail? It is a fascinating story."

'But I was fascinated by his heart and soul, and kept trying to discover for myself the spiritual functions of these. This for me was a constant miracle. Remember, Nikifor, simple, crippled and half blind, was trying to say more through his paintings about humanity than the great philosophers were able to say."

He stopped, and I saw on his face great bewilderment. "We don't know what we need for our soul. We search, fight, run around and we don't know that all for which we search is within us. This simple Nikifor was making fun out of the wealth of our world, and showing us through color and design the road to the immortal beauty of inner existence."

"One day I received a letter from Halina Królikiewicz. At that time I was Archbishop and Metropolitan of the Cracow region. Halina gave me lots of information about the artist, and mentioned that he was dying of tuberculosis. But he still clung to the hope that Pope Paul would visit him. It was a pointless, fruitless hope, she said in her letter; and she suggested that I visit in the name of the Pope, especially since this great primitive artist was constantly talking about some secret he would like to divulge to the Holy Father. I felt that I should take into consideration this suggestion without even consulting the Pope, and my reason was that I like his painting enormously, especially one called *Small Town*, which made a tremendous impression on me. This canvas represented a church, or maybe a three-story palace, with two towers on which two crosses were placed. In front of this church, or palace was a fountain, or maybe a monument, on top of which a woman stood, holding in her hands an urn from which water was sprinking on bushes and trees. The canvas was painted in green, blue, grey, yellow, yellow-grey and violet from which shone a silver glow. I am familiar with several languages, but cannot describe the emotions the paintings brought to my heart and soul."

When he said that, I looked at his face closely and never saw in any man such a puzzled yet inspired expression. It was not proper for me to interrupt his narrative with a question, so I listened.

"I knew this part of the Carpathian Mountains well. Many times I was on the Dunajec and Poprad rivers, drinking water from them and fishing. I also visited Piwniczna town as well as Żygiestów-Zdród and Muszyna, not to mention Krynica which was a not-much-frequented health resort before the war. But I didn't know that the primitive painter Nikifor lived in this town from 1920, or maybe many years earlier. I discovered him in the early 1950s, but I didn't know much about his spiritual inclinations. The long letter which I received from Halina Królikiewicz made me curious, especially his threat that the world would be destroyed if he could not divulge to the Pope his great secret. One day I said to my housekeeper, Maria Morda, and to my valet, Franciszek Wicher, that I was going away for a short time, but they

should not talk about this because people would think their archbishop was confused by going to see a deranged man who demanded to
meet the Pope. One hot day in August, I arrived in Krynica and went
to the dilapidated house full of papers, frames, pencils, canvases, paints
in various shaped jars, and remnants of worn-out clothes; everything
was impregnated with a specific odor mixed with the fragrance of freshly cut pine; when I entered, Halina appeared (I presume she was taking
care of the dying man). I approached the bed with its covers in dissarray
on top of which Nikifor sat with a canvas in his hands. Halina whispered to him that I had arrived, and imagine: he started to recite passages from my drama *Job*, written by me in such a way that shivers engulfed me, and I thought that my skin was covered with a burning
rash.

> You are here, thus I will tell you
> today my soul is howling in me
> so you will hear with howling
> which comes up and tears –
> o you, cursed day, cursed –
> when my mother took me inside herself
> I condemned the sun of that day
> I condemn the brightness of that day.
> This day should not have dawned
> this day should be lost in time
> such a heavy bane of life
> such misery and destitution –
> I curse my life. Excommunication be imposed upon it.
> I curse my days because they are closed to me
> and they are closed to fulfillment
> to roll, to discard,
> to forget...and to cover with a shawl.
> Because you come in, so I said
> what I was supposed to say to you –

"The words of my drama flooded my mind, and I replied to Job:

> We came in because we saw the light in the mountains
> we knew where your herds were,

Bishop Wojtyla (left, with glasses) with Franz Cardinal König and Ferdynand Machay in Cracow Cathedral, April 30, 1963.

Archbishop Wojtyla while on a kayaking trip on the Mazurian Lakes, 1965.

Archbishop Wojtyla taking a break on a bicycle trip, 1965.

Karol Cardinal Wojtyla, 1967.

where they were grazing in the valleys between
    the rocks
News came that Job was burning
that you became a beggar
we came in to visit Job in sadness

Job:
My songs have gone with the current of a tempest and
my daughters are lost
my helpers and my possessions gone too
I became a queer man to the people –
Something of a drag, something of a beggar.

"I could not stand more recitation of my drama, and I cried out to Halina and to Nikifor, 'Leave me alone, give me peace!'

"They were startled by my sudden outburst, and Nikifor raised his bloodshot eyes and said to me, 'Anyhow, the Holy Father came to me.'

"'What kind of Holy Father am I? I am only Archbishop of Cracow.' I felt fatigued, so I sat on the edge of the bed, stretched out my hand and took this living human miracle in my hands. Then I began to cry, and when Halina noticed that, she too burst into tears. But Nikifor, loosening himself from my embrace, said,

"'Yesterday an archangel visited me, and asked me when am I coming, because God is waiting for me; he understands my paintings, he understands my stuttering, and he is waiting although he would like to see more of my paintings, which show him this world more accurately than reports of his angels; especially priests who are behaving outrageously – arriving in expensive cars, and feeding themselves on expensive food; they do not behave like Jesus Christ, they do not walk barefoot, they do not eat fish, simply prepared. They enegetically support rich people, people who make wars. I have to capture this in my pictures, but I don't know if I have enough time.'

"He was talking faster and clearer, and in this fervor he lost his stuttering.

"'God said to me a few times through this archangel that I should come in for a while, and show him my paintings, then he will resurrect me, and again I will return to earth to paint the world. Then God said to me through the archangel that he will believe me more than anybody else, because I suffer a lot. I endured a thousand times more suffering than any man in the world. An archangel also gave me a message from God that after I am gone, temporarily or permanently, the world will be changed. That's the reason I wanted to talk with the Pope today, because I don't want to talk behind his back; otherwise I have to say bad things about today's Pope. I want to tell him to repent, to walk on this earth barefoot, to radiate more love, but if he would say to me that he cannot do this, God will strike him and he will die.'

"He stopped, rose from his bed and continued,

"'I am sure that you are the Pope, but you are afraid to admit it to me. Otherwise, why are you here? You know, Halina is a good woman; she has taught me a lot of useful things. But it is too late. I have to go, I cannot keep God waiting forever. I have to repeat to the Holy Father that He should roll up his sleeves and start pursuing Christ's work, and go after believers and nonbelievers, and ask them for help too, because, as you know they are people. People are people.'

"He returned to the bed, sat on the edge and whispered,

"'If the Holy Father will talk like that, and act like that, I will support him in front of God, and he will win, because God will be on his side, and I too.'

"Then he whispered to me, 'Tell me, please. Are you really not the Pope? Or maybe you are the Pope in a different guise.'

"I replied, truthfully, that I was not.

"He didn't give up and asked again, 'But, you know him?'

"'Yes, I do.'

"Then he mumbled, 'Please impress on him that God is waiting for better work, otherwise...' and he stopped.

"Nikifor didn't say anything more. He raised his painful face, closed his eyes, folded his hands to pray and sat motionless. Halina said to me, 'Let's go out. He's talking with God.'

"It was the first and last time I saw this fascinating man and artist. They made films about him and about his paintings. They wrote thousands of articles and books in many languages, and his paintings were sold in galleries all over the world and made people wealthy. He lived poor, and suffered much. When tuberculosis took over, and he was spitting blood, people brought him to the hospital to a warm pleasant room, where he painted from dawn until late at night. He gave his paintings to nurses and scrubwomen, to anybody who didn't look well-dressed."

"Finally, what happened? How long did he stay in the hospital?" I asked, excitedly.

"As you know, September in Krynica is always beautiful, full of golds and greens; there are excursions through the mountains, crisscrossing, lots of singing; wooden churches look inviting.

"Nikifor sat in his room near the window, painting and painting. One day smart doctors discovered that physical work together with mental concentration is bad for tuberculosis sufferers. So they decided to deprive Nikifor of paper, brushes and color, and told him to rest. He looked at them and stuttering, asked, 'Is this a medical decision, or God's decision?'

"Naturally, most doctors think they are gods, so they didn't even bother to reply."

"It was terrible, but he was receiving excellent care," I added.

"I guess he was, but not the kind he wanted; so, as a result, on October 10, 1968, Nikifor died. When I heard about it, I cried, and went to the chapel and prayed, asking God for forgiveness."

I said, "I wonder what the last conversation was between Nikifor and God."

"This is a secret between the two of them. We'll never know. But later, much later, I gave a tongue-lashing to the Pope."

30
Millennium

"A S PRIMATE," Cardinal Wyszyński began another of our many dialogues, "I was trying to explain to the Polish Episcopate that we would do everything possible to expose Archbishop Karol Wojtyla to the outside world during this Millennium of Polish Christianity – organizing trips that would enable him to demonstrate his intellectual and spiritual vitality to various cardinals and other leaders of Christendom. It was not a difficult task on Polish soil, but it was just as important to convince people outside of our borders who would ask the simple question, "Why Wojtyla?" I had a standard reply, "Because Wojtyla is the best product of our Church in Poland," and would complete my answer with a question, "Can you show me someone more pious and brilliant in today's hierarchy of the Catholic Church?"

"Very good," I said, "Very good."

"Preparation for the celebration of one thousand years of Christianity in Poland began much in advance of the official date which was April 14, 1966. One thousand years ago, in the town of Gniezno, King Mieszko accepted Christianity through marriage with the Czech Princess Dąbrówka."

"It was a tremendous undertaking, I presume, fraught with political undertones, was it not?"

"I anticipated trouble, because the government was afraid of large gatherings that could spark demonstrations. I went to the First Secretary of the Party Gomulka and said 'For a few years a *Picture of Visitation* has been travelling through various churches around the country; the faithful are praying in front of this picture and there have been no demonstrations.'"

"He asked, 'What is this *Picture of Visitation?*'"

"I didn't want to describe in detail this painting of the Holy Mother which had been blessed by the Pope and I simply replied, 'The people of the Church are praying for the country, their families, the Church and for you – that you should live long for the good of the country.'"

"'I trust you and will give you permission, but you will be my hostage if something goes wrong,' he replied with a twinkle in his eye, adding, 'above all no political or anti-Soviet demonstrations.'"

"'We are not interested in demonstrations. You have reports from your militia and other agents that the Church, under my leadership, is appealing for calm, work and justice, and I presume that there is no difference between your wishes and mine; the only difference is the method. You are a Communist patriot. I am a Catholic patriot. But our common good is Poland.' This simple outburst brought tears to Gomulka's eyes.

"During the long celebration of Millennium, we never had a single disturbance. What is more, many high Party and government officials took part in the celebrations and even carried canopies over the heads of bishops."

"Karol wrote a few touching poems in connection with this event which were published in newspapers and widely discussed, and not just by Catholic intellectuals, but because they had universal appeal. I will not quote them, because you can find these poems in various collections. But let me tell you that the culminating point of the Millennium celebration in Gniezno, King Mieszko's city, was Archbishop Wojtyla's celebration of the Holy Mass."

"Was this because it was performed at midnight and hundreds of thousands gathered in an enormous field and sang under the stars of electric lights?"

"You don't know what led up to it?"

"If I knew, I would not ask you."

"Karol was a far-sighted man. I am speaking naturally about a spiritual element, but I also have to mention the physical."

What was he talking about? I thought to myself. Aloud, I asked, "And, what next?"

"What next? My God. It was fantastic religion and also theater."

"What kind?"

"He arrived in Warsaw a week before my departure for Gniezno.

During this time he wrote, performed Mass, preached, conferred with various government officials and prayed; in other words worked from five in the morning until one or two at night without interruption. When the time came to leave for Gniezno he told me that he would take the train. I answered jokingly, "As Primate I give you the order to go with me in my car."

"He obeyed the orders and went with you?"

"Naturally, he obeyed the order. But when we left Warsaw we noticed that the roads were packed with walking women, children, old and young people, those on bicycles, in horse-driven carts, and some even in automobiles with government markings – I presume they were Party officials. The weather was nasty, as it always is in April. One moment it was raining; next snow fell on the bundled-up people. All of them walked slowly, but at a steady pace. Great crowds were spotted here and there with flowers, brightly painted women's kerchiefs, crosses made from pine branches, and others of boards decorated with flowers. There was the impression that thousands of people were going on a crusade. Their religious chants created mystery – even the heavens were curious, because from time to time the sun would come out and give luster and happiness to the human faces. This unique exchange of feelings between the heavens, bogged down and tortured by April's cold weather, and the faces of simple people continued for hours. Karol, riding beside me in the comfortable car, constantly looked through the windows; I was annoyed by his restlessness and said, 'You took part in many processions to the Bright Mountain of Częstochowa and many other places. Why are you so emotional now?'

"'I did, but I never had the feeling I have now. Riding in a comfortable car while hundreds of women and children walk through this terrible weather...' Without waiting for my comment, he said to the driver, 'Please stop the car!' The driver stopped and Karol hugged me, saying, 'Thank you for letting me ride in the Primate's car.' He opened the door, jumped out, and disappeared in the crowd."

"I said to the driver, 'Please don't let the Archbishop out of our sight.'"

"'I have already lost him.'"

"What am I going to do? I thought. It was also important for us to exchange views on various subjects and compare notes.

"My old driver posed a question, 'Maybe he did something wrong?'

"'He is not capable of doing anything wrong. For him God comes first, then the people. This is his entire world.'

"'Your Eminence will forgive me, but I have observed the Archbishop for a long time and for him God is in first place; but young people take second.'"

"'Because he is young; I was young sometime ago too. Besides, you forgot that young people are people too.'"

"'I hope nothing happens to the Archbishop in this tremendous crowd.'"

"I replied, 'I hope he will not disappoint me, and be on time for Holy Mass.'"

"On that note my conversation with the driver ended. We both were quiet, listening to the chanting of the people and watching the flowers and crosses swing over the heads of hundreds of thousands of pilgrims.

"When I reached Gniezno, everybody was talking about Archbishop Wojtyla; that he and people from Wadowice carried a wooden cross. Gradually, the amazing story developed a few twists; one that the cross was so heavy that he fell down a few times; people tried to help him, but he refused. Another was that he walked barefoot through the mud. A few more variations were that he was singing. Someone even said he fainted under the cross and that they took him to the hospital. He did not reach his Golgotha.

"At the beginning, I was upset, because of the sensationalism involved. Then I reflected, saying that I knew Karol well and everything he did was sincere and came from the heart. At the same time, I gave instructions to the people around me to play down the sensational aspects of this incident. I asked my secretary to find the Archbishop and ask him to visit me. The celebration of the Millennium should be dignified and full of substance because we were observing the victory of Christ's ideas over tenth-century paganism. At this juncture of our development, through this unusual national observation of one thousand years of Christianity, our desire was to unite people from all walks of life for maximum effort in building a just state."

"Even if Wojtyla did behave like that, wasn't it in the character of religious observation?" I asked.

A note of disappointment appeared on the Primate's face, "To my taste, it was too theatrical, although this man bursts with talent and desires to give those talents real form and body."

"Was he on time to celebrate the Mass?"

"He was early, and explained to me that when he saw people from his native Wadowice carrying a cross, he had to help them."

"'Everyone was there. I was riding comfortably in a car and they were walking in mud up to their knees with a heavy cedar cross on their shoulders. What would you do in such circumstances?'

"While he said this a group of bishops gathered around and looked at me; I glanced at them and replied, 'I would do the same.'"

"His midnight Holy Mass was a revelation because of his masterful performance and the tremendous sensation and joy he caused. This Mass spilled out of the Church all over the town and fields and every place where microphones could reach the hundreds of thousands of people who sang and prayed with tremendous emotion. Everyone looked at the cross leaning next to the altar, and this symbol of suffering burned with an unusual glow. The glow was induced by electrical devices, but if you added to it songs, praying voices, thousands of burning candles and flowers held by women and children shining in the light of those candles, you felt tremors through your body and were a part of God's tremendous community. Then I realized that he was a master of human emotions."

"Did you have a chance to talk to him and hear his opinion about this successful midnight Mass?"

"He did approach me afterward to say, 'I don't yet know all the corners of my country. Now is the occasion for me to travel from place to place, examining the source of our strains as well as spending time on church services and plain conversations with ordinary people. Would you give me permission to do this?'

"I placed both my arms around him and we stayed like that for a minute without exchanging a word. He knew that I approved of everything he was doing."

"On the third of May, the day of the Polish constitution, we had a grand celebration in front of the picture of the Black Madonna of Częstochowa."

"I know that you revere the Holy Mother of Christ," I said, "but why do you call her the Black Madonna?"

"I am sure you are familiar with history and with the invasion of Poland in the seventeenth century by the army of Swedish King Charles X?"

"Yes, I know that at that time, the ruler of Poland was King John Casimir (1648–1668)."

"In 1665 the Swedish King's army reached Częstochowa and some of his soldiers invaded the church at Bright Mountain where the picture of the Holy Mother was hanging. They plundered the church, assaulted priests and nuns, and one of the Swedish soldiers slashed the face of the Madonna with his sword. According to legend, the picture of the Madonna was covered with blood that gradually dried and become black in color. The soldier dropped dead at the foot of the altar. Quickly, the tale spread throughout the town and to neighboring villages, to every corner of the country. People rallied in a tremendous outpouring of national fervor to beat the Swedish army. The Polish King proclaimed that from then on the Black Madonna would be called, 'Queen of Poland'."

"A charming legend."

"You have to know that such stories are part of a nation's soul and important to the health and development of unity." With that he returned to the subject, "On May sixth at Karol's invitation, I arrived in Cracow and took part in the well-organized celebration. The center of the festivities was the veneration of Bishop Szczepanowski, who was assassinated on April 11, 1079 by King Boleslaw the Bold. This brutal act was a result of the heated dispute between ecclesiastical and secular circles. The King accused the bishop of invasion of his prerogatives and the Bishop claimed that the King encroached upon Church power."

"It was a clever method of informing state authority that church power is real."

The Primate commented on my observation in a subtle way, "Pope Gregory VI excommunicated King Boleslaw who, as the result of a well-orchestrated campaign against him, was forced to leave the country and spend his last years in the Celovec Monastery in Carinthia. I have to admit that the affair of St. Stanislaw looks different depending upon historical perspective. The Church, many hundreds of years after that, constantly interfered with the affairs of the state, and Christianity lost its divine inspiration."

"I presume you subscribe to the popular expression, 'moderation should rule the game'?"

"The Church today must not go into raw politics but follow the visions and aspirations of the people, help them to better themselves ma-

terially and develop spiritually. We as clergy have to support the people
in their fight for justice and freedom of conscience. Karol Wojtyla understands this perhaps better than anybody else. His celebration of the
Millennium in Cracow brought people into the streets in a well-organized manifestation, and showed the authorities that the Church has
a power which should be used only toward the economic and spiritual
betterment of our nation."

"Gossip circulated that you as Primate were jealous of Wojtyla's popularity. The reason, at least the well-publicized reason, was that you
were seriously thinking of maneuvering yourself into the Holy See, and
Karol Wojtyla was your most important rival."

"You know as well as I do that this was untrue. The government
spread this kind of information for the purpose of weakening and dividing the Polish Episcopate, to create the impression that Wojtyla was
dangerous to the political establishment. The Party carefully observed
the organizational talents of the Cracow Archbishop who divided his
region into four parts, each having a different bishop with freedom of
activity who reported directly to him. This type of reorganization was
not received favorably by some of the clergy, and especially by secular
authorities, because they immediately noticed the improvement and
vigor of the Church under Karol's jurisdiction. He also brought to life
the Pastor's Council, which included, besides bishops, the lowest ranks
of clergy from the most remote parts of his Archdiocese. This Council
which met regularly in the Archbishop's palace in Cracow, discussed,
analyzed and made suggestions for improving the spiritual activity of
the Church. If you expand this type of reform to include the whole
country, then you can truly appreciate Wojtyla's organizational genius.
Naturally, he consulted with me on a regular basis, and the organization which functioned almost perfectly, gave Karol time for his literary
and philosophical writing, his never-dying ambition."

"Why do you think he always had this dual desire?" I asked.

He smiled, "Because he thought that a good pastor should enlarge
his spiritual activity by constant studying and writing. Through books,
essays and poems he could influence people not only in his country but
all over the world. A good example is his three hundred twenty-five
page book under the title *Persona e Azione* which caused great ferment
in Italy, France, Germany and naturally in Poland.

"In this book there are polemics with Jean-Paul Sartre, Roman Ingarden, Martin Heidegger, and even with his much admired Max Scheler." The Primate listed the names with a proud smile, "There are also Greek philosophers, as well as St. Thomas Aquinas. Paul VI read the book twice and one day he said to me, 'I didn't know that such brains existed among our *confraters*.'

"Wojtyla also developed a following among the younger clergy. A priest by the name of Franciszek Blachnicki started organizing college and university students into so-called 'oases'; groups of young people whom he took on long weekend excursions or sometimes during summer vacations to the mountains where they worked on farms, prayed, discussed philosophical and social subjects, and performed some liturgy. They even danced and sang through the night around the campfire developing relations between themselves and God. Karol, as a high clergy official, visited with them many times and took part in all of their activities including the dancing. Subordinates who heard distorted rumors about his trips into the mountains were rather shocked, but they could not raise their voices against their boss. The movement grew and spread to other parts of the country. Around the same time, Karol Wojtyla created yet another movement called 'Sacredsongs,' which was composed of young people playing on guitars and singing religious songs at various church holidays and even during the Holy Mass. This movement grew to the extent that it even reached the ears of the Pope. When I mentioned it to my beloved Archbishop he said, 'Look at the churches on Sunday. Have you ever seen so many young people there during your lifetime?'"

Primate Wyszyński concluded in a tired voice, "This was a sure way for Karol to go to the Holy See. Prince Sapieha was right and I was privileged to help in this endeavor. When a man has freedom of thought, and of action, and has access to knowledge and truth, he can be, with the support of hard work, the source of inspiration for his nation and sometimes of the world."

31
Some Unknown Pictures of Tragedy

"I will never forget those eyes, burning with hatred one second and love the next, peeking through the tumbling down hair as the autumn sun created flecks of light through the trees... then I lost consciousness...I felt physical movement, and with the last drop of awareness I knew that she was pulling me from the road to the ditch to save me from the wheels of the Nazi vehicle. After that I do not remember how I got to the hospital. Later, somebody told me that she had left her address with the attendant to let her know at the kiosk in the center of the city if they saved me. Others told me that she showed up at my bedside when I was still unconscious, stayed for a while, then disappeared.

"Later, much later, when I had recovered, I searched for her all over Cracow. People whom I met during the search informed me that she was dead. Others said that she left for Western Europe, and others that she was in Israel. I am still looking for her. I will not stop looking, because I will never forget her eyes of mercy..."

When John Paul II told me this story about the incident on the road from Zakrzówek, or more precisely from the Solvay Chemical Works, where he was hit by the German car and left to die, I deliberated with myself; should I ask him whether that was when his attitude toward Jews developed, although he was not certain that the woman who saved his life was Jewish. He read my mind and replied,

"I do not think that Christians should hate Jews, not any other nationality. You recall that Dr. Janusz Korczak, a Jew who perished with his children in the Nazi ovens, is the symbol of universal morality and religion. From early youth I have had many Jewish friends."

I am sure he was going back in time to this incident on the road. I also remembered what Reverend Stanislaw Kotowski, a friend of

Wojtyla's had told him,

> In Warsaw at 3–9 Zytnia Street was the Church of God's Mercy.
> Through this church you could reach the ghetto, and we took the
> opportunity to save one thousand Jews, among them some of
> Doctor Korczak's children. In the churches of St. Augustine, All
> Saints, which was located in the territory of the Ghetto, the Jews
> received help from priests and nuns. It is a well-known fact that
> nuns from the Holy Mother of Mercy order were integrating
> Jewish children with Polish children and moving them out to the
> country. When the Nazis discovered this, they arrested them and
> burned down the churches.

I heard other stories also, such as that priest Wojtyla during the
occupation worked closely in Cracow and other cities with the sisters
of the Holy Mother of Mercy to hide, feed and transport Jews from
ghettos to the countryside. It was Reverend Karol Wojtyla's idea that
Jewish girls should be accepted into convents for the duration of the
war. Also, on farms owned by the church, many young Jewish males
and females were employed by various orders.

He and other priests presented a plan that churches all over the
country with parish buildings should construct hidden rooms in the
basements and attics to enable Jews to hide. As a result many
prominent doctors, scientists, artists and writers of Jewish extraction
survived the war. The internationally famous medical scientist, Dr.
Ludwik Hirszfeld lived with his wife and daughter in the two-story
building which belonged to the church of All Saints, and after the war
wrote a moving testimony. In some cities they organized Elders of the
Church whose members, in large percentage, were Jews. This way such
Elders of the Catholic Church could function openly, and on behalf of
the Church, and save their brothers. Among other devices used by
churches in Cracow and around the country were birth certificates
supplied by Catholic printing shops and signed by priests. Jewish
parents wrote the names and other particulars about their children on
these Christian documents and saved their offspring. For the Elders,
people of Jewish faith, the Catholic clergy perused the Register of
Death Certificates, picked up names and ages to correspond with the
vital facts of these living Jews, and supplied them with birth certificates.

Among the private papers of John Paul II, I found a document signed by a woman using the name Józefa Kosowicz, verified by the priest, and also notarized. I presumed that this story has some relevance to distant relatives of the Holy Father.

"When the Jews of Polańce were about to be arrested and removed to concentration camps, a Jewish woman and friend of my parents, asked if they could keep her daughter Marysia for the night, and the next day she would pick her up. My father was dubious, but my mother, who was expecting a baby, accepted the Jewish girl readily. As my parents anticipated, nobody picked up Marysia the next day, or any other day. So my parents decided to take her to relatives in the country. While travelling, a German patrol stopped them, and when they discovered that they were transporting a girl who looked different from my parents, questioned them. Only my mother's wit saved her, because she said that the girl was the product of an extramarital affair. The Jewish girl Marysia survived the war in the village, and later returned to Polańce town to join my parents. Because she was not a Christian the local priest suggested that he would perform the ceremony to convert her. Later, Marysia went to the local school, was a good student, and grew up to be a beautiful child. When she was eleven years old, a Jewish man appeared at my parent's house, offered them money and said that he wanted to take the girl away. My parents said that they didn't want the money, or to give away the girl, and asked him to return when Marysia was eighteen years old and could make her own decision. The man didn't give up, and a few weeks later returned with the Chief Rabbi of the Polish Army. When the girl discovered that they wanted to take her away, she began to cry and left the house to hide until the civilian and the Rabbi in the army uniform left.

'The girl survived this trauma, and after finishing secondary school and college, went to study medicine in Cracow. During her studies at the Academy a man from Belgium arrived and tried to convince her to go to Canada where her maternal grandparents were living. She decided to go, and during the summer recess travelled to Canada and, for the first time, heard about the history of her family. She cried, and when her maternal grandparents begged her to remain with them said she would give it a try for five months.

"Marysia, now grown up, did everything possible to adjust to her new and luxurious life, yet after seven weeks she was so lonesome for her adopted family and the austere life in her native country, that she returned. She plunged into her work at the Academy, finished medicine and became a doctor, specializing in contagious diseases. Marysia married and works today in the hospital in the town of Tarnów; from time to time she visits Canada."

Among the many documents from the Pope's file, I found a different variation of the same story which pertains to the Lustiger family, who, during the war, reached France where they were arrested by the Gestapo; but somehow Mr. and Mrs. Lustiger managed to send their son to friends in Orléans. Mrs. Lustiger died in Auschwitz, but her husband survived and died after the war. Their son, however, Jean-Marie, at the age of fifteen, became a Catholic, and today he is the Archbishop of Paris and a friend of John Paul II. There is a feeling among church people that tomorrow he will be a cardinal. During his visit to Rome, the Pope and then Bishop of Orléans spent much time discussing the continuity and development of Christianity from the time of Jesus, and today's renewal of the Roman Catholic Church.

The ecumenical movement reinforced through the Second Vatican Council (1962–1965) created a solid foundation for *rapprochement* among all religions of the world in the struggle for peace and social justice. At the end of this Council, Pope Paul VI announced a "Declaration on the Church and Non-Christian Religions—*Nostra Aetate*," that provided a blueprint for the Catholic viewpoint, and suggested how clergy should approach other religions in the spirit of cooperating for the common good. On January 6, 1964 in Bethlehem he said, "We look at the world with great sympathy. Even if the world hears that the Christian religion is foreign to it, Christians don't feel that the world is foreign to them. Our Church serves as an intermediary between the unmeasureable, miraculous love of God and His people." He knew that powerful forces were working against ecumenical cooperation.

John Paul II repeated to me, on various occasions, the words of Paul VI from his encyclical *Ecclesiam Suam*, that "the climate of dialogue should be friendship—more than that—service."

During his pastorate in Cracow, the Pope initiated a Cemetery Committee which later spread all over the country. These Committees were composed of young and old, intellectuals and clergy who assumed the responsibility of weeding and repairing Jewish cemeteries. They worked without fanfare, showing, in this way, their respect for their non-Christian brethren. This attitude, which began in a modest way with ordinary people, spread to intellectual circles of the country and included such individuals as internationally famous filmmaker Andrzej Wajda; the President of Warsaw University, Dr. Henryk Samsonowicz; writer and member of Parliament, Karol Malcuzyński; and many other scientists, artists and writers. Their efforts led to the Polish Government initiating a budget of $100,000 to sustain the Cemetery Committees. It was not a large sum, but a symbolic one. The idea sprang from the heart of the priest Karol Wojtyla.

The last time I saw him in Rome and asked about these Committees, he didn't want to talk about them, remarking that this was "not a Polish or any other nation's affair, but a private matter of one's own conscience." After a long pause, despite his reluctance, he returned to this question from a different perspective.

"When we talk about the Polish or any other nation's guilt, I should mention that Yad Vashem (Institute of Remembrance) in Jerusalem, has up to now presented about four thousand medals, 'The Just Among the Nations of the World' to individuals—including Germans—who saved Jews during the Nazi holocaust. Among the recipients, Poles consisted of one third. Remember, there are many other Poles, and some I know personally, who did not talk about the matter to anyone except God, because they thought that these deeds of mercy were their own affair."

"Do you think that by clearing weeds from a cemetery a person can redeem himself in the eyes of God, and regain the friendship of people, whose lives were interrupted by violent death?"

The Pope rubbed his forehead and with blue eyes widening softly said, "Only God can answer this question." He then went into a long silence and followed this with, "When a man is full of penitence…sincere penitence, when a man truly suffers for his sins…there is only God…"

Book Five: Cardinal in Action

32

Beretta Rosa

"WHEN Poles of the twentieth century think about our past, we reflect on historic political mistakes perhaps even more than our nineteenth-century ancestors during the partition of Poland; but more importantly, we ponder our sins and moral guilt. Correcting and building begins with an analysis of national conscience, almost akin to individual confession," mused John Paul II.

"Our continent's greatest sin was the Second World War, which was connected to 'the church crisis' in Europe. We have to apply the theory of human subconsciousness as in anthropology and ethics to social questions like colonialism, imperialism and war."

Pope Paul VI recognized the ability of this man early, and the Curia concurred with him. In 1966, Wojtyla was elected to the Papal Commission on Marriage and Family Affairs. A year later, he accepted nominations to the Congregation for the Affairs of Eastern Churches, to the Congregation of Clerical Affairs, and to the Cult of God. He was already consultant to the *Concilium de Laicis*. When he was invited by Paul VI to the Synod of Bishops, he was an official philosopher of the collegiate church government, which he regarded in this way,

> Everything is being done in a dual manner. First there is a dialogue among bishops, followed by closed conferences between the bishops conducted in a spirit of Christian brotherhood that does not impose a person's thoughts on the others. On the second level the bishops cooperate with the Holy See in preparing values, Papal suggestions and laws, according to the leading dictum *cum Petro* and *Sub Petro*.

Paul VI considered Wojtyla a valuable asset to the Church. The Holy Father in his recollections of the country often returned to Wojtyla's theme of "originality in Polish thinking." He had served for a short time in Warsaw on the staff of the Papal Nuncio, and learned a little of the Polish language and much of the Polish culture. Almost every time Cardinal Wyszyński visited the Vatican, the Pope asked him to read Wojtyla's poetry because, "I like the music of the language and his philosophical orchestration." He asked Wyszyński to translate into Italian Wojtyla's "Easter Poem," which he carried with him in his pocket, and displayed on various occasions to the cardinals:

> The human body died in history
> more often and earlier than a tree.
> But man, beyond the wish of death,
> exists in catacombs and crypts.
> He departs, but lives in those who follow him.
> The man who comes
> already exists in those who have departed
> He exists beyond the departure, and beyond the coming.
> He exists in himself and in You.
> Beings such as I, search for a body
> which You alone can give.
> Everyone in history loses his body and goes to You.
> But in time of departure each one is bigger than history
> which consists of fragments of one or two centuries,
> and are united in one life.

Then came July 26, 1967, at 9:00 A.M., when in the Consistorial Hall, Paul VI presented to his cardinals a list of twenty-seven new cardinals, with the words, "Che pensate (think about it)."

An hour later, the cardinals moved into the Auditorio Pio XII, where Amleto Cardinal Cicognani handed each new cardinal a formal nomination, called the *biglietto* that read:

> *Romae*
> *in aedibus apostolicis Vaticanis*
> *ante diem VI calendas iulas*
> *anno Domini MCMLXVII*
> *Paulus VI Pont. Max.*
> *creavit ac renuntiavit*
> *S. R. E. Presbyterum cardinalem*
> *Carolum Wojtyla...*

Two days later in the Sistine Chapel where Michelangelo reigns through his masterpiece *The Last Judgement*, Paul VI sat on his modest throne. To his right were old cardinals and to his left those newly nominated. No singing, no lighting in any building in the world makes such an impression on a visitor as this magnificent chapel full of art and emotion. New cardinals, slowly and with dignity recited the pledge of obedience, then approached the Holy Father, their heads slightly bowed. On each head he placed the *biretta rosa* saying,

> To the glory of God, the Father, to the glory of Omnipotent God, and for the glory of the Church, accept this sign of the cardinals' esteem, for which you have to be prepared to spill blood.

Each nominated cardinal received for his own parish a Roman church. Cardinal Wojtyla was the recipient of San Cesareo in Palatino, the oldest section of Rome, where the most illustrious had lived in ancient times. It was located at the beginning of the Via Appia Antica, known as the Queen of Roads because of its many monuments.

On the day of Saints Peter and Paul, June 29, over one hundred and fifty thousand faithful appeared in Piazza San Pietro to participate in the Mass performed by the Pope assisted by his newly nominated cardinals. The day was sunny, and naturally the most happy people were the cardinals and their loved ones. The Pope made a short speech to them and handed each a ring.

After this exhausting celebration the youngest cardinal went skiing. When he returned from this short vacation the entire Curia knew about it, and some Cardinals were rather shocked, complaining that the Polish Cardinal had lowered the reputation of high Church officials. "What would happen if this skiing cardinal were to break a leg or arm in the presence of young people? How does it look when this cardinal stays in a hotel? Is he not exposed to all sorts of temptations?" One cardinal, Giuseppe Siri, who already viewed Wojtyla as a rival to the Holy See, said in the presence of the other Cardinals, "Your Eminence goes skiing, moreover, in our Italy, and as a Cardinal!"

"Certainly. I could ski any place."

"Do many Cardinals ski in Poland?" pursued Siri.

"In my country forty percent."

"How come? In Poland you have just two Cardinals."

"You're right. One, His Eminence Primate of Poland, and I."

"But how about this percentage," asked another Cardinal.

"His Eminence Primate, who does not ski, accounts for sixty

percent, and I, for forty. It's simple; add forty to sixty, and you have one hundred percent of the Cardinals!"

When I told this story to Cardinal Wojtyla's old friend, and mine, the Reverend Mieczyslaw Albert Krąpiec, the head of Lublin University, he commented, "Karol was feeling his oats, and was sure of himself because of his intellect on which he worked hard all those years. He would not allow himself to be outwitted by anyone."

About that time I talked with Professor Henryk Piluś from the Polish Academy of Science, an authority on the Thomistic deliberations of Wojtyla and Krąpiec.

I asked, "Why is there so much interest today in Thomas Aquinas' philosophy?"

"Marxists," replied the Professor in one word. "The goal of contemporary neo-Thomists is to renew the traditional concept of man through confronting the atheistic concept, specifically the Marxist theories."

"What would you say about the concept of Wojtyla's Thomistic philosophy?" I asked.

"We have to state that he made a great contribution in modernizing it in anthropological philosophy. His goal is to know and understand man phenomenologically, through his own experience. He claims that through activity we gain knowledge of the person. The relation of human beings to their activity creates a specific praxis which Wojtyla takes as a base for his theoretical deliberations. In defining a person and his actions Wojtyla presents a unification of philosophical existence with the philosophy of awareness; he claims that a person's act presents itself differently on the basis of inner experience from the sphere of outer experience. According to him a person is more than individual physical substance. He claims that a person as *suppositum* is the synthesis of action and achievement. An analysis of activity of human beings in various interhuman relations leads the philosopher to the conclusion that understanding man's activity permits us to make a correct interpretation of interhuman relations. From observation and experience we conclude that activity of a human being does not exist in a vacuum, but only together with others. In unified activity man creates common activity together with actualization. This not only explains human phenomena and structure, but also its existential position among other beings. All philosophical and methodological efforts lead in the direc-

Cardinal Wojtyla with his secretary Reverend Dziwisz on a rainy day.

Cracow Cathedral, 1970.

Cardinal Wojtyla at Częstochowa, 1971. The elderly man behind him is Franciszek Gajowniczek, who survived Auschwitz when his place in the gas chamber was taken by Father Maksymilian Kolbe.

At Bachledowka, near the ski resort Zakopane, with Stefan Cardinal Wyszyński and Bishop Bronislaw Dąbrowski, 1972.

tion that the reason and goal of human beings is an Absolute and that the existence of man can be justified only through the ontological perspective of the Absolute."

His intellectual contributions to the body of Church thought helped Karol Wojtyla to further his contacts with the Princes of the Church, especially those Cardinals from the Third World who would play an important role in his future.

Before leaving Rome he bade farewell to many cardinals, including John Patrick Cody, who headed the Chicago archdiocese in the United States, and to other American cardinals, including John Joseph Król, Archbishop of Philadelphia, who said openly to Karol,

"You should be the next Pope."

While still in Rome, Karol had some friendly chats with Italian church dignitaries, including Giuseppe Cardinal Siri who was thirteen years his senior and on the conservative side, but with great influence in the Curia. This Italian Church Prince said to his Polish rival outspokenly, "I will do everything possible to prevent you from occupying the Holy See, because it would be a deep tragedy for the Church."

Wojtyla responded immediately, "Who told Your Eminence that I want to become Pope? On my part, I will support Your Eminence without reservation."

Cardinal Siri was dumbfounded.

Immediately after his investiture as Cardinal, Wojtyla traveled to Vienna, where he visited Cardinal König who was fifteen years his senior and who had become a cardinal in 1958.

"I don't know if you could be a successor to Paul VI, or the successor to the next Pope, but I have a premonition, and I am convinced that you will occupy the Holy See, not because I like you, but because you are the most worthy Cardinal living today. I will work hard among the German Cardinals for you. The German nation is guilty of crimes against the Polish nation; the German Roman Catholic church, quiet during the war, suffers today because of that, and the German hierarchy knows this. I will work, I think successfully, because I know their guilt complex, although every German Cardinal is being pushed by the German Government to try to occupy the Holy See. I will let you in on a great secret; the reason is that unification of both Germanies can succeed only with the help of a German Pope."

Wojtyla cried, and König embraced him; both were in tears. Immediately afterward, Karol Wojtyla returned by train to Cracow, and like a good farmer, plunged into the spiritual fieldwork of his archdiocese. He had an abundance of work because, from the start, he had created committees and symposiums, on the subjects of natural science, economy, law, psychiatry; even a group which occupied itself with the role of physical science in the development of man in the world. Outstanding specialists from other parts of the country and Europe were invited to various conferences organized by the Polish Church.

At the Cracow Curia a Family Institute was also organized in which young people of various professions took courses and participated in discussion of ethics, psychology, medicine and theology. During these discussions they analyzed *Humanae Vitae*, the 1968 Papal encyclical, which created much international controversy because of Church opposition to unnatural prevention of conception and birth control against pregnancy. The church standing was that a woman should practice the "rhythm method"; the opposition viewed this as "Vatican Roulette."

Karol Wojtyla wrote a paper entitled "Theological and Pastoral Commentary to *Humanae Vitae*," which pleased Paul VI and the Vatican Curia. It should be noted that Wojtyla's book *Love and Responsibility*, published in 1960, was to some extent a source for the Papal encyclical eight years later.

Wojtyla also organized an SOS Action for single mothers in his diocese, that gave advice on pregnancy and children. Despite his pastoral work Wojtyla did not abandon his duties at Lublin University as professor and head of the Ethics Department where a dozen bright students worked under his direction. People wondered how he could do all these things and survive. The only logical reply was that Karol was blessed with iron health and developed an unusual ability to apportion his time in such a way that he could spare parts of his days for skiing, hiking or swimming. Close friends compared him to Persian philosopher, Abu-All Al-Husain Ibn Abdullah Ibn Sina (980–1037), popularly called Avicenna, who had his litter hung between two camels. In this litter he also had necessary equipment to read and write.

Some friends did not fully appreciate the constraints upon his time. They even felt offended and criticized his behavior. One of his oldest friends, the novelist Wojtek Zukrowski tried to describe the situation,

"I left Cracow for Silesia, having finished my university studies at Wroclaw. Our roads parted. From time to time I sent my short stories and novels to Karol, and we exchanged letters. I was much impressed by him because I was just a lay Catholic, and he was Prince of the Church.

"One day when visiting Cracow, I noticed my friend on the street and yelled, 'Karolek, wait!'

"He turned, approached me and said, quietly, 'Wojtek, I am Cardinal here. Why yell so? If a market woman hears this, gossip will begin.'

"I, behaving like a clown, went on my knee and grabbed his hand to kiss the ring.

"Karolek whispered, 'Please don't play the comic here on the street. Let's go somewhere else—maybe to my place and have a vodka.'

Wojtek Zukrowski smiled and said, "Everybody places him on a pedestal, but I would like to say that he will always be for me, modest Karolek, open and friendly to everybody; never mind that he is a Pope."

33

The Socialist State and the Holy See

During Edward Gierek's decade of political rule (December 1970–September 1980), I visited Poland many, many times. Travelling around the country, talking with workers, peasants, intellectuals, clergy and especially Primate Wyszyński, I learned much about this country from simple people and from the powerful. Naturally, I did not neglect Gierek who for some reason hid this fact from his two secretaries–short Jerzy Waszczuk and sinewy Jerzy Wójcik. He behaved as if he didn't care to see writers, while simultaneously contacting me for long discussions over dinner, photography sessions and straight talks where only mineral water was served.

In personal contact he was simple and direct, and spoke with me about his modest daily meals composed of raw vegetables, fruits and lean, sauceless meats. Sometimes I would meet him in his private Warsaw villa, other times, but not often, in his hidden room at the Central Committee. Both places were furnished simply and decorated with paintings from the national museum. Our meetings were private; and if it was breakfast we would have carrot juice, oatmeal with milk, two soft boiled eggs, a piece of bread with butter, and *ersatz* coffee. Sessions at lunch time featured vegetable soup, a piece of boiled beef with potatoes, mixed green salad and fruit compote. Before sitting down to eat, he would say, "Don't worry, everything is prepared under the supervision of my wife." Our evening conversations were usually at supper and would consist of sliced tomatoes topped with onion rings, a variety of Polish cheeses and breads with butter washed down with herb tea. Sometimes we would start with a glass of vodka. Those meals were the starting point of our long dialogues. Gierek loved to talk while he ate. I asked, "Do you eat the same thing all the time?"

"I make exception for state banquets, but when I am with my wife or a special guest, I follow my diet. Wherever I am I do not overeat."

He was open and sincere with those he knew would not spy on him or ask him for favors. He usually began our conversation with a light story or anecdote. When I asked why, he replied, "I learned this American style from you"; then he would plunge ahead.

"When we decided to produce the Fiat 126P, a small car called Maluch, people asked, 'How do they decide to produce such cars?'

"'Autos should be impressive, big, cheap, comfortable, yet consume little gasoline. But this Fiat 126P, is so small it is afraid of a dog and would run away from him into a tree.'"

"Others commented, 'This Polish Fiat is too big and cannot be squeezed into an elevator or house.' This joke is rather poor and trivial, but people like the car and pamper it. I would not try to press more meaning out of this story, but you can see how it reflects Polish thinking and especially the desire for luxury." He wiped his mouth with a napkin, reached inside his pocket for a handkerchief, blew his nose loudly, and said, "I am waiting for a serious question." I noticed that he had prepared himself and did not want to wait any longer.

"Let us begin with your mistakes; later we will talk about achievements," I said.

"I like your honesty."

"I have seen a big separation between workers and the Party and your administration; I think with time this will destroy the system."

"You exaggerate. We noticed this some time ago, and are trying to correct it." Then he went into a tirade, "During the thirty-five years of people's authority we have finally secured our position in Europe by returning to our historical borders and establishing the demographic and ethnic unity of our nation. Our internal affairs, in the realm of economy, are well taken care of. As to industrial production we are ninth in the world. I know we have problems supplying housing for working people, that there are queues of young married people waiting for apartments, but this situation grew out of the war and was aggravated by rapid industrialization and the flow of workers into the cities. You have to remember that the desires of people grow faster than the economic possibilities of the country. Someone who used to live in a one-room apartment, now wants three rooms. It is understandable."

"I am referring to the attitude of society toward government; the feelings of a nation looking for its own road."

"Do not misunderstand. I am on the side of progress. If we did not have some minor polarization, we could not progress. It is important to have controllable discontent, but it is also important that the main goal not disappear from our vision."

Hearing these generalities, I tried to obtain concrete facts. I asked, "What was the real reason for the switch from Gomulka to Gierek?"

"Gomulka was near-sighted and a miser. He was afraid to borrow money for investment and shunned new things such as profiting through the achievements of the western world, especially the United States. He would lock himself in his office rather than discuss matters directly with the people. We did not forget about building homes for working people. This required production of housing materials, especially cement, whose production during the Gomulka era was twelve million and today is twenty-four million tons per year. Mind you, we did not neglect production of agricultural machinery in which we also invested large sums. I would say the country is now ready to tackle agriculture."

"It is difficult for me to talk about cement; I prefer to talk about people."

"But you must understand that cement is an element in satisfying human needs."

"To some extent you are right, but borrowing money left and right when you have limited resources, as well as limited foreign markets for your goods is economically dangerous. What I have observed is that nobody asks workers how they live, nor what kind or quantity of equipment they need for the improvement of their work; but Warsaw is preparing to ask workers to build factories with borrowed dollars; and then what?"

"We are borrowing money, but we will pay it back, because our production is growing; raw material exists in the country in sufficient amounts, but if we need extra, we can get it from the Soviet Union or other socialist countries. If you are talking about workers, I know their morale, because I travel all over, talking, observing, discussing their production problems."

"I am sure you remember the story about Field Marshal Potemkin who also travelled in the eighteenth century with the rulers of Russia all over the country, but before he went, gave orders to build special villages. You, too, travel throughout the country, but before you go on a trip, everything is prepared for your inspection, even the red carpets. Why don't you do as some Polish kings – travel incognito, dressing in peasants' rags and observe? Take King Lokietek or King Kazimierz as an example."

Gierek waved his hand in annoyance and replied, "We live at the end of the twentieth century and everything should be based on precise economic calculation and hard work."

"This means you are satisfied with your achievements?"

Then he went into a discourse about internal and external criticism of the country's economic situation ending with this observation, "The Party and I are grateful for objective criticism. We are not completely satisfied, but you have to admit, we have made substantial progress toward improvement."

Knowing that I would not learn much from him in the economic area I switched to religion. "What is your relationship with Primate Wyszyński?"

He began this way, "My mother was a simple religious woman. She almost forced me to make contact with Cardinal Wyszyński, and we became friends. Ask him if I am not telling the truth." At this moment, as I prepared in my mind a few specific questions about his dealings with the Primate of Poland and the Vatican, he asked, "Have you heard any good jokes about me recently?"

"Naturally I have, but I thought we would discuss serious matters."

"All right, we will. But, tell me a joke."

"One day you went for a walk on the streets of Warsaw with Prime Minister Piotr Jaroszewicz. When you passed the building where Wladyslaw Broniewski lived you noticed a plaque on which was engraved, 'Here lived the great poet Broniewski.' You turned to your Prime Minister and asked, 'I wonder what would be engraved on a plaque on the front door of where I live?'

"'The Prime Minister replied, 'House for Rent.'"

I pursued the subject. "Speaking about Jaroszewicz, you know that he is hated for various reasons, including his financial dealings and specifically, supporting his son's costly habit of car racing. Why don't you discharge him?"

"It is difficult because of his relations with our eastern neighbor."

"Is it he who is trying to prevent you from establishing good relations with the Vatican?"

"He and others who think that if we have excellent relations with the Church and especially with such clever cardinals as Wojtyla and Wyszyński that socialism will suffer. My idea is different. Almost ten years ago, I expressed my opinion that building a socialist country is the responsibility of all people, believers and nonbelievers, and that the Church could play a vital role."

"What signs did you have from the Vatican on the subject of cooperation?"

"John XXIII and Paul VI were friendly toward Poland. This was expressed in these words by the latter, 'We would like to engage ourselves in cooperation with the socialist countries and together build a just and peaceful world without exploitation and without war.' Under this declaration I am sure that every Communist, every man of good will, could sign his name. During the 1967 Vatican visit of Nikolai V. Podgorny, President of the Soviet Union, Paul VI said, 'I would like to have the best possible relations with your country.' This was the real beginning of Vatican dialogue with Russian churches. In our case, Wyszyński and Wojtyla were two great Church leaders with tremendous vision who didn't wait for a cue from the Vatican to work with our government in building a just country. On November 12, 1973 our Foreign Minister, Stefan Olszowski, had a long private audience with Paul VI during which the Pope supported the idea of Vatican cooperation with the Polish government and of acceptance of the political line of the two Polish cardinals. What's more, the Holy Father instructed the highest Vatican officials to discuss Poland's economic and political relationship with western Europe. As a result of these instructions the Vatican Secretary of State, Cardinal Jean Viollot, and Archbishop Agostino Casaroli, Secretary of Church Public Affairs Committee, spent a long time in conferences with Olszowski. Later *L'Osservatore Romano* published an article stating that the visit of the Polish Minister of Foreign Affairs was one of the thirteen most important visits of foreign dignitaries to the Vatican that year."

"What was the next step?" I asked with anticipation.

"In July of 1974 at the suggestion of the Pope, we sent our Vice Minister of Foreign Affairs to the Vatican to harmonize our cooperation with the Holy See. Paul VI even asked if he could be the intermediary between his office and Moscow, and when we agreed, he had a warm feeling about me which was related to me by Cardinal Wyszyński." A smile appeared on Gierek's face and he added, "My mother was happy that the highest authority in the Catholic Church liked me. She thought my place in heaven was secured."

"Who instigated this *rapprochement* between Warsaw and Rome?"

"It is obvious that in the Polish Church it was Wyszyński and Wojtyla. Thanks to them we built this solid ground not only in Poland, but also created the possibility for cooperation between Christian churches in all socialist countries and the Vatican. I cannot forget two other men who worked hard in this diplomatic effort: Bishop Bronisław Dąbrowski, as Secretary of the Polish Episcopate was ingenious and a tireless propagator of cooperation; and Bishop Andrea Maria Deskur, school friend of Karol Wojtyla who later became a close friend of Pope Paul VI. The Pope made him Head of the Vatican Commission for Mass Communication, and he was teaching his Holy Father the Polish language. As you can see, we were on strong ground in our relations with Paul VI."

"Since you know so much about this delicate diplomatic work and the Polish personalities involved, please tell me who was on the Curia's side."

"I guess we would first have to name Archbishop Luigi Poggi who worked with a representative of our government." My host got up, went to a mahogany chest of drawers and picked up a piece of paper. Returning to his seat, he said, "Poggi was very capable and I was certain he represented the conservative group of Curia officials. In addition to the activity of this Archbishop, there was another one by the name of Agostino Casaroli, who visited Warsaw many times and had a few private discussions with me. He said without any diplomatic double-talk, 'I believe that socialism is the only system to liquidate the economic misery of people and to stop wars.' Casaroli was also enlightened and honest, and liked by Wyszyński and me. When Wojtyla became Pope he made Casaroli his Secretary of State.

"The Catholic Church, beginning with John XXIII, concluded that it could work successfully with socialist countries, better than with capitalist countries, for eradication of social injustice. Pope John was a dreamer and visionary and Paul was an intellectual and realistic politician. Both supplemented each other and built a practical base for cooperation between the world's progressive socialism and the Roman Catholic Church."

"You have such a high opinion of those two Popes; why did it take them so long to invite you to the Vatican on December 1, 1977?"

I observed his face become tense and his legs slide under the table. He must have been thinking, 'Should I answer this question?' After a minute of restlessness Gierek said, "Bonn had tried for a long time to sabotage our good relations. The Germans convinced even Washington to prevent our normalization of the socialist states' relations with the Church. When they heard that the Pope was thinking of inviting me to Rome, American and German representatives asked Him, 'How could you invite an agent of Moscow?' The Germans and Americans were trying to convince Paris and London to support their side, but France refused, and the British government, under the pressure of the Anglican Church which was discussing the possibility of unification, also refused. Paul VI, a perceptive politician, understood the worries of the capitalist countries, but pursued his own policies. As a consequence, he not only invited me, but treated me well, and we spent almost two hours in private conversation."

"About what did you talk for such a long time?"

"Let me begin with a story about my wife, because this invitation created a problem for me."

I knew that Gierek, as a leader, always stressed his faithful relations with his wife and he had carefully built up his image as a family man. But I also knew that he had a few women on the side, one in Silesia and two in Warsaw. So I said, "Tell me the story any way you want to."

"You know, a wife is a wife and every one of us has various problems with them. Imagine, when she heard that I was taking her to visit the Pope, she said that she wanted to dress colorfully, because, 'They will take color photographs and since the Pope always appears picturesque why shouldn't I?'

"I asked if she were crazy. My secretaries had already coodinated our plans with Vatican officials including how we should behave, how we should dress, and everything else in minute detail. There was a specific request that we not dress colorfully, because it was not proper to disregard protocol, especially in the Vatican.

"She said, 'Edziu, I have your secretary in my ass. I cannot dress like your mother, always in black, Pope or no Pope. I must wear a colorful dress, and look young by using a lot of makeup. Our picture will be on the front page of all the European magazines. The Pope, in his garments, will look majestic, and you on one side with your big frame, will probably look majestic, too. But I, a short, plump woman in black will look like a little crow.'"

My host got up and walked around the room, waving his long hands. "'You mean you would like to look like an actress?' I said.

"She replied, 'Why not? There are a lot of worse looking actresses than me.'

"'You mean you would like to be Gina Lollobrigida or Monica Vitti?'

"'Why not?'

"'Are you crazy? Do you want to make a fool of yourself and finish me politically?'

"'What are you talking about?'

"'Didn't you read the article about those actresses and Pope John XXIII?'"

"'No, what happened?'

"This conversation we had about a week before our departure to Rome. I was extremely busy preparing myself for this unique visit, discussing all aspects of my meeting with the Pope, not only with my Party colleagues and Vatican representatives, but also with the Soviet Ambassador. And then during the same week, I had to spend many hours arguing with my wife about a dress. It was already established that she would wear a simple, modest dress and black veil over her head."

While Gierek was relating the problem of his wife to me, I recalled the 'Lollobrigida affair' with John XXIII. When this Italian actress, after a few attempts, finally received an invitation from the Pope, she dressed in a beautiful long black dress, and naturally, later, dozens of photographers took hundreds of pictures of smiling Gina with the stout, majestic Pope. The next week, these photogrpahs appeared on the front page of magazines all over the world. Then, readers discovered that Lollobrigida was wearing a black dress, but very sheer, so sheer that you could see every part of her body through it, due to powerful lenses and clever photographers.

"I know the episode concerning Lollobrigida," I said. "Also, when they asked the good-hearted Pope to comment on the subject, he put his head in both hands, smiled and laughed heartily. What I don't know is the story about the actress Vitti."

"I will tell you. Monica Vitti and a group of Italian actors were invited to an audience with the Pope."

"I presume she dressed modestly in a black, and certainly not sheer, dress?"

"Yes, she wore a long dress, but chic with a high slit on one side; and to minimize her large bust she wore a long shawl, which covered the slit as well. Everything went well until she kneeled before the Pope."

"The shawl covered her completely, didn't it?"

"Not exactiy. Monica was excited and when she knelt to kiss the Pope's ring, her shawl slid off and the beautiful actress showed not only the top of her bust but her shapely thighs."

I commented, "Knowing John XXIII, his character, modesty, and previous experience, he probably turned his head and ignored the whole situation."

"Not quite. He looked at her, and majestically and slowly said, 'Our daughter, please rise up quickly and let my old eyes look down.'"

"Wonderful response."

"What would people think, if I were in a situation like that?"

"Don't exaggerate. There is nothing wrong with your wife or her figure."

"When you have been married a long time, you try to forget how your wife looks or how she might try to behave," he replied with melancholy.

"Let us go from this plateau to the summit of your visit to the Vatican and your talk with Paul VI."

His face brightened and he began in an excited voice. "I, a simple coal miner, was treated unusually well by the Head of the Church with a two thousand year tradition. When I reached the Saint Damascus court, at the head of a dozen cars, the papal Swiss Guard dressed in festive uniforms greeted me like a king. I was moved and grateful. Can you guess to whom I was grateful?"

"Paul VI?"

"Yes, but initially to Primate Wyszyński and to Wojtyla. Without their help I would have been unsuccessful. What's more, without their work and influence on John XXIII and Paul VI, the Church would continue its Middle Ages philosophy and there would be no attempt to build a bridge between Catholics and Marxists. Their effort and support of socialist work in our country echoed throughout the Christian world which was so eloquently expressed by John XXIII in his *Mater et Magistra*: 'Common good should be translated into economic and social policy as well as into cultural activity. The function of the state should be responsibility to the people's common good.'"

"John XXIII in his *Pacem in Terris* suggested that Catholics should approach people outside the Christian faith, and loyally cooperate in the fight for a better existence. I, myself, as First Secretary of the Polish Worker's Party in Mielec, expressed the same sentiment; Paul VI agreed with me wholeheartedly."

At this moment, I tried to ask him to describe to me his impression of Paul VI. But I was not quick enough and my host asked me, "After twenty centuries, only one third of the people in the world have accepted Christianity, but after forty years, one third of the world's population identifies itself with socialism. Who said this?"

"How should I know? You prepared yourself for this conversation with me; you tell me."

"This was said by R. Houben, a professor at Catholic University in Louvain. Paul VI knew right away and elaborated, 'At Vatican II, I expressed Houben's sentiment in my pastoral constitution *Gaudium et Spes*. We are convinced that the mission of the Church should be extended not only throughout capitalist countries, but to socialist countries where this sincere dialogue is extremely important.' The Pope noticed that I was listening attentively and he continued, 'In my *Ecclesiam Suam* I underlined the positive activity of various Marxists in the direction of socialist humanism. Our Secretary for Unbelievers received an order from me to prepare the document which would stress the importance of our work not only in socialist countries, but also in countries of the Third World.'

"When I said to Paul VI that Poland is familiar with the achievement of Vatican Council II and its historic work in building cooperation between opposing systems, he asked, 'Don't you have opposition on the political left and right to our cooperation?' Without diplomatic ado, he added, 'You will see what will happen to you in a couple of years.' This shook me up. How could he know about an opposition toward my political moves? Before I could ask my question, the Pope continued, 'We were informed of your initiative and thoughtfulness in helping families in various ways, including building new apartments for newlyweds as well as your effort to raise the morality of young people.

We are pleased with your sincere attempts to work closely with the Church in Poland. It is also our deep desire that harmony should exist between the hierarchy of the Church and your government.'

"'This is not only my effort,' I replied, 'But most importantly it expresses the good will and sincere desire on the part of the Polish Episcopate.' At this moment, I tried to read observations to the Pope made by Primate Wyszyński at the third Synod of the Warsaw Archdiocese when the Primate talked about bringing up youth in an atmosphere of social responsibility. But when I saw my name in the text and how Wyszyński had praised me, I reflected, because I thought that it would be in poor taste."

"Didn't he mention to you his effort to establish better relations with the Soviet Union?"

"I had the feeling that this friendly attitude toward me at the outset was the basis for a discussion of politics 'toward the East.' What's more, before I left for the Vatican I heard from Comrade Brezhnev and his people that he might talk; I also heard from them that after John XXIII's encyclical *Pacem in Terris*, Moscow, seeing in this encyclical almost a communist program, approached the Vatican and tried to discuss the possibility of close cooperation in combating war and economic exploitation. But not much came of it, because the Curia used French and German cardinals, labeled American imperialist agents by Moscow, to torpedo John XXIII's efforts.

"This is interesting," I began. "Judging from my observations, any political *rapprochement* on such a high level has to be approved and all directives carefully screened by the Pope himself, who is the highest authority in these matters. Even the Vatican Secretary of State cannot make a political move without papal approval."

"I thought you knew more about the whole business and especially the manipulation of the Curia behind the Pope's back. But I was wrong. Let me explain to you our attitude, and especially the Soviet Union's toward Vatican politics. Through the ages their politics have supported the ruling classes. Even during the Second World War the official Church, seeing tremendous injustice and slaughter unprecedented in history, took a neutral stand. When John XXIII ascended to the Holy See, all leaders of the socialist countries, and especially Moscow, thought that the Curia under his orders would behave differently, and that Vatican policy toward socialist countries and toward the Third

World would be genuine and beneficial for both sides."

"Was it not?"

"Yes, officially everybody from the Secretary of State down claimed that, 'we have to work even with the devil to preserve peace and ensure just distribution of world wealth.' But, unofficially, the Curia's efforts were to soften communists and socialists, collect information on the weak points of their system, and share them with the United States. When John XXIII died, we consulted with each other and Comrade Brezhnev said to me, 'It will be important for us to know what the east politics of the intellectual Paul VI are.'"

"You don't say that John XXIII directed the Curia's maneuvering."

"No, he was an honest man and deep believer in social justice as well as in genuine peace. But he was in some way outmaneuvered due to his naiveté in practical politics, and we are certain he never received a truthful report on Church cooperation with socialist states. His successor, Paul VI, intellectually sharp, convinced us with his encyclical *Humanae Vitae* and with other pronouncements that his internal Church politics were generally democratic and his Eastern politics were based on political realism. He knew that Socialism was here to stay and that the Church must find a way to work with those states on an equal basis. As he said to me, 'Our politics should be in the form of service rather than domination. We should cooperate with various socialist governments to supplement each other in the development of a just democratic system.' During the same meeting, he added, 'I wish that during my lifetime we could establish genuine diplomatic relations with the Soviet Union and the rest of the socialist world. For us it is not important who is Marxist, we respect them and would like to help in a way that would lead to the betterment of humanity. We would not think of imposing our form of service and belief in God. We would merely like to stretch out our friendly hand to the leaders of the socialist countries and tell them that we, too, are interested in building a better world.' He concluded 'Please tell this to Mr. Leonid Brezhnev and other socialist leaders: that when they accept our outstretched hand, they should be sure that this hand is the hand of a friend.' The Pope told me this in great emotion. And when I listened to him, a physically small man, I thought that I was listening to a giant."

"What did you say to him at this private meeting in the Papal Library?"

"I said that my report to the Conference of Socialist Leaders will be so positive that they might even accuse me of being an agent of the Vatican." Gierek smiled. "But when I left this strictly private conference between two men and reached Clementine Hall, I said publicly that 'His Holiness Paul VI is a genuine man of peace. Although we have differences in viewpoint on specific questions we will slowly eradicate them and work together harmoniously, because we know that humanity, in the time of nuclear armament, needs cooperation between all to prevent war. In the case of Poland and the Church, there is no conflict and we have the will to cooperate. Cardinals Wyszyński and Wojtyla and I are working steadily for betterment of life in our country.'"

"For you as a politician, what did this meeting show you?"

"Careful preparation and execution of this meeting between the head of a socialist country and the head of the Roman Catholic Church created a model of how leaders of the Eastern bloc should deal with matters of mutual interest. Even the Soviets could learn how to work successfully with the Vatican. I emerged convinced that the Church could be helpful in defusing ideological tensions."

"Where would you place the United States?"

"Washington, as leader of the Western world, should tell its diplomats to stop criticizing Vatican policy toward the Soviet Union and other socialist countries; instead they should take a cue from them and contribute something positive. Practically speaking, the United States should be an equal partner of the Soviet Union and the Vatican in an effort to prevent nuclear armament. It should be a model for the rest of the world, so that religious, capitalist and socialist leaders can work harmoniously toward peace. Only close cooperation by those three powers can produce success."

"Those are noble words," I commented. "It looks like your mother won and made you a good Roman Catholic. The Pope engaged you in international *aggiornamento*." Gierek did not comment, and I saw that he was tired and thinking about something else. I asked, "Maybe we should finish with high politics?"

"Tell me a joke or let me know what people say about me, because my secretaries no longer report 'my opinion polls.' Even my wife does not relay gossip. I don't know what has happened."

"You can always rely on me," I ventured.

"Go ahead. Don't be bashful."

"When in 1970 you grabbed power and said to the people, 'Help me to build,' your popularity rapidly grew and people rushed to work hard and long hours. Now, when they see long lines in front of food stores and when they hear about the country's enormous debt, your popularity continues to decline."

"But my foreign policy is successful. So I should be a bit popular."

"How do you figure that?"

"I work long hours in my office and peek through the windows; I see people stop by my building and look up. I presume they are commenting, 'Edward is still in his office figuring out how to pull us through and bring the country to complete prosperity."

"They are not looking at your window, but at the roof of the Party building."

"Are you sure? How do you know?"

"There is a story spreading through the capital that if one goes to the Party building in the middle of the night one can see your wife dancing on the roof with a wreath on her head made of kielbasa. The price of the sausages is attached to the wreath, but it is the low price of your predecessor's kielbasa."

To my surprise, I saw a smile on his face, and he said, "I guess my wife and predecessor, Gomulka, are in on this joke. During his time there was plenty to eat, but no heavy industry. I built heavy industry and that's the reason for temporary food shortages."

"People also say that you have a problem with inflation."

"Certainly, I do."

"But they say..." and here I tried to be gentle.

"Go ahead, tell me, what are they saying?"

"That you have developed a new method for fighting inflation."

"What kind? You see, I don't even know myself. I have so many plans."

"People say that you gave the order to make holes in hundred zlotys coin and sell them as buttons. This is only the beginning," I said, quietly. "You know that all over the country strikes are spreading. People are dissatisfied. Somebody has to tell you the truth. If you borrow more money from other countries to build heavy industry, neglecting farming and light industry, you are in trouble, the whole country is in trouble. In such a situation, neither Wyszyński nor Wojtyla could help you. And you'd have to go."

"Perhaps *you* should go," was his reply.

I got up slowly and reaching the door, turned around. He was standing in the middle of the room. I asked, "Who created the black market? Who gave the order to exchange the tourists' dollar for thirty-three zlotys for which you cannot even buy a good cup of coffee in my hotel?"

From the center of the room he shouted, "Get out!"

I obeyed the order.

The next day PAP, the official news agency released a communiqué which appeared on the front page of all the newspapers stating that the First Secretary of the Polish United Worker's Party had spent time with me in friendly discussion.

34

In North America

"IMMEDIATELY after the nomination of Wojtyla to the College of Cardinals, I started thinking about how he should be introduced, in a natural way, to important officials of the church," Primate Wyszyński said, continuing his oral history. "It was necessary to show Wojtyla's intellect and piety to the entire Catholic world, especially those cardinals who were to take part in the next Conclave."

"A good idea," I replied. "The surest way would be to hire powerful publicity men."

"Are you joking, or poking fun at me?"

"I simply don't know the mechanism of publicizing cardinals."

"I received an invitation from the Congress of Canadian Polonia, whose president was a good Catholic, to deliver the opening speech on the celebration of this organization's quarter century existence, as well as to take part in commemorating the German attack on Poland. I contacted Karol and suggested that he go to Toronto. Initially, he was unreceptive; but when I convinced him that his old colleague from *Concilium de Laicis*, Cardinal and Primate of Canada Maurice Roy, would be a gracious host, he agreed. The Polish Episcopate and I suggested that there should be two friends in his entourage: Bishop Szczepan Wesoly, Reverend Professor Franciszek Macharski, and naturally, his personal secretary, Reverend Stanislaw Dziwisz. During my visit to Rome, I also discussed maximum exposure for Cardinal Wojtyla with the Holy Father, who suggested that the Curia offer technical help as well as inform the prominent clergy in Canada and the United States that Karol would be visiting. On August 28, 1969, Karol and his friends left Rome for Montreal."

"Canada overwhelmed me with its beauty and space," the Pope later told me, "Green, gold and various shades of those colors dominate the

landscape in summer and captivated me. I thought to myself, how re-
freshing it would be to walk for hours and hours, days and days, in
Canadian fields and forests, and drink the colors, smell the fragrance,
my ears filled with songs and voices of animals; to walk and walk and
walk in this stupendous country–I correct myself–this continent, in
the company of old school friends; and not return to civilization, but
to live with God, nature and close comrades; to subsist on berries and
mushrooms in forests, and on the banks of rivers help ourselves to
fresh fish. But let's return to reality; instead, I feasted on an elaborate
meal provided by Cardinal Roy, archbishop of Québec, and his *confrères*, and drank a small amount of Canadian whiskey to prove that I
was one of them."

"You could have cheated a little and had water on the rocks; or followed your old custom of half and half–wine and water."

"I did, but during my first speech in Toronto, I reached for a glass of
water to lubricate my dry throat, and someone handed me a glass of
straight vodka. I almost choked to death. This Canadian hospitality
pushed me to consume alcohol because they said that in their country
a little whiskey before breakfast helps prevent colds. As a result, I drank
in the morning after the first Mass."

"What did you see in Canada?"

"I travelled by cars, trains, planes and helicopters when visiting cities
and towns, including Ottawa, Winnipeg, Calgary, St. Catherine; and
across Canadian wheat fields, oilfields, and the Canadian Rockies. But
the most startling incident was in Edmonton when a group of Polish
Canadian farmers travelled hundreds of miles to greet me with a verse
of the Polish poet, Juliusz Slowacki. In the early nineteenth century, he
wrote,

> when nations quarrel and fight, God will ring an enormous bell,
> and will place the Slavic Pope on the Holy See, and he will give
> love to people as emperors today give arms.

We looked at each other, and I felt we were thinking the same
thoughts.

He continued, "These Canadian farmers insisted that the prophecy
must be fulfilled by me, and they kissed my hands and hugged me. I
did not have the strength to protest. Next, they begged me to send a
Polish priest to their region, and I solemnly promised that I would do

this as soon as possible. Then we knelt and prayed that God should give us happiness and the strength to work."

When the Pope said this, I saw tears in his eyes, and read his lips which whispered "Look at me; I am human too. Don't you think it is a miracle to find brothers in faraway Alberta province who bestow a prophecy on you, pray with you, and then...I might never see them again. When leaving the Canadian continent I said, 'I have to leave Canada, but I do not know how to leave her. This is the strange law of human souls. Part of me will remain forever.' If there could be a rejuvenation it might be on the enormous plains and Rocky Mountains of Canada, where people are close to earth and heaven."

"I see the poet won you over completely."

No comment from my host, but he continued his narrative. "The night before my departure from Canada to New York, which I had never seen, I had a strange dream about Canada's southern neighbor."

"Everybody has strange dreams. It's nothing unusual."

"I don't attach much significance to dreams, although, as the saying goes, pious people, and I consider myself pious, believe deeply in the meaning of dreams."

"What kind of dream did you have?"

"About cats."

I myself had a dream – about little abandoned kittens, but you dreamed about cats – grownup cats. Am I not right?"

He did not reply and described his dream,

It was a terribly severe winter in New York, the city completely covered with snow. Inhabitants were well and warmly dressed, and walking slowly along roads because cars, due to mountains of snow, could not be operated. I was happy that I could walk on top of the snow on avenues of white. In the middle of this street I could only see the tops of spruce trees."

As an old New Yorker, I interjected, "This was Park Avenue, because only on this avenue, around Christmas time are Canadian fir trees transported to New York and decorated for holiday festivities."

"Maybe you're right. But in my dream I didn't notice any festivities.

All my physical effort was spent on walking. To this day, pictures of huge apartment houses on both sides of the avenue are instilled in my mind, and the doormen quickly closing and opening entrance doors as though trying to prevent humanity and warmth from escaping. I could hear every voice, because there were no motor vehicles to interrupt the flow. People bundled up in green, orange, red, blue and other plastic uniforms moved like mannequins. Suddenly I appeared, for no reason, on top of a tower, to which was glued a big clock with golden arms. I looked at the clock and saw that the glow from its golden arms was more intense than the sun which I could not see, and that twelve o'clock was approaching. I was dressed in a modest black cassock, and this man-made glow made me nervous. I turned my back to the clock, shivered and looked up and down, trying to find the sun, but couldn't.

On top of the snow, I noticed a brown cat emerge from a side street and walk on the snow. I looked closer, and to my surprise, saw that this big cat was being followed by six small brown-and-white kittens, all of them following the big brown cat in a perfect line. The mother cat looked back from time to time to see if her babies were there, but her main concern was to reach the entrance door. I presume she was trying to find warmth for herself and her children, but as soon as she reached the door, a man in a well-pressed uniform, jumped at her with a broom and chased them away. I followed this procession and prepared to deliver a speech to the doorman. I opened my mouth and tried to complain, 'Where is your proverbial American generosity? Where is your American good heart and fair play? Let them in. Let them in!' I tried to speak, but the words would not come out. Maybe I was afraid of the doorman with the broom. I started searching my cassock pockets for a piece of bread, found some crumbs and put them on my palms, calling: Kitty, kitty, kitty. But the simple words would not emerge from my supposedly intelligent mouth. Instead, the wind blew the crumbs from my palm. I said, 'What can I do? I can't speak to the cats. I can't speak to the doorman. But there are many hungry birds. They might pick up the crumbs.' A second thought contradicted the first, 'How could the birds find the crumbs of white American bread on white American snow?'

Again, I walked after the cats, with a pain in my chest, feeling tremendous cold. On the left I saw a church building and thought, 'There we will find help.' The mother cat walked in the direction of the church. I heard singing and again, the idea occurred to me that 'it must be a Catholic church!' The music grew louder, as though trying to convince God that they were praying for Him. The mother cat jumped in front of me and climbed the stairs, followed by her kittens. I raised my head and saw a tall Jesuit shooshing the cats off the steps.

Although the story was exciting I asked my narrator, "How did you know it was a Jesuit who shooshed the cats from the steps?"

"You mean I, a Cardinal, couldn't recognize a Jesuit? I can recognize them even in my dreams."

"Excuse the interruption," I said, meekly. "It was a stupid question."

As I was about to shout at the Jesuit priest that I was a cardinal and give an order to accept the cats, the mother cat and her offspring ran behind the church, because from there came the appetizing aroma of broiled meat.

"Probably there was a kitchen."

Kitchen, dining room and the rest of the Jesuits' living quarters. But a second Jesuit appeared at the kitchen door and scared the cats away. They returned to the avenue and started walking north.

"It's not simple for some living creatures to find food, even in summer," I commented sadly, "and in winter, especially for animals, it's almost impossible, particularly in the city."

"But they were determined. You know how animals are; sometimes more determined than people.

They walked on the same side of the avenue as the Jesuit church and I followed. Then they reached an imposing red brick edifice under the control of the British queen. Probably no one noticed me because I was dreaming, and anyhow, for a long time the Anglican church didn't recognize Catholic priests. The Anglican bishop appeared, and said to the cats, 'My dear animal children. Please return immediately to your shelter. There is food for you and a warm corner. We Anglican clergy donate lots of money to the animal shelter, every year, at Christmas time.'

The mother cat and her kittens didn't even meow. They knew the authoritative voice of the Anglican bishop, through which could be felt the Queen's presence.

"They were probably raised in an Anglican family," I ventured. The Pope disregarded this comment.

They walked uptown and gradually the luxurious buildings disappeared, together with the doormen, and we saw drab dilapidated apartments.

"I presume they were in Spanish Harlem, or maybe Black Harlem." "I don't know," replied the Pope. "I have never been in Harlem." "Then, what happened?" I was curious about the end of the story.

As they walked and the buildings grew shabbier and dirty, a door opened, not by a doorman but by an old wrinkled woman in a cotton dress. She shouted, 'Oh mama mia,' and when she opened her mouth I saw she had no teeth.

"Was she Puerto Rican, Italian or Black?"

It is not important. She gently ushered the mother cat and kittens inside, who jumped happily about because the warmth of the house embraced them."

I never saw such a sad expression on the face of this man.
"Tell me, do you think that God's boundless wisdom would suggest Saint Francis for cardinal in New York?" Not waiting for my reply, he recited from memory, a prayer of Francis Bernadone of Assisi who left his wealthy silk-merchant father, became a soldier, and wound up taking care of lepers,

Lord,
make me an instrument of thy peace.

Cardinal Wojtyla with Stefan Wilkanowicz, editor of the monthly *Znak*, 1968.

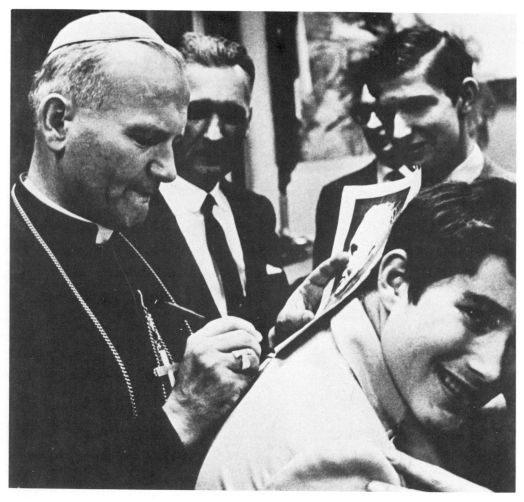

Cardinal Wojtyla signing a photograph in the United States, 1969.

In the United States, 1969.

Cardinal Wojtyla in Québec City, 1969; Cardinal Roy is at his left and his secretary, the Reverend Stanislaw Dziwisz, is at the photo's far right.

Where there is hatred, let me sow love;
where there is injury, pardon;
where there is doubt, faith;
where there is darkness, light
and where there is sadness, joy.
O divine Master,
grant that I may not so much seek to be consoled
    as to console
to be understood
    as to understand
to be loved
    as to love
For it is in giving that we receive;
it is in pardoning that we are pardoned;
it is in dying that we are born to eternal life.

"This means," I said, "that to be a cardinal in New York you have to be a lover of money."

"From there it is a long way to the Holy See," he replied softly, and looked beyond the window at the gently swaying trees. "My philosophy is simple. Only through service to people, without regard for race, color or creed, could I find the Love of God; I am lucky and blessed that the Almighty put on my life's road more than my share of great human beings such as Stefan Wyszyński, including the mysterious woman who saved my life on my way from slave labor in the Solvay quarries to my father's home. I don't know why God did this for me; why He blessed me."

I was moved, and could not reply.

He returned to reality. "Naturally, I value friendship of such Church people as John Joseph Cardinal Wright, who, as bishop, invited me to Pittsburgh a few times, or a man like John Joseph Cardinal Król from Philadelphia. But I also enjoyed Chicago, because next to Warsaw, this windy city has more Polish people than any other city.

"You met many other important Church people in America, did you not?"

"Certainly. I think I met them all. There was Joseph Francis Dearden from Detroit with his droopy chin, and in St. Louis, John J. Cardinal Carberry. He and I were nominated to the Cardinals College at the same time. Naturally, in Baltimore I renewed my acquaintance with Lawrence Joseph Cardinal Shehan whom I had met during Vatican Council II; he read an important declaration in December 1966 in which the Roman Catholic church cancelled the 1054 excommunication of the Patriarch of Constantinople. This act created good will between the Eastern and Western churches. During this ceremony in the Vatican, Nikodemus Metropolitan of Leningrad was present, as official representative of the Moscow Patriarch. After that, Cardinal Shehan, who was the chief delegate of the Vatican, went to the ceremony in Constantinople, and presented this official document to the Patriarch Atenagoras. As you can see, this Catholic official from Baltimore participated actively in *rapprochement* between the two churches that was inaugurated by Pope John XXIII.

"During my stay of one month in America, I travelled to many cities and was confronted with tremendous wealth as well as the enormous misery of the blacks in New York, Detroit and Chicago, and in California with the migrant workers from Mexico.

"As a Roman Catholic priest I always advocated that the church go arm-in-arm with black, yellow and brown races, with everyone who is oppressed, otherwise the Church should not call itself a Church of Christ. I discovered during my first visit there that the American Catholic Church was powerful materially, but some of the leaders were poor spiritually. I talked to them and expressed my opinions everywhere I went, including my lecture, 'Alienation or Participation' at Harvard University and Catholic University in Washington where I delivered another lecture entitled, 'Problems of Man's Autotheology'; I talked and talked until one of the American cardinals, I think it was Cardinal Cooke, said that guests should not express themselves in such a way. I replied, 'The truth should be said everywhere the same way; strongly and honestly. Otherwise God and people will condemn us, and we will perish!'"

"How did you like America?"

"I didn't spend a long time there. Besides, as a Cardinal of Polish extraction I was obliged to visit Polish communities, talk to Polish clergy and participate in various ceremonies. For example, during my visit to Orchard Lake in Michigan, I presented an urn filled with earth from Auschwitz Concentration Camp to the Reverend Walter Ziemba, Rector of the local Seminary."

"May I hear something about your impression of racial and religious minorities of America," I pressed.

"You mean Indians?"

"Not exactly, because we know that many of the Indian nations perished."

"You know that this is an enormous country with industrious people and tremendous wealth, and as I said, I visited homes of millionaires but also poor people."

"What about the majority of Americans – the great American middle class?"

"I visited them too. What impressed me most were American children. During my visit to an elementary school, I overheard a conversation between a mother and her five-year-old son. When the mother asked the boy to present the flowers he was holding to me, he refused for some reason. The mother was visibly upset and said, 'I will exchange you for a better behaved and more obedient boy.'.

"'You cannot do that,' he replied.

"'Why not?'

"'Because you cannot find a mother who will take a bad boy for a good boy.'

"Such American children will grow up and the majority will receive mediocre educations, just enough to make money; and possess just enough intelligence to place a smart ad, such as one I read in American papers about contraception: 'the unborn will bless you.'"

We laughed and the Pope asked, "What else do you want to know from me?"

"About American business."

"I don't know much about it, but I have noticed that in your country there is an abundance of bankers and not enough schools for black, Hispanic and white poor children to be adequately educated; due to this malady much great talent is lost. *C'est dommage* for the country. Again, overwhelming industrialization poisons the physical life of people, and exaggerated publicity and competition destroys their spiritual development. To illustrate this further I'd like to tell you a story: A robot entered a New York bank to cash a hundred thousand dollar check. When he completed the transaction, he left, and on the street another robot approched him with a gun in his hand, yelling, 'Your money or your battery!'"

"As a result of what you're telling me, organized religion in America is disappointing to God and abandoning humanity?"

"When we look at the history of the world, we conclude that the enormous drive to be wealthy kills the desire for spiritual richness, and obscures the vision of God and His goodness. This doesn't mean that America in the long run will succumb to this trend, and I have no facts to support my view, except maybe, I should quote Alexis de Tocqueville who visited the United States in the first part of the nineteenth century, and expressed an interesting opinion. Allow me to quote from memory:

> Americans are separated from all other nations by a common feeling of pride. For the last fifty years no pains have been spared to convince the inhabitants of the United States that they constitute the only religious, enlightened and free people. They perceive that for the present, their own democratic institution succeeds, while those of other countries fail; hence, they conceive an overwhelming opinion of their superiority.

Please tell me, does this opinion of de Tocqueville not apply today?"

Without waiting for my response he said, "In my view, *all* American Christian churches are disappointing because they support without criticism the political rulers of the country. If they do not begin sincere *aggiornamento* and deep renewal inside themselves and help the people regain dignity and spiritual integrity as well as justice, a great catastrophe will destroy them and everyone else."

This pronouncement of forthcoming doom brought to my mind Wojtyla's books and especially *Persona e Azione*, in which the author analyzes and interprets Christian doctrines and other religions of the world with equal if not superior foresight to de Tocqueville, who concentrated only on America. But Wojtyla devotes his studies to man in general and, according to philosopher Joseph Kockelmans, will have "a lasting impact on everybody concerned with the contemporary conception of man."

35
Curia's Corridors

"THE PEACEFUL village of Filetto lies in the Abruzzi Appennines. The highest peak of this chain of mountains is 10,000-foot Monte Carno. Through the Abruzzi Apennines, parallel to the Pescara river is the well-known pass, Pescara. From the town of Pescara the railroad went to Rome. The Apennines is not only a beautiful part of Italy with passes, mountain lakes and streams, but it also is the beginning of great Italian rivers such as the Tiber, Arno, Garigliano and Volturno. The climate of this region is severe, but below 1,500 feet there are plantations of olive trees and vegetables. And up to about 6,000 feet, chestnuts and oaks. The farming population is poor, hospitable and extremely religious."

Stefan Cardinal Wyszyński and I were sitting on the couch before a large oak coffee table with notes, pamphlets and books. It was our seventh meeting and we had scheduled for today a talk about the intricate mechanism of the Vatican administration. However, he was avoiding this topic, for the Curia had played tricks on him – for example, by preventing him from becoming Pope. A long time ago, I learned that when people in high positions have real or imaginary phobias, I should give them time to cleanse their souls because later they will return with a fresh start.

"The year was 1944. Germans fought on all fronts. Everywhere partisan movements were growing, including Italy. A detachment of the German army under the leadership of Captain Matthias Defregger arrived in the small mountain village of Filetto with an order to clear the region of partisans. Although the Germans were well-equipped, the Italian partisans defeated them because they knew the countryside so well. The remnants of the German detachment retreated, leaving their dead and wounded behind. But they returned with a larger force and killed most of the partisans as well as old women and children. Only a dozen partisans survived the attack, and took refuge in the mountains. Captain Defregger reported his victory to his superiors, yet the extermination of the Italian population in Filetto in no way delayed the final defeat of the German army. It only scarred the Captain's conscience, despite his attempts to convince himself that he was carrying out orders. When his conscience questioned, 'Why women and children?', Captain Defregger's mind lacked a logical reply. He was also frightened because when the war ended he discovered that the surviving partisans were outraged by the crime in Filetto."

"To be very Christian," I said to my host. "The history of war has had many Filettos and Defreggers through the ages."

"But this one was different. After the war Defregger entered the Roman Catholic Seminary in Munich and decided to serve God. He was a good student and was quickly noticed by his professors. I must add that his contacts with high army officials were kept intact. For those reasons, as soon as he finished the Seminary and was consecrated priest, he became the Chancellor of the Munich Curia. Reverend Defregger was introduced by friends to Julius Cardinal Döpfner. As the tale goes, the Cardinal, recognizing the talents of the former Nazi officer, suggested to the Vatican Curia that this bright man should be made Bishop. There were two sides to the story that surfaced later; one was that Cardinal Döpfner said he didn't know anything about Brother Matthias' past, and another that Defregger confessed to him everything about Filetto."

"It is rather unbelievable," I interrupted the Primate. "Because Cardinal Döpfner was known for his fairness as a scrupulous, honest man."

"Let's stick to the facts," said the Polish Primate. "During Pius XII's Pontificate, there was a beautiful and smart nun of German descent, named Pasqualina, who wielded great influence upon the Curia. Some malicious people called her Pasquinata, the name of a statue in Rome upon which, through time immemorial people had posted jests. This tradition intensified during the reign of Pius XII.

"Pasqualina was instrumental in keeping the well-known Nazi Bishop Carl Maria Splett as head of the Catholic Church in the Polish city of Gdańsk, although he lived in Germany. She also favored Cardinal Döpfner and many other Vatican Curia officials who expressed extremely conservative views. My own experience was minor, but I would like to tell you that in 1957 the Pope Pius XII called me to Rome for an urgent conference, and then made me – the Head of the Church of Poland – wait two weeks until he would see me."

"I presume he didn't like your political philosophy."

"You may be right, because the Holy Father was convinced by his conservative advisers that 'the Polish Church should sacrifice itself in fighting Bolshevism.'"

"At this juncture I would like to ask if it is true that his predecessor, Pius XI, was poisoned in 1939 by Germans, so that he would be succeeded by Eugenio Cardinal Pacelli, former Apostolic Nuncio in Munich and friend of Benito Mussolini, who as Secretary of the Vatican Department of State, signed a concordat with Hitler's regime in 1933."

"I see that you have some knowledge of European history," answered Wyszyński with a wry smile, "but you must know that Achille Cardinal Ratti who became Pope Pius XI was a lifelong conservative, and under his guidance Cardinal Pacelli regulated Church affairs with Fascist Italy and Nazi Germany."

"Yet isn't it true that during the last two years of his life, Pius XI lost complete confidence in the political philosophy of Pacelli, who believed Fascists and Nazis could be instrumental in fighting godless Bolshevism?"

"I would like to illustrate for the purpose of objectivity, what Cardinal Tardini, Undersecretary of the Vatican State, said during the war to Hugh Montgomery, Chargé d'Affaires of Great Britain. 'It is true that in the case of German victory, only Hitlerism will be the master of Europe and all other nations will suffer slavery and oppression. In the event of an Allied victory, Communist Russia would not be alone; she would have Great Britain and America to cope with. Nevertheless, the Communists would surely move West, destroying European civilization and Christian culture.' Vatican politicians convinced the Pope long before the war that the best approach to the complex political situation was neutrality. This neutrality was cleverly interpreted by the German Catholic Church and especially by German Jesuits such as Schneider and others."

"But, let's return to Pius XI, and clear up the mystery of his assassination."

"I do not know if I can clear up anything, but let me stick to the facts I know about firsthand. In December 1938, Pius XI was working on the encyclical in which he, a disillusioned man, was convinced that Mussolini's Fascism and Germany's Hitlerism were no better than Russian Bolshevism. The Pope kept this encyclical in strict secrecy and, as I said, worked on it without advice from the Vatican State Department. His Holiness was considering reading his document personally during the Christmas holiday. But for some reason, he postponed it until February 1939. Anyhow, despite his secrecy, news reached Berlin and Adolf Hitler gave a personal order to his intelligence organization to try to poison the Pope as soon as possible. I knew that such an encyclical, the original and four copies, was kept in the private apartment of the Holy Father. But, to this day, nobody in the Vatican can find any trace of it. Also, on February 9, 1939, after breakfast Pius XI lost consciousness and rolled on the floor in tremendous pain, holding his stomach with both hands. The next day, he was dead. For the first time in the history of the Roman Catholic Church, the Vatican Secretary of State, Eugene Cardinal Pacelli, who acquired the name of Pius XII, became Pope."

Primate Wyszyński rose from the couch. He was disturbed, and while holding his hands behind his back, paced nervously.

"Let's stop this conversation," I said, pouring mineral water into both glasses. He approached the coffee table, took a sip and replied, "Nobody knows where I am."

"Then, let's call."

"I am sure your telephone is tapped, and when they discover that I am here..."

"I would not worry about your secretary."

"Do you have something against him?"

"Not exactly, but I don't think he is a serious man."

"Who gave you that idea?"

"After exchanging a few sentences with him, I knew his only interest was in becoming a bishop."

"Practically everybody in my office wants to be a bishop. It is human nature to strive to advance oneself. But, I suspect that you have something else against him."

I argued with myself whether to talk to him about his secretary, because anything he said I thought would be anticlimactic after his bombshell about the Popes. The Primate insisted, so I finally said, "Some time ago this young man telephoned my hotel room and said in a condescending tone, 'If you talk with Communist officials about

Church affairs, you will be cut off from the Primate and will never see the Pope or anybody else important in the Church.'"

"I see now that he is rather stupid, but I forgive him and presume that you will too." He then became silent, sat beside me, and almost whispered in my ear, "You know that some Jesuits in Rome and in Warsaw, and my boy, Bronek, say that you are searching among high government officials in Poland and in Italy for scandalous stories about the Church. I know that you are a writer and should be able to talk to Fascists, Communists, Democrats, to anybody you want. I understand, but Jesuits..."

"I suspect that my good friend Jesuit Casimiro who works with Corda Cordi was eager to place me under his influence, which disturbed me very much.

"From my long experience, I know that when you try to pin down informers and ask them for the facts, they never come up with them. But, before I leave you, I would like to let you in on one more secret: the Holy Father John XXIII saved world peace despite the Jesuits' and Curia's advice to the contrary. Imagine that it was only because of the small matter of jealousy that Dominican Father Felix Morlion became intermediary instead of them."

I was shocked, but didn't have enough intellectual strength to pose a pertinent logical question. I simply said, "What is this all about?"

"In the fall of 1962 the Cuban Missile Crisis erupted and around the same time there was a Conference of East and West intellectuals in Andover, Massachusetts, in which Felix Morlion, under an assumed name, took part. President John F. Kennedy, knowing about Felix's connection with the CIA, asked him a favor. We should point out that Felix was one of the organizers of the Pro Deo anticommunist university in Rome, for which the CIA paid the upkeep. Another fact is that Norman Cousins, editor of the *Saturday Review*, was the intermediary between the President of the United States and Felix Morlion. On top of that, Felix claimed that without anyone's help he talked personally with Mr. Kennedy, who requested that he get in touch with Pope John XXIII immediately and ask him to take part in settling the Cuban Crisis by arranging a meeting between the leaders of the Soviet Union and the United States.

"Felix immediately went to Rome and got in touch with Bishop Igino Cardinale who at that time was Head of the Protocol Department in the Papal Office and had direct access to John XXIII. As a result of the verbal and later written plea from the President to the Pope, the Vatican Council, during the plenary session on October 20, prepared an 'Appeal to the World,' parts of which said that 'there is no man who did not hate war and who did not deeply desire peace. The Church is continually expressing its will to work for peace and to cooperate loyally with everybody who is striving for the same thing.' During the night of October 24, the Holy Father put the final touches on his letter to the governments of the United States and the Soviet Union. The next morning this personal note from the Holy Father was delivered to the Soviet and American Ambassadors in Rome. On the afternoon of the same day, the Vatican radio announced an appeal to those two governments, parts of which read as follows,

> We desire to remind those on whose shoulders responsibility for peace rests, that they should go according to their conscience and listen to the calls from all parts of the world, those of children, old people, individuals and societies: peace! ... We repeat this call and ask the governments not to be deaf and indifferent to their peoples' desire. The governments should do everything possible in their power to save peace. They should use their wisdom and common sense for which they will be blessed in Heaven and on Earth ...

I could wait no longer and asked Cardinal Stefan, "How do you know all these things in such detail?"

"I was there. Peace is very important for my country too." He continued in an emotional voice, but from a different angle. "On the morning of November 16, Dr. Pietro Valdoni, personal physician of the Holy Father was deeply immersed in reading works of the Fathers of the Church, David's Psalms, and letters from Apostle Paul. When I visited him, I saw on his enormous desk, among other books, St. Augustine's *Civitate Dei* and he pointed out a page to me where the author was talking about peace: 'that it should emerge from your house, from your Order, from a city, from society, and from a man.' Then he said, 'I am working intensely on my encyclical *Pacem in Terris* and am looking diligently for ancient wisdom in old writings; however, I am not neglecting Professor Pietro Pavan and the group of specialists who work under him, but I think to prepare this encyclical I must pray to God more to grant me wisdom. Current international politics are pressing me down.'

"He asked me to be seated and concluded, 'I should not abandon the hope and belief that countries of the Western bloc are expressing a positive desire for peace, and at the same time I cannot abandon hope of the same desire for peace by the Eastern bloc. I should be objective and support the dialogue wholeheartedly, as a constructive intermediary; otherwise the door will close and we will be confronted with an ugly war...'

"He didn't know about the thundering around him in ecclesiastical circles, especially from Jesuit black clouds and other black clouds from the Congregation for Propagation of the Faith, headed by Alfredo Cardinal Ottaviani, a personal enemy of the Holy Father. For the purpose of combating the Holy Father's ideas, Cardinal Ottaviani used an intelligent Dominican priest by the name of Luigi Ciapi who had powerful connections in the Curia. He not only used his own eloquence and knowledge, but through research and compilations utilized opinions of previous popes, Gregory XVI, Pius XI and Pius XII, to convince everybody that they were one hundred percent against Socialism or Communism; ergo, John XXIII was pursuing politics, not only against the present-day Curia, but against the tradition of the Church. The Jesuits were also undermining the efforts of Good John. One of them, a prominent Frenchman, G. Jarlot said, 'The most dangerous thing for the West is Communism, which in the case of its victory will bring Christian civilization to its end. Russia possesses an atomic bomb and at the present is trying to surpass the United States in controlling outer space. But, China who possesses enormous potential power is also reaching the international arena. Don't you think that in such a situation the defense of Western Europe is equivalent to the defense of Christianity?'"

Wyszyński stopped for a moment and after reflection said, "As you can see, the powerful forces in the international Church hierarchy, in addition to the bureaucracy of the Curia were *par fas et nefas* for confrontation with the East, without considering the grave consequences."

He returned from pacing the room, sat beside me, and putting his head in his hands, observed, "Sometimes I think I do not understand how the religious educational institutions produce priests like that."

"Tell me, please, what was John XXIII's opinion?"

"He would not stoop so low as to make personal attacks or reply to them. As Supreme Pontiff, he was far above that. 'We have something more important to do than to throw rocks at the Communists. Our entire energy must be put to work for a compromise between the ideologies and the states. As a result of this, we will achieve peace.'"

"Wasn't there an attempt on the part of some governments to prevent the publication of *Pacem in Terris?*"

"I only know about one incident," replied the Primate. "The German Bundestag sent a man named Eugene Gerstenmaier who tried to convince the Holy Father to rewrite the encyclical, but he did not succeed; nor did the *demarche*, delivered by the German Ambassador, Chancellor Adenauer, to the Vatican. Cardinal Ottaviani did not even listen to the personal instructions of the Holy Father not to interfere with the wishes of the Supreme Pontiff. He tried on his own to mobilize the Curia's forces, as well as more conservative bishops all over the world, especially in the United States, to prevent the encyclical from seeing the light of day. Despite all actions by the secular and conservative members of the Church, *Pacem in Terris* was officially published on April 11, 1963. On June 3 of the same year, John XXIII died..."

My guest stopped and looked around the room, as if he were searching for something, or perhaps just for words. "As you can see, I know how to talk long and chaotically." He then began to collect his notes.

"I am very grateful for those revelations." I reached for the bottle of Courvoisier. "Maybe you will take a sip of cognac?"

"You always insist on drinking. Go ahead and pour," he said with a smile.

Encouraged by this cooperation, I asked, "I would like to know what finally happened to Bishop Matthias Defregger. And, a second question is, how it came to be that the nuns from Collegium Teutonicum tried to exterminate Vatican cats?"

"The Defregger affair was significant from the viewpoint that German influences built during the Pius XII Pontificate were still strong in the Curia and did not reflect the progressive philosophy of John XXIII or even of his successor, Cardinal Montini who assumed the Holy See on June 21, 1963. Paul VI made a rather large mistake by nominating in 1965 Basque Priest Pedro Arrupe to become General of the Society of Jesus. Arrupe spent twenty-three years in Japan and was infected with that country's disease—servility and connivance. The latter characteristic is probably more a part of his own personality."

Although I could not redirect the Primate to my original question which concerned the German Bishop and nuns, I figured that he was leading me to one more interesting story and I would have enough time to go back to the original. So I followed him by asking my next question: "Tell me, on what basis was the power of the Jesuits and their general Father Arrupe built?"

Again, my friend started painting the picture on a broad canvas. "In the world there are eight hundred thousand nuns and a quarter of a million monks, among them about thirty-four thousand Jesuits whose General Curia is situated on Borgo San Spirito. Day after day, year after year, information, gathered by members of this Order, flows to this place from all over the world. The information is about everybody who amounts to something and is gathered by intelligent people. The Jesuits are the best educated group in the entire Church, and they are also in charge of one of the most important Catholic educational institutions, the Gregorian University in Rome. Most of the Bishops and Cardinals over many, many years have been educated in this university. There is no Catholic institution in which there is not, on some level, a Jesuit priest who, besides his regular duties, collects information for his Order and sends it, sometimes directly, to the main headquarters in Rome. There the information is processed and filed for future use. As a result, it is impossible to say that the Jesuits didn't know about the background of Bishop Defregger. This tradition of spying goes back many ages, and as you know, the Society of Jesus was created by St. Augustine in the fourth century; in the seventeenth and eighteenth centuries the Jesuits reached the peak of power when they controlled almost completely, education and science, and became advisers to the princes and kings of Europe. Their political influence in various European countries was such that they even disrupted the functions of some governments. As a result, France, Spain, Portugal and Austria approached Pope Clement XVI, himself a Franciscan, and asked him to curtail Jesuit activities. On August 16, 1773, the Pope dissolved the Order with his *Dominus ac Redemptor* brief. Over forty years later in 1814, Pope Pius VII restored it. You must understand that in some European countries, Jesuits were an important force in building education, especially in Poland when our country was occupied by three neighboring powers."

Cardinal Wyszyński bypassed my observation, "You are right, but referring back to the beginning of our conversation, Paul VI could have saved himself much trouble if he had not nominated Arrupe, but instead his confessor, Reverend Paolo Dezza, who was later the confessor of John Paul I. But those are the weaknesses of human nature due to belief in people."

This conversation with Wyszyński was conducted at the end of 1980, when the Primate disclosed an important fact to me, "Soon after Karol Wojtyla's ascension to the Holy See, I suggested to him that he remove Arrupe and nominate Dezza to take his place. Karol replied, 'I am thinking about it, but I have to be careful in this delicate matter...' I knew what he meant, because American Jesuits and the Vatican Curia were maneuvering to put Reverend Vincent O'Keefe from New Jersey in charge of the Society of Jesus. What's more, without permission from the Holy Father, the Jesuits in Rome sent news on August 10, 1981, that Reverend O'Keefe would be nominated Superior General. The Holy Father was surprised and much annoyed. On October 22, 1981, he announced that Father Dezza who, *nota bene*, was eighty years old, would be the temporary Head of the Society of Jesus, as 'personal delegate of the Pope.'"

"What were the reasons for such 'rivalry' between the Holy See and the 'Black Pope,' as Arrupe called himself?"

"There were many explanations going far back, but the most recent was that he didn't like some of the new reforms introduced by John XXIII and Paul VI. For example, the positions of bishops and cardinals in the Curia had been for life, but now they were for a duration of only five years, after which the Holy Father could keep or discharge them. In other words, neither Curia officials nor the Jesuit Order liked the papal strong hand and rigid control over Vatican bureaucracy and the independence of the Jesuits."

"This is interesting, but I am still puzzled about what happened to Bishop Defregger who took part during the war in the extermination of the Italian village of Filetto."

"This is a typical trick which the curia played on Paul VI. Somebody important in this organization removed a biography from Defregger's file and left only Cardinal Döpfner's letter of recommendation; the result was that a Captain in Hitler's army became a Roman Catholic Bishop in September 1968."

"That is rather embarrassing. I heard that the Jesuit dossier on Captain Matthias Defregger did not reach the Holy Father either."

"True, but what is even more embarrassing is that Cardinal Döpfner told me himself that he would like to see his protégé Matthias in the cardinal's purple robes occupying his place."

"What happened next?" I pursued.

"My good friend, Giovanni Cardinal Benelli, Archbishop of Florence said that the Franciscan Fathers, who have been rivals with the Jesuits for a long time, leaked the story of the Nazi Captain to the Italian press. The whole affair received tremendous publicity. Some people said that the Holy Father was the victim of Jesuit and conservative groups in the Vatican, and others that the Pope knew everything about it, but was trying to discredit Cardinal Döpfner who had high aspirations for his Captain."

"How did this finally end?"

"Bishop Defregger disappeared from sight and people said that under specific order from the Holy See he had locked himself in a monastery and the whole affair quieted down."

"*Rem acu tetigisti*," I said. "You have touched the point with a needle."

"This is not the end of the story. In 1970 the monk Defregger appeared in the village of Filetto and insisted that he should conduct a Holy Mass. When the villagers heard about it, they rallied around the Church, made a lot of commotion, and tried to stone him. The German escaped with his life and went back to the monastery."

For no reason, I said, "*Roma veduta, fede perduta* (See Rome and lose your faith)."

Primate Wyszyński rose from his seat and yelled, "That's not true. It's a lie."

"I am sorry."

He quieted. "This incident taught us a lesson, and confirms the Evangelical saying, 'Anyone who wants to be great among you, let him be your servant; anyone who wants to be first among you, let him be your slave.'"

"As we reach the premises of human interest stories, let me not forget to ask you what happened with the Vatican cats that were supposed to be exterminated by the nuns?"

"This is an entirely different event which has an interesting background, perhaps more interesting than the story. I heard about it from Cardinal Benelli who at that time was Head of the Papal Cabinet."

"And Undersecretary of the Vatican State?"

"Yes, but the most important thing was that Cardinal Benelli from Florence was hated by Cardinal Siri from Genoa, who was fifteen years his senior."

"Is he the same Giuseppe Siri who competed against Wojtyla for the Holy See?"

"Yes, Giuseppe saw Giovanni Benelli as competition because his colleague was younger and more intelligent, and above all, the Holy Father liked him."

While Primate Wyszyński drank mineral water, I thought, 'He always goes around the main narrative, but sometimes the background is more interesting than the story.'

"Giuseppe became Cardinal in 1953 and Giovanni in 1977. The older Cardinal did not consider Cardinal Wojtyla his most important rival at the beginning, because he was a foreigner from a socialist country. So he went after his compatriot Giovanni Benelli, and having many connections, not only in the Curia, but being a good friend of General Arrupe, he used the Jesuits working in the Vatican Administration to concoct a story about cats for the purpose of compromising Benelli who was close to the Pope."

I was so excited about this that I poured double cognacs for the Primate and myself; he resented this, being distracted from his account of the incident.

"You know as well as I that in Rome, and especially in the Vatican, there are hundreds of thousands of cats living at the mercy of good people. Especially in the Vatican, cats are well fed by brothers and sisters of the Franciscan Order."

"It is well known that Franciscans like animals more than anything, but Jesuits are fascinated by the human intellect." I couldn't resist making this ironic comment.

"You are unfair to the Jesuits, but you might be right. The hordes of cats running around Vatican gardens were killing birds without anyone's interference and fewer and fewer songs could be heard. So Cardinal Siri used this event to convince Jesuits that they should help find a way to exterminate the cats. Smart Jesuits suggested that they approach the nuns living in Collegium Teutonicum, who were famous for their cleanliness and order, that they should take care of the cats."

"It is a rather clever gimmick to destroy the reputation of Cardinal Benelli."

"The good sisters decided to call in a village boy for help. He was supposedly like St. Francis and could talk to animals. With his singing he could lure all the cats from the town like a modern 'pied piper' and lead them to the mountains."

"It is an ingenious project, but one for which they would have to receive permission from the Pope or at least Benelli. What would happen if the boy went around the Vatican singing and calling the cats, gathering them, let's say, on St. Peter's Square, and from there, leading them through Rome to some obscure village? Wouldn't it be embarrassing for the Pope to admit that he had to hire an illiterate boy to get rid of the Vatican cats?"

"Certainly. The whole affair would be ridiculous. First, the Italian press and then the world press would make fun of the Pope, because how could the Holy Father manage people if he cannot manage his Vatican cats? A lot of people would lose their faith in the Catholic religion. To top it off, country people would be horrified to see thousands of cats roaming around farms, devastating fowl, livestock, and wild birds. Villagers might rally and invade the Vataican; then the Pope would have to speak to them, but how could he explain that cats are good for villages but bad for Vatican inhabitants?"

"A grave problem."

"The sisters gathered together in the Collegium Teutonicum and discussed the matter thoroughly. They came to the conclusion that the only way out was to poison the cats."

"I guess that was the only way out."

"Unfortunately. So the nuns bought poison, and made meatballs inside of which they placed the poison. They divided the meatballs among themselves, and in the depth of night, were ready to insert the meatballs in various places in buildings, the Papal Garden and in any other spots where the cats gathered."

"Gruesome, but necessary," I interjected quietly.

"Yes, but the Franciscan Brothers discovered this plot and went to the press. As a result, the action was stopped."

"The cats were safe?"

"Yes, they were safe, because Giovanni Benelli gave orders not only to stop the plan to poison them, but also to deny that such a plan existed. The Holy Father heard about this amusing incident, called in Cardinal Siri and severely scolded him, 'You should work hard for peace in a world where there should not be any kind of killing."

"As you can see, sometimes even cats can curtail the ambitions of powerful cardinals and help others," Primate Wyszyński concluded.

36

The Quality of Renewal

"DURING my first vicarage in Niegowić parish I heard the confession of a young girl who said, "'I committed one sin…'

"I asked this innocent voice, 'What kind of sin?'

"'I wrote a story about a cat, but this anecdote resembles the story of my twin brother. The teacher punished me.'

"I asked, 'Why did you do that?'

"'Because we own the same cat.'"

I laughed and thought, what is the purpose of asking children to go to confession? But I didn't have time to phrase my question because John Paul II came up with another amusing anecdote.

"A fourteen-year-old boy came to confession when I was serving in the St. Florian church in Cracow, and said that he had entered a neighbor's house and stolen two suits, immediately adding that he would not do anything like that again. I asked, 'When you stole the suits didn't you think about your mother and father?' The boy replied, 'Yes, while stealing the suits I thought about my father, but in my opinion, they wouldn't have fit him.' "I am not telling you this for the sake of jokes; what I'd like to explain is that priests who hear such confessions should personally take part in leading young people to the right road. We should not occupy ourselves so much with the colorful forms of Christianity, but with its simple content. We should bring religion to the people, not wait for them to come to us. That's the reason the Second Vatican Council was so important; because this great gathering brought the church to the people and to the reality of the modern world. Today the Vatican Curia has to pay attention to the Synods of Bishops who bring new ideas from all over the world, directly to the attention of the Pope, that become the primary base for the Holy Father's conceptions for Church law, and his attitude to the world. The Curia, through the actions of John XXIII and Paul VI is confined to an executive position, and cannot interfere much with the legislative power of the Supreme Pontificate. What's more Paul VI internationalized Vatican offices to such an extent that sixty-three percent of the employees of the Curia are people of various nationalities from outside the Vatican. He gave more authority to the Vatican Secretary of State and other church organizations such as the Commission on Justice and Peace. This created healthy rivalry between them. The rearrangement of power enhanced the position of the Holy See. On July 8, 1970, Paul VI defined this power: 'According to Christ's purposes, power does not exist for those who exercise it, but for human beings who benefit from it... There is no just authority of man over other men if it does not serve the people.'"

John Paul II poured coffee in his library, where paintings of well-known Italian religious artists hung on two walls, "Museums, palaces, churches and the Vatican, together with the Holy Father now serve the common people. There is not much royal splendor or archaic custom. The Curia's dignitaries do not wear picturesque uniforms, and all the privileges which powerful people of the world once received from the Vatican are nil. Even the Palace of the Pope is now called the home of the Pope. All these things began with the reign of John XXIII about whom a friend of mine, the Primate of Belgium, Leo Joseph Cardinal Suenens said, after his death, 'Leaving us, he brought our souls closer to God, and made the earth a better place for people to live.' Paul VI later said, 'Before we convert the world we should talk to people on an equal basis, because the Roman Catholic Church recognizes the spiritual and moral value of other non-Christian religions, and is ready to join with those religions in the struggle for brotherhood, social justice and freedom of conscience. Such a dialogue we are initiating now.'"

The Pope searched his memory. "During the second Synod of Bishops, conducted in late 1969, he invited me for a private conference, asking how I imagined the position of the Holy See versus the needs of the people. I repeated almost his own words without hesitation. 'The Church should be a light for children, youth, scientists, for the world of workers and artists, as well as those in government and those who are governed. Atheism is the most difficult problem of our time, but atheism is often inspired by the desire for justice and progress. Because we are for the same thing, we should cooperate with them in building the new world. Non-Christians who are sincere and act according to their conscience should be respected. Unification of Christian churches should not be the result of the concept that one church should dominate another.'

"I added that I agreed with Cardinal Suenens who said, 'It is important to ponder why so many people are negating God and combatting religion. We should find the road which will lead us to a dialogue with them.' I reached for the pronouncement of other leaders of the Catholic Church as though I would show him, delicately, that I am not the only brain in the Holy Church. I spoke about Bernard John Cardinal Alfrink, Archbishop of Utrecht who said, 'The church should begin a dialogue with Communists and atheists to work together with all people in achieving common good.' Finally, I searched my mind for the pronouncement of Franz Cardinal König. 'Believers should work with atheists in building a new world, and show them that religious motivations help rather than lead people away from noble goals.'

"The Holy Father said, 'You could be a peacemaker among cardinals, and even better than I at the Holy See.'

"I bowed my head and replied, 'I do not have enough experience for such honor and grace.'

"He said, 'You are a good diplomat. I want you to be a leading spirit in the Synod of Bishops.' I thought of thinking, and searched for words, but he spoke first, 'You should go skiing. Where do you like to ski, Italy or Poland?'

"'Wherever the snow is better.'"

"'Even now you are a good diplomat. I will pray that you should live a long time, because the Church needs you.'

"Holy Father, I will be sincere when I say that I need the Church more than the Church needs me.' He embraced me warmly, and we parted as two brothers. I returned to Cracow the next day, packed my skiing gear and went to the Carpathian Mountains for a little relaxation."

"I presume this was the beginning of your complete involvement on the highest level of Church affairs?"

"In September I prepared myself to take an active part in the Church Synod of Bishops which began on the last day of that month in 1971. Two hundred and fifty bishops from all over the world attended this conference which dealt with a crisis in the ministry. The second, maybe more important object, was how to define Church doctrine which dealt with justice in the world."

"Those were two basic questions?"

"In my opinion a crisis in the ministry is strongly linked with an economic crisis of men. We have reached a point where people are divided into two definite groups; one has everything and the other doesn't know if he is going to have a piece of bread tomorrow. Priests are trying to reconcile these two groups, but they're unsuccessful because a hungry man cannot like a man who has everything. Church leaders should be on the side of hungry men. That was my position at the Synod of Bishops. One leader of the South American church, Bishop Jeronimo José Podesta from Argentina agreed with me because he knew the problem firsthand. 'In Latin America there is going to be a revolution. What's more, the continent is alive with revolutionary movements and we Catholics should not be for the status quo. We have to work with the people, otherwise, the Roman Catholic Church will disappear.'"

"What was the attitude of the Pope?" I asked.

"In a letter to the Belgian Cardinal Le Roy, head of the Papal Commission *Justitia et Pax*, dated May 14, 1971, Paul VI said that just distribution of material wealth in the world should be our goal; states should be arranged in such a way as to curtail brute force, and a pact between the states should have the good of people as a goal. In his letter *Octogesima Adveniens*, the Pope spoke about socialism as a positive force believed by millions of people, and to keep those people in the Church we should go out to them. This is how the concept of Christian Socialism was born and defined during his time on the Holy See. As a result of the Papal pronouncement, the French Episcopate in 1972 came up with a document entitled *Christian Political Practice* in which the bishops said that the Catholic church should not formulate directives for people as to how they should behave in political affairs. But Catholics should participate in all political groups, and in this way reinforce Church teachings among people of various views and beliefs. French bishops were for a division between religion and politics, but they were flexible in searching for new ways to improve human minds and the material well-being of people in general."

I was impressed by erudition, but at the same time I was tired of all those pious opinions of Church Princes about how they intended to improve the lot of working people. Sometimes I even have doubts about their sincerity in sacrifice for almighty God and ordinary laborers. I noticed on his table a book about winter sports entitled *Zakopane*, which once was a famous international ski resort.

I presume he read my mind because he said, "In a few days I returned to Cracow, and one early morning, I went skiing."

"By yourself?"

"I guess I must have. From the day I became Cardinal I thought it would be unbecoming to go with a group of young people, although I would enjoy it. However, I have much thinking to do. It would do me good to be alone in the mountains, close to God."

He went in complete secrecy, even from his personal secretary the Reverend Stanislaw Dziwisz. This physically small man had a talent for maneuvering people under the pretext that God gave him license to protect his Cardinal, later the Pope. Although I knew him well, I could not grasp him completely. Nor could sweet words, or a bottle of good whiskey change his mind. He was always uniformly suspicious and interested in others' affairs, no matter what gender. From childhood he had a detecting talent, and from the first day he met Wojtyla fell in love with him. But I still don't know for what reason Karol Wojtyla selected him to be his shadow and alter ego. Maybe at the bottom of the big heart of this small man lies a tremendous amount of love for the boss, or maybe just a simple desire to be a Cardinal. I do not know any other secretary who is feared by so many people, and deeply respected by others. All of them consider him a friend, and except for me, call him Stszek. He might some day die a cardinal, or an obscure monk in a forgotten monastery.

There was a blizzard in the town of Zakopane, which lies in the Tatra ridge of the Carpathian Mountains. Cardinal Wojtyla, dressed in his new ski outfit, with his equipment on his shoulder, took the lift to the Kasprowy summit. Snow and wind created a white wall, obscuring vision. He went to the restaurant to have a cup of tea and wait for better skiing conditions. When he entered, students from Jagellonian University recognized him.

He smiled and said, "Please don't betray the cardinal; otherwise I will complain to God."

They laughed, drank tea and ate ham canapés. After finishing his meal Wojtyla left the group. But snow was still playing its games with the wind. He put his skis on and decided to head down the mountain.

"I would have waited longer in the restaurant," he said, "but didn't want to remain with the young people; so I put my skis on, looked up and almost through a fog, could see from the top of Kasprowy peak, to Orawa-Podhale valley, dominated by the ridge of Gubalowka hill. Way at the bottom someplace was the town of Zakopane."

"How could you see through such terrific snow?" I asked.

"I was dreaming, and I saw in my dream," he responded. "I told myself, I had descended this mountain many times from the same place, and knew my way by heart. I decided to ski and experience communion with the wild nature of winter. The world looked tantalizing in all white. I started fast and right away the wind intensified its beating of my face and ski mask. But I did not look through it much. I felt lightness in my head, and music in my ears. This symphony of nature mingled with thoughts about those who tried to conquer the highest peaks of the Alps many years ago, such as Jósef Czarnota, the first European to climb Mount Demavend, the highest peak in Iran, at 18,600 feet! And I could not descend properly from Kasprowy summit merely 6400 feet. 'What kind of man are you?' I thought. My heart pounded, my eyes were confronted with darkness, although the snow was white.

"Suddenly, I found a religious experience in my subconscious; the Holy Father grew into a bright monster, and the Vatican II conference began losing its color and sense. I said to myself, 'Better stick to God.' When I went to God in my mind, my legs could not coordinate themselves, and I whispered, 'How could you lead millions of faithful if you cannot lead your two legs?' Again, for no reason, following this thought, a line from Horatius jumped to the forefront of my mind, 'Muse, if you grab somebody's neck, this person will never be caught by logic!..' I didn't know if this thought was Horatius' or not, because Slowacki, the romantic poet, interfered with it, saying to me in private, 'Anyone who chooses an eagle's nest on top of a mountain instead of his home is...' What this meant I don't know. I was in a panic. I stopped, toppled over and tried to remove my skis. I raised my head and began my conversation with God, asking Him to forgive my pride and my exaggerated belief in myself, especially when once I thought,

'How nice it would be to sit on St. Peter's throne.' I was arrogant. Although people did not know this, God knew very well. It was blasphemous on my part; then a picture of St. Francis entered my head, talking with the birds; but why here? There are no birds except the white wings of snow. St. Francis did not want to talk to me. He was busy with the birds. Blessed Father Kolbe appeared with Doctor Korczak, and above them Sister Theresa Benedictina with black hair and white wings, floating on air. And my father, mother, sister, brother and many other faces of loved ones appeared, but rather small and insignificant in their physical appearance, below the Saints. All of them were praying to God, and begging Him to forgive my sins. Although I could not see their eyes, nor their raised faces and hands, I knew they were crying.

"Suddenly, I felt better. My ski mask lost its shield of snow, and a spiritual *vade mecum* entered my soul. I understood the real meaning of faith and its beneficial implications in the mortal life of a human being. I heard the voice of a woman, 'Your Eminence got lost!" A masculine voice followed, 'Let's go together.' I didn't know whose voices they were. Maybe Doctor Korczak who was taking his children on the road to God? Or Sister Theresa who, directly from the crematorium, went to God; or maybe Father Kolbe? I am sure now that it was Father Kolbe, because I personally went to the Holy Father and begged Him to make this man a saint.

"I regained consciousness; looked to the left and to the right, and what did I see? Students kneeling over me, the same ones that I left at the restaurant at the top of Kasprowy summit. I heard the emotional voice of a woman. 'Although you are a Cardinal, you should not go by yourself in such a blizzard.'

"I said, with penitence, 'I got lost, not as a Cardinal, but as one of you.'

"Then, together with confidence, because you have to know that when you travel in a group you are more likely to reach your destination, we went not only to Zakopane, but far beyond it."

Skiing at Zakopane, 1970.

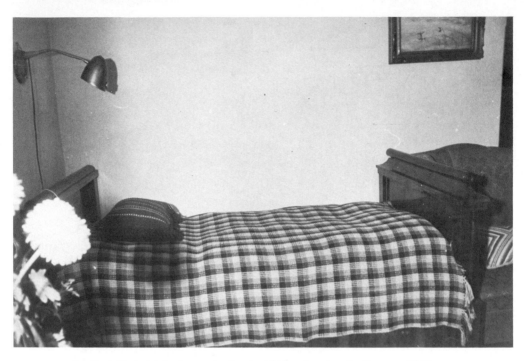

Cardinal Wojtyla's bedroom in the Archbishop's palace in Cracow, 1978.

The Cardinal has retired and his shoes wait for him to wake.

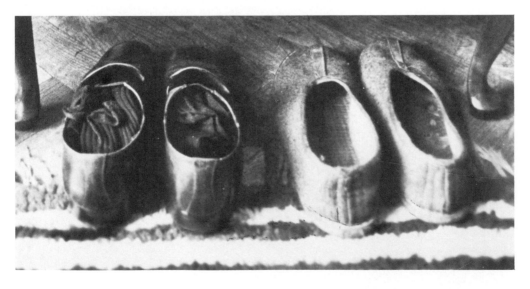

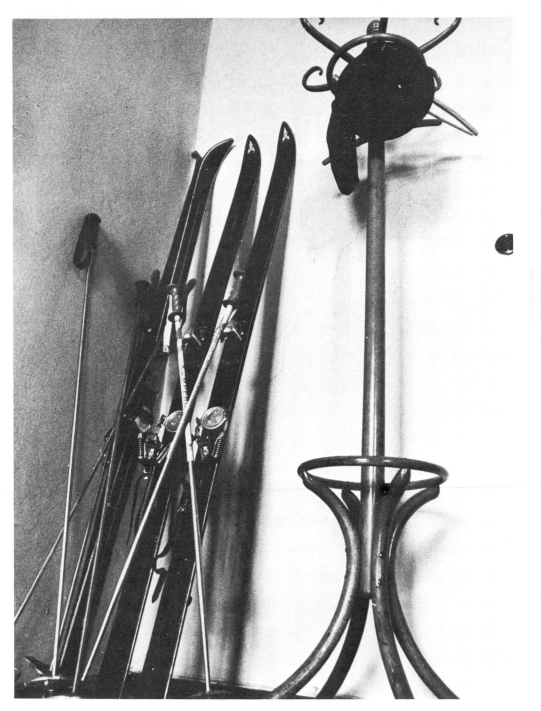

The Cardinal's skis, poles, and berets, 1978.

Rakowicki cemetery, Cracow. Pope John Paul II prays at the grave of his parents,
June 1979.

37

His Eminence Cardinal Rubin

W HEN I talked with Wladek Rubin for the first time after
World War II, he was a Cardinal and the prefect of the
Sacred Congregation for Oriental Churches. His predecessor, a Frenchman by the name of Pierre Paul Cardinal Philippe, received top information from him on secret dealings in the Middle East
during the war. No one in the Vatican knew this part of the world as
well as Wladek who spent the war years there, and was blessed with a
keen memory for faces, details and names.

This is his offical biography: Wladyslaw Cardinal Rubin was born on
September 20, 1917 at Toki in Lwów Province. His father was a farmer,
and Wladek finished secondary school in the town of Tarnopol. In
1935 he was enrolled as a student of theology and law at Lwów University, but the war interrupted his studies. Like many other Poles during the Stalin-Hitler pact, he was arrested and sent to a forced labor
camp. When Hitler's army attacked the Soviet Union Wladek was released and joined Polish forces being formed in the Soviet Union to
fight the German invaders. Soon after this, Polish legions were moved
from the Soviet Union to the Near East, and became part of the British
forces. The military vicar of the Polish forces was Archbishop Gawlina,
and he gathered together all the theology seminarians who had not yet
completed their studies, and sent them to Beirut where they earned
their degrees at St. Joseph University.

Wladek, a dark complexioned, pleasant man, with a ready smile soon
became a friend to professors such as Monsignor Ignace Ziadeh, later
Maronite Archbishop of Beirut, and Monsignor Michael Doumith,
Bishop of Sarba. His closeest contemporary colleagues at the University
were Antonio Joubeir, the Archbishop of Tripoli; Nasrallah Sfeir, Patri-
archal Vicar of the Maronites; Joseph Khoury, who became Maronite

Archbishop of Tyre; Chucrallah Harb, Bishop of Jounieh; and You-hanna Kabés, Bishop of Alexandria for the Coptic Rite. Many other students who are today serving in high offices in various Middle East countries are also comrades in Jesus Christ's legion of faith. Through them, he established a strong and permanent contact with various Christian groups within the Antiochene Patriarchate, which reached Christian groups in the Soviet Ukraine; the Archbishopric of Ukraine was located in the city of Lwów.

On June 30, 1946, Wladek received his priestly ordination in Beirut. His first assignment was in Lebanon for Polish displaced persons. He also worked as a chaplain in hospitals, and among young people. In 1949 in recognition of his unique ability he was sent to Rome to study at Gregorian University. After receiving his doctorate, he remained in Italy and from 1953 to 1958 was in charge of Poles in Italy. A year later he became the head of the Pontifical Polish College in Rome, where many Polish youths came to study theology and modern Christian philosophy, later to spread their knowledge in Socialist Poland.

During his stay in Rome he met Cardinal Wyszyński and Archbishop Karol Wojtyla. In 1964, Monsignor Rubin became a Bishop of Serta, and also Auxiliary to the Primate of Poland. There is probably no country in the world which he did not visit: Latin America, Australia, New Zealand, the Middle East, Europe, Asia, and his attentions were directed to all minorities in the various countries in which he travelled. Wladek not only observed the situations of those minorities, but made firsthand studies of their relations with the governments, their spiritual and material needs, their strengths and weaknesses. As a result, Bishop Wladek Rubin became a human encyclopedia, which was helpful to him in his work in the Curia, and when raised to the position of the Secretary of the Synod of Bishops by Paul VI in 1967.

As first Secretary of the Synod of Bishops he greatly contributed to the preparation of documents of much importance for church work around the world and to the evangelication and ministerial priesthood. Shortly afterward he became a member of numerous congregations in the Roman Curia, such as the Pontifical Commission for the Interpretation of the Decrees of the Second Vatican Council; also the Sacred Congregation for Catholic Education, Congregation for Bishops, and even the Pontifical Commission for the Pastoral Care of Migrants and Tourists. In recognition of his outstanding work, Pope John Paul II raised him to cardinal on June 30, 1979, and appointed him to the Sacred Congregation for the Doctrine of the Faith, to the supreme Tribunal of the Apostolic Signatura as well as to the Commission for the Revision of the Code of Oriental Canon Law; and, we must not forget, to the Congregation for the Causes of Saints.

One day I was sitting with Cardinal Rubin in his office at 34 via della Conciliazione, talking about old times. I thought it would be interesting to ask him about Wojtyla. I began innocently. "I never heard anything bad about Karol. What is the reason for this?"

"I am not here to praise a man who doesn't deserve it, but I will give you a small illustration. One day Karol Wojtyla agreed to meet with Alfred Cardinal Bengsch. You know Karol suffered a lot during the war from the Nazis; but this victim of Hitler showed up at the meeting with his colleague half an hour early, and the German Cardinal was much touched by the magnanimity of the Polish Cardinal; and from then on they became friends.

"Karol has a talent for beinging out the warmth in people. His friendship with Alfredo Cardinal Ottaviani began during Vatican II, when both were working on the Source of Revelation and other ecclesiastical subjects – although the Italian Cardinal was a conservative and the Polish, progressive; but they developed a friendship through cuisine. The amicability with Amleto Cardinal Cicognani, Pericle Cardinal Felici, and Monsignor del'Acgua, the permanent Under Secretary of State, began on a strictly intellectual level, because they admired Karol's knowledge. This developed into a close personal relationship, and Cardinal Felici, a man with thin hair and thick glasses, reached special distinction because he was the one who announced the election of Karol Wojtyla to the Holy See.

"As Secretary General of the Synod of Bishops, I had the opportunity to observe such Cardinals as the energetic Casaroli, the wise-eyed Cardinal Benelli, and the Curia's knowledgeable high priest, Pietro Palazzini; they respected Karol's sensitivity and intuition. Derek Worlock, Archbishop of Liverpool, described him as possessing great strength.

That is the overwhelming impression; spiritual and moral strength, as well as strength of intellect. He has a well-ordered and disciplined mind, that is undoubtedly the fruit of continuing study and reflection. I know him to be a good listener, often the last one to speak in a discussion. It is his custom to listen carefully, and weigh well all views expressed before delivering his own opinion or answer, deliberately and clearly, sometimes almost in tabulated form.'

Cardinal Rubin continued the Englishman's outpouring.

In debate, as in the rest of his life, he is humble and not self-assertive. But he can, and often does, defend his views resolutely, as when he sees the rights of freedom under attack. Wojtyla is a man of great principle who has learned to live his beliefs and to proclaim Christian truths, even in hostile circumstances. Somehow, he has managed to achieve a balance that has enabled him to live and to speak without compromise, and yet, apparently, without antagonizing unnecessarily or provoking unreasonably those who do not share his views.

"Although I will talk with you more about this colorful Casaroli later, I'd like to mention that the friendship between Agostino and Karol had its ups and downs, because this diplomat in a cassock tried to regulate not only State affairs between the Vatican, Yugoslavia, Hungary and Germany, but also went over the heads of Wyszyński and Wojtyla and attempted without our knowledge to meddle in Polish affairs; he even engaged two German cardinals, Höffner and Döpfner. When the two Polish Cardinals discovered Casaroli's role they concluded, 'Curia or no Curia, our relation with the German Episcopate and our politics with the Warsaw Government will be conducted by Poles, and no one else;' and they attempted to leave Rome. Casaroli's reasoning was simple. He said to Paul VI, 'If every Episcopate tries to conduct its own politics, we will have calamity.' The Pope agreed, and called in Wojtyla and Wyszyński, and again the two of them in one voice explained to the Pope, 'Through a thousand years of our history, Germans did much injustice to the Polish nation, and our people still boil with resentment that the Vatican did nothing to lighten the burden of brutal German occupation.'

"Next, Primate Wyszyński said, more or less apologetically, 'Your Holiness. We are not against the diplomatic vision of Casaroli, and we have no right to interfere with your Holiness' decisions, but we think that such an approach to German-Polish relations will be damaging to everybody.'

"When Cardinal Wojtyla was elected to the Holy See, he nominated as Secretary of State, Cardinal Casaroli, a man with a vast knowledge of the Curia, who had the support of this bureaucratic organization. But Wojtyla knew that Casaroli was a man of character and principles, and that he would faithfully obey the Pope.

"For the sake of chronology, let us return to February 1973. I would like to show you some personal notes Karol took in Australia when attending the Melbourne Eucharistic Congress."

Wladek handed me some sheets of papers written in longhand, and I began to read,

'On February 6, at 10:45 P.M., we took a Dutch airliner from Fiumicino Airport in Rome on the long journey to Manila. We stopped in Karachi and Bangkok, and at 7:00 P.M. the following day arrived in Manila. The same evening, Bishop Szczepan Wesoly and my chaplain, Reverend Stanislaw Oziwicz, celebrated Mass in Redemptorist Church in Manila where the church was overflowing, and many hundreds of people took Holy Communion. What struck me was that most of the faithful walked on their knees to be closer to the altar. At Port Moresby a group of Polish missionaries greeted us, but at Goroka we experienced an interesting ceremony during the Holy Mass. Part of the liturgy was in Latin, the homily was in Polish, and the rest in local dialect, in which the singing was inspired.

From New Zealand at 6:00 A.M., we left for Sydney, Australia, where we stopped for two hours. I couldn't see kangaroos, or many people, but in Wellington where we arrived in the afternoon I met, in a Polish National Home, many faithful who had emigrated from Russia, Germany and even the Middle East after World War II. During the meal, we exchanged observations on national politics and local troubles.

On Sunday, February 18, I became sick, due to weather and food, but I took part in the inaugural ceremony in St. Patrick's Cathedral. The most impressive Holy Mass celebration, however, was at the Cricket Ground in Melbourne's stadium, where the first Mass was conducted in Italian, the second in Polish, and the songs were sung in Danish, French, Croatian and Maltese. Prayers were conducted in Chinese, German, Maronite, Lithuanian, Latvian, Czech, Russian, Slovak, Ukrainian, Spanish, Hungarian, Irish and Portuguese. Hurray for Australia, above all nationalities, country of immigrants.

On Thursday, February 22 at 8:00 P.M. again at the Cricket Ground, there was a huge ecumenical celebration – plenty of color and words, but we have to wait for the spiritual results.

Friday, about one hundred and fifty thousand young people took part in a day dedicated to 'youth,' and there I discovered that young people, never mind the geographical location, have a common language – guitar playing and rock music.

Rubin looked at me and I wondered if he was thinking that I was only interested in stories, so he said, "During the Ecumenical celebration at the Cricket Ground, a man approached the Cardinal's entourage and asked if he could have a few minutes private conversation with him. The priests were suspicious, and the stranger began talking,

"'My name is Jack Adrian, I am a Lutheran, but my wife is Catholic and Polish, and we have five children...'"

"A typical intermarriage story," I murmured.

Wladek Rubin heard me and commented, "Polish women won't change their religion; and often they can't convince their husbands. But in the case of Mr. Adrian the story has a twist. He made a bet with his wife who was well versed in Wojtyla's writing, that if by chance Cardinal Wojtyla should arrive in their part of the world and christen his kangaroo, he, Jack Adrian, would change from Lutheranism to Roman Catholicism."

I roared with laughter, and Wladek said, seriously, "You have to know that this particular kangaroo was special."

"Why?"

"Because not only the children loved him, but also Mr. and Mrs. Adrian."

"That's understandable. People love animals."

"Certainly. But according to Mr. Adrian, if not for this kangaroo, he would have had no family. A year before the Cardinal's arrival in Australia, Jack Adrian went to Melbourne for his monthly shopping, got drunk and stayed overnight in the city. Mrs. Adrian, after a heavy day of physical labor on the farm, was sleeping soundly with her five children, when fire broke out in their house. Their pet kangaroo woke up Mrs. Adrian and went to alert the children, pulling the youngest out of the burning house."

"Amazing. How did he pull the child from the house – with his mouth, or if he was a her, did she pop him in her pouch?"

"I don't know exactly, but when Mr. Adrian returned the next day, and discovered the miracle, he comforted his family, and right away went to his Lutheran Pastor and asked him to christen the kangaroo. The Pastor rejected the idea in no uncertain terms, but Mrs. Adrian, knowing much about the Catholic Church, said to her husband that in her faith this can be done, providing she can obtain permission from the Bishop. She had heard on the radio that Wojtyla was in Melbourne and he was not only a Bishop, but a Cardinal, so she sent her husband to talk to him.

"Mr. Adrian arrived in Melbourne in his dilapidated truck, successfully reached Wojtyla and explained his predicament. The Cardinal looked into his eyes, and saw that this was an important issue for the man. So, secretly, he took some holy water and aspergillum, and departed with the farmer to his ranch."

"'I feel that you, my dear Wladek, have some reservations about this, but I am sure that St. Francis would have done this gladly; as a theologian you also know that animals with their bodies, gave warmth and protection to the Holy Mother and her son, Jesus Christ.'"

"And what of Jack Adrian? What of his christening?"

"When he said he wanted to convert to Catholicism, Wojtyla explained that on his return to Melbourne he would try to arrange for a priest to visit the farm and prepare him for the conversion."

"After Karol returned to the city, he talked with James Robert Cardinal Knox, Archbishop of Melbourne. The Australian Cardinal, in spite of some doubt, could not refuse the request of his colleague, who insisted he should send a priest immediately to Adrian's farm, to teach him the Catechism. But Jack Adrian was sincere in his belief. He not only took Catholicism seriously, but he, a good farmer with many friends, convinced about a hundred other Lutherans to convert."

"In other words, he became a modern apostle."

"True," said Rubin, seriously. "Who knows? Adrian became so engaged in the work of the Church, that given time, he might become a priest, and spread the Gospel beyond his region."

"Speaking about Lutheranism, you promised that you would give firsthand information based on your files about the Curia, Wojtyla, Wyszyński and Polish-German relations."

"We could talk on this subject not only days and nights, but weeks and months. I would not like to burden you with minute details which are a part of the rather tragic picture. I'd just like to show you a few incidents which occurred during World War II, when the Lutheran clergy, under the protection of the victorious German army, tried to convert the Catholics in various parts of the country where Catholic priests were arrested and sent to concentration camps. I won't delve into this subject deeply, because it would be against the ecumenical spirit of the Church, but one example concerned the Chelm Diocese, whose head Bishop Okoniewski was arrested and sent to a concentration camp, and his place was taken by pro-Nazi bishop, Carl Maria Splett of Gdańsk. The Polish Government's representative in the Vatican, Kazimierz Papée, protested to no avail. Also, when Archbishop Orseni, Papal Nuncio in Berlin, informed the Curia about the persecution of Jews and Polish people by the Nazis, Pius XII replied that the Vatican's intervention with the Nazi Government would be detrimental to the well-being of Catholics in the Third Reich. After the war, when Poland regained its Western territory and Chancellor Konrad Adenauer concluded that those territories were 'under temporary Polish administration,' Pius XII and the Curia agreed. As a result of the Second Vatican Council, but not until 1972, did normalization of the Catholic Church on Polish Western territory take place. As you can see, Wyszyński, Wojtyla and the rest of the Polish Episcopate, have a certain amount of animosity against the Vatican, but a man such as Cardinal Wojtyla possessed a greatness of heart, and tried to build a friendship between the German and Polish Catholic Churches. He had the courage to speak from his heart on German television: 'We still have to work hard for reconciliation and base our understanding on the fundamental principles of Christian morality.' Karol's friend, German Cardinal Höffner, was cooperative in building better relations between the two churches and the two nations, but when Paul VI publicly announced that he considered Wojtyla the most outstanding intellectual and theologian of the whole Roman Catholic church, the Germans and the Curia got the message."

"But why?"

"The Polish Cardinal was travelling all over the world, and reports received by the Pope were glowing. He recognized that the church had, in its midst, one of the most outstanding men of the century."

"How do you know that?"

"Paul VI personally asked me to prepare an intellectual *vade mecum* on Wojtyla."

"Why from someone with the same ethnic background?"

"You have been researching this book for some time, in Rome, yet you don't understand. The Holy Father asked for similar reports from Italian, German, French and Third World Cardinals, and maybe others."

"A smart approach."

"Simple logic."

"And, what happened?"

"The Holy Father read those reports and called him in. 'I could learn something from Wojtyla.'

"I, with an apologetic smile, replied, 'The Polish language?'

"Paul VI's face became serious. 'Wisdom.'"

"What was the final result of the Pope's high opinion?"

"In February 1976, Paul VI asked Cardinal Wojtyla to deliver a series of sermons between March 7 and 13, to His Holiness, a selected group of Cardinals, and high Curia officials. Karol had little time to prepare, but no way out."

Wladek reflected for a moment. "I was not there. Cardinal Benelli later told me that the Holy See and distinguished entourage were impressed with the wisdom and his manner when delivering the sermons."

"Tell me, Wladek, is it true that Wojtyla's book *Love and Responsibility*, was one of the sources of Paul VI's *Humanae Vitae*? I heard from Primate Wyszyński that the Pope told him so."

"Yes, that is the truth."

"So, the Curia, knowing this, paid more attention to Wojtyla?"

"But it doesn't mean that privately, high Curia officials did not dig ditches under him, and tried to convince other officials that reports about Karol's wisdom and importance were exaggerated by his friends."

"Looks as if competition exists in heaven too?"

"I don't know, but when I discover I'll let you in on the secret."

"Maybe you can shed a little light for me on Gierek."

"He attempted, especially when pressured by his pious mother, to see the Pope, and have good relations with him as he had with the Primate, Wojtyla, and the rest of the Polish Episcopate; because, he recognized early that the Church could play an important role in his brand of socialism. The Vatican Curia tried to keep him at arm's length, but in 1972, at the suggestion of the Pope, sent Cardinal König from Vienna to talk with the Polish Episcopate on the relationship between the Gierek government and the Vatican. As though trying to compare his views with mine, Franz König said, 'We have contacts with Marxist atheists in the West, and they express readiness to cooperate with us on a theoretical level, but we must not involve ourselves in discussions in political areas which will make difficult the development of more permanent dialogues. This goes doubly for Marxists in the East.'

"As someone who went through all kinds of experiences during the Second World War with the Russians, I listened to König without commenting, and encouraged by my silence, he continued his political attack inspired by the Curia. 'There is a danger for the Church when it becomes entangled in raw politics. Theology of salvation for radicals in the Church becomes theology of political liberation, and Gospel for them becomes instruction for revolution.'"

I recalled what Primate Wyszyński said to me when he met Cardinal König for a similar discussion some time earlier, and I repeated this to Cardinal Rubin. "'My dear Franz. We live from day to day in our country. For religious and political existence we are responsible to God, the Holy Father and our nation. As representatives of the Church, we work toward peace, secure decent living conditions, and love of our nation. We know better than most in the West what is good for Poland and for us. In short, people living on earth who are soaked with our brothers' blood, are not interested in throwing rocks at Communists who are working for a common goal.'"

"So, you know yourself, the attitude of the Polish Episcopate to the teachings of the Curia and its envoy, Cardinal König. And you also should know there existed a group in Poland under the name Pax, headed by Boleslaw Piasecki which utilized different strategems to provoke the Polish Episcopate to too much or too little cooperation with the Government. In doing this Piasecki could also justify his existence as mediator between Church and State.

"This reminds me a little of the situation in the West, where organizations sprang up to promote more active cooperation between the official Church and radical political groups."

Wladek Rubin rose from his antique chair, brocaded in delicate pastel colors, and went to his impressive Cardinal's desk. Searching through drawers, he pulled a bottle from one and papers from another. Slowly, he returned to his chair, put the bottle on the floor and handed me the papers, "I am sure you are thinking about Reverend G. Arroyo who is the founder of Christians for Socialist Society?"

"Yes," I said.

"Read it."

I glanced at the typewritten wisdom of the maverick Jesuit Arroyo,

The Church, that is, the hierarchy which directs it, conducts certain political functions in the orientation of Christian masses towards the actions and programs of various regimes.

Although in reality those Church leaders claim objectivity, in practice they serve conservative forces, or at best, important reformist political forces. The result is that although Catholics comprise the vast majority in countries such as Chile, Brazil, Mexico, Italy, Spain, and Central America, the populace chooses secular political actions with revolutionary tendencies. To survive and benefit the masses, the Christian religions should think about an alliance with socialist elements.

"But this switch to the left will make many Western powers, especially America, angry."

"Do you know why the Curia became angry at the United States?"

"I'm not privy to secrets, like you."

"When President Jimmy Carter visited Warsaw and was interviewed by the editor of the Polish Baptist Magazine, he said, 'The United States adheres to the freedom of religion as it exists in Poland.' On top of this, Mrs. Carter, in the company of Zbigniew Brzeziński, the White House National Security adviser, visited Primate Wyszyński, and expressed admiration for the freedom to practice religion in Poland."

"This only proves that the Catholic hierarchy in the United States does not have regular contact with the White House."

Cardinal Rubin replied, "There still exists isolation of the Catholic hierarchy from the ruling class, although not as much as before. The

Protestant Churches, Masonic and Jewish groups exercise more influence on the White House than the proportionately larger group of fifty million Catholics under the leadership of three hundred and fifty bishops. You know who I blame for that?" He got up, went to his desk again, pulled out two glasses and a corkscrew, and returned to his seat, putting the bottle on a round Renaissance table, "American bishops, the majority who are poorly educated, and worse, unmotivated."

He uncorked the bottle of wine, filled two tall Venetian glasses, and spoke his last words, which astonished me. "What I just said is not for publication..."

He looked at me with an expression I have never experienced, raised his glass, touched mine and said, "I don't know if I am going to see you any more."

I could barely speak.

"Why?"

"I am dying."

38

Making of a Saint

A T THIS meeting we were supposed to talk about the mechanics of beatification and canonization. I was obliged to wait for the conversational opening by the Holy Father; nevertheless, I spoke first,

"To be a saint you have to apologize to God all your life; in front of Him you are never right; at the same time, you have to apologize to man, with whom you are always right."

My host asked, "Do you believe in life after death?"

"I do."

"Explain this to me," he said, gently pushing a bowl of fruit toward me. I noticed he was upset. Confronted with a tough question, together with grapes, oranges and apples, I knew not whether to reach for fruit or to reply.

"Are you going to answer my question?"

I thought the best answer would be, "Last month, when working with a lawyer on my will, I said that an orchestra should play at my funeral. The smart attorney asked, 'What would you like to hear?' I replied, 'Chopin.' Turning to the Pope, I asked, "Is this not sufficient proof that I believe in life after death?"

For the first time I saw that he was experiencing inner rage which he could not articulate. Silence reigned, and I did not know from which angle to begin.

I said, "Looking through reports and clippings, I have discovered that you as a Cardinal have calmed the West German Catholic hierarchy, and then later pursued East German Catholic circles, starting with localities such as Erfurt, Görlitz and Dresden. Is this at the suggestion of the Pope, Curia, or is it your own design?"

He didn't like my introduction to this session, but replied anyhow, "I approach West and East Germany in the same way, with caution, because I suffered during the war. When I received in Cracow an invitation from the Bishop Auderbeck of Erfurt, an old city which was founded in 741 by St. Boniface with a university dating to the fourteenth century, I could not refuse."

"Understandable," I said.

He continued, "I am sure you remember that Martin Luther, the Augustine monk, once lived in this city. And in 1808, the Congress of Erfurt was opened and attended by Napoleon. Erfurt was taken by the American army in 1945. So you can see that I visited a very interesting city, not only full of history but beautiful gardens."

"Please tell me why, in three days, so many German bishops courted you, such as Huhn, Meisner, Schaffrau, Weinhold and more?"

"I deduce that you feel I'm not telling you the whole story."

"I have no such notions."

"My desire to go to East Germany was, in the first place, to bow to the thousands of people who perished in the Buchenwald concentration camp; and I, as a Cardinal, cannot be ignored by German bishops. I took this opportunity to demonstrate in the presence of high Church officials my deep feeling against oppression and murder."

I felt humiliated, "I remember your speech in front of twenty thousand people in the square of the Erfurt Cathedral..."

He did not wait for me to finish the sentence, and quoted from memory, "Here, on earth, we all are pilgrims on the road to our Father, directed by Jesus Christ. On this road we find our life in a definite sense. I wish, with all my heart, that each of us could find the reason for existence, to discard our blindness, to be brothers to each other..."

He turned to me with an explanation. "Certainly, I wanted to see how Catholics in Socialist Germany lived, and I gave a report to the Holy Father as well as shared my observations with the Primate of Poland. Every Cardinal, and especially Polish Cardinals, should have a good *rapprochement* with the heirarchy of the German church, and not be divided into separate East and West groups."

Although I believed him, I posed one further question, "It was urgent because you left for Rome right away, was it not?"

"Not true. I went a few weeks later, in the company of Primate Wyszyński, who led a pilgrimage of twenty bishops and a few hundred priests, among them one hundred and thirty Polish clergy, former prisoners of German concentration camps. We went to celebrate the Holy Year. The Pope took part in a Mass, during which he beatified three priests and one nun."

I, who consistently press the Catholic hierarchy to give more exposure to nuns who do such great service to the Church, took this opportunity to ask, "What was the name of the nun?"

"Maria Teresa Ledóchowski," he replied.

I knew that a General of the Society of Jesus was called Ledóchowski, and this name brought to my mind a multitude of feelings and stories from my youth. Pictures of enormous fields of ripe rye and wheat, green forests and blue skies of Wolynia province, a beautiful girl, and myself, thin and timid. On top of those reminiscences I wondered if I should interject my personal story of a teenage boy who was equal to other teenage boys, but a servant nevertheless. I went to the same school as Leon Ledóchowski. During the day I lived in his father's mansion as a tutor, boot polisher and messenger for Leon. Secretly, I was in love with his sister Ewa, who was a few years older than I. Every morning, Leo, Ewa and I went from the estate of Ledóchowka to the city of Wlodzimierz to attend *gimnazjum*.

John Paul II in his perceptive way, noticed I was witholding something, and said, "Go ahead, make a confession."

"It was a balmy Sunday and we all attended Holy Mass in the mansion chapel. Afterward, Count Ledochowski, the cousin of the Head of the Society of Jesus, took my arm, and we went for a walk in the fields. He recounted the history of this very old family which went back to the first quarter of the sixteenth century with achievements in wealth and oppression, as well as service to the Church. Naturally, he did not forget to mention that Wlodzimierz Ledóchowski (1866–1942) was the General of the Jesuits from 1914 until his death, and loved to call himself 'A Black Pope.' His sister was Maria Teresa, the nun. In a proud voice, Count Ledóchowski told me that she had chestnut hair, and deep blue eyes, but 'she was not as beautiful as my daughter Ewa.'

"I politely asked the handsome Count why all the members of his family were so good-looking.

"He replied, 'Because, by some design of God, the males in our family always marry beautiful peasant girls.'

"Hearing that, I tried to think of myself and Ewa. Meanwhile we continued to walk, and pick wild flowers for the ladies. When we were close to the mansion, the Count took me in a fatherly way by the neck, and whispered in my ear, 'I know you are in love with Ewa.' I blushed and began to tremble. He noticed this, and said, 'It is beautiful.' I regained my composure, and again the Count continued his thought in a paternal voice, 'Why don't you sleep with Ewa?'"

"Unbelieveable," the Pope interjected.

To reinforce the true story from my life, I added, "He didn't ask me to marry Ewa because of my lowly status, and I later discovered that she was already promised to a member of another aristocratic family. As you can see, my story is moral, and I am not taking responsibility for the Count's ethics, although, when an influential aristocrat steals or lies, we say he made a mistake; but when a poor man makes a mistake, we say he has stolen or lied. But all those things returned to my mind when I read your emotional speech during the closing session of the beatification of this Polish nun."

The Pope, as though to demonstrate his photographic memory, started repeating his speech,

When we hear the name Maria Teresa Ledóchowski, before our eyes, generations of sowers appear, who were connected with numerous names, among them her sister, Urszula, and brother, the General of the Society of Jesus; also, her uncle, the Primate of Poland, Mieczyslaw Cardinal Ledóchowski. Those names bring to mind the spreaders of the gospel. We are happy that Maria Teresa worked among black people in Africa; to this day she is called 'Mother of Africa,' although she was the daughter of the Polish nation, at that time, enslaved. Africans knew that she experienced slavery in her own heart. Other members of this illustrious family fought in Europe 'for our freedom and yours' but she sowed the Christian belief among people of Africa who yearned for freedom and independence.

"Well expressed," I exclaimed, "but it upset me slightly that you expressed noble feelings for this aristocratic family, and did not mention that she was the child of a simple peasant woman."

"How do you know?"

"Because Ewa's father told me."

Pope John Paul II and John Cardinal Krol, 1981.

Wladyslaw Cardinal Rubin and the author in Rome, October 1980.

The author and Bishop Bronislaw Dąbrowski, 1980.

Józef Cardinal Glemp, Primate of Poland and the author, May 1982.

"It isn't important."

I thought to myself, 'He will be annoyed, but I have to tell him to round off the picture.' After a short pause, I remarked, "According to what I heard, Maria Teresa travelled many times from Vienna, or from Salzburg where she was lady-in-waiting in the Toscanian Court to her cousins in Wolynia; one summer she fell in love with an ordinary peasant laborer."

"Don't tell me anymore," sighed the Pope. "I know..."

Nolens volens, I said something else, "I have a suggestion for the Vatican, and because you are progressive, will place this in your hands."

"Something else bizarre?"

"Not terribly."

"I have suffered much from you, I might as well suffer some more..."

"In 1968, Pope Paul VI established January 1 as an International Day of Peace; in general, I see the Church going to the people; what's more, even dethroning some saints, such as St. Patrick, who is no longer a saint, nor a Patrick."

"What happened to you today? What are you trying to say?"

"We have many saints, many blessed, most of them are of royal background, noblemen's background, or Popes and other church dignitaries."

He interrupted me, impatiently, "I don't understand. What are you trying to convey?"

I felt concerned that I had infringed too much on his hospitality, but having gone so far I thought I'd finish, "We have monuments to unknown soldiers in practically every country. Why can't we have a monument to unknown saints who symbolize all the goodness of a simple man who worked for his country, and his fellow man, and about whom nobody knows, not even the local priest. Except God. Let's say we would have a momument in Rome to an Unknown Italian Saint, or a monument in Berlin to an Unknown German Saint, or any other country in this world. People could search their minds for whom this monument had been built, and it would make them feel good, united, inspired. Even if they made mistakes it would be a human mistake. But the Almighty would know who deserved this monument in each capital. Don't you think it's enough for Christians to feel that God knows about it, and people to worship it?"

The Holy Father looked astonished, and said, "It's no good serving two masters."

"Is this your reply to my question?"

My illustrious host looked at me again with his kind blue eyes, and said nothing.

"I am waiting for your reply."

Not a muscle moved in his face, except that his eyes gave me a message of pity.

I am still waiting.

39

From the Vatican to Philadelphia

POPE Paul VI asked Cardinal Wojtyla to conduct special religious exercises during Easter week of 1976 for cardinals, high Curia officials and himself. It was a great honor for the Polish Church Prince. The Pope was sending signals to the cardinals that his days were ending that they would have to think about a candidate for the Holy See; in doing so, they should seriously consider Karol Wojtyla.

There is no doubt that the priest from Cracow understood the intentions of the Pope, but would not compromise even in the presence of the Holy Father. In his speeches to the distinguished gathering, he said that Roman Catholic priests should not 'wash their hands' and avoid political reality, but should roll up their sleeves and work with both hands for the good of the people.

> The verdict of guilty was given by Pontius Pilate under the pressure of priests and a hostile crowd. He washed his hands to show that he was acting under duress, as before the verdict he talked about truth. In both cases Pontius Pilate was trying to preserve his independence, and 'stand on the side.' But this was only the appearance of independence. The meaning of the cross to which he condemned Jesus of Nazareth, as well as the real truth of Jesus' Kingdom not only had to touch the core of human existence of one man, but of everybody through the ages. Such was the reality then, and so it is today. We cannot wash our hands of responsibility nor stay on the side and be neutral.

Later, Karol Wojtyla collected his series of speeches and published them under the title, *Segno di Contraddizione*.

Although the philosophy of those addresses was in line with Paul VI's thinking, a lot of Cardinals objected and saw the unwritten message that the Polish Cardinal would be a serious candidate for the highest position in the Church. A group of American clergy was against Wojtyla, not because of his philosophy, but because they were openly lobbying for John Patrick Cardinal Cody, Archbishop of Chicago, and Terrence J. Cardinal Cooke, Archbishop of New York. They claimed that either could be a good Pope, especially at a time when the Vatican needed a lot of money for its missionary work. When the Pope heard about this, he said to Cardinal Wyszyński, "I know the biographies of those two American businessmen well, and I can tolerate neither their shallow piousness nor their meager intellect." When Wyszyński expressed his surprise at such a characterization, the Pope added, "I have faith in only one man and his name is William Wakefield Baum, Archbishop of Washington; and I will make him a Cardinal right away."

During one of my meetings with Primate Wyszyński, I asked, "Why was Paul VI so against American bishops?"

"He was not against American bishops specifically, but he was against many clergy in the Western world who, according to him were impregnated by 'shallow American civilization,' best illustrated by expensive cars, beautiful apartments and luxurious meals, to which cardinals, bishops and the rest of the clergy, naturally, with minor exceptions, were flying like bees to honey. 'Where is the food for the heart, the soul and for the intellect?' he would ask."

The Primate looked at me, and I said, "This is a difficult situation. Everybody is human and we all are susceptible to this kind of weakness."

"You have the wrong impression that the Holy Father was against only the luxurious lives of American bishops. He was upset when he heard jokes and negative comments about high Vatican officials who travelled in expensive cars on which the plates had three letters: SCV. Roman citizens interpreted these letters as *Se Cristo Vedesse* (If Christ Would See It). Expensive restaurants were frequented by high Vatican officials dressed in civilian clothes and the Pope wondered where they were getting the money to pay the bills. On the other hand, during the Thomistic Congress in Rome and Naples which was conducted to commemorate the seven hundredth anniversary of the death of St. Thomas Aquinas, the Pope heard that the only Cardinal that did not travel in a car, but in a dilapidated bus from Rome to Naples, was Karol

Wojtyla. He was excited and I thought he might have a heart attack from joy."

"Did Karol do this for publicity?" I asked the Primate.

"Not at all. The Congress was attended by eighteen hundred philosophers and scientists from all over the world, and when he heard that some of the younger ones were travelling by bus to Naples, Karol joined them, thinking that during this trip he could exchange views on various aspects of Thomistic philosophy. Naturally, Karol was dressed in civilian clothes, and when they stopped for a meal in a village restaurant he did not eat, but went from table to table, talking to clergy from various countries, asking them about the Christian educational systems and especially about teaching Thomism in their particular area. The questions were intelligent and travellers started asking left and right, 'Who is this man?' One of those questions reached a professor from Lublin University. He replied, 'This man is my colleague.' Then somebody else added, 'He is also a Cardinal.'"

"Do you think such behavior has something to do with Karol's love for theater?"

"If it does, it is not a premeditated attitude or artificial pose. You can see in him and his actions tremendous sincerity supported by deep knowledge. As an example, I would like to tell you that during Holy Mass in the town of Fossa Nuova where St. Thomas was born, Karol made a speech about the philosophy of this apostle of Christian faith. This speech was not only original and full of unknown facts, but it had a new and different approach in the interpretation of Thomism for the modern world. After that, one or two Italian Cardinals and a French scientist who had heard this homily, approached Wojtyla, congratulated him, and a Cardinal said, 'You should be Pope.'

"'There are other Cardinals, surely wiser and more pious than I...'

"The Frenchman expressed his opinion this way. 'A man should perform a service for God instead of praying and begging Him for things he wants; he should go out into the world and work for them.'

"The Polish Cardinal asked, 'Are you American or Canadian?'

"'Why should I be American?'

"'As I heard it, Americans are the best go-getters, who spend a lot of energy acquiring material things and have no time to pray to God.'

"'I am French-Canadian, from McGill University,' said the stranger, mumbling his name, 'Listening to you lecture, I have discovered that you are the most enlightened Cardinal living today, so I would like to ask you what you think is wrong with the American Catholic Church, and what a layman should do to enhance its image?'

"'I do not know much about America,' said Cardinal Wojtyla, 'but I am going there shortly and will try to learn more about that country and its enterprising people. As to the second part of your question, I would answer in this way: only through recognizing his own mistakes, through suffering and praying can man achieve excellence and wisdom.'"

On July 23, 1976, Karol Wojtyla departed for the United States to attend the Eucharistic Congress. Four days later, July 27, he delivered a lecture "Participation or Alienation" at Harvard University, during which he posed the question, 'After people have satiated themselves with material goods, what should come next? – a spiritual vacuum? – anti-love?'

From the packed hall somebody yelled, "Marxism solved that problem."

Wojtyla paused and with visible irritation replied,

It is well known that according to the teachings of Marx and his disciples, humans are not alienated only by the system of private ownership, but by working in the system, and by the institutions which serve this system, and by the government. To this we can add that several of Marx' disciples in my country, too, have become convinced, and have expressed this conviction, that the transformation of the social, economic, and political system has not eliminated various types of alienation, but rather has created new types.

He noticed that the audience was listening attentively,

This understanding of the human being in his total richness, the understanding of the human being as a personal subject who is capable of self-determination on the basis of self-awareness, who wants to find fulfillment in reference to the transcendental powers of his soul, and who strives in different ways toward this goal, is the basic condition for a conscientious and creative participation in the current 'struggle for man.' This struggle has been caused to a considerable extent by the concept of alienation. I am of the opinion that this concept, which is used in Marxism in various and not always contestable ways, does not have its significance in relation to the human being as an individual of the species *homo*, but to the human being as a personal subject. The human being as an individual of the species, is and remains a human being without regard for an arrangement of circumstances. On the other hand, the human being, as a personal subject, can in various circumstances be 'dehumanized,' and he actually is, often to a high degree. He is robbed of his objectively inalienable rights. He is robbed of that which constitutes his human nature. All this is contained in the concept of alienation or is derived from this concept.

He looked at the spellbound audience, and took a sip of water,

It is well known that Marx also looked upon religion as a source of alienation. The human being who feels himself particularly duty-bound in context to the realization of Marxism, who thinks deeply about the problem of the human being as a personal subject, is led to the ever clearer realization that the only world in which one can attain victory over human alienation is that world which we find in the Gospel – and no other. Only in this world – in this dimension of understanding, reason and ethical sense of duty – does the human being find liberation from that which 'dehumanizes' him. Everything that 'deifies' him in this world certainly does not cause his dehumanization, since God's image is the basic measure of the human being.

Finally, he observed,

There is no other way for a man but to return to God. I think that a special path for theology and the Church in the contemporary world is opening, one which is emerging with all the tension of the growing 'struggle for man.' A special appeal is coming from this direction, an appeal which theology must not ignore.

When people asked him to comment on culture, he replied,

Man creates culture, relies on culture and develops through culture. Culture is an acquisition of facts by the exclusive means of which Man expresses himself. He expresses himself for himself and for others. The products of culture, which outlast Man are a testimony to him. They are a testimony to his spiritual life, and for the spirit of Mankind, which not only lives through mastery over things material, but is also life within itself, through the means to which only it has access and which only it can understand. It lives through truth, goodness and beauty—and can express this inner life without, and is able to objectify its actions. And that too is why Man, as the creator of culture, bestows a special testimony on Mankind. For over two thousand years, Christianity has been a great source of cultural inspiration. What we must ensure is that this same inspiration can be discerned in the events of our own times as well as in years to come.

Even a cleric as knowledgeable as Wojtyla could not prevent himself from speaking to a secular audience on religious and even parochial subjects. "We live in an epoch in which the world proclaims liberty of conscience and religious freedom, in an epoch in which the struggle against religion is defined as 'the opium of the people,' and is carried out in such a way as to avoid as far as possible the creation of new martyrs. Thus, the program of the new epoch is persecution. But, to judge from outward appearances this persecution does not exist and there is 'full religious liberty.'"

He paused for a moment, reflected and thought, 'I have gotten through to them.' "'Take the course opposite custom and you will almost always do well,' I think Jean Jacques Rousseau said that." Then, his religious training took over.

Moreover, this program has succeeded in arousing in many the impression that it is on the side of Lazarus against the rich man, and hence, on the same side as Christ, although it is above all against Christ. Yet, can we really say 'above all'? We would like to be able to affirm the contrary. Unfortunately, the facts show clearly that religious struggle exists and that this struggle is the untouchable dogma of the program.

It also seems that the means most necessary for the realization of paradise on earth are to be found in depriving men of the strength which they draw from Christ. This strength in fact has been clearly condemned as weakness, and unworthy of man. Unworthy and somewhat uncomfortable. The man who is strong in the strength given him by faith will not easily allow himself to be pushed into collective anonymity.

There is in this world great faith and a considerable margin of liberty for the mission of the Church, although often it is only a matter of the margin. It is enough to observe the principal tendency dominating the mass media; enough to pay attention to who is passed over in silence or what is said in a loud voice; enough to lend an ear to that which comes in for most opposition, to see that even where Christ is accepted, there is opposition to Christ.

People want to mold Him, to adapt Him to their own dimensions and to the dimension of man in an era of progress, and to the program of modern civilization, which is a program of consumerism, not of transcendental ends.

When I started checking and rechecking Wojtyla's various pronouncements, speeches and conversations with me and others, I concluded, and here I state again, that he had a talent for remembering various things, that many times he repeated himself in almost the exact words.

During one of my meetings with him, I mentioned this and he smiled and replied, "I don't know if this is a gift, or not, but I am blessed by God in various ways. At the same time I remember what a German philosopher of Polish descent said, 'Blessed are those who forget, for they thus surmount even their own mistakes'."

"Nietzsche?"

"Yes, that is the culprit."

After the Harvard lecture, a photograph of Karol Wojtyla appeared in the local paper with a caption, "Probably the Successor to Paul VI.'

On July 22, he spoke at the Catholic University of America in Washington, D.C., on the subject "The Auto-Theology of Man." In this lecture he expressed the idea that man, having rich inner spiritual possibilities, should look into himself for his own approach to God and to people. Organized religion could help him solve his spiritual, philosophical or even daily life problems; but, when a man looks inside himself for the deeper meaning and explanation of his existence on earth, confronted with the difficulties of resolving it, he should approach other men and together they could search more meaningfully for real humanity and the infinity of life, leading them toward the wisdom of God. This human personalism of probing one's thoughts and soul functions differently in each of us and expresses itself in various ways, such as profound poetry, unshakeable confidence, or strong faith in the other man. Whenever we work hard toward the goal of improving ourselves, and our attitude toward our environment, this leads us toward a higher inner achievement as well as toward a deeper engagement in human endeavor. The knowledge that we are serving God and people enables us to gain inner content and happiness.

In various appearances in the United States, Wotyla stressed the fact that Paul VI, by establishing in 1967 the *Commission of Justice and Peace* indicated that awakening people of the world to support justice and social equality was the real sense of Christian love.

The Eucharistic Congress in Philadelphia that met August 1–8, 1976, brought together many cardinals, bishops and theologians to deliberate on the status of the Catholic Church in the world. The procedures of the Congress were divided into three parts: the first was liturgical, during which a Holy Mass was celebrated for the faithful in three Philadelphia sports arenas. The second part was scientific, composed of lectures and discussions conducted by prominent clergy and scientists. The third was dedicated to entertainment with, among the participants, famous singing artists like Ella Fitzgerald.

The organizational center of the Congress was located in the Civic Center of Convention Hall. From there the threads of operation went all over the city, which had been invaded by a hundred thousand people from all over the world. They required among other things accommodations for a week.

The theme of the Congress was hunger – spiritual, freedom, truth, peace, justice, bread – but overall the subject was the hunger of people for God. Participants of this Congress were not only Roman Catholics, but members of the Protestant churches the world over, including the United States. The undertone of the discussions was ecumenism.

I did not want to ask the Pope about his opinion of the United States because he had already presented it to me after his first trip in 1969. I would not forget what he said about his short excursion. "Beautiful country, good people, an abundance of wealth." I thought, 'A wise man giving me such a standard description.' He read my mind and added, "Wealth, most of the time, has been acquired by dishonest means and lies, but love cannot be gained in such ways. What you need in America is more love between American races and more compassion and understanding for people of the world."

When Cardinal Cooke asked Cardinal Wojtyla a similar question, he received the following reply, "What I like in America is the cafeteria style system where all people are treated equally."

"I'm not sure I understand," Cardinal Cooke said.

"I liked the fact that during this Congress practically every Cardinal went to the cafeteria, picked up a tray and stood in line to get his food, like every other participant of the Congress." Cardinal Wojtyla said.

"You did the same thing?" queried Cardinal Cooke, peering over his gold-rimmed glasses.

"Why not? We are all servants of our brothers, to whom we teach Christian love. When I sit down at a meal, mind you, I do not want to impress you with my humility, but I always think about those who are eating their sumptuous dinners in concentration camps."

Then I asked the Pope, "What did you like best about the Congress, if I could ask you a question like that?"

"Certainly. Two women and one bishop."

"You mean there were over a hundred thousand participants and you liked just three people?"

"...and one black girl."

"But didn't you talk to President Gerald Ford, who delivered the welcoming remarks? Didn't you discuss a ski trip to Colorado with him?"

"No, because they said that he had received an urgent message to return to Washington because there was trouble in Nicaragua.

"I do not know your impression of President Ford, but I feel he is an honorable and moral man."

"I agree with you wholeheartedly, but at this moment a quotation of a great American, Ralph Waldo Emerson, comes to my mind, 'When the guest talks about honor and morality, the host should count his silver spoons.'"

"Can you tell me about the interesting Bishop of the Congress whom you mentioned before?"

My host ignored the request. "Going to the Black Community Mass, conducted by my friend, Maurice Cardinal Otunga, from Kenya, I met a little black girl and her mother. They came in to listen to the great jazz singer, Ella Fitzgerald, and the black chorus, five hundred members strong. The mother was happy, but the six-year-old daughter was crying. I took the girl in my arms, gave her a picture of the Black Madonna of Częstochowa and asked, 'Why are you crying?'

"'Because my Mommy said we are going to Georgia to see my grandfather and drink fresh milk.'

I looked at the mother and she explained, 'Anytime I go places she asks whether we are going to visit her grandfather in Georgia.' Then she whispered in my ear, 'Last year her grandfather was killed and the farm burned down, so I came upon the idea that Grandfather retired from the farm and figured out that in a year or so when my daughter gets older I would tell her the whole story.' She paused and then continued, slowly recollecting, 'When my daughter visited our farm in Georgia the first time, she saw a cow being milked and she asked, where the cows get their milk...'I saw no grocery store around here.'

"The black girl, seeing her mother whispering in my ear, wiped her tears and looking at the Black Madonna, asked, 'Is this Lady in the picture like my grandfather, retired too?'

"'The next time I pray to this Lady, I will ask her.'

"The resolute girl posed a new question, 'What is retired?'

"'It is a man or lady who after many years of work stops working and gets a pension,' I replied as simply as possible.

"'I'd like to retire too and get money, and go to my grandfather's in Georgia and drink fresh milk.'"

This is how Cardinal Wojtyla saw America.

"How did you like Ella Fitzgerald's singing?"

"I was overwhelmed by her beautiful voice and the great chorus. It was a tremendous spiritual experience. The Black Community Mass was staged in a multitude of colors, fantastic rhythm of drums and voices which expressed in a unique way a return to God. Black people are talented in many ways, and the Church should stretch both hands to them, because in their hearts there is a lot of room for love of the Almighty and people."

"Who was the second woman you mentioned?"

"She was an unassuming, small woman, dressed in white, who spoke softly in heavily accented English. But what she said was tragic. Her name was Mother Maria Teresa of Calcutta...'One day an Indian mother came to our orphanage with four children and pleaded with us to keep three of them; when I asked her, could she leave the fourth which she held in her arms, she replied, 'This one I am not going to give to you.' When I asked why, she replied that the child was a cripple and needed much love and care. The Indian mother left with tears in her eyes, hugging the child, and I heard her murmur to herself, 'If we die, we have to die together.'

"Mother Teresa concluded her speech, stating that every day in Calcutta a few hundred children die of starvation and disease, and she was appealing to us for help."

I did not ask the Pope, but asked myself, 'How could I reach Cardinal Cooke and persuade him to sacrifice a few dollars for Mother Teresa's orphanage in Calcutta?'

My thoughts were interrupted by John Paul II. "How many Teresas do we have in the world who help hungry people? Is the Church doing enough in preventing human tragedy by persuading powerful politicians to curtail their armaments? Where are the Christian Churches who are supposed to shape the face of the earth and make human life more human? Are we really human, are we really children of God?"

Silence fell between us. I searched for a suitable reply but the Pope did not give me enough time to respond. "At the Eucharistic Congress, I also met an unassuming man with great spirit. His name was Archbishop Helder Camara from Brazil, and he had been harassed by his own government. But how can you silence the torrent of the Amazon River? How can you dry it up?

"Helder Camara was indignant in his speech about the misery of Latin Americans, of dictatorships and persecution of good Christian-minded people, and he finished his fiery speech in these words. 'We have in Latin America many dedicated people who work and dream about the future. But remember, if one man dreams, it is an ordinary dream; but when many people have the same dream, you are convinced that a new, better reality is coming into being.'"

John Paul II looked at me and concluded. "During this Eucharistic Congress in Philadelphia, we exchanged millions of words full of wisdom and anger, but also words of love. We, the Roman Catholic clergy, following the ancient Christian custom, washed the feet of our Protestant brethren. When I bent over the feet of a black Protestant bishop, I noticed scars on his feet, and I thought that he probably walked without shoes in his youth and suffered hunger and deprivation; I could not prevent myself from saying out loud, 'We both came from the same human misery, you a Protestant and I a Catholic. Let's work together.' The black Bishop replied, 'Amen.' Then we embraced each other."

40
Pope Paul VI and Cardinal Wojtyla

"WHEN Karol returned from the Eucharistic Congress in the United States, I asked him his impression of America; he replied with two words, '*Sapere aude*.'"

I said to Primate Wyszyński, "You mean he just answered, 'Have courage to be smart'?"

"Then he smiled and a puzzled expression appeared on his face; so I pursued the subject, 'You must have some impressions?'

"His smile lingered and he replied, 'A week in such a huge country is not enough time to have definite impressions, as I was busy with Church business. But here are two interesting stories by our two mutual friends, which you will enjoy and will allow you to form your own impressions.'

"Karol told me that Cardinal Cody, who is known for his love of good food, was sitting one evening in an exclusive Chicago restaurant, and overheard a conversation between two men at the next table. After greeting his friend, the first asked, 'How are you doing?'

"'Not bad, as a matter of fact, very well.'

"'You mean only two months ago you got out of jail, and are doing all right?'

"'I'm lucky. Last week I bought myself a Rolls-Royce, and today, or this morning to be exact, I bought the Chicago Police Chief!'"

The Primate and I looked at each other and I asked, "Is this Cardinal Cody's America?"

"It is not, but probably an interesting observation of a Cardinal who has lived in America all his life."

"What else pertaining to this powerful country did Karol tell you?"

Still smiling, Wyszyński answered, "He also illustrated to me a different aspect of American life, or rather, American education, by repeating the tale of Cardinal Król which he claimed he heard some time ago from the great composer Stravinsky."

"He was not only an important composer, but also a practical joker and good story-teller."

"I think you should hear this didactic anedcote."

"Naturally, a story of a genuine composer related by a colorful Cardinal from Philadelphia must be interesting."

"One day when taking a taxi in New York City, Igor Stravinsky noticed a plaque which bore his name. He was puzzled, and asked the driver, 'Do you know who Stravinsky is?'

"'This is the name of a friend who owns this taxi; he is sick, so I'm doing him a favor because he wants to keep the car in circulation to make money.'

"Without identifying himself, composer Stravinsky began talking about the great Russian composer and his achievements. The taxi driver listened patiently for some time, and finally said, 'Mister, I don't know anything about music; please don't bug me about it because I got my own headaches.'

"The composer complied with the request, and arriving at his destination, paid the fare and gave a generous tip to the driver, who was so overwhelmed that he began to make apologies.

"The passenger said, 'My name is Stravinsky; what is yours?'

"'Puccini.'"

When my host and I stopped laughing he said, "On the basis of those two stories, do you know the conclusion Karol arrived at?"

"How should I?"

"'I don't know who inspired the American government to work to achieve the goal of full stomachs and empty heads. I pray God it was not the Roman Catholic hierarchy.'"

Hearing this I commented, "From my first meeting with Karol Wojtyla I discovered that he has the ability to present the history of a country, a society, or even a person in one sentence."

"I'm sure you are not the first or last to recognize his ability and personal magnetism. That is probably the reason why, at any time or any place he appears, people of every social status try to consult him."

"Even Cardinals."

"Yes. Cardinals of such stature as Albino Luciani who, as you know, later became Pope Joannes Paulus I, not to mention your Americans

Cody and Król."

"He does have personal magnetism. Even after our first meeting, he instilled in me complete confidence. As a matter of fact, after that meeting he made a rather strange observation, 'Not many people are worth arguing with.' And when I began to dispute this, he asked, 'Do you love life very much?'

"I was dumbfounded. When I turned the question around in my mind, the answer was obvious, 'I do.'

"He said, with a twinkle in his eyes, 'To love something more than life means to work at it so hard that it becomes something more than ordinary life.'"

"In this sentence is the complete Wojtyla," Primate Wynzyński exclaimed. "He was the idea-man in everything he organized, such as Bishops' Synods and Family Institutes. What's more, he worked harder than anyone and still had time to spend with young people, writing poetry or philosophical commentaries on Pope Paul's encyclicals. When a Roman Congregation of Faith Teaching issued a declaration *Persona Humana*, he wrote an interesting article entitled, "Anthropological-Theological Aspects of Man's Maturing." At the same time, he was trying to solve the family problems of his valet Franciszek and housekeeper Maria. When I met Paul VI on my usual visit, he was amazed by Karol Wojtyla, and inquired, 'How does he do so much in a mere twenty-four hours?' I replied, 'Your Holiness, forgive me for saying this, but please see him and ask him yourself.'"

"I guess we could say that this type of man was born with an old head on young shoulders."

"You might be right, because I, as a Primate, received a few *honoris causa* degrees, which nobody made a fuss about. When Karol received his distinction from the Gutenberg University in Mainz, not only the German press commented, but the echo went all over the world.'

To raise the Primate's morale, I said, "It was the five hundred year anniversary of this University."

My host, Primate Wyszyński bypassed my comment, and said, "His article in *Osservatore Romano* was read all the time by the Holy Father, and when *The Truth About Man* appeared in which Karol talked about the United Nations Charter of Human Rights and the Helsinki conference, the Pope was so excited that he exclaimed to me, 'I have to see Wojtyla!' I politely suggested that maybe it would be a good idea if His

Holiness' secretary would call and invite him. A few weeks later a note appeared in the Italian papers, 'Il Card. Karol Wojtyla in udienza privata dal S. Padre Paolo VI a Roma il 31, III, 1977.'"

"As I recall, at that time the Holy Father was suffering not only from serious cardiac ailments, but also arthritis."

"Many times when kneeling during the Holy Mass he couldn't rise, and we had to assist him," replied my friend, "He complained about pains in his spine and in his joints, and had to wear a specially made corset to support his back. He drank prescribed mineral water, but at the same time loved good wine. This latter was not beneficial for his illness. On top of this, due to the reforms he introduced, he had to argue constantly with cardinals, especially those who were past the age of eighty. After this age, with few exceptions, he deprived all of them of any Church activities, particularly from taking part in the election of the Pope. Because of this decision, French Cardinal Eugène Tisserant commented, 'As we know, cardinals at the conclave express the will of the Holy Ghost. Is it possible that cardinals after eighty have no communication with the Holy Ghost?'"

"I presume that Paul VI did not apply this rule to himself?"

"You are right, but he had so much on his mind that he forgot about his age," replied the Primate with a smile.

"Did he not limit the number of cardinals who could participate in the conclave?"

"Up to one hundred and twenty—the magic number. The cardinals and the Curia objected, but could not do anything because the Pope is Supreme Pontiff! And besides, although he was physically small, he did have the stubbornness of a dozen men in him. But you don't know what made the biggest uproar?"

"How should I? I'm an outsider."

"His reorganization of saints."

"What?"

"Yes. You probably don't know that Paul VI loved to read biographies of the saints in his spare time, and we have a lot of them in our church."

"I presume it's difficult when you go back, to verify who was a saint and who was a poltroon."

"Maybe it is too drastic, but I'll give you one example. A long time ago, when I was reading about St. Simeon, I came to a paragraph in which a situation was described. For some years, this particular saint sat on top of a tree stump. Today, medical scientists describe this behavior as 'catalepsy'—someone who considers himself inspired by God. God tells him to sit there, and through him He sends a message to the people. But, in actuality, it is the condition of a man showing signs of loss of voluntary motions and suspended animation."

"To be frank, I'm hearing this for the first time, and from such high clergy as you, Primate."

"From the time of early Christianity, there have been Simeons, such as Simeon Magnus, who claimed that he was a god, and his woman, Helen, of Venetian background, who claimed to be a virgin.' The faithful had to pray to them at the statues of Zeus and Athena, and during these prayers, Simeon was called Kyrios or Lord, and Helen, Kyria or Mistress. And anybody who forgot their names was labeled a spy or traitor and treated accordingly."

"Judging by the tone of your voice I do not think that you have exhausted all the Simeons?"

"I can recall one more Simeon. He was a Dominican traveller and diplomat who, on the orders of thirteenth-century Pope Innocent IV, undertook missions to the Mongols of Persia and Armenia. According to the records this Dominican Simeon was a sacrificing and pious servant of the Pope. But I don't know if he sat on a tree stump."

"I see you don't have a high opinion of non-Simeons," I said.

"Let me see. There was a virgin from the second or third century, a member of a wealthy Roman family. Her name was Sta. Cecilia, and according to the legend, in childhood she promised God to remain a virgin. But when her family arranged for her to marry a wealthy pagan by the name of Valerian, eventually she agreed under one condition; that he would respect her wishes, which were supported by an angel who would tell him personally that she promised God to remain pure. But there was also one more important condition. She would prepare for a meeting between her husband and the angel providing he would embrace Christianity. He agreed. When Valerian returned from the christening he found his wife talking to an angel, and was so surprised that he related this story to his brother, Tiburtius; Tiburtius who had never seen an angel promised to abandon paganism also. As a result of Cecilia's purity, she converted two brothers to Christianity. When the Roman prefect Almachius heard about this, he gave an order to execute the brothers. Sta. Cecilia was greatly grieved. She gave her property to the poor, and was about to leave Rome, but the Prefect Almachius apprehended her, and condemned her to the stake. To everyone's surprise, the fire did not touch her body..."

"It is a tragic story," I commented.

"This is not the end. Almachius did not give up, and condemned her to death a second time by beheading. The execution was carried out, and the Christians, under cover of night, took her body and buried it in the catacombs. After a long search, ninth-century Pope Paschalis I discovered her body and buried it in the church which is today called Sta. Cecilia in Trastévere."

"Is there a record of the fact that she performed miracles after her death?"

"I do not recall, but a tragic legend persists to this day."

I became sad too, and exclaimed, "Many faithful Christians throughout history were condemned and died for their beliefs. They never became saints, and nobody knows about them. They do not make problems for the church or for living believers."

"You're right," said my host, "but imagine how much commotion was created by wise, just and pious Pope Paul VI."

"What do you mean?"

"For example, instead of leaving St. George alone, he questioned his sainthood. What's more, he questioned his existence."

"This is too much for me. Please explain more precisely."

"In the early years of Christianity, there was supposed to be a martyr whose name was George, who risked death defending a virgin from a dragon, and who eventually died in Lydda, Palestine. Much later, in the thirteenth century, his name appeared in various writings, and in the fourteenth century, Edward III made St. George the Protector of the Order of the Garter."

"Do we know why the Church made him a saint?"

"The reason is foggy and so is the story of his existence."

"Since we are spending this meeting talking about the saints, a neighbor of England is Ireland, which produced St. Patrick, about whom we probably don't know any more than we know about St. George."

"It must be your habit to collect material on dubious things?"

"You might say so, and memorizing, but let's be fair and finish with St. Patrick. Apparently, he was born in 389 and died in 461; the story

about his career was created much later. There are practically no historical facts other than that of his existence, although the legend says he
was in the business of exporting Irish wolfdogs, and spent time in Lér-
ins Monastery in the Mediterranean Sea, near Cannes, France. He decided to return to Britain because he heard a voice of a man named Victorious, who said, 'We pray thee, Holy youth, to come and walk again
amongst us as before.' So St. Patrick went to a monastery in Auxerre,
in the northern part of France where he prepared himself for ten years,
to become a missionary in Ireland."

"Where did you hear this?"

With a naive smile, Stefan replied, "From a monk who, along with
other *confraters*, received the order from Paul VI to research and prepare
material from the Vatican Library. This was for the Congregation for
the Affairs of Saints, and was to verify lives and deeds of various dubious benefactors of faith and mankind."

"I presume things like that made the Catholic Church stronger in the
long run, but in the meantime created much commotion and problems for the Holy See?"

"You are not a pious man, but sometimes you say the right thing. For
example, Maurice Cardinal Roy Archbishop of Québec told me about
a classical problem with Sta. Philomena. When travelling to consecrate
the Sta. Philomena church, he called his office and was told they had
just received a message from the Vatican *Congregazione per le Cause Dei
Santi* that researchers had just concluded that Sta. Philomena never existed. But there were more serious problems with the saints, such as
San Gennaro, whose Holy Day is observed with great pomp each year
in 'Little Italy' in New York City. He also is the patron saint of Naples.
In the cathedral of this beautiful Italian city, there is a golden sepul-
crum in which the blood of San Gennaro is preserved."

"How could you preserve the blood for so long?"

"This blood is now a brown powder, but twice a year at a certain time
this brown powder takes the form of liquid. The reason is that tremendous belief and prayers of the faithful produce this transformation.
What's more, if this transformation were not accomplished, the legend
tells us that a great cataclysm would invade Naples, and the Vesuvius
volcano would erupt and cover Naples, as happened with Pompeii and
Herculaneum. In the meantime we heard just recently, that scientists
from the *Congregazione per le Cause Dei Santi* established that such

transformation is impossible on a regular basis. Again the Italian faithful are in an uproar that their compatriot, Paul VI, deprived them not only of a miracle, but also of the saint who performed it."

"I think that the Holy Father should leave the dead alone, and concentrate on helping people living their lives on earth."

"There is certain wisdom in various acts of John XXIII and Paul VI that led to reforms by having the Church face problems of humanity more realistically, and to participate more energetically in human endeavors on a worldwide scale. At the same time, some conservative forces in the Church are doing everything possible to prevent liberalization and humanization of the Church, and to reach the proclamation *Sede Vacante*, as soon as possible."

"What do you mean?"

"I will be frank. They hope the time will soon come when this progressive Pope will die, and there will be a chance to elect a conservative who will not rock St. Peter's boat."

"Since we have mentioned the word 'dead,' I have an urge to ask you why, after a Pope passes away, there is no post mortem?"

"I could not reply for the simple reason that never, during my time of serving as a member of the Holy College of Cardinals, has even one member raised this question; although once, in Warsaw, Karol said when I spoke about the strange circumstances of the death of some of the Popes, 'To light the night is to emphasize the darkness.' I thought this a philosophical approach to post mortem."

This gave me intellectual pain because, through conversations with John Paul II, I dug up some ingenious abbreviations with which one could begin a book, but my train of thought was interrupted with the continuation of Wyszyński's narrative.

"After the Pope's death his tremendous power is put into the hands of the College of Cardinals. But the process of verifying the Holy Father's departure is simple and traditional. When the news reaches the cardinals who are in Rome, they go to the bedroom of the deceased and the cardinal who holds the title of *Camerlingo del Apostolico Camera* slowly approaches the bed with a little silver hammer and taps the body of the Pope three times, asking each time 'Are you sleeping?' When there is no answer, the announcement of the Holy Father's departure is proclaimed. This means that the Holy See is vacant—*Sede Vacante*; a conclave is then called to elect a new Pope. But let's return to those living on earth."

"Right. You are supposed to tell me about the private audience of Karol Wojtyla with Pope Paul VI."

"It would be better if you asked Karol himself."

"I'll do that, but first I'd like to hear it from you."

"Why?"

"Because he would probably be reluctant to talk to me about this, and would minimize his relationship with the Holy Father."

"I don't know how to approach the same subject from different angles for your maximum benefit," began Primate Wyszyński. "But you know that the fever started in the Curia during John XXIII's reign, and intensified during the reign of Paul VI, especially in 1976–77, when it was known that the Pope was very ill. You have to know also that the Curia and all the Italian cardinals were insisting on an Italian Pope of conservative lineage. To this you have to add German aspirations; and, Cardinals Cody and Cooke were pushing themselves in this direction; and there were also Third World possibilities. And, Paul VI was still alive!"

"Some time ago you told me that Paul VI was following Karol Wojtyla's intellectual and ecclesiastical blossoming, and that he considered Wojtyla a possible candidate to occupy the Holy See."

"The Holy Father was thinking about the future when there would be harmonius cooperation between Socialist countries and the Vatican; and the only man in his opinion to codify this mesh of ideas and actions would be the young, energetic and pious Karol Wojtyla.

"What's more, a few times Paul VI repeated to me with joy in his voice some clever expression of Karol's such as, 'The longer I am a bishop, the stronger I feel that I am *below* rather than *above*... Every life is a gift of God, and we should protect it with our life...' Because he was, even as a Pope, enchanted with youth, he cherished the expressions of Karol,

> In this time of hypocrisy, young people would like to breathe the truth, and go with it to meet the future; and they are not afraid of anything the future will bring. They believe the most important thing is to be yourself, to be faithful to your heart, to your soul, and to Christ.

"When, on March 31 he saw Karol, he said, 'I would like to see you as my successor because you will do more for the Church and for humanity than any of us.' Karol didn't have words to thank him, except that he knelt and kissed the Fisherman's ring.

"The Pope continued, 'The Curia who is working right now twenty-four hours a day, would like to have their own man, and Siri is working hard to be this man. No doubt Cody and others are working underground. I am still alive, and it seems I could help elect a Pope of my choosing, but I have no strength to do this.' Saying that, he handed Karol a few sheets of paper, asked him to sit beside him, and explained the contents. 'Here are three groups of cardinals, the one on the first page will vote for you because they are of the same philosophy; the second group is on the border; if you talk to them they will be on your side; and the third, only the Holy Ghost could enlighten them; otherwise, they will work for Siri.'

"Karol, according to my impeccable information, replied, 'Your Holiness, my conscience would not allow me to do that.'

'The Pope gave him a piece of his mind. 'On one side is the future of the Church and humanity; and on the other is your single conscience. What would you choose? Siri, Cody, Bertoli, or some unknown cardinal, or even sick Luciani who could not make up his mind on anything in a hundred years? A weak individual in the hands of the Curia would be a disaster. Please help save the Church and the simple man. I am asking you in the name of Christ.'

"Karol was extremely moved, but regained his composure and clearly explained with tears in his eyes, 'Holy Father, if God, if Jesus Christ wanted me to occupy the Holy See, then I am sure that Providence would act accordingly, ' and he put the list of cardinals back on the Pope's desk.

"'Go ahead and wait for the act of Providence, but in the meantime, take from your superior this list, and put it in your pocket.'

"Karol obeyed the order."

"I am much obliged to you for this inside information," I said to the Primate of Poland, "but I cannot understand your confidence in me, the perennial sinner."

My friend, Stefan, smiled enigmatically and continued his story. "On September 25, Paul VI told me and a few other cardinals, 'I am approaching my eightieth year, and my life on earth is coming to a close. This event directs me toward more humility, to a plea for God's mercy, and to look for help in the prayer of good people.'

"Suffering from rheumatism and grave heart problems, he would live less than a year after the day he spoke these words. The summer of 1978 was hot and humid. The people of Rome escaped the climate for the mountains or forests. The Pope left for Castel Gandolfo, and naturally the high Curia officials dispersed all over to expensive resort areas.

"It was Sunday, August 6, early evening. The Pope went to his bedroom to make himself comfortable and began reading various papers that a messenger had delivered to him from the Vatican. The more charitable people said that he was reading a religious book; others, that he was going through the report on Cardinal Cody, which upset him. He slumped, and never woke up. Such was the end of Pope Paul VI, who occupied the Holy See for fifteen years and forty-six days."

We looked at each other, and I thought this was a proper place to end our revealing conversation. But Stefan Wyszyński evidently did not think so. He said, as though replying to my unspoken question, "Karol Wojtyla was on vacation, an excursion with young people in the Carpathian Mountains region of Bieszczady. He heard about the Holy Father's death on the radio in his tent on the riverbank. Right away, he returned to his Cracow archbishop's palace and called me.

"On August 7, the Polish Episcopate and I issued a communiqué in which we praised Paul VI for his wisdom and far-sightedness, and for his courage in estabalishing good relations between the Apostolic See and the People's Republic of Poland.

"Before Cardinal Wojtyla departed to attend the memorial services in Rome for his most admired Pope, he performed a Holy Mass in Wawel Cathedral on August 10, during which he eulogized,

> The Supreme Shepherd of the Catholic Church should be mourned the world over by all people. We should do the same with our hearts full of grief, because Pope Paul VI had a difficult time during his Pontificate in the crucial period of our Church and during the time of Vatican Council II. He showed great serenity, sacrifice, love and humbleness. In his long life he did not travel much, but as a young priest he worked for a while in the Nuncio's office in Warsaw, and many times during his Pontificate he recalled those months in the capital of our country with deep nostalgia.

Together with the Primate of Poland, Cardinal Wojtyla flew to Rome; they were driven by car to the summer residence of the Pope in Castel Gandolfo. The simple wooden casket was mounted for adoration by the faithful. In this palace on Lake Albano, thirteen miles from Rome, built during the reign of Pope Urban VIII, you could hear only shuffling feet and whispering mourners who came to pay their final respects to this unusual man who had given strict orders that there should be no flowers or candles, no ornamentation or elaborate ceremony to mark his departure.

From Wednesday, early in the morning, thousands of people poured into St. Peter's Square, and during the next few hours the multitudes of people filled the Via della Conciliazione and spilled out from Borgo Sant' Angelo to Borgo San Spirito.

"I don't think St. Peter's Basilica remembers a time when the casket of a deceased Pope was not displayed within," John Paul II said. "After the Holy Mass was performed and people said good-bye to the Christian leader, the pine coffin was carried inside the Basilica and then to the Donatello Chapel that is located under the nave of the church. It was placed in a deep grave because Paul VI had said, 'I would like to lie on earth near John XXIII. There we will have time to solve many church problems.'"

"Why exactly did Paul VI insist on being buried in the Donatello Chapel?"

"Because Donatello was a giant of the Renaissance, and his bas-relief of the Madonna and Child adorn this chapel. The Pope, who had a tremendous feeling for classic and Middle-Ages art, was always lyrical in his description of Donatello's work. Each time he was in Florence he went to see the *Annunciation* Tabernacle in Santa Croce as well as the *Cantoria*, which Donatello created for the Florentine Cathedral. Today it is displayed in the Cathedral's museum. Donatello, who lived a long life and whose creativity never ceased, left his work all over Europe, including America. You can find his masterpieces not only in Rome and Florence, but in Naples, Siena and Venice. His *Delivery of the Keys to Saint Peter* can be found in the Victoria and Albert Museum in London, the *Pazzi Madonna* in Berlin's Staatliche Museum, and the *Shaw Madonna* in the Boston Museum of Fine Arts."

"How do you know so much about Donatello?"

"Even as a seminary student I collected postcards which represented Donatello's work, and before I knew that Paul VI admired the beauty of Donatello, I discovered and absorbed his particular feeling for God who spoke so beautifully through the sculptures of this fifteenth-century Italian genius. When I was young I used to dream of seeing his originals, and I was greatly desirous of travel and space. Now, I have one simple desire: to have more time."

41

The Three Poles

DURING our many meetings, Edward Gierek and I exchanged arguments and sometimes insults, but they were of a political nature and at the end we would always patch things up and see each other again. Once, I said I would bring some pronouncements by Primate Wyszyński and Cardinal Wojtyla and would like him to make an intelligent response.

"I will even read Max Scheler," he replied triumphantly, trying to indicate that he knew something about this German philosopher, a propagator of 'theological ethics of value,' and adherent of Pascal's 'logic of the heart.'"

Gierek noticed the surprised look on my face. "I know Wojtyla is fond of Scheler and wrote about him. I will tell you something else; although I am not a literary man I read everything about and by my adversaries."

"You, a communist, have adversaries throughout the world," I said, "and they have written much about communism and socialism. How do you manage to absorb all this information?"

"This may be an overstatement, but I try to know everything about people like Wojtyla and Wyszyński who are privately very charming, but whose political pronouncements are critical and sometimes even vicious. I don't mind because I like to keep Polish prisons free of political detainees and would never persecute real patriots who are helping us build a socialist country; but they are often intolerant of our viewpoint."

For no reason, he switched the conversation, "Do you know who François Rabelais was?"

The question startled me, although I knew that, because of his work in the French coal mines, Gierek was fascinated with the culture of France. In interviewing important people, I always showed great patience, so I replied meekly, "A great sixteenth-century satirical writer."

"So, you do have some education!"

"But my knowledge of Rabelais was cut short at the college level."

"Oh, I love him, especially because of his poking fun at King Francis I and French cardinals—sometimes even at the Pope."

I noticed he had prepared himself for our conversation about Wojtyla and Wyszyński more deeply than I had thought. "What kind of fun?" I asked.

"Once, Rabelais was in Lyons, and didn't have money to pay for a coach to go to Paris. So he stole some sugar from the local inn where he was staying, for which he could not pay either, and dividing the stolen sugar into three little bags, labelled them: 'Poison for the King,' 'Poison for the Queen,' and 'Poison for the successor to the Throne.' He left them in the room, and after a while they were discovered by the innkeeper who called the royal guard. Rabelais was arrested, and sent to Paris under guard. Naturally, he did not pay for the inn or for his trip because he was in the hands of Royal authorities. When the prosecutor threatened him with the death penalty for attempting to poison the royal family, Rabelais opened the bags, put some of the contents into his mouth and began to eat. Everyone was startled, especially when Rabelais said, 'Le sucre.'"

"You mean you like to show that authoritarian governments were so stupid at that time that they did not even examine the contents of the bags?"

"Yes and no," replied Gierek triumphantly.

Here, I discovered that when people said that Gierek's Achilles' heel was not in his foot but under his hat they were wrong.

"Do you know that NATO's intelligence branch uses sugar today, among other things, to destabilize our good relations with the Catholic church?"

"How?"

"Recently, we discovered that Wyszyński, Wojtyla and other important members of the Polish Catholic Curia received gifts from abroad, various sweetened products, and when we analyzed them in laboratories we discovered that the sugar contents in the products was tainted with a powerful poison."

"Do you think I should believe you?"

"You don't have to because I just talked about sugar. Last night, I read *Gargantua* by Rabelais, and figured that this humorous author should give an interesting introduction to present-day gruesome things, and the reality of power politics between the Soviet Union and the Western world, of which we, as a small nation, are victims. You know perfectly well that the Catholic Church and their leaders are critical of our socialist attempt to build a just society, but I am also sure that Wojtyla and Wyszyński are great patriots and like we, they would like to see a fair and prosperous country."

"How would you respond to Wyszyński's pronouncement that you, as leader of the Workers' Party live in luxury similar to a medieval king, using a gold table setting, while in some remote Polish villages peasants use wooden spoons?"

"You have eaten meals with me, and didn't notice luxury, but when entertaining foreign leaders, as first person in the country, I think I should show the same hospitality they offer important guests."

"What would you say to Wojtyla's statement that political power has corrupted you? 'That physical might is admired only by small people through which they believe they will make themselves great. The really great man, even when he possesses power, uses this power to be a servant of the nation.'"

"I admit that sometimes I lose my equilibrium and show off, but then I look at my mother's photograph and return to reality."

"It's interesting that your mother's humility brings you to size, but Wojtyla thinks that you do not show respect and understanding for the peasants who, with little machinery, produce bread; and without keeping a balance between industry and agriculture you will destroy the country."

"I think you are an agent of the church, and don't understand the mechanism of the Polish economy!"

So as to ensure that our session would run smoothly, I decided not to answer him, since he would not believe me and would be annoyed. I preferred for him to become angry over something worthwhile, "Can I read you a statement by Karol Wojtyla?"

"Go ahead. I still have patience with you..."

"Then, I would like to comment on it.

Human rights are important not only in our country but in the world. Those rights are indispensable, and they are not a gift of the State or the Church. Those rights are given by God, and should be respected by everyone. We cannot solve the problems of human conscience by oppression; police intervention is not the answer, and the solution does not lie with the enlargement of State security forces. There is one road to Peace and national unity, and this road has to be paved with the rights of citizens. Citizens should not be divided into believers or nonbelievers, into mere members of the Church or party. The Church is not, should not, and will not seek authority. The Church only bears witness to the truth about God and man.

Patiently and quietly Gierek replied, "I agree with his idealistic pronouncements, and am sure every honest man, not only in our country but in every other country would agree. But do we have enough inner strength, we, the small people, we the small countries, to fight with bare hands, those who possess military might, and those who play power politics?"

He stopped, reflected and added, "Give the message from me to Wojtyla that we might be successful if the Catholic Church, together with all other churches of the world, concentrate on their work, and inspire people to engage actively in an endeavor for peace."

He smiled ironically, "Let us return to present-day reality. I don't know if I am correctly paraphrasing Wojtyla's beloved philosopher Scheler, who, someplace, some time ago, said that we are living in a spiritual realm of self-poisoning. This creates suggestive truths which are not accepted by the opposition, and critics condemn, although they give the impression that they would like to do something good. Critics don't want to correct wrong things, they use their activity for the sake of controversy."

Then Gierek went into a tirade about raw politics. "Maybe biologists will some day create 'homonucleus' but, for God's sake don't let them create him in their own image! I would like to work even closer with Wyszyński and Wojtyla and not see them play saints in front of people. I know what they like to do. They like a good fuck and good food like everybody else. I know they are patriots. I'm a patriot too, but I don't want another situation like what they did to me on June 8, 1978, when, during Corpus Christi day, they had a little meeting with Archbishop Luigi Poggi, who looks like your American actor, Mickey Rooney. They discussed religious activities in the Soviet Union. Imagine how much trouble I have been getting from then on, from our great Eastern neighbor who accused me of participating, or at least condoning, the long-range strategy of 'cooperation' between Russian churches and the Vatican. Poggi flew in especially for this meeting, and we were hospitable toward him, and as repayment he involved me in a conspiracy. Neither Primate Wyszyński nor Cardinal Wojtyla explained anything to me, although my information was unimpeachable. I feel personally hurt. I know also that a long time ago they developed a strong connection wth various dissatisfied workers' groups, and started organizing certain underground societies through which they would pressure the Party, government, and me, to estaablish a 'renewal movement,' which they said would neutralize the dissent. I don't know now whether or not they want to destroy our system of government."

I was surprised that the 'First Person' was confused, so for the sake of conversation I said, "Some of us spend too much time being suspicious and run away from something that isn't even chasing us."

"To that, I will reply differently. The Church really is going too fast, and with less and less consultation with me, and this is no good for anyone. They are so Americanized that when I travel through the country I see on some churches, such signs: 'Come in and have your faith lifted.'"

"The economic situation is worsening, and people are organizing in opposition to your policy of rapid industrialization and dependence on the American dollar. Their psychology is being shifted toward the West and the Council of Bishops and especially, Wojtyla and Wyszyński."

"How do you know that?"

"For example, yesterday I was invited to a dinner. I thought I would go a little early, walk around Warsaw, smell the atmosphere, feel the bright sun, and engage people in discussion. When I appeared at Unia Lubelska Square, I saw flower and berrysellers. These women sat at the corners of converging streets, praising the freshness of the flowers and brightness of the berries. When I come to Poland, I always buy a new suit, and because of my good command of the language I could be taken for a native..."

"Suddenly you become modest. Continue the story."

"I approached one of the ladies, pulled from my pocket some zlotys and asked, 'How much for a bouquet of roses?'

"She looked at me and replied, 'I will not sell to you.'

"Why not?"

"'I cannot...'

"I went to a fat lady wearing a colorful print dress, and asked, still holding money in my hand, 'How much is the basket of blueberries?'

"'It's not for you!'"

"I was puzzled, but didn't want to argue, so I asked both ladies a neutral question, 'Where is Wieniawski Street?'

"Both shrugged, so I asked again, 'Are you not local merchants?'

"'We are, but we are special.'

"I looked at them. There was nothing special about them. Two middle-aged fat women, one blonde, one brunette, with beautiful roses and extremely large fresh blueberries – sitting like mother hens around their chicks. Then, I repeated my question, 'Why are you so special?'

"'Because we sell only to foreigners, for dollars,' replied the brunette.

"'Where can I buy flowers and berries for zlotys?' I asked still clutching in my perspiring hand, a bundle of Polish currency.

"'In the back streets behind the square,' replied the blonde woman. She looked at me, trying to size me up, and said, 'You must have dollars. The berries in the back streets are sour, the roses, wilted. You must have dollars.'

"You see, it is a rather stupid story, but illustrates today's situation in a country whose leaders develop a dollar psychosis."

Edward Gierek said quietly, "You, and probably Stefan Wyszyński, Karol Wojtyla and others spit at this, while sitting before your heretic, but by doing this you are extinguishing the national stake. Do you think I want to borrow dollars to buy machinery to industrialize our country? However, we had no way out."

"I realize that, but you forced development of heavy industry, and by doing that you destroyed agriculture, and neglected light industry. As a result, inflation is growing, people are working harder and longer hours, and when they go to shop, the stores are practically empty."

"Go ahead, accuse me of treason," commented Gierek.

"I'm not accusing you of anything, and I don't even have the right to criticize you, but I feel that someone has to tell you the truth if you don't see it yourself."

I figured I should tell a little story to ease the tension between us.

"Remember when I went to my friend with the flowers and berries?"

"Yes, it was a strange story."

"This man works in the Ministry of Heavy Industry, and has six children to support. When I asked, following a meager supper, how he managed, my friend replied,

"'I work eight hours in the Ministry, and spend the second eight hours as an ordinary worker in a factory. Then six hours teaching, and on top of it five hours in a private garage fixing cars.'"

"I said, 'Stop! That is already twenty-seven hours!'"

"He smiled and replied, 'I usually get up early!'"

Gierek looked at me and remarked, seriously, "Your friend is not working well in any of his jobs. He must of necessity cut corners, and when you multiply this by millions, you can see why production in the country is reaching a new low and people are demoralized."

"Why cannot the government, the party and you recognize this and with the help of well-meaning people and especially the Church, get together and reorganize the economic system in the direction of more productive and more profitable results, which will commit and satisfy the majority of the nation?"

"I had a serious talk with Wyszyński, Wojtyla and the rest of the Polish Episcopate. They agreed with me. Wyszyński even made a few speeches pleading with the citizens to support the government effort. But behind my back the same Wyszyński, the same Wojtyla are helping to organize strikes in the Polish seaports, in the Silesian industrial basin, and other parts of the country through which they disrupt the economic life of the country. The government could lock them up, but we have no political prisoners and we are proud of this. We don't like to use force because we think that reasoning and persuasion with honest people is sufficient. I don't know what they want from me."

"I talked to them and they say that you and the Party pay lip service to suggestions of reorganization, for the simple reason that the people who hold political power in the country, with you as leader, think that this wave of strikes and discontent will be over shortly. Putting it bluntly, the workers, the peasants and the Church do not see that you are capable of introducing complete and honest renewal."

"Do they want me to introduce capitalism and sell the factories to foreign investors? Then, will they be happy?"

This was a difficult question, and as a result, uneasy quietness reigned between us. We began talking about personal matters.

A wave of strikes did rock the country in the summer of 1980 and on August 31, with the help of Wyszyński and the Polish Episcopate, a workers' organization under the name of Solidarity came into being in the port city of Gdańsk. The leader of this organization, Lech Walesa, was a young man with a thick mustache who wore a picture of the Holy Mother on his lapel. This image of the Black Madonna of Często-chowa was a symbol of his and his organization's adherence to the Christian teaching and subordination to the Polish Episcopate and the Primate of Poland.

When I asked Wyszyński, "Who is this man?" the Primate, as always, honestly replied, "A charismatic simpleton, who never in his life read a book but had a golden tongue and complete trust in us."

I repeated the same question to two other leaders. Wojtyla said only, "A good man."

Gierek reacted differently. "I don't know how this foolable army private who doesn't know the difference between the handle and barrel of a gun, can discuss state matters with a well-educated general."

Exactly a year later, the United Workers' Party—the Communist Party of Poland—issued the following communiqué,

> The Ninth Extraordinary Congress of the Party brought to account people guilty before the nation and before the Party. Delegates made a decision to exclude Edward Gierek and others from the Party ranks. The newly elected Party authorities received mandates in the most democratic election in the history of the Party. Among new members of the Central Committee are Stanislaw Kania, Wojciech Jaruzelski, Kazimierz Barcikowski, Stefan Olszowski and Mieczyslaw Rakowski.

Some time later, a new communiqué appeared charging Gierek with irresponsible conduct in managing state matters. In his reply, Gierek admitted his responsibility for the socioeconomic development of the country in the 1970s, saying that he was guided in his actions by the welfare of the people, the necessity of creating new jobs, and the need to quickly modernize production potential. He stated at the same time that control by the Political Bureau and the Government had been insufficient in such spheres as drawing credits (the country's indebtedness exceeded by far its payment capability), developing investments, and distributing the national income, which caused deep economic imbalance in key branches of the economy such as power, industry and agriculture.

This communiqué full of generalities concluded:

> Edward Gierek saw the cause of many economic setbacks in improper functioning of the leading government agencies, toleration of ministry and industry particularism, and lack of effective control which hindered the termination of responsibility for decision making. Gierek gave a particular self-critical assessment of his responsibility for the personnel policy in the party and the state. All those shortcomings and adverse influences on decision making were of key importance for the country. After 1976 there was no analysis of the mounting crisis which made it impossible to draw proper conclusions.
>
> Assessing the functioning of the Party in the 1970s, Gierek pointed to his numerous contacts with the workers. He said that today he was aware that not all of them had been true reflections of the public opinion and moods. Regarding interparty activity, Gierek underlined shortcomings in educational work and the practical obligation of the principles of consultation, as well as weaknesses in organizational work . . ."

The Polish Episcopate supported the new Government and its effort of renewal, and appealed directly to the nation for greater effort in rebuilding economic life. The Government, the Church, and Solidarity began to assemble all the positive elements in pulling the country out of the deep material and moral crisis. At the beginning, those three powerful elements received complete support of the people in various stratas of endeavor. The Holy Father gave his approval and blessing for this peaceful cooperation.

42

An Eyewitness to the Conclave of Glass Angels

THE END of August 1978 was hot and sweaty. The half-empty streets of Rome were punctuated with black garments of priests and nuns running in various directions and you could feel the nervousness and smell the perspiration, but above all, you felt that something important was going on in the Eternal City. All ranks of priests and many tourists came every day to the Vatican for the Conclave, among them Cardinal Wojtyla.

Wojtyla was staying in his usual place, the Collegio, and was getting up sometimes at 5:00 A.M., even earlier than in Cracow, because he was swamped with work, meetings, writings. Despite this he still had time to go swimming with his friend, Bishop Andrea Deskur, confidant of the deceased Paul VI who was extremely knowledgeable about the Curia. Andrea brought Karol the latest gossip concerning almost all the one hundred and eleven Cardinals preparing to elect a new pope. Names of various cardinals were popping up as potential candidates, the *papabili*; among them Giovanni Benelli, Sebastiano Baggio, Paulo Bertoli; the Austrian Cardinal König, Holland's Willebrands, the Argentinian Pironio, Poland's Wojtyla; although the last name was supposed to be, according to Pope Paul's promise to Wyszyński, up front on the *papabili* list.

Three cardinals nominated by Pius XII; eight by John XXIII and a hundred by Paul VI were taking part in the Conclave, but the thoughts of the Holy Spirit and the intricate operations of the Curia were kept in complete secrecy. Benelli, Baggio and Bertoli, employees of the Curia, were eager to occupy the Holy See. Different groups of Vatican circles mentioned the names of the two Americans, Cody and Cooke, whose backing came from Vatican and American financial circles. Wy-szyński's name appeared in gossip columns of Italian papers as the only cardinal who had skillfully developed a *modus vivendi* between the Church and a Communist government.

Three other Italians also appeared as *papabili* possibilities: Pericle Fe-lici, Giuseppe Siri and the not too well-known name of Venice's Patri-arch, sixty-six-year-old Albino Luciani.

The custom of electing a pope goes back to the thirteenth century when in the town of Viterbo in the northern part of Latium province, seventeen cardinals got together in 1268, and lived for two years at the expense of the town, trying to arrange a successor to Clement IV. The citizens of Viterbo finally locked up the cardinals (*cum clavis*) and fed them only bread and water until they elected Pope Gregory X in 1291. This method of locking up cardinals for the purpose of electing a pope has survived to this day.

Many changes were introduced by Pius XII who announced his con-stitution *Vacantis Apostolicae Sedis* on March 8, 1945; John XXIII added his own suggestions by announcing *Summi Pontificis Electio*, on Sep-tember 5, 1962. Finally, Paul VI, on November 21, 1970, proclaimed that cardinals could not participate in the Conclave after they reached the age of eighty. In 1975, he also specified who could attend the Con-clave: the Secretary of the College of Cardinals, the Holy Father's Gen-eral Vicar for the City of the Vatican, the Pope's Master of Ceremonies, a few confessors, the priest who helped the deaconal Cardinal, two medical doctors, two male nurses, the architect of the Conclave with two technicians, and two other technical persons. As we can see, a new, revised, expanded and modernized Conclave came into being to-ward the end of the twentieth century–for better or for worse.

A few days before the Conclave, workers prepared accommodations in the Vatican Palace for one hundred eleven cardinals; and, except for two entrances, sealed the Vatican Palace so nobody could enter and ob-serve the proceedings, except the Holy Ghost.

The beginning of the Conclave was solemn and colorful. All cardinals who took part in the election entered from the Pauline Chapel and walked majestically through the Royal Hall toward the Sistine Chapel. Only from the Royal Hall could foreign diplomats and journalists see their pious faces. The Sistine Chapel, where the election took place was guarded by a specially selected group of Swiss Guards; nobody but cardinals could enter. After Holy Mass and a modest breakfast, cardinals were summoned by a melodious bell to take part in the voting. The election could be achieved by acclamation or compromise; that means one hundred eleven voters could select from among themselves from nine to fifteen cardinals from which they would in turn elect a pope. Whichever way it's done, the election of the Pope has to be approved by two thirds plus one of the voting cardinals. Scrutators, verifiers and infirmary representatives were also selected by voting cardinals; the duty of these people was to check the votes as well as to pick up the ballots from the cells of sick cardinals.

The ballot card has a printed line: I select for the Pope...and there written in longhand is the name of the candidate for whom the particular cardinal votes. Then the ballots are placed in an antique box on the altar, and performing his duty, each cardinal solemnly proclaims, "I take Jesus Christ as a witness who will judge that I am selecting this candidate which I am convinced in the presence of God should be elected."

In the astonishingly beautiful Sistine Chapel where Michelangelo's *Last Judgment* overpowers the distinguished gathering you can barely hear the echo of the solemn words and shuffling cardinals' shoes. The colors of the masterpieces on the walls, the muted sounds, and the coolness of the air bring to some minds a feeling of insignificance of the human body and the almightiness of God; but a person who takes his religion more rationally experiences the power of the old Vatican and its rigid rules. One of the cardinals put it this way:

> If the Pope is not elected during the day of the votings – two in the morning and two in the afternoon – the Cardinals return to their cells to pray and rest. If, after three days of this routine, the successor to the Holy See is not chosen, the fourth day is an intermission, during which Cardinals pray, eat and trade candidates. On the fifth day, they return to the Sistine Chapel to vote again. If, after the seventh ballot, the results are not positive, then the so-called camerlinger Cardinal addresses the rest of the brethren and suggests that they should select from amongst themselves nine to fifteen delegates, who, according to the rules should vote on one of two top ballot candidates. When the successor to the

Holy See is elected, the Dean of the College of Cardinals or his Deputy, or, if neither is attending the Conclave because of his age, the eldest cardinal approaches the elected Pope and in the name of the Holy College of Cardinals asks, "Do you accept the election to the Holy See which has been carried out according to Canon law?"

When the response is 'yes' he asks the newly elected Pope what name he is going to choose. The new Pope announces his name to the members of the Conclave and the chorus sings *Te Deum*. Following this, all the Cardinals, one by one, approach the newly elected Pope and pay him homage. Simultaneously, from the little stove which is placed in the Sistine Chapel, the white smoke of burning ballots wafts outside, while many thousands of people, gathered in St. Peter's Square, know that the new Pope is elected. At the same moment, the Deacon Cardinal appears on the balcony and announces to the excited crowd that the new Pope is elected. Afterward, the Pope-elect appears on the same balcony and gives *urbi et orbi*, his first blessing to the City of Rome and to the entire world.

The Holy Father selects the day of his Coronation during which a great procession takes place. He is borne along on the gestatorial chair, called *sedia gestatoria*, and again blesses the great crowd, among whom are people from all over the world, including nearly all heads of state.

Up to now, Coronation festivities have been performed in Saint Peter's Basilica in the morning, but Pope Paul VI changed this routine and the ceremony of his Coronation was carried out in the evening in St. Peter's Square, where according to his wishes, more people would be able to share his joyous election. In his case, there were eighty-three heads of state of the world. When the procession reached the altar, the master of ceremonies faced the new Pope and burned a handful of cotton with these words,

"Holy Father, this is how the glory of the world passes."

During the Coronation, the first of the Cardinals put the triple tiara on the Pope's head and announced,

"Remember that you are the Father of princes and kings, and the world leader, Vicar on earth of our Savior Jesus Christ for whom we proclaim respect and glory forever."

On September 29, 1964, during the audience for foreign diplomats, Paul VI said that this "Father of princes and kings" is an expression in a moral sense, and he would try to represent the deep desire of humanity for peace and truth which should embrace all nations and political systems. As a symbol of good intentions he requested that his tiara be sold, and the proceeds be given to the poor.

The political goodwill was expressed in numerous antiwar speeches, as well as by sending Archbishop Agostino Casaroli to Moscow – from February 23 to March 1, 1971 – to discuss religious and political affairs with Russian leaders. Jean Cardinal Villot as well as Casaroli had been personally ordered by the Pope to steer Vatican diplomats into international activity through which they could enhance peace and freedom of conscience. The result of this order was Church participation in the 1973 Helsinki International Conference. At that time Paul VI said that Church participants are "personal representatives of the Holy See who are trying to intensify the possibility of serving people."

The continuation of this activity was the presence of a Vatican representative in the United Nations at the New York headquarters, the Red Cross in Geneva, UNESCO in Paris, FAO in Rome, as well as in the International Bureau of Atomic Energy, the European Council for the Common Market in Brussels, the Council for Cultural Cooperation and the United Nations Bureau for Displaced Persons, World Council for Work Safety, the World Council of Health to fight malaria, and many other U.N. organizations, such as the International Association of Doctors, Committee for the History of Arts, and the Congress of Anthropological and Ethnological Sciences. A substantial financial contribution was made by the Vatican to all these organizations, and the Pope expressed his sentiments clearly by stating,

> We are not neutral. The Holy Gospel does not permit us to be indifferent when the question of the good of man is being considered – his physical health, mental development, the basic material and spiritual law. We cannot be indifferent when people of some countries live under conditions which endanger their well-being, or when an international organization needs help.

At the suggestion of Paul VI, Albino Cardinal Luciani established contact with Cardinal Wojtyla to discuss the problems of Eastern Europe. As a result of these discussions, a deep friendship grew between this quiet and well-educated Patriarch of Venice, who had been elevated to this position by Paul VI, and the Polish Cardinal Wojtyla.

For some reason, Cardinal Albino's background was a well-kept secret. His father was a staunch socialist, and glass-blower by profession. When he lost his job because of his beliefs, he emigrated to Switzerland, but didn't have success and returned to Italy where by accident he secured work in a Venetian glass factory; as we know, the glass masterpieces produced on five small islands in the lagoon of Venice are world famous. Young Albino Luciani almost swallowed, with his big lustrous eyes, the stories his father told him about the creation in liquid glass of delicate angels. When smoke and clouds from the heat subside, the angels of dreamy shapes would shine with permanent rainbow colors.

"My father was an ordinary worker, a simple glass-blower," Albino said in his quiet voice, so as not to awaken the dreams of his youth, "but he was a great artist. My father was a creator of angels."

This was how he began his story, during the hot and humid afternoon of August 1978, to his friend, Cardinal Karol, who later, as John Paul II, related it to me:

I never saw a man who could talk about a glass-blower's work with such enthusiasm and love. But he divulged the secrets of his passion only to a select group of people. When I ask, 'Why are you telling me?' he replied, in almost a whisper. 'You are from the East, and for me your country presents the enchantment of the unknown. What is more, you captivate me and have my trust.'

But Albino was telling me something which, at the beginning, I could not comprehend or explain. He said that his 'glass-blower father created angels in fantastic poses, clothed in white or shining black or red; all colors under the sun, but representing priests of various religions. The most impressive angel, however, was an angel in a white cassock who had the body of my mother, whom I once saw naked…' One afternoon, my friend, Cardinal Luciani said that 'for an inexplicable reason they all have my face and in my dream fly around my bed, the house and around me.' I thought, 'Does my father make a joke of me? Is he a real father? The angels were imitating my talk and gestures, and they merged into one angel in a white cassock. I woke up; but I couldn't tell anyone – not even my mother—because she would say to me, 'Albino, you are crazy,' and I didn't want to worry her. Quietly, my father approached one day and put his hand on my head,

'Albino, I have a feeling that the angels are persecuting you.'

'I replied, Yes father.'

'He said, I know why the angels are angry with me; because they would like to be created not by a socialist, but by the Pope, or by God, So they turned against me, the creator. I don't know why they are against you, a little boy. I am going to ask them.'

'We did not speak again about the angels, but my father became sick, and I never had the courage to disturb him with my dreams.'

Karol Wojtyla asked, "You as a writer, what do you think about Albino Luciani's dreams?"

"The question should be directed to a psychiatrist," I replied, rather strongly, because we were in the season and atmosphere of dreams. Then I brought myself and Wojtyla back to reality by saying, "Nothing is wrong with Albino Luciani. He was elected cardinal."

"I agree with you," replied Karol Wojtyla. "Albino told me that the dreams stopped a few weeks before his nomination as cardinal, but they began again, and to obliterate those dreams he said that it did him good to talk about communism, socialism, capitalism, all political movements which annoy the angels but give him intellectual respite. I presume the angels prefer a status quo."

"Possibly," I replied. "On the other hand, he is looking for information or psychological support from a man like you, whom he described as 'a man from the East.'"

"There is validity in your observation," replied Karol Wojtyla. "But I wonder who the angels would pester if Albino Luciani were to be elected Pope."

"Who would elect him?"

"With the cardinals it is a difficult business, because you not only have to know their minds, but you have to know the mind of the Holy Ghost."

"You have had a better chance with the Holy Ghost for sure, but with the cardinals too!"

Wojtyla smiled, as if to say thank you. "In the best situation, an Italian is in first place; second is the Austrian König; then, a few Germans;

and don't forget the Americans, and a Pole at the end. But even then, I put Wyszyński first."

"Most of the cardinals are smart and devoted to the Church, and they will search for an intelligent candidate for the Holy See. Who has such a reputation? Who is well-respected and admired?"

Wojtyla did not reply, so I answered my own question. "You!"

"No," he whispered in sadness. "I prefer to write and study, to go deep into the nation's soul, and search for a realistic roof for my spiritual deliberation on the future of humanity. For me the Curia's bureaucracy will be an insurmountable obstacle to directing the Church into progressive activity."

I came up with a brutal reply, because I knew that he did not have knowledge of how much I knew.

"You can deny it, but I know from the Primate that Paul VI promised him that he would do everything possible to influence the College of Cardinals. Because you are closer to the ideals of John XXIII and Paul VI than anyone else."

"What are you talking about? The Pope is in heaven and we are dealing here with the reality of earth, and a group of cardinals who although in the majority was nominated by Paul VI, would not listen because Paul VI is in heaven, probably discussing more important problems with St. Peter than the election of the new Pope."

"Where is the conscience of the cardinals? They know that they should elect you for the good of the Church."

"I will tell you honestly that I would not like to be Pope."

"Why not?"

"Because deep in my soul I have a tragic feeling that if I were elected it would be bad for the Church and for me. I have a premonition of disaster. God is my witness that this feeling is genuine."

"I do not deny that. But I see that you were influenced by the glass angels, and this feeling is not healthy."

Wojtyla did not reply, although anyone could see that my explanation was provocative. I did not give up.

"Many people will be disappointed. I am not talking about two deceased Popes or a few cardinals who are in heaven; I refer to your friends, Rubin, Deskur and cardinals from the Third World who would like to see you Pope and spiritual champion of their countries, in addition to some of the Italian cardinals. I am certain Albino Luciani would work for you at the next Conclave."

"To be a 'Bishop of Rome' is a great responsibility, but I would prefer to be a 'Bishop of Cracow'; anyhow, let's stop talking about this."

For some reason he was annoyed or maybe he knew things about the Conclave which I didn't know. In the meantime, human affairs in the Vatican were acquiring new dimensions.

August 25, 1978, was a peculiar and oppressive day. A hazy sun did not give much heat, but for no particular reason one felt a heaviness in the chest and brain. From time to time a breeze appeared, almost ruffling one's hair, and then a friend said,

"Oh, this is the wind that comes directly from the Apennine mountains, and I can almost smell the chestnut trees and the Apennine oak." He mumbled that this was not his own description, but he had heard these exact words a few minutes ago from an old friend of his, a Jesuit priest.

I concluded aloud, "I presume the Jesuits know best and the Pope will be Italian."

My disappointed friend asked, "You mean, they are still talking in symbols, and the weather has something to do with the election of the Italian Pope?"

"Listen to me. I am wearing tight shoes, and do not see the beauties of the world – not even the magnanimity of Jesuits! Anyhow, I discovered a long time ago when the Conclave elects a Pope who is supposed to perform his duty differently and better, before you turn around you discover he is acting just like his predecessor."

During the first balloting it was obvious that Curialists Benelli, Baggio and Bertoli were strong candidates for the Holy See. All three were trying to convince the rest of the cardinals that they would go against the progressive directions of Paul VI who had ruled for fifteen years, and would develop a moderate, if not conservative attitude, toward the existing situation in the world, and 'would not rock St. Peter's Boat.'

Three other cardinals: Siri, Felici and Wojtyla were mentioned as potential *papabili* – together with the Frenchman Villot, catalyst of the Vatican Secretariat of State. He was Cardinal Camerling in the Conclave, and at eight o'clock in the morning, during the Holy Mass, said in his homily, "Jesus looks into the eyes of each of you and demands from all the cardinals, unity and adherence to His will and His love."

Despite this, the deadlock continued. The clear majority was not achieved by any of the three cardinals whose names began with a 'B'.

Then, the name of Albino Luciani, Cardinal from Venice, appeared in the balloting.

It was Saturday morning, August 16. Smog and humidity hung over the heads and stuffed the lungs of the tremendous crowds in St. Peter's Square. Nervousness and perspiration exhausted the gathering outdoors, but the crowds still grew both in multitude of colors and languages, all looking up in anticipation of the 'goat.' Bottles of mineral water, sandwiches and fruit were consumed in great quantity. Italian television showed the Sistine Chapel, but instead of white smoke, only black smoke emerged. The Pope was not yet elected! Tens of thousands of people and cars packed in the Via della Conciliazione and the back streets in the direction of St. Peter's Square. Everybody was trying to be as close as possible to the center of the action. But this action only manifested itself in louder conversations, arguments, and more food and drink to assuage the anxiety.

At 7:00 P.M. light grey smoke appeared over the Sistine Chapel and almost immediately a roar went up from the excited crowd. Some seconds later on the balcony of St. Peter's Basilica a few bishops appeared, among them the round face wearing horn-rimmed glasses of Pericle Cardinal Felici. The roar was hushed; everyone turned his ears and her earrings toward the balcony.

Did you ever hear a soundless crowd of two hundred thousand?

Through the silence, the voice of Felici boomed through the microphones, "*Annuntio vobis gaudium magnum: Habemus Papem!*"

The roar of voices, mixed with thousands of clapping hands, shook the ancient monuments, columns and buildings of the Vatican, followed by a deep stillness. Cardinal Felici, as if to gain strength from the crowd, pronounced emotionally, "*Eminentissimum ac reverendissimum Dominum, Dominum Albinum . . .*"

Again, a tremendous roar rose toward the polluted skies!

"*Sanctae Romanae Ecclesiae Cardinalem Luciani.*"

Here, a simple priest, without any specific talents, 'Man of the terrain' became the 253rd (or 264th, depending on how you count) successor to the Holy See, choosing the name of Joannes Paulus I.

His first task was to reconcile Curia Romana conservative cardinals with those cardinals who were domiciled in other parts of the world, because the last Conclave showed a large discrepancy in political views which could endanger the well-being of the Church. He began quite successfully, and partly because of his nature and this initial achievement he was called the 'Smiling Pope.'

The next day John Paul I appeared in the window of the Papal apartment, and after his first *Angelus Domini* said,

"Yesterday morning I went quietly to the Sistine Chapel to vote. I never dreamed that this would happen." He had, however, realized, in the back of his mind, that the conservative cardinals supported him because they thought he was one of them and would forget about the reforms of his two predecessors, whom he characterized as follows,

> I do not have the wisdom nor heart of Pope John; I do not have the background nor culture of Pope Paul. Nevertheless, I am in their place. As a result, I have to do everything possible to serve the Church. I beg you to support me with your prayers.

"On September 3, the official ceremony of the enthroning of John Paul I began in St. Peter's Basilica," Cardinal Wojtyla told me. "The Pope went outside to accept his homage from the mighty all over the world, as well as the humble people of Rome. I returned to Cracow, where on September 6 I performed a Mass for the well-being of the new Pope, and at that ceremony in Wawel Cathedral, I said, 'It is certain that he, who bore on his shoulders the heavy load of St. Peter and pastoral responsibility for the whole Church, at the same time, bore on his shoulders a heavy cross. We wish to be with him from the beginning of his ardous journey, because we know that this cross belongs to world salvation as the gift to us from Jesus Christ.'"

"I have a feeling that your—Wyszyński's and Rubin's and the others'—trip to Germany after the election of the Pope was deliberate. Primate Wyszyński told me that, according to his informants, German influences in the Vatican were growing rapidly, and shortly after the election of the new Pope, the German Federal Republic government would ask the Pope to make an announcement about the unification of Germany. Upon learning of this, Wyszyński maneuvered his old friend Herman Cardinal Volk to invite the Polish delegation to the German Episcopate Conference. According to Wyszyński, during this conference, you, he and others from the Polish Episcopate would intensively campaign for peace."

"I must admit that I am hearing this for the first time. No doubt I was talking about our neighborly cooperation, and at the same time I did not forget the war in my speeches. On the other hand I will tell you honestly that I myself never had such crowds, maybe over one hundred thousand, that Wyszyński drew in front of the Cologne Cathedral. Then he shouted to the German clergy, young people and government officials, 'Europe should not and could not become an ammunition factory. If you want to work against this, you must not waste time, but work for disarmament and peace. Neither should you forget about the suffering of many nations during the Second World War, and all of you should visit Dachau and other concentration camps and pray for the souls of the killed and the killers.'"

"Primate Wyszyński told me that the Germans were puzzled as to why you, an entirely Polish delegation, travelled so much and repeated the same antiwar speeches. The Bonn government was extremely upset with the German Episcopate for inviting the Polish high clergy to remind them, not about the unity of Germans, but about German war guilt. What was the opinion of John Paul I?"

"I do not think that at this early stage he had a definite opinion on the unification of Germany or our Episcopate attitude to this problem. I know one thing, that he began working hard to create unity in the College of Cardinals, and second, and here you might be shocked, he asked the high Vatican officials to submit to him reports on the financial situation of the Curia."

"Talking to people about your life and your idiosyncrasies, I have discovered that you never borrow money. Why not?"

"Borrowing is a poor busines," he replied. "You take somebody else's money, but you have to give back *your* money. You borrow for a short time, but you give it back forever."

"What happens if you really have to borrow money?"

He laughed. "If you really have to, the only way you can make a profit is by not returning it. But again, this is dishonest. So now you can see why I don't borrow money."

"Let's get back to John Paul I. Why did he decide to check on the Vatican's financial state?"

"For some reason the IOR was poorly managed, and to keep various charitable organizations going, the Vatican treasury was running into deficit and borrowing money."

"What is the IOR?"

"Istituto per le Opere de Religione. This means, the Institute for Religious Works. It is the only Vatican bank. Such a peculiar name."

"Who is responsible for the poor management of this bank?"

"This is a complicated story. You have to go back to Pius XII and his nephew Carlo Pacelli as well as the German-Swiss banker Paul Niehans, and Count Enrico Galeazzi, Marquis Giulio Sacchetti, and the latest, illegal currency dealer Roberto Calvi; also, Michele Sindona who had mysterious financial connections with several American bankers. For some inexplicable reason Luigi Mennini got involved with those people, and Mr. Mennini was the highest layman in the IOR."

"Because of the manipulation of various laymen with Vatican money," I concluded, knowing this was painful for Wojtyla to talk about, "The Church administration received bad whispered publicity."

"Right now I do not have the real facts, and I would not try to build my opinion on gossip and presumption."

"Who knows, you might..."

He looked at me, said nothing, and poured two cups of coffee.

"What next?" I asked.

"When I returned to Cracow I plunged into pastoral work in which I had many dedicated helpers, among them two bishops, Stanislaw Smolenski and Franciszek Macharski. You have to remember that in my archdiocese I had four hundred and ninety groups studying various aspects of spiritual and social life. I call this system 'a learning church' which was unique in the Christian world. I began this type of communal intellectual endeavor a long time ago, even before the Holy Father expressed his desire that the attitude of the Church to the world should be enlightening, based on equal terms with the community."

"You started this type of work before the announcement of *Pacem in Terris* or *Populorum Progresso*?"

He ignored my question to go into strictly personal matters. "At the time I had a thirst for more prayer to purge myself of physical and emotional desires. One of the reasons was the anniversary on September 28 of my appointment as a suffragan-assistant bishop of Cracow. I locked myself in my chapel to pray all day without seeing anybody, because I thought that I needed to converse with my Maker and the man who brought me to this position.

"When I prayed on this particular September day, I didn't know that the Holy Father was dying, or dead. Later, his secretary, Reverend John Magee, described his last hours.

"'On the evening of that day, after supper, John Paul I gave an audience to his Secretary of State, Cardinal Villot, who brought him some documents. The Pope went with those documents to his bedroom. As we know, the Pontiff was an early riser, even earlier than 5:00 A.M.' When Reverend Magee knocked on his door and heard no voice, he knocked again, and entered. He saw the light and approached the bed. The Pope's face was white and motionless. Beside him on the bed lay an open book *Imitation of Christ* by Thomas à Kempis. On the page, in Latin, was written 'When morning comes, remember that you might not reach the evening. During the evening do not promise yourself the dawn so eagerly. Always be ready and live in such a way that when death comes he will not find you unprepared.'

"'So many people die suddenly and unexpectedly. At an hour when no one is anticipating, the Son of Man is coming'."

We looked at each other and I thought about this strange coincidence, that Wojtyla was praying in Cracow at the same time that the Pope was dying in Rome.

John Paul II then added, "I heard about the passing of the Holy Father early the following day from my driver, Józef Mucha, who came to my room and said, 'The Holy Father died last night. God, who will be the next?'"

"I know your reply to your driver . . . 'Unpredictable are the decisions of God, and we all have to bow our heads to him.' I wonder if the 'Smiling Pope' was thinking about the glass angels created by his father at the hour of his death, especially the one in the white cassock who reigned above all others?"

43

Finances and Ethics

ILISTENED attentively to Primate Wyszyński.

"In my long Church mission I have always had great interest in the integrity of politicians and cardinals. But I find two different standards of judgment being used. When President Nixon lied, people remarked, 'How dishonest Nixon is'; but when a cardinal says something stupid or evasive, the same people comment, 'How hypocritical the Roman Catholic church is.'"

"This is unclear to me."

"Meaning that in the cases of politicians, journalists and others one would not condemn the political system, but with regard to cardinals' mistakes, the whole Church is condemned."

"Most of the time it is a question of Church money which the Vatican keeps in complete secrecy," I ventured.

"The budget of every state is more or less secret, but only a small group of people connected with it know for sure how much money goes for espionage, subversive activities, armaments and other devilish endeavors to sow revolution, counterrevolution, destabilization of countries, general demoralization and murder. In the case of the Vatican budget, about seventy to seventy-five percent is designated for charitable, missionary and peaceful work; about twenty-five percent is spent on administrative expenses."

"Why does the Camera Apostolica which has administered Church properties from the time of the eighth century act in such secrecy?"

"Your information is not exactly accurate. Already in the twelfth century a list of all Church properties existed, and this document entitled *Liber Censuum* can be found in the Vatican Library, as well as the Lateran Treaty which regulates relations with the Italian government. In this treaty there are exact figures of money which were paid for Church properties acquired by the Italian government. These are two examples, but you can find many more in the Vatican Library which will support the openness of Church financial status and dealings. I do not mean that individual Popes and cardinals were eager to broadcast their material wealth. Church officials are human too and God will deal with them individually."

"Were there many fiancial wizards among the Popes?"

The Primate rose from his chair, walked around the table and looked at the four walls of the meeting hall covered with pictures of saints, popes and villages. I presume he was pondering historical examples, although he could have referred me to the extensive library that exists in his official palace. He smiled, paused and said, "Sixtus V, who ruled at the end of the sixteenth century, with the help of a Portuguese Jew named Lopes, not only tried to 'modernize' Curia finances, but sold to wealthy Roman families various administrative positions in the Camera Apostolica for sizable sums which enriched the Vatican treasury. Signore Lopes was a descendent of Fernão Lopes, a famous chronicler and keeper of the Portuguese royal family archives. Various branches of the Lopes family built their financial empire not only in Lisbon but in Madrid, Rome and other western European capitals. They were financial advisers to princes and kings."

"I see you are well-versed in the monetary history of the Vatican."

As though prompted by this comment, the Primate looked at his notes and continued.

"Yes, seventeenth-century Alexander VII was a skillful persuader and knew how to approach European bankers to lend him money at low interest rates. With this capital he bought numerous properties, made improvements so they became attractive commodities, and then resold them for a handsome profit. This business prospered to such an extent that the pope engaged some of his nephews to help him. Even as a cardinal, Urban VIII during whose time St. Peter's Basilica was finished, made lots of money as a landlord with the help of his brothers, nephews and other relatives. When he became Pope he intensified his financial activity for the good of the Church. Naturally, his relatives prospered as well. If you know little about the financial situation of the Vatican in the eighteenth and nineteenth centuries I will suggest some material to read, but I am sure you know a good deal about post-Second World War developments. Pope John XXIII discovered that the Vatican budget was in the red and asked his secretary to submit to him the files of those cardinals who were known as 'good money collectors.'"

"I remember that he was touchy on money matters, and many times would repeat after Saint Matthew, 'It is easier for a camel to go through the eye of a needle than for a rich cardinal to enter heaven.'"

"Yes," replied the Primate. "Relatives never visited him to talk about material problems. He didn't help anyone in financial matters; he lived modestly and died poor, but his interest in wealthy cardinals was obvious. When he received this list, he looked at it, saw a few Germans and Americans; but he did not see the name of Cardinal Spellman, so he asked his secretary, 'You mean this wealthy New Yorker is not on the list?'

"'We looked under Spellman in our files,' replied the Pope's secretary jokingly, and under Spelly and under New York, but could not find the name of Cardinal Spellman.'

"'Did you check the special file called *Real Estate?*'

"'We did not think of it,' replied the surprised secretary.

"'Go and look yourself.'

After a while the secretary returned with a folder under his arm and said to the Holy Father, 'Success! We found it under *Real Estate of Cardinal Spellman.*'"

Primate Wyszyński finished his story. "That is the reason why Paul VI nominated Bishop Terrence J. Cooke, friend of Spelly's to the position of Cardinal in 1969."

"Why did they wait so long?"

"I presume the Curia was collecting and analyzing information about His Eminence, Archbishop Cooke and his real estate talents."

"Did he have any other abilities?"

"Like Spelly, he wanted to be Pope, but how could you elect a cardinal to the Holy See only on the basis of real estate ability?"

"But shouldn't St. Peter's successor have administrative talents?"

"It is advisable, but most important is piety and intellect which would help him understand, analyze and help people of the world. I am sure among three hundred and fifty American bishops, there is someone like that, and he will eventually surface. Also, you have to consider the inspiration of the Holy Ghost during the Conclave." He paused as though thinking about something else; instead he returned to the original subject. "Naturally, finances are important for the

Church which represents hundreds of millions of Christians, because our work is based on love and charity."

Again my host paused, and I felt he was trying to say something different, so I prompted him, "I will be poorer if you do not tell me what you would like to say. You are withholding something, are you not?"

"Not exactly, I just feel there is no other cardinal today like Wojtyla."

"Please clarify this."

"Very simply, Karol Wojtyla possesses one pair of everything, except shoes, of which he possesses two pairs – one good and one full of holes; and if he fixed them he would think he was spending money unnecessarily. All the royalties from his writings and other financial remunerations, he has given away for scholarships or to charitable institutions. Can you imagine, if all cardinals were like that, the Vatican could not function."

"I think it would function better. People all over the world would think that cardinals were real apostles, and their money and wealth would be distributed for better causes than the high living of Church Princes."

"From a moral viewpoint, it would be a great victory, but I do not think that depriving wealthy churchmen of their possessions could cover the tremendous expense of five thousand Vatican employees, diplomatic services, international gatherings such as bishop synods, church orders, the Vatican radio, publications, and so forth, that consume each year about two hundred million dollars. There is no way to bring the rest of the cardinals to Cardinal Wojtyla's way of thinking. Materially, demoralized cardinals would stifle the international activity of the Church."

"I think there is a dilemma between the rigid characteristics of the modern apostles of Jesus Christ and the materialistic world where everything is based on profit."

"I am glad that you as a layman understand this, and am sure you know that the Church cannot invest its money in armaments or other industry connected with war."

"What are the sources, besides voluntary contributions of the faithful, of the Vatican treasury?"

"After the Lateran agreement between the Italian goverment and the Vatican, the Church treasury was enriched by money that came from confiscated Vatican property. This is the core. Then the Curia engaged various financial specialists and with their help, invested money in real estate, bonds, and industrial establishments, including the armament industry. This was during the reign of Pius XII. A man by the name of Count Enrico Galeazzi became the president of the real estate organization called Società Generale Immobiliare, and manager of other Church properties. He became wealthy, but to this day, nobody knows how much money he delivered to the Vatican treasury. The second important financial adviser to Pius XII was his nephew, Carlo Pacelli, who even received the title of Prince, but again only the Holy Ghost knows how much money Pacelli's family made on Church investments. I presume that the most important swindler was Dr. Paul Niehans. Almost like Rasputin, who captured the mind and soul of the emperor and empress of Russia, so Niehans captured the mind of Pius XII who was enchanted with the history of aristocratic families. When Niehans discovered this, he convinced the Pope that he was a descendant of the fourteenth century Dietrich of Nieheim, personal adviser to Urban VI and Gregory XII, who spent most of his life in the Curia as a 'Papal Chancellor.' To everybody's surprise, Dietrich appeared at the Council of Constance as 'adviser of the German nation.' Paul Niehans had the upper hand because as a medical doctor he treated Pius XII not only with German imperialistic philosophy but also with the needle. From time to time when the fragile Pope felt weak, the doctor injected into the Holy Father's veins extracts from animal genitalia without prior analysis of blood or any physical examination, on the basis that he would feel like a young man after each injection. During these 'medical conferences,' Paul had long political and financial discussions with the Holy Father and convinced him that the Vatican should invest money in the German heavy defense industry as well as international armament concerns.

"At the same time Carlo Pacelli advised his brother Giulio to take an important job in the Banco di Roma where the Vatican had substantial shares, and whose president, Vittorino Veronese, a friend of Pacelli's family and head of Catholic Action, was one of the important figures in UNESCO. Under the control of the Pacelli family and their friends were various enterprises such as an insurance company by the name of Unione Italiana di Assicurazione; Ceramica Poggi which produced bathroom accessories, toilets and baths; a macaroni factory, Pastificio Pantanella; and the gas company Società Italiana per il Gas. There were many more companies in which Pius XII's nephews were instrumental in investing Vatican money, such as the pharmaceutical outfit SeRono, and the financial concern Società Generale Immobiliare International which financed housing complexes in Italy, the Watergate Hotel in Washington, Lamas Verdes in Mexico, and Montreal's Stock Exchange Tower; commercial buildings in various parts of Africa, and in numerous other European and South American countries."

"Rather extensive holdings."

Cardinal Wyszyński ignored my comment and went on with reading his story.

"The Pacelli brothers, having complete support of their uncle, the Pope, engaged more people in their financial empire. They were instrumental in appointing Marquis Giulio Sacchetti to head the Banco de Santo Spirito in which there were large deposits of important international financial outfits as well as Italian government and Vatican State funds. Because of his connection with Shell Oil, Massino Spada was a useful acquisition to the Pacelli family's network. But Banco di Roma per la Svizzera operated independently in Switzerland and made various international deals on behalf of the Vatican.

"To those men we have to add Prince Plinius Barberini, president of the savings bank Cassa di Risparmio di Roma, and Enrico Galeazzi, the Italian representative of the Radio Corporation of America in which the Vatican also invested much money; this corporation was organized a long time ago by our *landsmann* David Sarnoff. Chase Manhattan, First National, Morgan Guaranty Trust and other financial conglomerates were also involved in Vatican enterprises. Heavy holdings in stocks of IBM, General Motors, TWA, General Electric and other American industrial giants are giving headaches to Vatican financiers, although they can get a discount in various Hilton hotels and rest on the sunny side of luxurious swimming pools."

My interlocutor was allowing himself to become upset by his own account, but he continued anyway. "A large group of financial speculators and political agents who represented powerful anti-Catholic forces in the West were trying to discredit and subjugate Christian philosophy and control anything that threatened international monopoly and private enterprise. It is well-known that the Church is neither on the capitalist side nor the socialist side, but following the teachings of Jesus Christ, supports justice and equality of man; above all, the Church is not and never will lean toward those political powers which are for the exploitation and domination of people. But in recent years, powerful Western countries have been trying to convince us to join them in fighting revolutions and socialism. We could not do that; we support a just distribution of wealth and freedom of conscience; then there would be no base for revolutions or socialism. Oppression in the East and West is a result of injustice, and we, as believers in Jesus Christ and His teachings, can only lead the cause of freedom that exists in human hearts. We also cannot say that injustice in the West is better than in the East or vice versa. Our impartial and compassionate attitude toward humanity is being challenged by policy makers of the world, and because we do not want to engage in the bloody rivalry between capitalist and socialist countries we are being marked for diversion, destabilization and destruction. The main accusation in the West is that we lean toward communism."

I was dumbfounded by this pronouncement from the Prince of the Church, whom I thought reflected the view of the middle-of-the-road wing of the College of Cardinals and thousands of ordinary priests in Third World countries. But my question was unpolitical. "What does this have to do with Vatican finances?"

"Plenty. These sinister forces figured out that if the finances of the Church were in disarray, our activities on behalf of the oppressed and poor would have to be curtailed. People all over the world would start saying that the Roman Catholic Church, the most powerful Christian organization on earth, is sitting on the fence and watching people being oppressed and hungry children die. You have a group of naive cardinals who were duped by sinister men and unknowingly helped them achieve their goal. An example was Sergio Cardinal Gueri and Archbishop Giuseppe Caprio, good friend of international financier Michele Sindona; Roberto Calvi, president of the Banco Ambrosiana; and Licio Gelli. Those three men, according to the best Vatican sources, were agents of political and financial groups in the West who set out to discredit the Roman Catholic Church. But naturally, while doing this political job, they also enriched themselves. Mr. Sindona was able to steal a hundred million dollars from the Vatican bank; Mr. Calvi, through various manipulations diverted a few hundred million dollars from the Banco Ambrosiana; and Mr. Gelli, who claimed that he was a good Mason, was not only engaged in various financial speculations from which he benefitted, but also headed a secret international group under the name of Propaganda II, which engaged in disseminating misleading information about the Church, the Pope, and the Cardinals. Imagine, clergy such as Gueri, Caprio and others had helped them reach the highest Vatican circles."

I noticed signs of pain and sadness on the Primate's face and deliberated whether I should proceed with my questions. But he said, "During a three-hour conversation on April 9, 1951 with His Holiness, Pius XII, he asked me what he could do for Poland, and I replied that the Polish Episcopate needed money to build housing and schools for blind and handicapped children. The Pope replied, 'I have to tell you with embarrassment that I do not know whether we can get you the money.' He shuffled papers on his desk and asked, 'How much?' I replied that we figured out that twenty-seven million dollars would be sufficient.

"'How did you arrive at this figure?'

"I replied that we carefully developed a plan, and the figure reflected our calculations. I added that we would like to borrow the money.

"'We could not spare such a large amount, but I will talk to my Pacelli cousins, and they will help arrange a loan on good terms, if not in the Institute for Religious Works, perhaps in the Banco Ambrosiana or Banco di Roma.'

"I thanked him sincerely, and after a few more words left the Appartamento Pontificio full of hope and returned to my country. I waited and later made delicate inquiries, but years passed and I never received any communication on the subject of a loan from either the Vatican or from the Pacelli cousins. In the late summer of 1958 I received information that Pius XII wished to see me in the second part of October, and that I should bring to him the complete plan for orphanages and schools for handicapped children. I was so happy and began arranging papers and plans as well as financial figures. Then, on October 9, the Holy Father died."

We both became sad because I knew the effort and how much of his own private meager funds Wyszyński had put in through the years toward helping Polish blind children. His place for them in Laski was the closest thing to his heart, but there was no reason for me to rub salt into the wound. I posed a realistic question, "Which Pope really began reforming Vatican financial institutions?"

"John XXIII ordered the Curia to get rid of armament industry stocks but did not have much time for other financial alterations. When Paul VI reached the Holy See, he removed the Pacelli family from any influence over Vatican finances. Then he told the managers of the Istituto per le Opere di Religione to sell all gold in the bank's possession and distribute the money to various charitable institutions. A further step in clearing up this operation was taken by the Holy Father in liquidating various secret accounts belonging to Roberto Calvi, Giulio Sacchetti, Enrico Galeazzi, Paolo Baffi, Mario Sarcinelli and others whose names were associated with various financial and political dealings detrimental to the Church and contrary to Christian ethics. Naturally, we don't know if Luigi Mennini, the highest layman in the Vatican bank, dropped his contacts with international financial speculators. But I guess Cardinal Casaroli watched him carefully. Caprio and Gueri, who were close to Sindona and Calvi, were also removed from any influence, and their contacts with the international political world were cut off completely. Strict orders were given to all Vatican officials to break contact with General Rafaele Giudice, chief of the Italian Finance Police, as well as the sinister and conniving fascist, Licio Gelli, founder of the organization Propaganda II."

"There was an American-born Archbishop Paul C. Marcinkus, of Lithuanian extraction, who was supposed to be financially astute. What is his position now in the Vatican?"

"The Holy Father had discovered his financial talents as well as his piousness and scrupulous honesty, so in 1969 he made him the president of Istituto per le Opere di Religione."

"Up to now you haven't said how large the Vatican budget actually is."

"I am not really privy to these matters, but I presume around four hundred and ninety million dollars. Naturally, we have to consider adjustments and world inflation."

"How much money is being designated for charitable work, minus administrative expenses?"

"I would assume over two hundred million, with about fifty million dollars being collected every year the world over. The largest sum is from the United States – close to twenty-five million.

"The Italian Church with its innumerable and unique art treasures is probably the richest Church because you cannot put a price on Michelangelo or other masters displayed in churches all over Italy. It is in a class by itself from a financial viewpoint. But the greatest contribution to the Vatican treasury comes first from the United States, next from Germany, and third, I suppose, France; I think, however, over sixty percent of the Vatican budget is based upon investments in consumer industries.

"As a result the Vatican, in its religious and social activity, has to be careful not to alienate the capitalist system in the rest of the world, because investments are there, and profits likewise. It must be careful not to step on the toes of powerful capitalist or socialist bureaucrats. In my old age I have concluded that no nation should look for salvation and help from other nations. It is not worth weakening your moral and social fiber to expect others to come to your aid without recompense. What would happen if you could not repay them?"

"But you must take into consideration that the Polish Church paid Peter's Pence for a thousand years, and Pius XII, putting it mildly, did not show great anti-Nazi courage during the Second World War. His Holiness should invest a few million in Polish orphanages."

Stefan Wyszyński's face reddened and his lips tightened.

The Primate got to his feet and said, "God will forgive you. But I don't know if I will!

He grabbed me in his arms. He said nothing else.

44

To Have a Dream

"IT WAS raining in Cracow, the day sad and depressing. I was overworked and overtired, not only with ecclesiastical affairs but with my writing. Everywhere people walked with deep thoughts and somber faces. I had been working without interruption on a paper in which I was supposed to present my ideas on the renewal and improvement of conditions in our Republic to be presented to the Polish Episcopate for discussion. I reached a blank spot in my mind, and could work no more. I turned to sports to recharge my mental batteries."

"As many people do," I said, reaching for a piece of tropical fruit in a crystal bowl placed on the antique table before John Paul II and me.

"Many times when I went skiing in Zakopane, I stayed with the Ursuline Sisters at Jaszczurówka; I did the same this time. Before I left, I called the Sisters, and they informed me the snow was good for skiing. I called my former student, Reverend Tadeusz Styczen, who was good not only for skiing but for philosophical discussions, which I felt I needed at this moment. We went together to Zakopane, and before sundown had climbed Turbacz Peak. We descended the mountain quickly; wind and snow striking our faces, and the blades of the skis making pleasing music. My soul had been cleansed of intellectual pollution, and when I looked at the face of my young friend Tadeusz I was sure that he was experiencing the same feeling.

"After such exericse I thought I would sleep like a log, but I did not. Following an initial forty-five-minute deep sleep, I started tossing in bed; my head was full of ideas, peculiar projects and unholy thoughts. I pluged into poetry, and remembered lines of my poem written ten years before:

There is a Night when we keep vigilance
    beside Your Grave
Then we are very much with the Church –
It is a Night of struggle, this struggle between
    despair and hope is going on in us.
This struggle which is going on in us is topping
    all the struggles of all the ages
And filling them up
(All of them – are they losing their sense?
    Or are they gaining it?)
During this Night, the mystery of earth is
    reaching its beginning,
A thousand years is as one Night:
Night of vigilance beside Your Grave.

"I got up, this fragment cruising inside my head as I washed myself. While I shaved I looked into the mirror and behind me, pictures of Christ's life appeared. I began composing a new poem about the suffering people of my country, the suffering people of the world, and Jesus' sacrifice. After shaving, instead of going out, I lay on top of my bed. I was perspiring profusely. I closed my eyes and saw half-human, half-animal figures in my subconscious. Among them appeared a devil in iron armor encrusted with bright stars, but his face was the face of a wolf. When the devil opened his lips, he showed a row of clenched teeth through which he said, 'You will never win! Stronger men than you tried through the ages and they failed! He grabbed the spear lying on the ground beside him and in almost lightning speed, plunged it into my chest, yelling, 'Don't try to mediate between the people! Don't try to make peace between systems! You will never turn sinners into angels! You are only dreaming about power. I have death for you!' I pulled the spear from my chest. Blood burst and at that moment I woke up."

Even now my interlocutor was pale and visibly shaken. It was difficult for me to comment except to ask an insignificant question, "Did you cut yourself while shaving?"

He looked at me with surprise and said, "Naturally not. If I had I would have remembered. You should leave your psychoanalysis in your hotel room. To this day when I have difficulty solving problems, I

I think about this nightmare and instead of being depressed, I feel a resurgence of energy, work harder, and pray more deeply. I am becoming more stubborn as though I were trying to say to this monster with the spear that I would not give up even an inch of my chosen road. My lips get tighter, my hands become clenched, and my belief in God and man becomes stronger with every living day. I have had so many such warnings in my life, and although I disregard them, for the time being, Providence has saved me because I think Providence believes that I am, although an insignificant man, a committed servant of humanity and as such I should live on this earth a while longer. This particular problem of mine is between God and my soul. I could spend days and years talking about it, but my mind is too limited to grasp the wisdom of the Almighty. Only the future will decipher the miracle of man. I am one of millions."

"Would you permit me to observe that when you are in the Carpathian Mountains you always experience extraordinary energy and inspiration to create and to pray. But this experience always begins with a dream."

He looked at me and I noticed in his blue eyes a strange reaction which I could not define. John Paul II did not comment; instead he reached toward others' reality.

"We have many problems in our native country, and I wish those problems would not lead to bloodshed. The nation wants more justice and better division of its daily bread. At that time, I was in the Carpathian Mountains to develop on paper a definite plan for a renewal which I would first discuss with the Primate and the Polish Espicopate, and then submit to the Government. Gierek, during our meetings, stressed industrialization, and we told him that the patience of the nation was exhausted, that we were on the edge of catastrophe. He didn't listen, and instead said that everyone loved him and there were no political prisoners in the country."

"What did you and the Primate reply?"

"That we would have to go along with the nation. His reply was simply that the nation did not have an adequate sense of the need for industrialization, and since he did, we ought to go along with him."

"It sounds like a vicious circle."

"We told him the populace should be invited to participate in various governmental decisions, to be involved on the level of the factory and the farm, to have a chance to speak through the radio, press, television. As a result of this exchange between citizens and rulers, Polish socialism would be humanized.

"'If we do that,' he responded, 'the farmers will ask to divide State-owned farms; workers will demand that the factories be owned cooperatively; the next stage will involve the Soviet Union, who, I guess will accuse us of restoring capitalism. And even if the Soviet Union does not intervene, other Eastern European states will criticize us severely. Eventually, the Soviet Union will be obliged to act in concert with the rest of the socialist countries.' Then Gierek added, 'And what will happen to Christian Poland?'"

"This is a pertinent question. What kind of reply would you wish?"

"A good question, Gierek's and yours. I don't read Soviet minds, but I know that they experience similar difficulties: heavy industry is stressed to such an extent that light industry production suffers and people stand in lines in Moscow as they do in Warsaw. So I imagine that Russian leaders should look favorably on Polish experiments. The Church did not look forward to the counterrevolution and abolition of socialism, but tried to help in a humanistic way to solve economic problems. Today's priests are definitely on the side of the workers, where we would like to see the smoke of incense mix permanently and equally with those of industry in such a way as to create a solid bridge between the working masses and the churches. Then we might contribute a brighter life for the common people. The Church should not give its blessing to caesars or would-be emperors. Christ never blessed them. He only bestowed blessings on men with simple hearts. This should be the order not only for ordinary priests, but for the Pope. Otherwise, we will assist nuclear catastrophe."

Our minds seemed headed in the same direction, toward the night when he had his awful dream. The following day he decided to cut his vacation short in Zakopane and return to Cracow. When he bade farewell to the Mother Superior of the Ursuline Sisters he did not look at her face, but instead at the picture of St. Ursula, legendary Italian martyr, who founded this Order in 1537.

"I have to return immediately." Then he left.

When getting into his car he felt a pain in his chest as he did when he was speared by the devil in his dream. The pain persisted. Later he told me that maybe it was not physical pain, but 'clairvoyant' pain.

Leaving the outskirts of Zakopane, he noticed a young mountaineer, poorly dressed, carrying ski poles on his shoulders. He tapped his driver Józef Mucha on the shoulder, and cried out to the stranger,

"Stop! Do you have skis? How well do you ski?"

The boy, dumbfounded by this clerical yell and seeing a priest in the car pulled off his hat. "I know how to ski."

"Where are your skis?"

The boy shivered from emotion or from the cold, and did not reply right away, as though he were ashamed to be carrying poles without the rest of the gear. Cardinal Wojtyla didn't wait for his response, but opened the car door, and handed him boots and the rest of his ski outfit.

"Get inside and dress."

Naturally, the boy was much surprised but obeyed the order. The most surprised man was the driver, who got out of the car and began to untie the skis and put them at the side of the car.

Józef Mucha was a good driver because he knew his boss' mind. When he completed this unrequested task, Józef returned to the driver's seat. Cardinal Karol asked the young mountaineer, "I am sure you don't have skis. Take mine."

"Father," said the boy from outside the car in his too large ski outfit, "I will have no trouble borrowing from my friends." He stuttered in embarrassment, "Father, you might need them. You're not going to ski? I am sure you will – you're young. You're not coming back?"

The Cardinal looked at the astonished boy and smiled, "I don't need them and I don't know if I'll ever be back."

The boy, trying to grab the hand of the priest, slid down and hit the running board with his chin. Cardinal Wojtyla helped him get up, the boy clutched at the priest's hand and kissed his ring.

"What is your name?"

"Józek Gasienica."

"Can you promise me something?"

"Yes, father."

"Promise me to ski well, so well that I will read about you in the sports magazine."

"I promise, with all my heart," said the boy.

Wojtyla touched his hat, said good-bye, closed the door and left. Sitting comfortably in the car he commented to his driver,

"He really is young and does have the figure for a first-class skier."

Mr. Mucha was surprised, not by the comment, but by the name of the boy, because there was a well-known family of skiers who had the same name. He was thinking of saying something to his illustrious passenger, but the passenger had spoken,

"I have finished with sports. I have to start working with all my energy and destroy the devils with sharp spears..."

Driver Mucha, frightened, looked at his passenger through the mirror, and quickly stepped on the gas.

Book Six: Christ's Deputy

45

A Man From a Far Distant Country

AFTER considerable coaxing, Cardinal Wyszyński agreed to recall his eyewitness account of the behind-the-scenes election of the successor to John Paul I.

"Until the last moment Karol Wojtyla refused to be on the list of *papabili*, explaining that the potential for economic and political catastrophe was growing in Poland, and at such a time he should be with his nation.

"I said we would manage somehow without him, that there was no other candidate for the Holy See his equal and that the Christian world was searching for a dedicated individual who understood social changes in the world and possessed compassion as well as piety.

"He answered, 'I know such a man.'

"'Who is he?'

"'You, you are.'

"I replied that I was too old, too sick and not an intellectual. Wojtyla launched into a tirade explaining that today's world needs a church leader who would be a symbol of courage and heart.

"I continued my persuasion, going back to Cardinal Sapieha, who predicted a long time ago the possibility of his being the most important man in the church. 'Prince Sapieha and I prayed and worked and dreamed that you would some day occupy the Holy See. As for me, a seventy-seven-year-old man with cancer would not do service to the Church nor to the people.'

"'I realize that Sapieha and you worked and prayed that some day I would be the chosen man in Slowacki's daydreams. Besides, even if I possess the ideal psychological disposition I would not succeed because members of the Curia are talking about a successor with the same character as the deceased Pope. Even the first speech of John Paul I was written by the Curia. Although he was a man of great heart, God took him home early. I am not considered a steady pastor, acceptable in the corridors of power.'"

Wyszyński looked at his notes and said, "It was difficult to argue with Karol, so I reached for help from heaven and said, 'I am sure the Holy Ghost has decided that we must have a man on the Holy See who is versatile in international politics, young, and energetic.'"

Listening to Wyszyński recount his conversation with Wojtyla, I felt that the latter was desirous to be Pope, but his realism took over. When I expressed this opinion to Wyszyński, he said, "You have to know the psychology of priests who spend a good part of their lives praying and serving people and finally discover that they are not being rewarded properly by God while on earth. They don't want to blame the Holy Ghost, so they turn to their peers and try to maneuver them into recognizing them as a little more than equal. Karol did not escape this human weakness, and looking objectively at all the candidates for the Holy See, he was the most deserving.

"I said to him, 'The whole Third World will work for you. I am sure that the Holy Mother of Częstochowa will talk to the Holy Ghost and persuade Him to influence the College of Cardinals in such a way that maybe on the seventh, eighth, or ninth ballot, you will be elected. You know, even in heaven, we have an influential Lady.'

"Karol smiled and said, 'You mean, after four hundred and fifty-five years and likable Adrian VI, miracles should happen? You know what became of this Dutchman?'

"I did not comment on this particular foreign Pope, but went into statistics, trying to convince him that there had been many foreign Popes. 'Up to now we have had about two hundred and sixty-three Popes, among whom were fifteen Greeks, six Syrians, six Germans, five Frenchmen, three North Africans, three Spaniards, two Goths, two Dalmatians, a Thracian, a Portuguese, an Englishman, one of indescribable nationality, and this tragic Dutchman. Now is the time for a Polish Pope.'

"We were travelling by air from Warsaw to Rome when this conversation took place. Karol did not comment on my recollection of all these Papal nationalities; he only turned to the window and looked out aimlessly, his hands placed on the open breviary, twitching nervously. I noticed a muscle tense in his face. I returned to my notes and jotted down some ideas about which cardinals I should approach first, what tactic I should use with the Germans, what with the French, and how I should convince Cardinal König instead of being a candidate, to be a vote-getter for a Pole.

"Karol turned to me and asked, 'Do you know what the Dutch curse is?'

"I looked at him and in a split second discovered that he was thinking only about *papabili*. I said, 'This is what the Curia christened Adrian VI, am I right?'

"'At that time the Hapsburg dynasty was fighting the Valois dynasty and Adrian was poisoned by the Germans. This is the story in a capsule, but if you want to go into detail, let's begin this way: The German Lutherans and Spaniards were preparing to take Rome. Adrian knew about it and tried to prevent this. But he only slowed it down, and in 1523 died mysteriously. Four years later they took Rome. Spain would not forget that the Pope who, thanks to the Spaniards achieved a high position in the church, was against their politics. Pope Leo X, a great art lover, saw in Adrian Dedel fine material, and made him a Cardinal and pastor of SS Ioannis et Pauli; and Cardinal Dedel was unanimously elected Pope. Immediately after the election Cardinal Dedel, who took the name of Adrian VI turned against Protestant Germany and the Roman Curia because, in his opinion, this institution, instead of scrupulously observing Canon Law, was spending its time and energies on·financial speculation. In December of the same year the Pope sent his emissary Chieregati to Germany with instructions to organize Catholics against Martin Luther, explaining to the German Catholic nation that Luther was a heretic. Later in his pronouncements, Adrian VI blamed the Curia for Martin Luther's activities.'

"You mean that historically you can prove that the idea of removing Adrian VI from the Holy See was conceived in Rome?"

"'The conspiracy of poisoning the Pope was conceived by Germans in Nuremberg, but the Curia knew about it and did nothing. There could have been two explanations for this: first, the Curia did not attach much importance to the rumors of the assassination of the Pope, and did nothing; and second, that powerful Curia officials were having so much trouble with the high moral standards set for them by the Pope, that they wished for his disappearance as soon as possible. In August 1523, the strong-willed Pope experienced severe stomach pains. Somehow he survived by constant prayer and fasting, because he said that he must live to conclude the successful reforms of church administration and eradication of the schism in Germany and Switzerland. In September, the second attempt on his life was successful, and on September 14, 1523, he died in agony from poisoning. Giulio de' Medici was elected Pope and took the name of Clement VII, but Martin Luther in Germany and Huldreich Zwingli in Switzerland accelerated the Reformation.'"

At this point our airplane began circling Rome and Wyszyński, as if trying to emphasize how valuable a source he was for my book, said, "You recorded the first eyewitness account of the election of the Pope. Let's go to the latest eyewitness account of this most important function of the cardinals. Then you will be able to evaluate the developments of the Conclave, based on personal observation of its participants. It would be best if I could look at my notes and read them to you.

Wednesday morning, October 11, 1978: A meeting of the General Congregation of Cardinals which decides to adhere strictly to the Paul VI constitution of October 1975, *Romano Pontifici Eligendo*, which prohibits any Cardinal who has passed age eighty from participating in any Conclave. This Constitution also states, 'During the Conclave, the Church is in especially close contact with Cardinals who are electing their highest priest and begging God that the new head of the Church should be the gift of His Goodness and His Providence...' Taking as an example, the first Christians about whom it is written in the history of the Apostolic Universal Church that they were united with the Holy Mother of Jesus, and prayed that the election of the new Pope should be a special act of the people of God performed by the College of Cardinals, but in a certain sense as an act of the whole Church.

Thursday, October 12: Before the meeting of the Cardinals, which was supposed to take place at 11:00 A.M., Cardinal Felici asked me if Boleslaw Cardinal Filipiak would join us from Poznań. I replied that I did not know because he is very sick. He said, 'There will be one less ballot for Wojtyla.'
"'I responded, 'My dear Pericle, the Holy Ghost will place a dozen healthy Cardinals on the side of Karol.'

"'Remember, Stefan, the Italians will not give up. This is old Siri's chance and he is determined. Benelli is young but in a hurry. Baggio cracks jokes saying that only when he is in the Appartamento Pontificio can he get good wine, but Pappalardo thinks he could bring lots of sun from Palermo to the Vatican. Add to these two Americans and a few from the Third World. Now you can see that the College will be very divided.'

"'I presume because of our old friendship that you, Pericle will see the light from the Holy Spirit and work for Karol, who, as you have said many times is the best candidate.' We embraced, and he left with a smile.

"I searched for other Italian Cardinals; especially waiting to talk with Siri. I went to Holy Mass for the soul of John Paul I, which was the closing of *novendiales*, the official mourning ceremony for this 'smiling son,' whom the Curia was eager to make Pope. They succeeded, but only for a short time, and now we are confronted with the question, who is next? I spent all my time talking and campaigning for Karol. Most could not refuse me because for the last twenty-five years I have remained in close contact with all of them and developed deep friendships. I promised Sapieha, and don't remember when I ever broke my promise.

"One hundred and twelve cells were prepared for the electorate and Wojtyla's is number 91. Just this moment I heard that Cardinal Filipiak will not attend the Conclave beacause of his grave illness; also ill was John Joseph Cardinal Wright from the United States. Today, for the first time, *L'Osservatore Romano* dropped the black borders. The period of mourning after the death of John Paul I has ended; flags went up and we are returning to normal life. *Tempora mutantur, nos et mutamur in illis* (Times are changing and we are changed with them).

Friday, October 13: During the meeting of the Congregation of Cardinals, which began punctually at 10:00 A.M., Jean Cardinal Villot, Secretary of State, gave us beautiful medals designed by an artist named Nicola Morelli. I noticed the Holy Ghost symbolic Dove with the inscription, *Veni Sancte Spiritus*.

"Just received the news that yesterday in Poznań, Cardinal Filipiak died. We were waiting for news about Cardinal Wright. The rest of the day and a good part of the night I talked to potential candidates, explaining that Karol Wojtyla, in the present world situation, would be the best for the Holy See. Everywhere I turn I hear that Cardinal Rubin is active on behalf of Karol; Cardinal König is pushing the Germans in the same direction; and Dominic Ignatius Cardinal Ekandem, sixty-year-old Bishop of Ikot Ekpene, Nigeria, is working on Cardinals of the Third World.

Saturday, October 14: At 10:00 A.M. in St. Peter's Basilica a Holy Mass for *pro eligendo papa*, led by Jean Villot. After the Mass the Cardinals walked slowly from the main altar of the Basilica, crowds greeting them warmly on both sides. Karol was among them and behind him was his young secretary, Reverend Stanislaw Dziwisz. At 4:30 P.M. during the continuous singing of *Veni Creator Spiritus* electorate Cardinals emerged from the Pauline Chapel and through the Royal Hall reached the Sistine Chapel. At that moment sad Dziwisz dropped out and the American Cardinal Wright joined us in a wheelchair. Now we will have one hundred eleven cardinals to elect the Pope.

"At the altar of the Sistine Chapel, Cardinal Villot prayed aloud for all the present electoral cardinals: 'Almighty, the Protector of our Church, give us your great Spirit of Wisdom, Truth and Peace so that we may recognize with full heart what pleases You. Then we will act courageously, through the spirit of Jesus Christ our Lord. Amen.'

"I looked at Karol's face. It was flushed with spiritual emotion. At 4:55 P.M. in the Sistine Chapel, the Master of Ceremony, Monsignor Virgilio Noè declared the beginning of the Conclave by pronouncing the formula of *Extra Omnes*. The youngest Deacon Cardinal, Luigi Mario Ciappi, adjusted his two-tone frame glasses, touched the front of his half-bald head, and in this way gained enough physical strength to close the doors to the Sistine Chapel. We were now locked in for the duration of the Conclave. At 5:00 P.M. activity began according to Paul VI's constitution, *Romano Pontifici Eligendo*. We were supposed to vote four times every day, twice in the morning, twice in the afternoon.

Sunday, October 15: I did not sleep all night but spent the time in deep prayer, begging God that Karol should be elected. At dawn I was exhausted, physically and spiritually drained, but still held on to my hope. After the Holy Mass at 9:30 A.M. the first voting was held: Siri, thirty-four ballots; Benelli, twenty-five ballots; Wojtyla, six. The rest were divided among Giovanni Colombo, Archbishop of Milan; Ugo Poletti, Vicar of the Holy Father in Rome; König of Vienna; and Arnau Narciso Jubany, Archbishop of Barcelona. Altogether, twenty-five Italians presented a united front, nineteen from South America will probably go half for the Italian candidate, and half for the non-Italian; thirteen Cardinals from the United States and Canada were divided, although they have their own candidate which is Cody; I didn't hear much about Cooke. Eleven African Cardinals and nine from Asia, Oceania and Australia—they might go for Siri.

"The second voting was more dispersed than the first, but at that moment, Sergio Cardinal Pignedoli, head of the Secretariat for Christian Affairs, recieved a few votes. But Siri, and then Baggio, have the greatest possibility.

"The technician in charge of the 'goat' received the order to release the black smoke; hundreds of thousands of people were waiting for the results. Nobody else has so much trouble with this goat as the Vatican, because sometimes the smoke is gray and people are confused. Journalists received instructions that the first smoke to appear was of vital importance, because later it could turn gray, and people would be bewildered. Three minutes before twelve, after counting the ballots, black smoke appeared, and at twelve o'clock we decided to have lunch in the Borgia dining salon. Then we waited until 4:30 when the third and fourth votings were carried out. Counting! Siri on top; then Benelli, followed by Colombo, Poletti, Wojtyla and Baggio. About 6:20 P.M. the goat again produced the *fumata nera*. In the meantime wardrobe-keepers were dusting and preparing three sizes of papal garments, together with shoes and hats. They were nervous. No one was sure how the clothing would fit the new pope, because no one yet knew his name. I asked people in Poland to pray constantly for the new pope in churches throughout the country. I was sure they were much affected. But the two hundred thousand in St. Peter's Square were increasingly nervous, and greater crowds were pouring into the side streets. Before I was locked up I received the news that every hour a new airplane was landing at Leonardo da Vinci Airport with Wojtyla's friends from Cracow, Wadowice, Lublin and other parts of the country, coming to St. Peter's Square to kneel and pray.

"Suddenly, tremendous consternation. The electorates were bewildered and confused. Somebody spread a rumor. The older of the Philippine Cardinals Julio Rosales was supposed to have convinced his colleague Jaime L. Sin to whisper to the other cardinals that Siri, at this moment, the strongest candidate, was to deliver a new article to *Gazetta del Popolo* in which he strongly criticized the Vatican Council II and especially Paul VI. Cardinal Rosales, who did not like Siri, thought that the non-Italian Cardinals would go completely against Siri. Under my leadership and with the great help of König, Third World Cardinals were leaning toward Karol.

"The three hundred thousand people gathering in St. Peter's Square and the surrounding streets discarded the Holy Ghost and Third World feelings and discovered Cardinal Siri's power. They chanted, '*Romano lo volemo! Romano lo volemo!* (We want a Roman!).'

Monday, the day of St. Hedwig, October 16: From early in the morning I prayed for Karol's election. At 9:30, the fifth and sixth balloting began. To elect a pope we need seventy-six votes. A group of European Cardinals was divided. Now Benelli, Siri, Baggio and then Wojtyla. The Third World (forty-three cardinals, I think) were scattered also. Thanks to my dear König the Germans will vote for a Pole. I am losing my head because we do not have enough ballots. Nothing left for me to do except to pray to the Holy Mother of Częstochowa and to St. Hedwig who performed miracles in Silesia from where Karol's mother came. My knees were hurting but I still prayed that the Holy Mother would ask the Holy Ghost to influence the electorate.

"Four-thirty P.M. The beginning of the seventh and eighth vote. In the seventh ballot Willebrands of Holland together with König and Jubany miraculously convinced the Cardinals of the Third World to cast their votes for Wojtyla. Benelli discovered that he did not have a chance and supported Karol. What's more important was that the ambitious Cooke, with the help of Cardinal Król, told me that he and the other American cardinals would vote for a Pole...

"Cardinals passed by me, smiled and grabbed my hands; I could barely hold back my tears. I knew in my heart that Karol would be the next Pope. My body trembled. The counting of the ballots moved slowly. But at 6:00 P.M. I was certain that my Karol was elected Pope with one hundred and four votes. I could not walk. I felt faint and sat down. Many Cardinals approached me and asked about my health. I did not remember who they were or if Karol was among them; only Siri in strong words said to me, 'Forgive me, forgive me.' I could barely stand up to embrace him.

"Karol had already confronted the electorate with a surprise. He asked them to stay overnight because he said that he wanted to tell them something and read his proclamation *Urbi et Orbi*..."

Now let us return to St. Peter's Square, where over three hundred thousand people spilled into the neighboring streets and squares. Human tension was on the verge of explosion.

Six-nineteen P.M. In the chimney white smoke appeared. Hundreds of thousands of voices shouted, "*È bianca. È bianca. È inequivocabilmente bianca!*"

And then, "*Chi è?* (Who is he?) *Polacco!*"

Somebody with a portable radio yelled, "*È il Polacco! Polacco!*"

Dissatisfied murmurs hovered above the crowd. Then you could hear some resigned voices shouting, "*Un Papa straniero!* (A foreign Pope!)"

According to *Annuario Pontificio* for the year 1978, if you count Popes, the two hundred and sixty-second Pope was elected. But if you count Pontificates this was the two hundred and sixty-fourth, because Pope Benedict IX occupied the Holy See three times.

At 6:44 P.M. in the central loggia of St. Peter's Cathedral, Cardinal Felici slowly appeared in front of a microphone with a distinguished entourage and in a clear voice announced, "*Annuntio vobis gaudium magnum habemus papam: Eminentissimum Ac Reverendissimum Dominum, Carolum Sancte Romanae Ecclesiae Cardinalem Wojtyla qui cibi nomen imposuit Joannem Paulum Secundum.*" In translation this reads, "We announce with great joy that we have a Pope in the person of the most eminent and venerable Master Karol, Cardinal of the Holy Roman Church, Wojtyla who selected the name John Paul II."

Wojtyla, thanking the electorate said, "I recognize the seriousness of these times, and I realize the responsibility of this election. Placing my faith in God, I accept. Due to my great love for John XXIII, Paul VI and John Paul I, who were my inspiration, I will follow in their footsteps and choose the name of John Paul II." Then he accepted from the Cardinals gathering in the Sistine Chapel, the promise of *ubbidienza*, not, as in the past, seated on a throne, but standing up and personally greeting each Cardinal and exchanging a few pleasant words.

Father Romeo Panciroli, head of the Apostolic Press Bureau, issued a communiqué which began, "Karol Wojtyla is the new shepherd of the

Universal Church, Vicar of Christ and Bishop of Rome, successor to the Prince of Apostles, the base and foundation of the unity of God's people..." Then the titles came.

The bells of Rome and the bells of Poland were ringing, and in St. Peter's Square hundreds of thousands of voices were clamoring: "*Polonia! Bene! Benissimo! Polacco! Molto Bene!*"

L'Osservatore Romano, the Vatican newspaper with the yellow border, appeared at 7:00 P.M., and on the front page was the portrait of Karol Wojtyla. At 7:25 P.M., Karol Wojtyla, preceded by a priest carrying a cross and in the company of Cardinals, approached St. Peter's Basilica loggia, from where, slightly more than forty minutes earlier, Cardinal Felici announced the election of the new Pope. On his right were Cardinal Wyszyński; Cardinal Villot, Secretary of State; and Monsignor Virgilio Noè, Master of Ceremony; and, on his left, Cardinal Prodeacon Pericle Felici and other Vatican officials. They walked toward the balcony barrier, the Pope looked out over the heads of the swarming masses and began speaking in almost perfect Italian.

"*Sia lodato Gesù Cristo*. Let Christ be praised! Dear brothers and sisters, we are still grieving after the death of our beloved Pope, John Paul I, and here venerable Cardinals call in the new Bishop of Rome. They call him from a faraway country. Far away, but always near because of common faith and Christian tradition. I was afraid to accept this selection, but in complete faith to His Mother, I eventually agreed in the spirit of obedience to Our Lord Jesus Christ. I don't know if I will be able to express myself well in your...our Italian language... If I make mistakes please correct me." Tremendous roar and applause from hundreds of thousands of voices and clapping hands.

"I stand before you to confess my faith, my hope and trust in the Mother of Christ and Mother of the Church, and also to begin a new historical road—with the help of God and the people..."

The next day, when journalists by chance met Cardinal Benelli walking to his car, they asked him his opinion of the election. He was not only abusive, but insulting, and a few hours later when the same journalists talked with Cardinal Siri, he said, "I am much surprised by the election of Wojtyla." When the same reporter asked what he thought about John Paul II, he replied, "I don't know. I forgot already."

In his farewell speech to the electorate Cardinals, John Paul II said that he would strictly adhere to the collegiality and before making decisions, would ask the bishops for their opinion; the cornerstone of his activity would be the provisions of Vatican Council II. He warned them about dangers from the political left and the political right, and said that he would support everyone who fights against economic and political oppression for the freedom of conscience and the dignity of man. The new Pope paid special attention to the growing fascist dictatorship in South America, and communism in Europe and Asia. This five-foot-eleven man, with blue eyes, the physique of an athlete and the voice of an actor, showed himself right away to be of a decisive nature in the service of humanity.

Telegrams and congratulatory letters poured into the Vatican from all the mighty of the world, including the President of the United States, Jimmy Carter, who said, "You, as a theologian, pastor and worker understand the difficulties which life brings. Your Holiness knows also what the struggle is, for faith, freedom and for life... During my visit to Poland with Rosalynn, we were convinced of the spiritual power of the nation which has given Your Holiness to the world..."

President of the Soviet Union Leonid Brezhnev sent the following telegram: "Please accept Your Holiness my wishes on the occasion of your election. I wish you fruitful activity in the interest of international relaxation of tension, friendship and peace between nations."

On Tuesday, October 17, at 5:00 P.M., John Paul II travelled through the streets of Rome in an open car to visit his friend, Bishop Andrea Maria Deskur in the Agostino Gemelli Clinic. This bishop was a man of tremendous intellectual capacity and *joie de vivre*, which probably caused his stroke, and eventual paralysis, but Paul VI often relied on his advice, and Deskur would have played an important role had it not been for his serious illness which confined him to the hospital, and later to a luxurious apartment in the Vatican. The Pope spent eighteen minutes beside the bed of his friend from Cracow, and later made a speech to the workers of the Gemelli Clinic, which overjoyed them. But the Pope forgot to bless the people and said,

"You probably noticed that Archbishop Caprio leaned toward me and whispered. Don't misunderstand me. He wasn't conveying gossip, but merely reminding me to bless you – and God knows, I forgot! You see how the Pope behaves. So, let me bless you:

Sit nomen Domini benedictum
Ex hoc nunc et usque in saeculum
Adiutorium nostrum in nomine Domini
Qui fecit coelum et terram.
Benedicat vos Omnipotens Deus,
Pater et Filius, et Spiritus Sanctus.
Amen.

After the election, stories circulated around Rome: one was that the Pope gave orders to open all the windows in his apartment and when the workers came many problems arose because some of the windows had not been opened for many years. Others said that in the Vatican gardens an open pool was being built, including a basketball field. When they asked the Pope who would play ball with him he replied, "Anybody who wants to be a cardinal."

Other Roman citizens commented that early in the morning in St. Peter's Square they could smell fresh bacon and eggs, adding, "Finally, we have a young and healthy Pope and what is more miraculous he thinks like an Italian, speaks like an Italian, and not only does he understand international politics, but understands us as well."

My conversation with Wyszyński had reached its end, and he said, "On October 23rd, before noon, the Holy Father gave a long audience to Henryk Jabłoński the President of Poland. He arrived in Rome as head of the Polish delegation to attend the inauguration of the new Pope which took place the day before. During this friendly conversation the Pope promised Mr. Jabłoński the help of the Church to solve Poland's internal difficulties. President Jabłoński said that he would do everything in his power to help the Pope establish better relations with the Soviet Union.

"Later in the St. Martha Hospitium which is located on the border of the Vatican where many bishops from foreign countries resided, the Holy Father took part in a dinner to which I was also invited. After the meal the Pope took me by the arm and the rest of the guests followed us to the enormous Nervi Hall where a few thousand pilgrims from all over the world, most of them from Poland, awaited us. As soon as we entered, the lights of hundreds of cameras flashed. The guests began singing, '*Sto lat. Sto lat.* (A hundred years! A hundred years!)' And religious songs. The Holy Father lowered himself into the chair located on the pedestal, and smiling through his tears waved to everybody. I, as the Primate of Poland, made a farewell speech because the next day we were all returning to our native country and Karol would remain for the rest of his life in Rome.

"'Holy Father, we know how much this decision has cost you and that it was not easy for you to leave your country, especially your beloved Cracow. You loved your Tatra Mountains, forests and valleys, your lonely excursions that gave you so much happiness and rejuvenated your strength. All this now rests on the pyre of your sacrificing heart…'"

The Primate, who through the years put so much effort into electing Karol Wojtyla to the highest position of the Roman Catholic Church, humbly thanked him for his work in the Polish Episcopate, for his scientific and professorial work and promised that the whole country would pray for him. At the very end he asked for blessings for himself and for all the people gathered together in Nervi Hall and all over the world. The old Primate kneeled and kissed the Papal ring. At that moment the Pope bent down also, and took the old Primate in his arms for a few moments. The roar of the applause was deafening, and when it subsided you could hear people sobbing. Later, Primate Wyszyński confided, "I was embraced so hard by the powerful arms of the Pope that together with my inner emotional exhaustion I thought I would lose consciousness and fall to the floor."

"It was like a scene from a Shakespearean drama."

"Do you know what John Paul II said to me when we got up from our knees?"

"How could I?"

"Here are his exact words: 'You probably recall that some time ago there was an artist named Jan Styka who painted a portrait of the Holy Mother while on his knees. When the Holy Mother saw this she came down from heaven to his studio and said, 'Don't suffer so much painting me on your knees…better to paint me standing up; but paint me well.'"

46

The Coronation of John Paul II

"T HE prophecy of the poet Slowacki made in 1848, a year before his death, was fulfilled," I said to Pope John Paul II and quoted from memory:

When perils abound, Almighty God rings an enormous bell
opens up His throne to a Slavic Pope
his face will shine like a beacon in the night
and lead new generations to the light of God
just as nations turn to arms
love will be his arm.

With melancholy he replied from behind a majestic renaissance desk, "I don't know if I can live up to the expectations that are placed before me, or if I can mobilize the Church's moral resources against the evil in the world today. People are feverishly searching to solve economic and political problems, to prevent war and build a lasting peace. Because of this the Church is under siege by evil forces who insist on more and more profit; sinister forces are bent on destroying and obliterating everything that stands in the way of this goal – even our Church."

"Your Holiness pictures a bleak future."

"This opinion is based on my personal observation and knowledge of facts that are frightening. Consider that enemies of Jesus Christ are directly and indirectly threatening the foundations of the Church and using all kinds of criminal devices to destroy Christianity and to eliminate even physically the leaders of the Church. Do you know that our enemies are not only trying to use conventional arms against our Church leaders but have developed undetectable carcinogenic drugs?"

"Frightening!"

"But with great love, wisdom and intelligence we might tame the devils or at least neutralize them."

"For that reason you were elected Pope." I made this pleasing comment, trying to dispel the gloom of my illustrious host.

"I am committed to the collegiate decision-making process because I think there is in the present-day world no possibility for one man to embrace and penetrate so many worldly problems and solve them justly to the satisfaction of the human soul and body. I know my limitations and the enormity and complexities of today's society. My immediate problems are local ones; to be more specific, I have to gain one hundred percent cooperation of the Roman Curia, and also to convince the Italian people that I will not act against the best tradition of their nation."

"Is it not true that Paul VI internationalized the Curia and yet for some reason you too are concerned with their opposition to your Pontificate."

"To some extent."

When he did not come forth with specific facts I looked at my notes and said, "On October 16th, just after your ascension to the Holy See, the Dean of the College of Cardinals Carlo Cardinal Confalonieri said, 'I believe that the election of the new Pope is a real blessing for the Church; even the selection of the name John Paul signifies the existence of a continuation of a sincere and positive attitude toward needy people which we witnessed during the short Pontificate of John Paul I. The world will be happy by the selection of the Holy College. The new Pope is a man to whom everyone can talk, brother to brother. He is understanding, knows the Italian lauguage, speaks many others, possesses great culture and knowledge of theology, and we know that he is revered by the Polish Episcopate and Bishops from other countries."

He smiled with embarrassment and looked at the pen that he rolled in his fingers; it was then that I reached for more quotations.

"Cardinal König, immediately after the election, remarked that, 'Karol is the right man at the right place who will succeed even in these difficult times, because he is blessed with exceptional gifts and talents.'

"Archbishop Loreto Loris Capovilla, former personal secretary of John XXIII made the following observation, 'The new Pope will be a magnificent symbol of unity and understanding between Catholics, and an initiator of brotherly dialogue among other Christians as well as the other peoples of the world. He will fulfill the prophecy of the Holy Scripture notation, *Salus ex Oriente* (Salvation is coming from the East)!'"

I pursued my observations, perhaps because the Pontiff did not react; he constantly played with his pen but his mind seemed as though it were touching other problems.

"The Director of the Vatican Press Bureau, Father Romeo Panciroli visited Bishop Deskur in the Gemelli Clinic a few days ago..." When I mentioned his name the Pope's face lighted up as though his thoughts travelled to the happy days he spent with Deskur in Cracow. "Father Panciroli said to me, 'After the Holy Father's visit to his friend in the clinic, he regained his speech and when I asked him what he thought about the election, Bishop Deskur replied, 'How surprising it is that this holy man became a Pope.'"

I made a comment on this conversation between Panciroli and Deskur, "Not only are they making you an unusual man but a saint."

My host raised his head and stopped playing with his pen; almost in anger he remarked, "'I am equally poor as Job, my Lord, but I am not so patient.' I believe Shakespeare said that. All of you should give me peace with your admiration; I have accomplished nothing yet." His eyes looked misty. "Tears are like pearls, you are never sure if they are genuine." After this he made a conciliatory comment, "*Bene*, good. I might agree that I have a little acquired knowledge, but you must remember that no knowledge is a tragedy, misused knowledge is a catastrophe, but knowledge without action is like a tree without fruit."

"I understand. But you have not had time enough to show your true colors and what you can accomplish; good-willed people are judging you on past performance."

"I am afraid that the Curia and the administrative problems of this Vatican machine will take so much of my time that nothing will be left for social and political affairs of the world, let alone writing and philosophical deliberations. What I know up to now is, there is a ready-made protocol, or method, for the Pope. I am sure that there was no intention of previous Popes—some of them were rebellious in a good sense—but rules prevailed. Certainly, it is not God's doing!"

I also observed various ancient ceremonies that had nothing to do with religion or God, coming to the conclusion that even Karol Wojtyla, a man with a soccer-player look and the brain of a first-rate philosopher will have insurmountable difficulties in the implementation of his human ideas and sooner or later somebody somewhere will try to neutralize him. But I did not say this knowing that he might reply, "Are you a prophet too!"

At the beginning I had detected that he liked the color and pageantry of the church customs and observances, in which he could show his uniqueness and brilliance; an early example would be in Consistory Hall in the Apostolic Palace on October 20, 1978, Friday at 11:00 P.M., where the Holy Father gave an audience to the Diplomatic Corps. The Dean of the foreign diplomats, Luis Valladares y Aycinena, Ambassador of Guatemala, in the name of the foreign representatives to the Vatican made a passionate speech and the Pope replied in French, not using *we* but simply *I* which pleased the gathering. This is a form he used previously during his first audience, the College of Cardinals.

In the first place I would like to say that every representative of his country should feel that he is being accepted sincerely and personally by me; and if there is a place where all nations should meet in peace to receive respect, sympathy, dignity and a sincere desire for happiness and progress this place is in the heart of the Church and the Apostolic Capital which is established for the purpose of giving witness to truth and Christ's love. The Church has always wished to take part in the life of the people and nations and help in their development. The Church always appreciated the richness in the variety of cultures, their history and their languages; in many instances the Church helps to bring specific elements in developing these cultures, but the Church believed and still believes that international relations should be based on respect of every nation's law...

When we talk about diplomatic relations we think about permanent contacts based on courtesy, discretion and loyalty. This does not mean that I necessarily approve or disapprove of the particular systems; it means that I recognize the positive values, the desire of dialogue with those who represent the legal rights to work for the good of their society...

The Church and especially the Apostolic Capital asks all nations and all governments to concern themselves more with the needs of people. We are appealing for this in unity with local episcopates

not only for Christians but different people living in your countries that they should on a just basis practice their own beliefs and
have the right to religious cults and be considered loyal citizens
and have full participation in social life...

There is plenty of physical and moral misery derived from negli-
gence, egoism, blindness or indifference. The Church through
peaceful means, through ethical education and through the activity of Christians wants to lessen the evil...

In this spirit, I hope I can sustain and develop further, friendly
and fruitful relations with all the countries which you represent
here. I encourage you and your governments to make greater efforts in the direction of justice and peace, in the spirit of love for
your countrymen, and in the spirit of opened minds and hearts
for other nations...

After the speech, the Pope in the company of two of the Vatican's
brightest diplomats, Agostino Casaroli and Giuseppe Caprio approached each representative and spoke to them in their own language
about their well-being and their country's affairs. When he appeared
between the French and Spanish ambassadors he told them a puzzling
story.

"Talleyrand worked in secret on the possibility of a political union between France and Spain. Because he had great trust in his secretary..."
Here the Pope turned to Casaroli and smiled. "...he asked his confidential secretary to read his report and give an opinion. The next day
Talleyrand's secretary said, 'It's well written.'

"'I am glad that you like it,' replied Talleyrand, taking the report from
him; then the secretary finished his thought, 'But sir, I don't know if
your report is for the union or against the union of these two countries.'

"'Thank you for your valuable opinion,' replied Talleyrand. 'This is
exacatly what I wanted to hear from you.'"

The two diplomats started to laugh and the Frenchman said, "It is
amazing, your Holiness, that you told the story in the French language
of Talleyrand's period."

The Pope concluded, "Do you know that Talleyrand made peace
with the Church during the last days of his life?"

When the Pope left, the representative of the French Republic asked
his colleague, the Spaniard, "How did he know we are agnostics?"

During the same diplomatic session the Pope spoke to Robert Wagner, the former mayor of New York, who was the special American representative to the coronation of John Paul II. Curia sources said that Mr. Wagner was boasting about American wealth and prosperity to such an extent that knowledgeable people in the Vatican State Department were disgusted with Mr. Wagner's behavior. This boasting reached the ear of the Supreme Pontiff, and when he talked to this American diplomat about the intricate relations between Protestant Washington and Catholic Rome he discovered that Mr. Wagner's political knowledge was nil. So, to be a pleasant host he said to him, 'One day Mark Twain walked on the streets of Hartford with a cigar box under his arm and he met a wealthy lady who looked at him and said, 'I see that you are now prosperous.'

"'Madam, why do you think so?'

"'Because you are buying expensive cigars, not one or two but in boxes.'

"'This is only a box for expensive cigars; inside are my personal belongings.'

"The elegant lady grimaced and Twain clarified, 'I am moving to a different apartment.'"

Mr. Wagner also made a face because he could not immediatly relate his own behavior in the Vatican to Mark Twain's behavior in Hartford. The Pope noticed this and with a chuckle continued, "I also moved to a different apartment with a cigar box under my arm."

The Italian press wrote much about the new Pope including his culinary habits. "In contrast to his predecessors, instead of having breakfast composed of coffee and rolls this Pope consumes a hearty breakfast of eggs, sausage and fruit."

Other papers said, "This Pope is not satisfied walking in the Vatican gardens; he prefers skiing and excursions to the 'Roman mountains.'"

L'Osservatore Romano, expressing the Curia's authority said, "We do not have a negative attitude toward sports which enable athletes to demonstrate their high skills, courage and psychological endurance. Because of the many tragic accidents that have occurred we should not be passive and we cannot be quiet. Sports should be the showcase of human physical possibilities and above all should be the glorification of life which is a priceless gift of every human being."

In this delicate way Vatican officials expressed their concern about the Pope's unusual behavior.

On Saturday, October 21, at 11:00 A.M. the newly elected Pontiff held a press conference attended by hundreds of journalists and photographers from all over the world.

The first question was, "Will you make many changes in the Curia?"

"Not immediately because I am newly elected."

"Is skiing on your schedule?"

"Yes, if they permit me."

"Are you pleased with Vatican circles?"

"If things go as they are now, I might endure."

When beseiged by hundreds of cameras and lights, the Pope, rubbing his eyes remarked, "You are really giving me a lesson."

At the end nearly every television reporter received on camera a special greeting in his own language. Saying good-bye he reflected and added, "Again I forgot..."

The closest reporter said, "What did Your Holiness forget?"

"Don't you know what? To bless you all!"

The spontaneous behavior of the Pope captured the hearts of all those present and everyone made favorable comments about "the man from the East." But the Curia was not pleased and delicately complained to Reverend Stanislaw Dziwisz, the Pope's secretary. The Boss replied indirectly, "*Deus Misereatur* (God be merciful), *Deus Mirabilis* (God is wonderful)."

Rome, on Sunday, October 22, was sunny in the early morning, but soon clouds attacked the light and at times there was a feeling that it might rain. The thousands of people pouring into St. Peter's Square did not look up; their minds were on one thing, the coronation of John Paul II which was to begin at 10:00 A.M. The liturgical calendar said that the color green was proper, because it was the 'world day of missionaries'; but for Karol Wojtyla it was the anniversary of the death of August Cardinal Hlond and Archbishop Walent Dymek; such thoughts raced through his mind on this auspicious day. "I have a deep desire to humble myself before the Secret of the Highest Birth, the most complete birth which is in God Himself. I have a deep desire—as much as man can have—to pay respect to the Son Who is born of the Immortal Father. He is the Guarantor of our life; a Base of our tradition. He decided that the past of the Church always gives birth to the future."

At the top of the enormous steps leading to St. Peter's Basilica, workers placed the modest papal throne in front of an altar. On both sides of the throne chairs for Cardinals were located. Behind them were places for patriarchs, bishops and leaders of twenty-four non-Catholic churches, heads of state, diplomats and representatives of international organizations. Television cameras from forty-six foreign countries were strategically placed on the Via della Conciliazione, St. Peter's Square and on the steps of the Basilica. Journalists were assigned to their places among the Bernini Columns. Between these points stood a sea of humanity from all over the world, a fourth of whom held umbrellas.

The first to arrive were delegations of the Italian Government, headed by President Allessandro Pertini, and the official Polish group with its President, Henryk Jabloński. Other heads of state followed: the President of the Austrian Republic, Rudolf Kirchschläger; King Juan Carlos and Queen Sophia of Spain; President of the Republic of Ireland Patrick J. Hillery; Lebanese Republic President, Ellias Sarkis. Then the reprsentatives of heads of state such as Gerhard Stoltenberg, President of the Bundesrat of the German Federal Republic, the Prince of Norfolk from Great Britain, Prince Albert of Belgium, Imelda Romualdez-Marcos of the Philippines; deputies of heads of states: Rezsó Trautmann of Hungary, Kurt Furgler of Switzerland, Gerald Götting of the German Democratic Republic, Ćvijetin Mijativić of Yugoslavia, Mainza Chona of Zambia. The Premiers were: Raymond Barre of France; Giulio Andreotti of Italy; Andries A. M. Van Agt of The Netherlands; and the Vice-Prime Ministers of Canada, Egypt, Turkey, and the Republic of Gabon. Besides these, in the ranks of ministers and ambassadors were representatives of the United States, the Soviet Union and hundreds of other states. The United Nations delegation consisted of Dr. Luigi Cottafavi, Deputy to the Secretary General; Ralph Phillips from the Organization of Nutrition and Agriculture; Frederico Mayor from UNESCO and Tadeusz Wójcik from the National Atomic Organization.

At 10:00 A.M. the sun's rays started to pierce the clouds and with its arms began embracing four hundred thousand faithful who had arrived in Rome to witness the great pageantry of the Catholic Church.

Thousands of Italian, Polish, French, German and flags of other nations were flying over the heads of the crowds, together with various plaques of youth organizations, one of them, *Unione e Liberazione*, that read, 'Union and Liberation Greeting the Pope!' Religious songs in many languages echoed in the buildings around St. Peter's Square. There was tremendous activity, but the empty chair in front of the Basilica facade waited for the new Pope, who, inside this magnificent church knelt beside St. Peter's tomb and prayed, asking God to help him to be a worthy successor to Apostle Peter, whose remains are preserved to this day in a special receptacle placed in a 'graffitti wall'.

It was 10:00 A.M. when John Paul II finished his pleas to God. He rose, encircled by the Cardinals and Curia dignitaries, among them Wyszyński and Felici, slowly left the Basilica and went to the outside altar. The Schola Cantorum chorus sang *Veni Creator Spiritus* and *Laudamus* together with all the gathered people who prayed to the Holy Trinity and asked that protection be given to the new Pontiff who, on reaching the altar, placed the liturgical kiss on top of it, wafted incense, and greeted the multitudinous people with the sign of the cross.

At this moment, and if I were not there I would not have believed it, I saw the bright sun emerge, and deepen its rays into a rainbow of colors. I was moved by the harmony of voices, hues and incense, as I would be moved by the tragic death of a saint or a criminal.

Cardinal Protodeacon Felici approached the Pope who was sitting on his modest throne, and pronounced the formula,

"Praised be God who chose you as Shepherd of the whole Church, trusting in you with apostolic service. You should shine in the glory of long years on this earth until the moment you are called by the Almighty to achieve immortality in heaven's kingdom." Simultaneously, he put on his shoulders a *pallium*, which is a long white woolen shawl with black crosses. The Bishop of Rome's pallium is woven from wool by nuns of the St. Agnes Convent; the lambs who give the wool are blessed every year by the Pope on January 21 during the Feast of St. Agnes. Next, for almost an hour, all Cardinals, young and old, slowly approached the Pope and knelt on both knees, with bent heads. The Pope, with a gesture of descending from his throne, exchanged a few words with each Cardinal. The old Cardinals were prevented by the Pope from getting down on their knees, and noticed that with some of these the Pope lingered in conversation, while with others he spoke less. When Wyszyński, who was the second in line after the oldest cardinal, Carlo Confalonieri, reached the Pope to pay his *homagium* and to kiss his ring, the Pope took him in his arms and kissed his hand. They remained immobile for a moment in this embrace.

During this whole *homagium*, the Schola Cantorum sang continuously, *Tu Es Petrus* and *Benedictus Deus et Pater Domini nostri Jesu Christi*.

Then came the emotional moment when the Pope left his seat and approached sick and disabled Cardinals, taking them in his arms, whispering words of encouragement and faith. Hundreds of thousands of voices in various languages cried, *"Humilitas! Humilitas!"*

After this interchange between the Princes of the Church and the Supreme Pontiff, the Pope in his baritone voice, began to sing,

"Gloria in Excelsis Deo."

The liturgy began from the Book of Isaiah (52: 7–10), "How beautiful upon the mountains are the feet of Him that bringeth good tidings..."

Following this, the chorus sang Psalms 33 and 116 and then came the reading of the Gospel of St. John (21: 15–17) in Polish. When the reading was finished, the Latin deacon harmonized with the sound of the Slavic language his Latin words,

Cum ergo prandissent, dicit Simoni Petro Jesus: Simon Joannis, deligis me plus his? Dicit ei: Etiam Domine: tu scis, quia amo te. Dicit ei: Pasce agnos meos.

Dicit ei iterum: Simon Joannis, diligis me? Ait illi: Etiam Domine: tu scis, quia amo te. Dicit ei: Pasce agnos meos.

Dicit ei tertio: Simon Joannis, amas me? Contristatus est Petrus, quia dixit ei tertio: Amas me? et dixit ei: Domine, tu omnia nosti: tu scis, quia amo te. Dixit ei: Pasce oves meas.

The dramatic intoning of the Greek deacon using the same words, ended this segment of reading and singing, and the Pontiff, having blessed the Evangelic Books brought to him by the deacons, turned to the faithful, and bestowed upon them his benedictions. He then returned to his throne, which with its simplicity, contrasted with the pageantry of colors, voices and music that reverberated through the columns and walls of the ancient Basilica. From the throne he began in Italian, *Papal homilium.*

Today the Bishop of Rome solemnly begins his service and mission of St. Peter. In this city, Peter performed his mission entrusted to him by the Almighty, and here, He achieved. According to the old tradition (which has been presented in a literary work of Henryk Sienkiewicz), during the Nero persecution Peter tried to leave Rome; but the Master prevented his departure by meeting him on the road, and when Peter asked the Master,

'*Quo vadis, Domine?*' the Master replied, 'I am going to Rome because they will crucify me there for the second time."

Peter returned to Rome, working there until his own crucifixion.

Brothers and sons, Rome is St. Peter's capital. Through the ages many bishops came here, and today a new one comes to St. Peter's Basilica, trembling because he is aware of his unworthiness. How could you not tremble in the face of this great calling to the Roman capital?!

Today into St. Peter's in Rome, enters a bishop who is not Roman. He is a son of Poland, but from this moment he became Roman. Yes, Roman! Since he is a son of the nation which has a thousand years of uninterrupted tradition and history of deep attachment to St. Peter's capital, he does have a right to call himself a Roman, because his nation was faithful through the ages to the Capital of the Church. The judgment of God's Providence is unfathomable!

Then, in dozens of languages, he greeted pilgrims from the many different lands who had gathered for his coronation in St. Peter's Square:

French: *Aux catholiques des pays de langue française, j'exprime toute mon affection et tout mon dévouement!* . . .

English: To all of you who speak English I offer in the name of Christ a cordial greeting. . .

German: *Einen herzlichen Gruss richte ich an die hier anwesenden Vertreter und alle Menschen aus den Ländern deutscher Sprache* . . .

Spanish: *Mi pensamiento se dirige ahora hacia el mundo de lengua española–. . . A vosotros, hermanos e hijos queridos, llegue en este momento solemne el afectuoso saludo del nuevo Papa* . . .

Portuguese: *Irmãos e filhos de lingua portuguesa: como ,,servo dos servos de Deus", eu vos saudo afectuosamente no Senhor*. . .

Russian: Господ да будеть со всеми нами со благодатию и человеколюбем своего милосердия.

Slovakian: *So srdca pozdravujem a zehnam Cechov a Slovakov ktori su mi tak blizki.*

Ukrainian: Зі щирого серця вітаю і благословляю всіх українців і русиніб у світі.

Lithuanian: *Mano nuosirdus sveikinimas broliams lietuviams. Bukite laimingi ir istikimi Kristui.*

The clouds disappeared, and in heaven this was a typical day; but on earth, in St. Peter's Square, hundreds of priests mingled with the tens of thousands of pilgrims from every part of the globe. They offered Holy Communion from golden chalices to all those who nodded acceptance. Through this participation a unique feeling was enhanced, and a tremendous electric energy grew between priests, people and their common goal. Mystery was the foundation of this deep faith.

The hymn *Christus vincit* sung by thousands of voices, powerfully engulfed the end of the Holy Mass. Then a torrent of clapping hands, and the Pope blessed again from the altar steps before descending to the people. First, he reached the sick and invalids in wheelchairs and on stretchers and then the children. He slowly passed by, talking, shaking hands and blessing. Eventually, he boarded the open white car, and cruised about the square, greeting enthusiastic people before disappearing between the colonnades of the Vatican.

It was 1:23 P.M. This part of the ceremony was over. But the masses were halted by a certain expectation. Two, three minutes passed, and in the open window on the third floor of the Papal Palace, John Paul II appeared. A roar of applause greeted him.

"Dear brothers and sisters, together with you, I want to share *Angelus Domini* . . ."

Then a short prayer.

"Now it's 1:40 P.M., time for your dinner, and time for mine!"

The square shook with laughter and clapping hands. Smiling broadly, he blessed them for the last time, and disappeared.

The window was empty, but Rome was full of pilgrims, laughter and joy.

Monday morning, October 23, the Pontiff granted audience to church dignitaries from the Socialist countries, and in the afternoon to secular leaders of those countries, including the diplomatic representative of the Soviet Union. To both of these audiences he said,

"I want to work with you, for peace and brotherhood among all nations."

47

Shadows in St. Peter's Square

WHEN on June 3, 1963, John XXIII passed away, emptiness and sorrow engulfed the world. During the almost five years of his pontificate the "good grandfather" nearly succeeded in reforming the Catholic Church by making people more aware of the necessity of brotherhood. His loss created a global emptiness that proved difficult to fill, even among those who were not believers.

After this "interim Pope," the Holy See was occupied by the ascetic and intellectual Paul VI who ruled more than three times as long as his predecessor. He introduced many of his own reforms, as well as enlarging and improving upon his predecessor's plans. But he lacked charisma and the spiritual enchantment that would move humanity. To some extent, the void left by John XXIII still persisted.

The third Pope, John Paul I occupied the Holy See for only thirty-three days. The sorrow caused by his premature demise mingled with the desire and competition among national world churches to finish with Italian Popes and select a representative of a different nationality such as German, American or someone outstanding from the Third World. This competition began in the fall of 1958 when Pope Pius XII died, but the Italian Curia's well-organized bureaucracy succeeded in postponing such a decision by suggesting a temporary Pope who would be sufficiently aged and benign so that the "cardinals of foreign extraction" would have time to think and evaluate. That is how John XXIII was elected and thanks to the Holy Spirit, caused trouble for conservative members of the Vatican establishment.

The powerful Curia successfully fought pressures from Bonn, Washington, Paris and other centers of political power who were insisting on a non-Italian Pope. This atmosphere steadily grew until the fall of 1978 when German, American, French and South American cardinals were seriously considering putting their own man in the Holy See, the road to which was paved by John XXIII and Paul VI's modernization of the Church apparatus.

Rome. Tuesday, May 4, 1982. A gray depressing sky could be seen through the windows of a large high-ceilinged luxurious room where I sat with Wladyslaw Cardinal Rubin. Little sound reached our ears from the Via della Conciliazione. The hour was early and the smog and humidity forced the street sounds to the ground. On such a gloomy day it is easy to recall the early years of your life, your young hopes and disappointments. In such a mood I asked my friend Wladek, "What is left from all those things which we dreamt about many decades ago. How can we bring the memories, smiles and recollections to this day?"

His light brown face acquired an olive hue and he said, "*Post obitum*...after death we all will have plenty of time to recollect...," then moved his hand from the arm of the chair and placed it onto his stomach.

I didn't persist. "Let's talk *pro bono publico*. Let's return to our conversation of yesterday about Germany, if you do not want to talk about our youth in Eastern Europe."

"You know well that the unification of Germany is a most important question. A German Pope would be a great help. But a German cardinal could not succeed; an American would do better; and toward this goal diplomatic and intelligence services diligently work in Rome. Even an Italian or a Pope from the Third World would be acceptable to the international powers if he would not openly support the idea of dialogue between nations and states of various political persuasions—if he could be tilted in his thinking toward confrontation..."

"Was there such a possibility?"

"If during the last Conclave, eight ballots were required to elect a new Pope, what do you think?"

"It would be a tremendous shock for Christians and other believers if the Holy Father (Volk, Höffner, Bengsch or Ratzinger) announced *Urbi et Orbi* to this city of Rome and the world, that eight hundred million Catholics should pray for German reunification *und so weiter*...and so forth...et cetera..."

To this Cardinal Rubin quickly replied, "Russia would never agree, and the risk of war would be intensified; the Church would only lose from this situation. I was therefore pleasantly surprised when Karol

Wojtyla was elected to the Holy See."

"I presume that everyone in the world," I asked, "was surprised Wojtyla was elected–and why someone almost immediately tried to destroy this remarkable man."

"Please tell me, before I forget, Toni, you said to someone in the Curia a while ago that before the Holy Father's visit to Poland on June 2, 1979, that Edward Gierek received a call from Leonid Brezhnev, who told him to take good care of the Pope because the Holy Father might experience a tragic end in Warsaw."

I was surprised that in the Vatican more than other places, I must keep my lips tight.

"As you know, I was in Warsaw in the sumer of that year, and Gierek granted me an interview. He complained that Primate Wyszyński categorically refused cooperation with the Polish authorities to protect the Pope. What is more, Wyszyński demanded that the government remove the militia from the cities and states when the Pope visited, and instead allow Church organizations to take care of the safety of the Holy Father. At that time, Gierek told Primate Wyszyński that Comrade Brezhnev called in May and detailed to him a plot being organized in Bonn to assassinate the Pope for the purpose of compromising Moscow and Warsaw. According to Gierek, Brezhnev offered Warsaw a group of Soviet experts who would organize the protection of the distinguished visitor. Wyszyński became so indignant that he said to Gierek, 'I will protect the Holy Father with my own body. I will give my life for him.'

I observed that the face of my friend Wladek had regained color and went on, "As you know, early June was politically and otherwise calm; only the religious fervor of the populace was extremely high, and the manifestations emotional and colorful. It is difficult to place the responsibility on one pair of shoulders; we should place it on thirty-six million people."

"The splendid Church organization," interrupted my questioner, "which did not disappoint us, as it did not disappoint us in January 1979 in Mexico; September in Ireland; October in the United States; or November in Turkey. In all those countries except Poland and Ireland were numerous attempts on His life, yet our brother priests protected him.

"We live in a period of high social and economic conflict which is the result, to quote John Paul II, of 'unjust distribution of the loaf of

The papal apartments.

John Paul II and the author in front of St. Peter's Basilica.

Joźef Cardinal Glemp showing the author a document pertaining to the book.

Pope John Paul II and the author.

bread.' Western and Eastern countries possess nuclear armaments although Western countries may have better ones as well as a higher standard of living that comes from an abundance of goods. But the East and the Third World have a much greater population. A fundamental fact is that the Church is on the side of man and his well-being, otherwise it cannot call itself a Christian Church. Yet, in the West there is a notion historically explainable, that the Vatican and especially the newly elected Pope should organize their episcopal methods in such a way as to support without reservation, the political and military efforts of the West to curtail the desire of the less fortunate people in their attempt toward economic independence. I heard from many Western dignitaries that peace and prosperity lie only in free enterprise."

"But how did these influential people think they could succeed in placing a man of their liking in the Holy See?"

"They tried, through various diplomatic, financial and intelligence means during the last three Conclaves to persuade the cardinals, as you can see without apparent success. The influences during the election of the last Pope were strong, the divisions among the cardinals sharp too, but even a nonbeliever has to say that some Divine Power—and I, as a Christian, would say the Holy Ghost—decided to place a human being from the East in the Holy See—a philosopher, humanist and pious man whom no state in the West nor the East, except Poland supported. The hearts of some cardinals were bleeding because the Holy Ghost gave them the order to vote for humble Karol Wojtyla…"

"With whom could you compare him?"

"It's not easy. Probably there has not been such a Pope in the history of the Church…" I noticed that my friend, the Cardinal was searching his memory for a particular figure; he said, "Maybe from a literary viewpoint, or a humanistic approach you could compare him with Pius II of the fifteenth century, who, before becoming a priest, wrote under the pseudonym Aenas Silvius a satirical play, maybe even a naughty play, called *Chrysis* as well as a novel, an imitation of Boccaccio. This novel entitled *De duobus Amantibus Euriolo et Lucresia*, was also in a light vein."

"When he became a Pope I presume he regretted his venture into risqué writing?"

"There is no record of regret, but his explanation was clever. When asked why, he replied that he wrote this fiction 'to reform our views on Venus.' He was an excellent diplomat and supported the Crusades. As we know, Pius II was not only a talker, but a doer and one day he decided to take a personal part in the Crusades and travelled to Venice from where he was to take the boat to the Middle East, but he died in 1464 in the town of Ancona of a mysterious high fever."

"He loved to travel?"

"Very much. He had decisive views on everything including politics which at the end was the reason that the Turks and Germans hated him and wanted him removed from the Holy See."

"There is some truth to the popular saying that history repeats itself," I interjected.

"As I said before, after the departure of John Paul I an emptiness and uncertainty ruled Christendom. The world desired a charismatic figure who would capture the imagination of the people and direct them toward the future. Despite the intricate and sometimes bitter struggle at the Conclave, the cardinals selected Wojtyla. Again, I emphasize the role of the Holy Spirit because it is difficult otherwise to explain that he was elected Pope. The powerful rulers of the world did not want to see a humanist in the Vatican, a man with a great mind and heart who was ready to give his life in defense of the landless peasantry in South America or the black man working in the South African gold mines. This type of charismatic Pope was not useful to the political manipulators of the world. But he won the Holy See. And, his first two encyclicals, the one from March 1979, *Redemptor Hominis* (Redeemer of Man), and the second from December 1980, *Dives in Misericordia* (On the Mercy of God), are documented proof where John Paul II stands."

I wanted to ask Cardinal Rubin to describe to me the mechanism of writing these two encyclicals as I had heard that they were written in longhand and in Polish; but instead he read a portion of the first encyclical to me:

Does not the previous unknown immense progress—which has taken place especially in the course of this century—in the field of man's domination over the world itself reveal—to a previously unkown degree—manifold subjection *to futility*? It is enough to recall certain phenomena, such as the threat of pollution of the natural environment in areas of rapid industrialization or the armed conflicts continually breaking out over and over again, or the prospectives of self-destruction through the use of atomic, hydrogen, neutron [bombs] and similar weapons, or the lack of respect for the life of the unborn. The world of the new age, the world of space flight, the world of the previously unattained conquests of science and technology—is it not also the world *groaning in travail* that *waits with eager longing for the revealing of the sons of God?*

We have before us here a great drama that can leave no one indifferent. The person who, on one hand, is trying to draw the maximum profit and, on the other, is paying the price in damage and injury is always man. The drama is made still worse by the presence close at hand of the privileged social classes and of rich countries that accumulate goods to an excessive degree; the misuse of those riches often becomes the cause of various ills. Add to this the fever of inflation and the plague of unemployment—those are further symptoms of the moral disorder that is being noticed in the world situation and requires daring creative resolves in keeping with man's authentic dignity.

Such a task is not an impossible one. The principle of solidarity, in a wide sense, must inspire the effective search for appropriate institutions and mechanisms, where the laws of healthy competition through trade must be allowed to lead the way on the level of wider and more immediate redistribution of riches and of control over them, in order that the economically developing peoples may be able not only to satisfy their essential needs, but also to advance gradually and effectively.

This difficult road of the indispensable transformation of the structures of economic life is one which will not easily go forward without the intervention of a true conversion of mind, will and heart. The task requires a resolute commitment by individuals and peoples who are free and aligned in solidarity. All too often freedom is confused with the instinct for individual or collective interests or with the instinct for combat and domination. Obviously those instincts exist and are operative, but no truly human economy will be possible unless they are taken up and directed by the deepest powers in man, which decide the true culture of peoples. Those are the sources of the effort which will express man's true freedom and which will be capable of ensuring it. Economic development must be constantly programmed and realized within a perspective of joint development of each individual and people. Otherwise, the category of *economic progress* becomes a superior category subordinating the whole of human existence to its partial demands, suffocating man, breaking up society and ending by entangling itself in its own tensions and excesses.

Cardinal Rubin stopped abruptly and said, "Through these words I am trying to show you that a man of Wojtyla's character cannot be drawn into partisan politics, nor global political maneuvers, that this man is not interested in capitalism, socialism or communism, but only in God and in human beings living in peace with their own conscience and the rest of society."

I then tried to steer my host's attention toward a more specific subject. "I spent lots of time with Primate Wyszyński, whose untimely departure still greatly hurts me. Also, you were extremely generous as was the Holy Father with his time, so I know the subject well. I would like to have from you facts and opinions which led to the young Turk, Mehmet Ali Agca's assassination attempt on the life of the Holy Father, May 13, 1981, in St. Peter's Square."

To my surprise the Cardinal ignored my question, and I discovered that he had prepared himself on this particular day to talk to me about John Paul's social and political philosophy. Reaching to my past experience, I convinced myself that it was not profitable from the viewpoint of an investigative writer to be persistent with his questions, but to wait for a moment when the interlocutor, having exhausted his own pronouncements, was ready for questioning. It was a moment when I thought that I should excuse myself and leave, but instead, my intuition told me to stay and endure.

The Cardinal pulled papers from the inner breast pocket of his cassock and continued, "In his second encyclical *Dives in Misericordia* the Holy Father said that 'an eye for an eye and a tooth for a tooth is a distortion of justice.' He went further saying, 'It is obvious, in fact, that in the name of an alleged justice the neighbor is sometimes destroyed, killed, deprived of liberty or stripped of fundamental human rights.' The Holy Father said that society would be more human if they introduced, 'not merely justice, but also that *merciful love* which constitutes the messianic message of the Gospel.'"

The cardinal raised his finger and slowly recited, "In January 1979 during his visit to Mexico this leader of eight hundred million Christians said loudly, 'The Church feels the duty to proclaim the liberation of millions of human beings!... the duty to help this liberation become firmly established!!'

Then he suddenly said, "One of my contacts in Rome's diplomatic circles told me, 'You Cardinal Rubin, and the other cardinals should look around for a new Pope.'"

Cardinal Rubin continued, "The year 1980 was an active one for the Holy Father. He was doing much writing on his encyclical as well as spending time on administrative and diplomatic affairs and travelling: Africa and France in May, Brazil in July, the Federal Republic of Germany in November. During all these travels he received a warm response, but at the same time we had to contend with numerous conspiracies directed against him. Incidentally," and here he directed a question at me, "On October 28, 1980 you told the Holy Father to watch out because in six months to one year he could be killed; and everyone knows what happened almost seven months later. How did you know?

"If you knew about this conversation with the Holy Father then you must know that I mentioned to His Holiness a saying of John D. Rockefeller III's which was told to me many years ago by this American philanthropist, 'We don't like people who rock the boat.' Because of the Holy Father's clear identification with social progress I told him that he is 'rocking the boat' too much. This Pope has certainly been accused of that, and this has led to hatred being directed against him in some quarters. A case in point is during his February 1981 visit to very poor and very Catholic Philippines, there were two attempts on his life.

"Yes, though the Holy Father granted an audience to President Marcos and his wife, Mrs. Marcos presented a plan to the Pope to build an enormous basilica for forty thousand people in Manila."

"What did the Pope say?"

"You know him, he always asks about costs. So the beautiful Imelda excitedly replied, 'Not much; a little over one hundred million dollars.'"

"And what was his reaction?"

"The Holy Father politely replied, 'Generous madam, for this enormous sum of money, you could liquidate Manila's shanties, build schools, and the remainder could be given to the poor, because God exists mainly among the destitute rather than in elaborate basilicas.'"

Rubin then slowly added, "In the world today there is a trend among the most powerful circles not only to weaken this particular Papacy but to bring the Roman Catholic Church to complete financial ruin, so as to eliminate work on behalf of peace and justice. There have been many attempts on the life of the Holy Father, wild accustions about the Vatican's mismanagement of finances, as well as concentrated propaganda against the Church organization and her spiritual leaders. But concurrently we are finding important high-minded individuals who are sincerely interested in helping us. In the meantime I would like to give you a moving description of the tragedy which occurred in St. Peter's Square." He handed me a few typewritten pages. "This could be useful to you because it is to some extent unusual and written by your friend Jerzy Hordyński, the Polish-Italian poet.

I began to read:

May 13, 1981, seventeenth hour, the precise time when the city of Rome stopped breathing and shortly thereafter the world was shaking!

The Pope was making a second round of the crowds before his Wednesday audience. He was standing in an open, white automobile and bending to touch the friendly hands and faces and kiss the children mothers were holding up; the noises of the cameras, flashing bulbs, clapping hands, singing and enthusiastic cheers characterized the feelings of the people and the atmosphere of St. Peter's Square. Suddenly, shots were heard. Three bullets hit the Pope in the stomach and hand. The assassin used a 9mm Browning pistol. The Pope slumped over. His face showed a grimace of pain. The car moved faster from under the right colonnade of the bronze gate to the other side. The police followed behind. The ambulance which was always present at the Square quickly took John Paul to the Policlinico Gemelli. The Pope was bleeding. His white cassock was covered with blood. I don't know why they took him to a hospital so far away, if they have Santo Spirito only a few steps away. They took two American tourists who had been hurt in the gunfire, one of them in grave condition, to the latter.

Twenty-three-years old, a Turk, Mehmet Ali Agca, while trying to escape, tripped and fell; the Browning slipped from his hand. The crowd tried to lynch him, but the *carabiniere* saved his life. One witness was a nun standing not far from the assassin. She did not collect her reflexes quickly enough to hit him on the hand when he pointed the gun at the Holy Father, who at that moment had stopped in front of a child held up for a greeting. The rest of the tragedy was moved to the hospital; television, radios and newspapers. We knew about the tremendous alertness of Reverend Stanislaw Dziwisz, the personal secretary of the Holy Father, who tried to stop the bleeding, protecting him with his body as well as performing the last rite. The first news about the wounded Pope was misleading and contradictory. Then, information reached me that the Holy Father had undergone six hours of surgery during which a large part of his intestines was cut out and many other surgical measures were taken by the surgeons of Gemelli Polyclinic. A bullet had gone through his right hand and hit a finger of the left hand. This was the first stage of surgical procedure; then after twenty days the patient returned for more surgery, but the prognosis was still uncertain because the question of infection was on the minds of the doctors, who were amazed at the physical strength of the Pope as well as his inner spiritual peace. Although medical bulletins were cautious, the doctors had an optimistic outlook. The Pope began to read the breviary from the bed and listened to the Holy Mass; he even accepted visits from his Secretary of State and other Vatican high officials. The enormous stamina and optimism were constantly punctured with tremendous pain. During these painful seizures, the Holy Father spoke in Polish with Jesus Christ and later someone said that he asked Jesus why he, as a mortal man, should have such terrible suffering. Two secretaries, Reverend Dziwisz and the Irish Reverend Magee, sat beside the Pope's bed round-the-clock.

At this moment, instead of reading the pages handed to me by the Cardinal, I returned in my memory to Jerzy Hordyński with whom I had a long meeting, during which he described the next phase of the Pope's recuperation.

Four rooms were prepared for the distinguished patient on the tenth floor of the clinic. Floors were covered with a red carpet and on a wall was a picture of the Holy Mother of Częstochowa. Beside the Pope's bed was a telephone. Three other rooms were allocated for his personal doctor, secretaries, and for two nuns from Cracow who discreetly watched over the Holy Father's needs. I spoke with the Pope many times about his personal safety. I even had a conversation with the chief of the Vatican police on this subject and he said to me, 'When we suggested to the Holy Father that he should wear a protective vest he replied that by using such a garment we would deprive the Guardian Angel of work.' I also talked to Cardinal Confalonieri, dean of the College of Cardinals and asked him to use his influence with the Holy Father to convince him to take more precautions, but the senior cardinal replied, 'He would never agree to curtail his contacts with people because it would not be in accordance with the Church's teaching; neither would he avoid controversial subjects which bring him so much trouble because this would be against his character and against the teachings of Christ.

Once more I returned in my mind to the meeting with the poet Hordyński, who recounted to me, "Not many people know that following the assassination attempt, Signor Pertini, President of Italy, stayed up all night in the hospital with the Pope. He returned many times to the hospital to watch silently, and later when the Pope could talk, exchanged a few words with him. With the passing days there were longer conversations and their friendship grew into mutual admiration and affection."

When I had completed my rumination, I returned the pages of Hordyński's manuscript to the Cardinal and commented, "It is a mysterious coincidence, but we should recall that fifteen days after the attempted assassination of the Pope, on the Feast of the Ascension (May 18, 1981), Cardinal Wyszyński died in Warsaw, and tales went through the Vatican that he had been poisoned by carcinogenic substances although he had had stomach problems for a long time."

Wladyslaw Cardinal Rubin looked at me with anger as if he would like to say, why are you meddling? But I do not give up so easily and thought that it would be appropriate to show him a leaflet which I had received a few days before in Warsaw. I pulled a sheet of light green paper with single-spaced type from my briefcase and said, "What do you think about that?"

He read aloud, "'October 31, 1981, Secret Vatican Report Which Unmasks the Perpetrator's Attempt on the Life of John Paul II...'" He glanced at the bottom of the page, "'w/g H.d.B. Review of the News,'" and asked "Who gave this to you?"

"An honest clergyman."

"If it is clergy I must know his name."

I employed various arguments so as not to divulge the name although the person who had handed me this leaflet did not ask me to keep his identity a secret.

"If I am on the level with you then you should be with me too. I am sure.this is not the work of clergy or anyone connected with the Vatican but a forgery. In all honesty, you should tell me the name of the person who is passing out such documents."

"I do not want to tell you, as I do not want him to get into trouble with his superiors, although I will divulge that this clergy received this from Warsaw Solidarity circles and that he does not agree with the contents of this leaflet."

Still holding this clandestine paper in his hands, Cardinal Rubin turned to the situation in Poland today.

"You should probably know that Solidarity was formed by worker-activists with the definite participation of the Catholic Church, the Polish government and with Soviet knowledge. The sole purpose of this organization was to improve the standard of living by increasing production, and defuse social and political tensions as well as create a more liberal model in the socialist structure in which the workers would feel like masters of their factories and their country."

"You mean that neighbors in the East were sympathetic to this idea?" I asked. Simultaneously, I remembered that this particular philosophy of the "Polish experiment" was expressed to me some time ago by Primate Wyszyński, Bishop Bronislaw Dąbrowski as well as by Wyszyński's successor, Primate Józef Glemp on the first day of May 1982.

Rubin continued, "Soviet economists were thinking that the Polish model of a deeper involvement of workers in production could be adopted into their system and would highly improve all production."

Now I realized that this type of thinking was spread all through the higher echelons of the Catholic Church in Poland because it was the cornerstone of the Pope's original philosophy on "Christian socialism." These ideas have spread widely since John Paul II's ascension to the Holy See.

Cardinal Rubin said, "The beginning was promising until the leaders of Solidarity thought that improving the country's standard of living could not be achieved without taking political power. When the communist party discovered this, they began maneuvering, defusing and compromising the organizers of Solidarity, which in a short period of time enabled them to build their organization to almost nine million members. With growing tensions, strikes and bloody riots, the Church tried hard to mediate between the government, which did not want to give up political power and Solidarity which was reaching for it. As you can see, the Polish Episcopate did not succeed; on December 13, 1981, martial law was imposed, Solidarity lost physically, and the government lost morally. But returning to your leaflet, I will repeat again that this document is not prepared by the Church or even by Solidarity..."

"First please read it."

He looked at me in puzzlement as he held this crumpled leaflet in both hands.

A secret report prepared for the Vatican convinced the Holy Father, John Paul II that the man who fired at him on May 13 did not act alone. For the Catholic Church it was important to know what kind of forces were behind it. Italian authorities were less interested because they were not comfortable with the implication of facts. A high official of the Italian police said, 'The more questions we ask him, the less information we get.' The perpetrator gave contradictory replies and tried to confuse stories. But the persons conducting the investigation at the Vatican's request were not easily led astray. The Vatican authorities requested Papal Nuncios the world over to collect information on the assassin Mehmet Ali Agca, as well as exchange information with Western intelligence. As a result of this effort, a secret report was prepared which was in complete contradiction to all the information disclosed during the trial. The most important undertaking was to trace the road of Agca after he escaped from a Turkish jail on February 24, 1979. It is known that this escape was accomplished with the help of a high official from outside. Between this date and the day Agca fired the gun in Rome, he visited twenty-five countries as well as spent time in the Palestinian Liberation Organization camp where he underwent training. It was also established that on February 1,

1981 he crossed the border of Iran and there he got in touch with another Turk by the name of Timur Selouk. Agca claimed that he hadn't stayed in Iran, but in Lebanon, where he spent three thousand dollars. Then he crossed the border and went to Symferopol in the Crimea where he was schooled in terrorist activities in a special Soviet KGB training center. No Russian was used, only English, Turkish and Arabic. It is surprising information that exists in this secret Vatican report that the decision to remove the Pope was undertaken in November 1980 during the secret meeting in Bucharest of the defense ministers of the Warsaw Pact countries. Marshall Kymitryj Ustinov, minister of Soviet defense, presented this project as the only way to weaken the spirit of the Polish nation whose growing stubbornness endangered the Soviet state. The East German delegation supported Ustinov completely, but the Hungarian and Romanian delegations were opposed. Ustinov's argument was that taking an action to scare or remove the Pope was essential to quell the situation in Poland. As a result of this decision in Bucharest, Ali Agca received an order to go to Symferopol. During this training he practiced shooting at a cardboard image of John Paul II, aiming at the lower part of his body and legs. This schooling included fast shooting and moving in a crowd.

After completion of the course, Ali Agca resumed his well-financed travelling. He visited Rome several times to study Saint Peter's Square as well as the possibility of escape. During this time he visited Austria and Switzerland where he established contact with a Turkish terrorist organization, the Grey Wolves, who helped to finance his terrorist action. About two hundred members of the Grey Wolves live in Western Europe and the majority of them in Germany where there are a million and a quarter Turkish workers. The gun used by Agca during the assassination attempt was not delivered to him by any organization, but he bought it in the town of Molderhof in a store of Otto Tintner's almost at the last minute in April of 1981. Ali Agca did have four partners in his assassination attempt, among them a German woman. The assignment of the partners was to organize and protect him during the attack and to help in the escape. When they discovered that Agca had been captured, they dispersed in various directions. They are not yet captured [one of the four was captured in January 1982 in West Germany], and the pursuit of the others was continued by various police organizations and Vatican agents.

When he finished reading, the Cardinal raised his hand, looked at me and quietly said, "Russian atheists are practical and no doubt they want to destroy religion, especially a well-organized Roman Catholic Church. But at this historical juncture, when they have so many economic problems in the Soviet Union, they would prefer to have peace in the East European Catholic countries. They would like to avoid any confrontation with the Church which is deeply entrenched in the hearts of the people. As a result they gladly accept the cooperation of the Church, for example, in Poland to help solve its economic problems. This particular report which you have shown me is clever but shallow and is trying to make Church investigation officials look like imbeciles who confuse and disorient people and their authorities. On the other hand, everything is possible in today's world and to illustrate I will give you a minor but rather cynical piece of information about how some people think in the West." He pulled a piece of paper from his breast pocket. "I have read in the *Wall Street Journal* of December 21, 1981 that Mr. Thomas Theobald, senior executive vice-president in charge of Citibank's international division, when talking about Poland's financial difficulties said, 'Who knows which political system works? The only test we care about is: can they pay their bills?'" Cardinal Rubin added, 'I presume the same question can be asked by Moscow bank officials?"

"But please tell me, you are a knowledgeable church prince in all those matters, why are all the West European media beaming about the Soviet secret police and Agca connections, while Moscow and the Vatican are quiet?"

"The Vatican's position is simple: we are collecting documents from which at the proper time the Curia will develop a paper for the Holy Father with suggestions about what kind of position he should take. But the Holy Father himself forgave Agca and all the people standing behind the assassin. The Holy Father does not want to use his energy to even think about it. The material and special report I presume will be ready shortly for the Holy Father's eyes. After he finishes reading it, this document will be placed in the Vatican Library for future historians, or maybe with the permission of the Holy See to be also examined by men outside of the Church."

I did not have any questions and he continued, "I know from Primate Glemp that in May of this year he gave you a handwritten letter addressed to Stanislaw Dziwisz concerning your audience with the Holy Father, but I beg you not to mention anything about Agca or any of your or others', speculations about the people standing behind the murderer. This is sincere advice which you should take under consideration if you want to be accepted in the Vatican. If not, then use your own judgment."

I arrived in Rome from New York through Bonn, Ankara, Istanbul, Warsaw and heard during my travels from various Church and secular people that the Pope's behavior and changed since the tragic incident on May 13. He was more restrained, aloof and talked little, not only to casual acquaintances, but also with friends. In Warsaw, Archbishop Józef Glemp with whom I had a long conversation on May 1, 1982, said to me that when I see the Holy Father I will see a different man and might even have difficulties getting to him soon or maybe never. By his own volition he gave me a letter asking if the Holy Father could see me privately. I received a similar letter with equal urgency from my learned Benedictine friend, Karol Meissner, to Reverend Dziwisz who is probably the man closest to the Holy Father today. I was surprised to hear about the "changed behavior" of Wojtyla, and tried to understand how anyone could sustain his will to fight and live after so many attempts on his life. As a result, I decided during the flight from Warsaw to Rome not to engage the Pope in heavy conversation. That it would be proper to walk into his library, kiss his ring, and if he didn't ask me questions, to tell him about my meeting with his Excellency Bülend Ulusu, Prime Minister of the Republic of Turkey whom I saw on April 14, and with whom I started a political conversation in such a way: "Why in today's Turkey, where almost everything is built on tradition and superstition, is your society abandoning punishment of unfaithful wives?"

The good-natured prime minister replied, "Are you referring to this tale in which an unfaithful wife was put in a sack with two cats by her husband and his family and dumped into the Bosphorus Strait?"

"Yes. Why did they not do the same with unfaithful husbands? Is it because of religion and the belief that women do not count as a one hundred percent human being equal to a Turkish man?"

"On the contrary. I think the reason is that we don't have enough cats."

I changed my tactics because I thought this kind of story would be too frivolous to narrate to the Pontiff. Instead, I considered waiting for a sign on what subject the Pope would like to speak. On the other hand, I could ask questions about his third encyclical, *Laborem Exercens* (In the Exercise of Work), issued on September 14, 1981, "to highlight– – perhaps more than has been done before – the fact that human work is a *key*, probably the *essential key*, to the whole social question, if we really try to see that question from the point of view of man's good."

In this encyclical the Pope states that profits should be honestly divided between the management and the workers, that the joint ownership of the means of production will be resolved in the near future. He condemned "multinational and transnational companies" for "fixing the highest prices on their products, while trying to fix the lowest possible price for raw materials." About unemployment he said, "it is an evil and when reaching a certain level, can become a social disaster."

Laborem Exercens was not well received in the industrialized countries of Western Europe or the United States. A typical response could be illustrated by an article *Unfair to Capitalism*, in the November 2, 1981 issue of *Fortune* magazine.

The encyclical's references to capitalism are almost uniformly hostile. The Church opposes what is called 'rigid' capitalism, whose commitment to exclusively private ownership of the means of production is identified as dogmatic and archaic. The Church believes that, since capital is 'the product of the work of generations,' there must be a 'joint ownership of the means of work'– a way for labor to gain ownership rights. The threat of unemployment requires 'overall planning.' Indeed, planning should ensure 'the right proportions between the different kinds of employment: work on the land, in industry, the various services, white collar work, and scientific or artistic work…' The capitalist alternative which has markets allocating resources and more rationally than planners and moralists, is never described fairly.

In its formulations about international economic issues, *Laborem Exercens* evidences a preoccupation with the agenda of the U.N.'s Third World majority. There is a reference to 'peoples who, after centuries of subjugation are demanding their rightful place... in international decision-making'—demands that 'will require a reordering and adjustment of the structure of the modern economy...'"

Then the author of the *Fortune* article complained further by repeating himself as if to emphsize his point about the Pope's philosophy: "There is a gripe about the tendency of multinational corporations to seek the highest possible prices for their products, while paying as little as possible for raw materials; the context makes it plain that such business-like behavior is reprehensible. There is that familiar complaint about the widening gap between rich and poor countries and the call for 'a leveling out.'"

In conclusion, the Holy Father was deprecated by the *Fortune* people for this economic philosophy. "The Pope is a moral leader, not an economist, and an encyclical on labor obviously won't be based mainly on economic analysis. The encyclical itself argues that 'economism' is an obstacle to social justice. Yet there is no escaping economics on the issues about which the Pope is prescribing. *Laborem Exercens* has an implicit economic model. Its promises are largely socialist, and trying to think of ways in which they might be implemented we have difficulty envisioning outcomes that look like social justice."

While waiting for an elevator to take me to Appartamento Pontificio I deliberated with myself, should I or should I not ask the Pope about assassins. I heard the elevator come down and lost my thoughts. The doors opened and I saw two nuns dressed in black habits. One was old and wrinkled and the other slim with a beautiful pale face. When I looked in the eyes of the younger nun I recalled that this was the same young girl in the white blouse and colorful plaid skirt whom I had met almost two years ago on a corridor outside the Pope's private chapel on my way to attend Holy Mass performed by the Supreme Pontiff. I even recalled the words, I had asked her then, and asked her now, also in Polish, "Can I speak to you for a moment?" She replied in the same language in the same words, "Later, I am in a hurry," then whispered something to her companion and both quickly left. A stocky elevator man nodded that he was waiting for me and I entered, my head spinning. I was hurriedly trying to develop a set of questions and how I should pose them to St. Peter's successor. At the same time I was thinking about this girl who was always in a hurry.

Upstairs, I was greeted coldly but politely by Reverend Dziwisz who said, "Don't you think you should have arranged your appointment with the Holy Father through me instead of through Primate Glemp?"

"I should but Archbishop Glemp suggested an introductory letter himself because he said it would be difficult to see the Holy Father privately because of the May 13 tragedy and as a result of the Vatican State's strict rules."

Reverend Dziwisz who is well known for his protective attitude and deep love of the Pontiff started giving me instructions in a stern voice, "Please, if you would like to continue your relations with the Holy See do not ask the Holy Father about Agca, financial affairs of the Vatican, about alleged contacts of Archbishop Marcinkus with Michele Sindona, Licio Gelli and the Banco Ambrosiana. Do not bother him with questions about the KGB, the CIA or Marshall Victor Kulikov and the Warsaw Pact. Also, don't ask questions about NATO and its secretary Joseph Luns because the Holy Father doesn't know much about it, he is not interested, and it would be improper for you to inquire."

All those restrictions he showered on me while I was standing in the corridor. I endured rather well the rudeness of this young man and sheepishly asked, "Could I talk to the Holy Father about a gold coin with his image on it which the Polish Government is planning to issue in a hundred million dollars value to sell on the world market?"

This question startled him, he looked at me in puzzlement and quietly said, "Maybe . . . but please talk only with the Holy Father on the subjects which are not controversial, and follow his lead."

"Thank you," I said, meekly. "Times are changed, people are becoming different."

"Yes, you should know the times will not repeat themselves," replied the Reverend Stanislaw Dziwisz, about whom the people in the Vatican claim is good-hearted. To whom? I asked myself. Certainly not to me.

It was Wednesday afternoon on May 5, 1982 when finally I saw the Pope. As I entered his private library, he was standing behind the desk, smiling. I approached him, kissed the Fisherman's ring, and he asked me to sit on the other side of the large antique table. On top were books, a few pieces of paper and a pen.

"We haven't seen each other for a long time," he began. I looked at his face; it had lost its roundness and fullness and I even noticed that his cheeks were slightly sunken and pale. He lifted his hand from the desk and touched the top of his nose. I noticed that his hands were shaking a little, presumably as a result of the medication he was taking. Returning to his face, I noticed lines and a sharper nose, but his eyes were shining more persistently and his lips were tighter. John Paul II's hair was thinner and whiter; he had lost, although I didn't ask him, about twenty pounds. His movements were slower as if to preserve energy for greater things. The Pope was now careful with his words, but when you looked at him, you felt that he was close to you and that deep love was radiating from his being. You could experience it by touching his hand.

How could a man develop in such a way as to brim over with such warmth, understanding and love? Is this the result of constant prayer, or is one born with those rare characteristics? I had the feeling that he deciphered my thoughts and wanted to change the subject.

"I heard that you have two grandsons?"

"Yes, two very young," I replied, joyfully.

"What are their names?"

"John and Daniel." Encouraged by this question I continued. "John, the older one heard that I was going on a plane to see Your Holiness and asked if he could come with me..."

The Pope smiled and said, "Perhaps some day, if God is willing, we will meet." He paused and concluded, "Although it is nice to hear about John and Daniel, I am sure it was not your intention to come here for that purpose."

"Of course not, but I received instructions from Father Stanislaw that I should not ask any questions which would upset Your Holiness."

A veil of sadness covered the drawn face of the Pope and he commented, "At this time, nothing more can be said about the incident. From the depth of my heart I forgive all the participants in the attempts on my life and I hope that God would also forgive them. I am going on with my ministry...the curing of souls...with this heavy work I am really going forward. I also strongly believe that humanity slowly but surely will be convinced that antipeace instigators are their mortal enemies, that the Almighty will punish them because Christ's justice must win! We, people of God, should work harder to seek peace and good will in the world. I repeat, we have to work extremely hard toward this goal."

Seeing the determination, and at the same time a deep sadness on the face of my host, I decided to stop questioning and instead reached for a lighter moment. "*À propos* 'hard work'... my older grandson said to me before my departure for Europe that he wants to be a Pope and I replied that to be a Pope is *hard work*."

"'I take pleasure in hard work,' John exclaimed."

The Holy Father smiled broadly, reached inside the drawer and pulled out a small brown bag, "Give him this rosary,"

Knowing that I had limited time and restrictions on political questioning, I decided to be obedient not for any other reason than to have a chance to see the Pope sometime later. As a result, my first question was rather benign, "Did your Holiness change your daily habits, your outlook on the world and man?"

He looked at me with an ironic smile, "You know me well, better than many people – how could I change myself?" Without waiting for my reply he continued. "The mortal fight with Satan is now more intense and needs a tremendous amount of spiritual and even physical energy. I have only rearranged my priorities; now I do not occupy myself much with Church reforms or with administrative problems although I keep my eye on these matters; but almost all of my energy goes to fighting evil in the world. I am writing, mobilizing people, making suggestions, and praying to God that He should save us from the cataclysm of nuclear war. This does not mean that social and political ideas have no place in my thinking and activities."

He moved around in his chair, looked at me, and I thought this was a sign that I should leave. Instead, he said, "I know what you are fishing for. You are a political creature and look at everything through the glasses of international politics and the economy. But you must be more patient for what you are searching in the Vatican. Important facts will reach you... maybe sooner than you think."

"How? When?" I asked, curiously.

He got up and I did the same. Walking toward me, he put his arms on my shoulders, "I'm sure you know the simple Polish proverb, that the obedient calf...?"

I completed the saying, "...getting milk from two cows..."

He switched the subject, "Why do Americans put 'In God We Trust' on their currency?"

I was surprised with this question and replied, "Taken from an historical viewpoint...I think those early idealistic Masons..." At this moment the doors of the library opened and the Pope's secretary appeared. The Holy Father took his arm from my shoulder and looking straight into my face said, "If they really wanted to, they could have saved me from those wounds and physical pains...Anyhow, I forgive them all and pray hard to transfer my physical pain into spiritual power..."

On Mother's Day, Sunday, May 9, 1982, one hundred thousand people gathered in Saint Peter's Square where the Pope during his weekly blessing said that on May 13 he would pray at the shrine of Fátima in Portugal, "Above all, I respond to a heartfelt need that presses me to be at the feet of the Mother of God at Fátima on the first anniversary of the attempt on my life, and thank her for her intercession in saving my life and for the return of my health."

During my many years of association with clergy of various rank and different churches I concluded that the fear of death exists among them as much as among laymen. This fear of the unknown which forces us all in varying degrees to think about immortality and God who in his undefined moods enchants and induces man to deeper contemplation and analysis of the various phenomena which engulf us. Through these processes we create metaphysical and philosophical theories which are often precursors of pure physical sciences. But when we reach to the origins of all those mental deliberations and processes, most of the time we cannot define them in physical terms and as a consequence we are lost in the shadows of metaphysics.

One of the many phenomena that engulfs man and his historical development can be the history of Fátima, daughter of the prophet Mohammed and his first wife Khadija, born in 606 in Mecca. Although she died young in Medina she was a woman of great intellect, heart and spirit. Her hands, by touching, performed miracles. To this day, in various religious manifestations 'the hands of Fatima are always shown.' Her followers called Shi'a are known as moral and pious people. Their rulers adhering to the veneration of Fátima governed in Africa, especially Egypt, where they called themselves Caliph or Mu'izz, and they were famous for their wisdom, love and justice.

Fátima's husband and sons were first Imams of Shi'ite Islam and they proclaimed that some day Fátima would return to earth as divine Mahdi to rule the people with complete justice. When we compare the legend of Fátima with the story and veneration of the Virgin Mary in the Roman Catholic Church we immediately see a continuation of human inspiration and desire for immortality which those two holy women through their goodness and love bestowed in our hearts and souls.

And now, let's make a mental break from the age of Fátima Bint Mohammed's death to 1917 to the village of Fátima in central Portugal when in October of that year the Virgin Mary revealed herself to three peasant children: Lucia dos Santos and Francisco and Jacinta Marto. During this vision the Virgin Mary told the children that people should pray for peace in the world and build a chapel in this place. After that first vision the Virgin Mary appeared on the thirteenth day of every month to those three children as well as to many villagers who were gathered to say the rosary and pray for peace. From then on many miracles happened such as crippled persons completely regaining their faculties, and mortally ill persons who were pronounced incurable becoming well when they were brought to the place of the Virgin Mary's appearance. The fame of the village Fátima first spread all over the province, then engulfed the whole country. In October 1930, the Bishop of Leiria in whose diocese this village was situated announced with the permission of the Pope that Fátima village should be a place of pilgrimages and prayers to the miraculous Virgin Mary of Fátima. In 1953 a Basilica was built beside the small chapel with a two hundred and thirteen foot tower, on top of which was a bronze crown with a crystal cross. Around the basilica enterprising people built hospitals and hotels to accommodate pilgrims from all over the world. Miraculous healing from incurable diseases were checked by non-Catholic medical doctors, but the Roman Catholic Church did not express an official opinion on the happenings in the village of Fátima. Skeptics confronted with miraculous cures explained that due to tremendous mental concentration and constant prayer, physical abnormalities, even mortal afflictions sometimes would be corrected and cured. To this day, religious people and agnostics agree that the village of Fátima is a center of miraculous happenings which cannot be scientifically explained.

At Lisbon airport, on May 12, 1982, many Church and lay dignitaries gathered with the country's president Antonio Ramlho Eanes to whom the Pope, after kissing the ground, said, "Hail to Portugal, its honest, generous, patient, hardworking and dignified people, land of martyrs, saints and heroic servants of the Gospel of Christ!" After individually shaking hands and exchanging words with hundreds of people who had gathered, he traveled slowly through the thousands of people lining both sides of the road to greet and sing for him.

That evening after Mass at the holy shrine of Fátima, the Pope spoke to three hundred thousand people against, "...every kind of injustice in the life of society...against famine and war,' and "hatred and demeaning of the dignity of the children of God..." and against "a nuclear war and incalculable self-destruction..." The enormous crowd was excited and there was almost no end to the cheers, singing and various forms of manifestations for the Holy Father. He mingled with and warmly greeted and blessed the thousands of human souls. Suddenly, in the entourage of the Holy Father appeared a man. He pulled out a German-style bayonet, lunged toward the Pope and started yelling that the Holy Father was helping to spread communism...that he destroyed Polish Solidarity and was evil in the white robe of a saint. The would-be assassin was apprehended, but the Pope was shaken and asked his entourage how this could happen, as almost exactly one year ago, another had tried to shoot him.

Apprehended by the clergy, the would-be assassin was turned over to the Portuguese police who discovered that the thirty-two-year-old man held a Spanish passport issued in Buenos Aires. During the interrogation he said he had arrived from Paris the day before "to kill the Pope." He was supposed to be a Catholic priest of German extraction with the name of Juan María Fernández Krohn.

The following day the distinguished guest of Portugal went on a tour of the country whose ten million people are devout Catholics. In the town of Vila Viosa, district of Alentejo, on the borders of Spain where enormous agricultural estates and hunting fields are situated, and where landless Spanish and Portuguese peasants live, he said, "The state of absolute poverty of certain human groups in many countries with backward agricultural economies, offends the dignity of millions of people forced to live in conditions of degrading misery..." He then spoke about military conflict, "The contemporary world, despite enormous scientific and technical progress lives in terror of a great catastrophe, which could reverse those great successes if war prevails over peace."

When reporters who were accompanying him asked why there had been so many attempts on his life he replied, "Because the Church supports the poor and disinherited in their fight for their rights and for everything to which they are entitled. I do not worry about my life because my life is in the hands of the merciful God who orders me to serve oppressed people."

His thirteenth trip abroad was partly pastoral, partly political and lasted six days. On Friday, May 28, early in the morning, his airplane landed at London's Gatwick Airport. After the customary kneeling and kissing of ground, and greeting Church and government officials, he commented on the British-Argentine War in the Falkland Islands.

My visit takes place at a time of tension and anxiety, when the attention of the world has been focused on the delicate situation in the South Atlantic. During the past weeks there have been attempts at settling the dispute through diplomatic negotiations, but despite the sincere efforts of many the situation has developed into one of armed confrontation..."

The tragic situation has been of serious concern to me, and I have repeatedly asked Catholics throughout the world and all people of good will to join me in praying for a just and peaceful settlement. I have also appealed to the authority of the nations involved, to the Secretary-General of the United Nations and to other influential statesmen. In each case I have sought to encourage a solution which would avoid violence and bloodshed. As I stand here today, I renew my heartfelt appeal and pray that such a settlement of the dispute will soon be reached.

At this moment of history we stand in urgent need of reconciliation between nations and peoples of different races and cultures; reconciliation of man with himself and with nature; reconciliation among people of different social conditions and beliefs, reconciliation among Christians. In a world scarred by hatred and injustice and divided by violence and oppression, the Church desires to be spokesman for the vital task of fostering harmony and unity and of forging new bonds of understanding and brotherhood.

This was the first visit of the head of the Roman Catholic Church who desired that the sixty-five million members of the Anglican Church could find a common denominator with eight hundred million Roman Catholics. In 1534 Henry VIII broke ties with Rome because Pope Clement VII did not permit him to divorce Katharine of Aragon and marry Anne Boleyn. Four-hundred and forty-eight years later in Westminster Cathedral., Pope John Paul II made a significant pronouncement,

> Today, for the first time in history a Bishop of Rome sets foot on English soil. I am deeply moved at this thought. Through the preaching of the Gospel, this fair land, once an outpost of the pagan world has become a beloved and gifted portion of Christ's vineyard.
>
> Yours is a tradition embedded in the history of Christian civilization. The role of your saints and your great men and women, your treasures of literature and music, your cathedrals and colleges, your rich heritage of parish life speak of a tradition of faith. And it is to the faith of your fathers, living still, that I wish to pay tribute by my visit...

Then he commented on the impertinence of Rome,

> Christians down the ages often travel to that city where the Apostles Peter and Paul died in witness to their faith and were buried. But during the four-hundred years the steady flow of English pilgrims to the tombs of the Apostles shrank to a trickle. Rome and your country were estranged. Now the Bishop of Rome comes to you. I truly come at the service of unity and love, but I come as a friend too, and am grateful for your welcome..."

He also touched on the history of religion which unites the two churches,

> In baptism we are given a name — we call it our Christian name. In the tradition of the Church it is a saint's name, a name of one of the heroes among Christ's followers — an apostle, a martyr, a reli-

gious founder like St. Benedict, whose monks founded Westminster Abbey nearby where your sovereigns are crowned. London is particularly proud of two outstanding sayings, great men also by the world's standards, contributors to your national heritage, John Fisher and Thomas More.

In this England of fair and generous minds, no one will begrudge the Catholic community its pride in its own history. So I speak last of another Chrstian name, less famous but not less deserving of honor. Bishop Richard Challoner guided the Catholics of this London district in the eighteenth century at what seemed the lowest point of their fortunes. They were few. It seemed that they well might not survive. Yet Bishop Challoner bravely raised his voice to prophesy of a better future for his people. And now, two centuries later I am privileged to stand here and speak to you, in no triumphal spirit, but as a friend, grateful for your kind welcome and full of love for you all...

In conclusion he pleaded,

I ask you to join me at each step of my pastoral visit, praying for a peaceful solution to the conflict, praying that the God of peace will move men's hearts to put aside the weapons of death and to pursue the path of fraternal dialogue."

The Most Reverend Robert Runcie, Archbishop of Canterbury together with John Paul II, knelt at the altar of the majestic Gothic chapel of Canterbury Cathedral and they merged in deep prayer for the unity of both churches. In the meantime, Christopher Hill, political counselor to Archbishop Runcie, in such words characterized the visit of the Bishop of Rome to England, "The Pope's goal is simply to restore confidence and identity in the Roman Catholic Church. We Christians need to see a personal figure of unity. We see the value of one man. A personal focus of communion. So we are beginning to see the point of the Pope for worldwide Christian churches..."

But the Archbishop of Canterbury was more specific in his characterization of the visit of the head of the Roman Catholic Church. After warmly embracing the Bishop of Rome the Archbishop said,

Our unity is not in the past only, but also in the future. We have common vision which also breaks up the lazy prejudices and easy assumptions of those present. The Chapel of the Martyrs of the Twentieth Century is the focus for our celebration of a common vision. We believe even in a world like ours which exalts and applauds self-interest and derides self-sacrifice, that 'the blood of the martyrs shall create the holy places of the earth.' Our own century has seen the creation of ruthless tyrannies by the use of violence and of cynical disregard for truth. We believe that such empires founded on force and lies, destroy themselves.

We remember all the martyrs of our century of martyrs, who have confirmed Christ's church in the conviction that even in the places of horror – the concentration camps, prisons and slums of our world – nothing in all creation can separate us from the active and creative love of God in Jesus Christ Our Lord.

During John Paul II's visit to Coventry, completely destroyed by the Germans in the Second World War, he observed, "Today the scale and horror of modern warfare – whether nuclear or not – makes it totally unacceptable as a means of settling differences between nations..." Then he appealed for justice with mercy and paraphrased Shakespeare, "That in the course of justice, none of us should see salvation."

When I heard those words I thought that brutal daily life is ignoring all the desires and pleas of outstanding fighters for peace and justice and is going its own way. But again, stubborn people like John Paul II would never give up their fight. I would remember for the rest of my life what he said to me the last time I saw him, "Some day all the chains will break, even the strongest ones, chains of greed and hate."

"In the meantime we have to experience suffering and dying," I said.

"Not necessarily. If you have deep faith, imagination and intelligence, plus the desire to work hard you can expect unusual things, you can expect immortality."

"You mean when a bird flying over Lake Gennesaret, or any other body of water, catches a fish and brings it up to the sky, this bird is performing grace for the fish?"

There was no reply. Silence reigned.

Index